THE AMERICAN CULTURE

Approaches to the Study of the United States

The America

Culture

APPROACHES TO THE STUDY OF THE UNITED STATES

Edited by Hennig Cohen
UNIVERSITY OF PENNSYLVANIA

HOUGHTON MIFFLIN COMPANY · BOSTON
NEW YORK ATLANTA GENEVA, ILL. DALLAS PALO ALTO

PRINTED IN THE U.S.A.

PREFACE

ALTHOUGH ITS ORIGINS as a recognizable academic movement can be traced to the 1930s and its theoretical beginnings to the turn of the century, for all practical purposes American Studies came into being shortly after World War II. It was then that the first curricula leading to baccalaureate and graduate degrees were formulated, creating something that, while not exactly an autonomous discipline, was at least a definable subject area. At the same time interdisciplinary research involving American subject matter and research based upon unconventional documentary evidence was being undertaken in appreciable quantity. The main causes of the emergence of the American Studies movement were the enhanced status of the United States in world affairs, the general advancement of the American scholarly community and the rapid growth of specialization with a consequent fragmentation of knowledge and breakdown in communication. Among Americanists a provocative assumption gained credence: every aspect of the culture and all of its artifacts might be used to derive information about the culture. It appeared that some source materials could be made to yield up information more readily than others — or at least scholars could learn to handle them more readily — and that the techniques of one discipline could sometimes be applied effectively to the problems of another. The richer texture and confirmation available through different kinds of evidence and different methodologies seemed desirable. Disciplines were no longer secure behind impregnable walls; ideas, institutions and physical objects became "documents," the equivalent of inscriptions on vellum or bound files of newspapers, to be "read" for clues to the state of the culture.

Because traditional slots were not always suitable, editors of learned journals and program chairmen of scholarly societies found much of this new research hard to place. The predictable followed. *American Quarterly*, devoted to "studies in the culture of America," began publication in 1949. Two years later, a committee of scholars obtained a charter for an "American Studies Association." An early promotional brochure forecast, accurately as it has turned out, a membership of specialists who "approach American Civilization from many directions but have in common the desire to see America as a whole rather than from the viewpoint of a single discipline." By 1952 *American Quarterly*, founded at the University of Minnesota, became the official publication of the American

Studies Association with which it was sharing an office at the University of Pennsylvania.

Now in its twentieth year, *American Quarterly* is itself something of a document, for its files show the broad outlines of the substance and method of American Studies and preserve instances of its most useful findings. This is reflected in the present anthology. However, the essays collected here were chosen primarily because they illustrate some of the ways in which the American cultural experience is organized and expressed, major forces that bear and shape American culture and the typical approaches of American Studies scholars. The categories, therefore, include the mythic and imagistic capacities of the culture and the impact of ideas, of technology and of communications. A final section contains essays exemplifying typical interdisciplinary research: covert political convictions as revealed in schoolbooks and children's literature; public address as evidence of attitudes toward technology; the business side of birth, marriage and death viewed from an anthropological standpoint.

The American Culture does not presume to cover the full range of American Studies scholarship, but it is intended to be a coherent unit. It was planned as one of two volumes, each a separate entity, becoming in combination a longer work with its own integrity. The volume with which *The American Culture* is paired is *The American Experience.* It places somewhat more emphasis on the origins of American Studies and is more obviously related to the classroom experience. Its subheadings are: "Defining the National Character," "A Problem: The Use of the Past," "A Theme: Innocence, Adolescence, Experience," "A Political Movement: Progressivism," "A Hero: The Cowboy," "Angles of Vision: America at Home and Abroad" and "Toward Method." In a number of instances essays under one rubric might have appeared appropriately beneath another in the same or in the companion volume — admittedly untidy but not without advantages.

A byproduct of the process of selecting the essays and establishing a structure for the two volumes was the accumulation of rough statistics on the disciplines and present professional affiliations of the authors. There has been much shifting about. Men who were in departments of economics when their articles were originally published are now in government service. Professors of English contributed articles on architecture, child rearing, motion pictures and popular music. Recipients of doctorates in American Studies are found mainly in departments of history and English but they may turn up almost anywhere, even in American Studies departments. Approximately one-third of the contributors are members of departments of history and one-third of departments of English. The remaining one-third are scattered among departments of sociology, American Studies, economics, political science and religion in the order listed. A significant number of contributors hold joint appointments in a department of American Studies or indicate administrative responsibilities in American Studies, despite a primary association with another department. In short, there is crossing of lines.

A year after the Battle of Yorktown a Frenchman, Hector St. John de Crèvecoeur, writing for an English audience, devoted a book to a pressing question: "What, then, is the American, this new man?" *The American Experience* and *The American Culture*, both subtitled *Approaches to the Study of the United States*, are one more document affirming the continued importance of Crèvecoeur's inquiry.

All the articles in this volume and in its companion, *The American Experience*, appeared originally in *American Quarterly* and are reprinted here by permission of the authors. Typographical errors in the original have been corrected, but the articles have not been revised. Contributors were given the opportunity to amend and supplement their articles in brief Afternotes.

Hennig Cohen

UNIVERSITY OF PENNSYLVANIA

CONTENTS

Mass Society

Varieties of Cultural Evidence

THE AMERICAN CULTURE

Approaches to the Study of the United States

Images and Myths

Alan Trachtenberg

The Rainbow and the Grid

WRITING IN HIS JOURNAL BEFORE 1800, GENERAL JEREMIAH JOHNSON OF Brooklyn noted that "a gentleman of acknowledged ability and good sense" had proposed to erect a bridge across the East River in less than two years. General Johnson himself felt that the project had some merit, but wrote that "the idea has been treated as chimerical from the very magnitude of the design." [1] Nothing more is known about this "chimerical" plan, but the tone of General Johnson's remark is revealing. The "magnitude" of the undertaking gave it a visionary aspect; it would require a bold, imaginative and dedicated builder. If such a bridge would ever arise, it would be a monumental feat. Here indeed was a challenge, not only to American technology, but to American patriotism; through a project of this sort, the new energies of the young nation could show themselves to the world. To span the East River would be more than a physical act; it would be symbolic of national destiny.

It is not surprising that the next proposal for a Brooklyn Bridge should have precisely this lofty tone. It was made in 1811 by a New Yorker, Thomas Pope, in *A Treatise on Bridge Architecture.*[2] A child of the Enlightenment, Pope made his proposal as the exemplum of a theory of bridge construction; from a comprehensive study of the history of bridge forms, of bridge science, of new world geography, he distilled a method for American bridges. His book is the first historical study of bridges to appear in America, surely an appropriate vehicle for the first recorded plan for what became the New World's greatest bridge.

Like his more famous namesake, Thomas Pope frequently spoke in rhyme. His epigraph blazoned on the title page:

1 Quoted in D. B. Steinman, *The Builders of the Bridge* (New York, 1945), p. 297. Also see Harold Coffin Syrett, *The City of Brooklyn, 1865-1898* ("Columbia University Studies in History, Economics, and Public Law," No. 512 [New York, 1944]), p. 146.

2 The full title is, *A Treatise on Bridge Architecture: in which the superior advantages of the Flying Pendant Lever Bridge are fully proved.* (New York, 1811). All page references are to this edition.

Exulting Science now disdains
The ties of custom's proud controul,
And breaks the rude and barbarous chains
That fetter'd down the free-born soul.

Like Jefferson, Pope respected "the ancients," but respected "experience" even more. In a study of the past, he pointed out in his Preface, we discover "those fundamental rules which have, in later times, governed the improvement of every age." But the past cannot answer the questions of the present. There is no standard except "experience," "whereby to resolve or proportionate the formation of any article of convenience, that man by his necessity might be led to contrive" (pp. ix-x). The practical men, the craftsmen, are the true men of science; the academicians are "unskilled pretenders."

There is nothing distinctly American about Pope's ideas of science. They were prevalent throughout western Europe in the last half of the eighteenth century, when applied science was making great advances. The work of men like Perronet in France, and Rennie and Telford in England, demonstrated that the new age of steam required a marriage between theory and practice, between architecture and engineering. But in advocating that such a marriage take place in America, Pope adduced reasons derived from America's unique historical and geographical conditions. For example, much like Horatio Greenough in the next generation, he criticized the Georgian style of public architecture on behalf of a native vernacular style. About façades he writes, "we have the painful mortification to witness the whole of an extended front, though built with marble, crowded with glaring absurdities from one end to the other." This situation ill bespeaks "the wisdom, grandeur and correct taste of a great nation" (p. xxi). Pope blamed this on the academic imitators, the "gentlemen of the gown," "those flimsy pretenders to Science, and enemies to the useful Arts, who now strut about like so many crows dressed in a few borrowed plumes, which only serve to make their deformity more conspicuous" (p. xxii). His solution is "a combination formed of ingenious mechanics and learned mathematicians." Although a man of obvious learning, Pope refers to himself as a landscape gardener and architect, a craftsman rather than a scholar or historian. Likewise, the list of subscribers to his *Treatise* consists mainly of New York masons, carpenters, stone cutters, shipwrights and merchants, although the professional and educated classes are also represented by the notable names of Governor Daniel D. Tomkins, Lieutenant Governor DeWitt Clinton, James Renwick, Robert R. Livingston, the President of the New York American Academy of Arts and several faculty members of Columbia College.

Pope's main concern, however, is bridges, and his *Treatise* is a preface to the leading motifs of the internal improvement period about to begin. Written in four parts, the study consists of a historical account of the development of bridges, a description of Pope's own patented invention, a cantilever "Flying Pendant Lever Bridge," a pioneering appraisal of the structural possibilities of native materials, like timber, stone, brick and iron, and an extraordinary conclusion, a verse essay of 210 lines of heroic couplets repeating his proposal made in an earlier section, for a model bridge at New York.[3] On the eve of the nation's first period of technological change Pope enlists history, invention, science and poetry in America's campaign to master the continent.

Pope's historical account of "sundry bridges" is comprehensive enough to remain even today a major source of information. It also serves in the *Treatise* to prove a special destiny for America, where the history of bridges will reach a new phase. Here, geography makes bridges essential to the nation.

> It is a notorious fact that there is no country in the world which is more in need of good and permanent Bridges than the United States of America. Extended along an immense line of coast on which abound rivers, creeks, and swamps, it is impossible that any physical union of the country can really take place until the labours of the architect and mechanic shall have perfectly done away with the inconvenience arising from the intervention of the waters. (p. 127)

If nature created the problem, it also provided for the solution, in the abundance of natural resources on the continent.

> Our forests teem with the choicest timber; and our floods can bear it on their capacious bosoms to the requisite points. Public spirit alone is wanting to make us the greatest nation on earth; and there is nothing more essential to the establishment of that greatness than the building of Bridges, the digging of canals, and the making of sound turnpike roads. (p. 127)

From this argument, which echoes Jefferson's second inaugural address, Pope proceeds directly to a "mathematical description" of his own invention, a prefabricated timber bridge which can be mass-produced and assembled on the building site. Using the method of his masters, Archimedes, Galileo and Newton, Pope demonstrates through axioms and deductions the practicality of his vision. Furthermore, the mathematical nature of the plan, together with the reliance upon native timber, meant

3 Reprinted in *Quest for America*, ed. Charles Sanford (New York, 1964).

that the "flying pendent lever bridge" was universally applicable in America. He proposes this bridge as a national form.

The bridge itself was a very flat arch, consisting of twin cantilevers, joined at the center, and stiffened with a diagonal bracing. The two cantilever arms were series of longitudinal ribs constructed into a solid girder and covered with a diagonal sheathing. Pope claimed that such a structure could be extended 3,000 feet across the Hudson River; if the principles were mathematically sound, he felt, only the strength of the material would limit the size of the span. In another section of the *Treatise,* Pope describes a 94-foot model of a "flying pendent lever bridge," or, as it came to be known, the "rainbow bridge," which he exhibited as a proposed East River bridge. He included testimony by a group of New York shipwrights about the soundness of the plans. The "rainbow bridge" was to soar 1,800 feet from shore to shore, 223 feet above high water—dimensions which exceed even Roebling's bridge.

Pope did not design his bridge to fit any specific place; it was an invention in the broadest meaning, a contrivance which could be used wherever a bridge was needed. In this sense it can be spoken of as a "pure" bridge, a formal principle. This made its national significance all the more dramatic for Pope. His bridge represented the "free-born soul" which "breaks the rude and barbarous chains" of academic tradition. For Pope, the bridge was a symbol of America itself.

In the long poem which serves as his conclusion, Pope writes:

> Let the broad arc the spacious HUDSON stride,
> And span COLUMBIA's rivers far more wide;
> Convince the world AMERICA begins
> To foster arts, the ancient work of kings.

The poem is a plea for the chance to build one model bridge (in this case, over the Hudson River, which has the double virtue of being wider than the East River, and of fitting the metrical pattern of the line). The very boldness of the plan was, Pope thought, its most characteristic feature.

> Stupendous plan! which none before e'er found,
> That half an arc should stand upon the ground . . .
> Like half a rainbow rising on the shore,
> While its twin partner spans the semi o'er,
> And makes a perfect whole, that need not part,
> Till time has furnished us a nobler art.

About half of the poem describes the technical aspects of the bridge, the "simple rules" upon which this self-evident structure is based. The rest of the poem is taken up with a dialogue between the author and a skeptic, who wonders "how to reconcile those novel truths,/With what the *Doctors* teach their college youths." The poet argues on behalf of experimental science and freedom against those "fools" who teach "That nothing strange or new can e'er be brought,/ But what in ancient times were known or wrought." Pope casts himself and his bridge in the role of defenders of truth and scientific discovery against ignorance and superstition.

> Yet, science has her sons in every age,
> Her babes of skill, her striplings, and the sage,
> And daughters too, on which her hand bestows
> Sublime discernments, that no stranger knows;
> Though bastards oft intrude and steal the bread
> With which the sons of merit should be fed,
> Array themselves in ep'lettes, swords and gowns,
> And strut about like showmen's drest-up hounds;
> And if you ask them a new work to view.
> "Oh, sir," say they, "it never can be true;
> "Besides, I have no time to spare, to look
> "At schemes like these; they're not within my book."

Thomas Pope did not get a chance to build his bridge. Although his structural principles were sound enough and were used in later cantilever bridges, either the Hudson or the East River would have been impossible to span in wood; the rainbow would have collapsed of insufficient weight. This weakness, however, is less important than the poetic vision of a bridge in America's leading city as a symbol of America itself. Illustrated in the *Treatise* (Figure 1), the Hudson River version of the "rainbow bridge" is a flat, graceful arch, made of two gently tapering arms connected in the center. It has two spirelike towers flanking the New York abutment, with no traditional form, although the slender, tapered arms of the arch call to mind the delicate cast-iron arch which Thomas Telford designed to replace London Bridge in 1801, and it foreshadows the thin, stark lines of Maillart's reinforced concrete arches in Switzerland. Pope seems to have been concerned exclusively with the form of his bridge, with its fitness and its "mechanical beauty," rather than its actual service as an urban bridge. He never bothered to describe the roadway, or the kind of traffic it could handle. It was a pure structural form, an ideal possibility for America to use in its building program. To "cultivate its growth," as Pope writes in the last line of his poem, would be a noble act; it would be a tribute to science and to art, and to America for fostering both.

A better sign of what America was fostering in 1811 is the report of a New York commission appointed four years earlier to propose "Improvements touching the layout of streets and roads in the City of New York." This report established the familiar gridiron street plan for Manhattan, a plan which, according to one historian, "marks the division between old and modern New York." [4] If Pope's vision belonged to the eighteenth century, the commissioners' report, whose sole concern was efficiency, belonged to the nineteenth. They make a nice contrast in values.

The gridiron plan of 1811 has been blamed in the twentieth century for many of the unpleasant features of modern Manhattan, the narrow east-west streets, the congestion and, especially, the unimproved condition of riverside areas. The plan became a vise, restricting the chances for large-scale horizontal planning along natural contours, and forcing the city to build vertically. Strictly speaking, it was not a city plan at all; compared to L'Enfant's plan for Washington, it was simply a street map. One modern planner has likened it to a drainage system.[5]

It is interesting to compare the style of the 1811 plan with the style of Pope's "rainbow bridge." The gridiron had its own touch of grace, as one might put it, in being totally devoid of any pretension to art or beauty; it was a pure application of plane geometry. Its only intention was to subdivide the land and lay out streets. Unlike Pope, the commissioners were unmoved by thoughts of national grandeur; their motive was avowedly commercial and utilitarian. Explaining their choice of the gridiron pattern, they wrote that they had considered "whether they should confine themselves to rectilinear and rectangular streets, or whether they should adopt some of those supposed improvements, by circles, ovals and stars, which certainly embellish a plan, whatever may be their effects as to convenience and utility." [6] Embellishment was so far from their purpose that a tone of disdain appears in their use of the term.

The commissioners made their assumptions quite clear; utility meant nothing more or less than a straight line between any two points. Speaking of themselves in the third person they wrote:

> In considering that subject, they could not but bear in mind that a city is to be composed of the habitations of men, and that strait sided and right angled houses are the most cheap to build, and the most conveni-

[4] I. N. Phelps Stokes, *The Iconography of Manhattan Island, 1498-1909* (New York, 1918), III, 478.

[5] Thomas Adams, Harold M. Lewis, Lawrence M. Orton, *The Building of the City, Regional Plan of New York and its Environs* (New York, 1931), II, 51.

[6] Quoted in Christopher Tunnard and Henry Hope Reed, *American Skyline* (New York, 1956), p. 57.

ent to live in. The effect of these plain and simple reflections was decisive.[7]

Likewise, economy was a matter of the *cash* value of land, rather than any other salutary values—the *disposal* rather than the use of land.

Those large arms of the sea which embrace Manhattan Island, render its situation, in regard to health and pleasure, as well as to convenience of commerce, peculiarly felicitous; when therefore, from the same causes, the price of land is so uncommonly great, it seemed proper to admit the principles of economy to greater influence, than might under circumstances of a different kind, have consisted with the dictates of prudence and the sense of duty.[8]

The same geography which moved Thomas Pope to dream of a rainbow, becomes an excuse to surrender "prudence" and a "sense of duty" to the demands of commercial efficiency.

The peculiar style of the 1811 plan is, then, its unrelenting adherence to the single motive of efficiency. In this it was unambiguous; the landscape *had to be subdued,* not for the sake of achieving a harmonious life between man and nature, but for the sake of the rapid development of a commercial city whose single unit was the private building lot. A modern city was to be imposed upon the island; nature itself was granted no say in determining how that city should grow and organize itself. As an exasperated critic of the plan wrote in a pamphlet in 1818, the gridiron platte ignored the changing levels of land; only the courses, widths and lengths of the streets were designated, and the land was expected to surrender its individuality to the platte. The city seems, this irate citizen wrote,

resolved to spare nothing that bears the semblance of a rising ground. . . . These are men, as has been well observed, who would have cut down the seven hills of Rome, on which are erected her triumphant monuments of beauty and magnificence and have thrown them into the Tyber or the Pomptine marshes.[9]

The land was a hindrance in the minds of the commissioners; it had to be transformed into geometry.

How did the gridiron plan serve the city? Mainly, as a means of earning public revenue. Late in the seventeenth century, the city corporation had been the leading landowner on Manhattan Island. Land tax was the corporation's major source of revenue. The easiest way to raise large

[7] *Ibid.*
[8] Quoted in Stokes, p. 478.
[9] Quoted in Stokes, p. 482.

sums of money for public projects, such as swamp reclamation, was either to lease or sell packages of the land.[10] In the eighteenth century, the city used both methods; long-term leases were issued with the expectation that improvements upon the land would increase values and thus rents and taxes. The city continued this practice throughout the eighteenth century, disposing of its public lands either through outright sales or through long-term leases. At the beginning of the nineteenth century, there were lots scattered at odd points across the island, most of which was still wilderness. At this point, as one historian writes, "New streets were needed to serve the land already sold and to open up the common land still in city ownership." [11] In 1807, the legislature authorized a commission to design an efficient method of expediting the further sale and exploitation of the land for public revenue, as well as to encourage private building, in order to increase the tax value of existing lots.

The plan of 1811 was, in short, a big step toward the transfer of ownership of the island from public to private hands. After 1811, municipal ownership and the leasehold system were on the way out, and the real-estate speculator, of which John Jacob Astor became the prototype in the 1820s, took over control of the city's land. In 1844, to settle an enormous public debt, the city finally disposed by auction of what remained of its original heritage of common land.

One of the major consequences of the 1811 plan and the sale of the common lands was the city's surrender of centralized control of planning and building on the island. This handing over of the control of city development to private investors affected all future building. As the *Regional Plan* of 1931 put it, the division of the land into salable packages made individual profit rather than "architectural control in the interests of the community" the decisive factor in the city's growth and appearance.[12] One specific effect of the gridiron plan was that it ruled out the residential square, popular in London; another was that it ignored the residential development of waterfront lands, one of the most blatant of missed opportunities of New York planning.

Another consequence of the 1811 plan is less obvious. The architectural needs of the city were necessarily based on the limited horizontal space available for commercial structures. Limited space, together with the great danger of costly fires in crowded sections, made the rural New England methods of wood-frame construction risky, and led to the more appropriate iron-frame methods of Badger and Bogardus in the 1840s.

10 See Cleveland Rodgers, "The City as Landlord," *New York Plans for the Future* (New York, 1943), pp. 34-53.

11 *Ibid.*, p. 42.

12 Adams, p. 50.

This in turn began the development toward the steel-skeleton tall building. This line of architectural development, based primarily on the internal structure of single narrow buildings rather than the treatment of spaces wider than the individual lot, became America's unique contribution to modern architecture. One interesting result of the emphasis upon a uniform internal structure is that monumentalism in building was reduced to the design of the façade rather than the arrangement of buildings in relation to each other, and the construction of large building units. The gridiron, for example, prevented the fusion of the separate geniuses of Bogardus and Frederick Law Olmsted to create a zone of buildings in relation to nature; instead, Olmsted's Central Park is set aside from the essential life of the city, in its own rectangular space, and Bogardus' iron front developed into a standardized pseudo-Renaissance form that paraded the crowded streets of lower Manhattan.

The 1811 plan helped to fix the character of New York as a New World commercial city. The plan conceived of man facing only raw nature on the island; there was no visible past to build around, or even to destroy. It prepared the way for large-scale real estate speculation; it also prepared for expansion into the wilderness lying at the northern end of the island. Moreover, it prepared for traffic, making every street a potential thoroughfare. Thus, along with Thomas Pope's rainbow, it prepared for Brooklyn Bridge.

The antagonism between the rainbow and the grid was a germ of what Van Wyck Brooks called a hundred years later the tragic split between "high ideals" and "catch penny realities." In this early case, the rainbow was itself an effort to overcome the split, to fuse vernacular materials and building crafts with loftiness of design. But the grid was devoted only to the needs of commercial growth. Such narrow devotion to "efficiency" resulted not many years later in all the urban diseases we still suffer today, crowded living quarters, congested thoroughfares, blight, hazards to health, and ugliness. These are the outward signs of an inward bifurcation of the impulses to wealth and to welfare. The split between aesthetics and business, between heart and mind, is, of course, not especially American. But given the naked landscape as a field for aggrandizement of the human will under the name of progress, the split widened into a virtual way of life in the New World.

It is wrong to assume that the nineteenth century had no ideal of community life by which to criticize its own practice. Pope's proposal to combine native materials with originality in design to serve public aesthetic needs was such an ideal; it belongs in the line of organicist thought embracing Horatio Greenough and Frank Lloyd Wright. A high dramatic moment in that line was the opening of Brooklyn Bridge in 1883. For John A. Roebling was as deeply aware of the split as Thomas Pope, and followed his predecessor in proposing to join two growing commercial centers, New York and Brooklyn, with a rainbow. By promising to build a beautiful bridge as well as a sound one, Roebling tried deliberately to overcome the separation between utility and art. But this is to state in merely the simplest terms all the divisions and conflicts in post-Civil War America Roebling hoped to overcome by his bridge. The symbolic reaches of the bridge are unlimited once the metaphors of crossing over and connecting are recognized. Thus the Opening Ceremonies orators set the tone for future celebration, including Hart Crane's, by addressing Brooklyn Bridge as a herald of the future, yet a link with the past, as a healer of the breach between labor and capital, a sign of the victory of honest Americanism over Tweedism, as a link between city and country, east and west, and even, as one speaker put it, between heaven and earth. Yet the bridge was unmistakably a traffic bridge in the least complicated dimension of its existence; it carried trains and carriages, and allowed four hundred million citizens a year to pass over the river to and from the business sections of the cities. It was, in short, a symbol rooted in actualities, a marriage of the rainbow and the grid.

But to have thought that Brooklyn Bridge truly solved the vexing problems of the late nineteenth century was absurd. It is true that the troubled history of its thirteen years of construction, its shift from private to public hands, was an excellent lesson to the city in the management of major public projects, a lesson applied in the 1890s when New York sponsored a municipal transportation system. But there were deeper problems that remained untouched, perhaps even exacerbated by the bridge. One of these was the very subtle and complex tensions between city and country. By looking at this problem, even somewhat hastily, it will be clear that the marriage of the rainbow and the grid, like all marriages, was not without its own profound conflicts.

In the period after the war Brooklyn was known as a "city of homes," a dormitory suburb of Manhattan. But by 1880 it was already a full-scale city in its own right, with more than a half-million inhabitants. Its growth had been even more rapid than Manhattan's. In 1810, Brooklyn had about three thousand people, and covered about one square mile on Long Island; at the end of the century, it had close to a million people, and was the third largest city in the country. Much of its sudden increase in size was based on the absorption of twenty-five other villages during the century, but industry and commerce were also major factors. By 1880, Brooklyn was third in the nation in number of manufacturing establishments, fourth in the total amount of capital invested in industry,

Figure 1. Thomas Pope. THE RAINBOW BRIDGE. 1811.

Figure 2. John A. Roebling. ORIGINAL DESIGN FOR BROOKLYN BRIDGE. 1869.

fourth in total value of manufactured products and second in average wages. It had over five thousand factories; twenty years earlier, it had less than five hundred.

In spite of its industrial and commercial growth a vigorous village pride persisted throughout the century, and has remained, if only in a sentimentalized form, to give the city its unique tone in the twentieth century. In the early years of its expansion, however, the spirit of localism had a decidedly defensive tone, as members of the older generation set their teeth to resist the encroaching metropolitanism represented by Manhattan.

New York and Brooklyn have nothing in common, not in "object, interest, or feeling," argued General Jeremiah Johnson in 1833.[13] Johnson, a revered member of the revolutionary generation, spoke of Brooklyn as though it were a distinct region, set apart from the commercial center across the river. In fact, he felt, geography would preserve the uniqueness of the region. The waters that flow between the two cities, he wrote, "form a barrier between them which, however frequently passed, still form and must forever continue to form an unsurmountable obstacle to their union." This was surely an anachronistic point of view in 1833, at the height of the internal improvement period, when nature's obstacles seemed to be invitations to surmount them, and when the continent's waterways seemed to guarantee national unity rather than the preservation of regional peculiarities.

Although General Johnson's localism soon gave way to a more ambitious civic boosting, the sense of something lost in the rapid shoals of nineteenth-century progress disturbed some citizens. There is some evidence of ambivalence toward progress. One apparently optimistic citizen was Walt Whitman, who had grown up in the rural sections of Long Island as well as in Brooklyn village. Whitman passed back and forth between city and country throughout his youth, and his poems between 1855 and 1860 reflect in their images and rhythms an intimacy with both ways of life. In "Song of Myself" (1855) the protean self of the poem has easy access to both the "blab of the pave, the tires of carts," and the "big doors of the country barn . . . the dried grass of the harvest-time." There is no conflict, no fear of the city, no nostalgia for a landscape buried in the past. Whitman always identified himself as a New Yorker, meaning one who knew both the countryside and the sea as well as the crowds. In *Specimen Days* (1882) he cites as one of the "leading sources" of his character precisely this "combination of my Long Island birth-spot, sea-shores, childhood scenes, absorptions, with teeming Brook-

[13] Quoted in *New York City Guide,* American Guide Series (New York, 1939), p. 431.

lyn and New York." With its excursions into the country and its loving description of flora and fauna, *Specimen Days* itself testifies for the enduring appeal of nature to the cosmopolitan Whitman. To the end of his life he maintained this apparent unity of opposites.

I will not suggest that it was not a true unity. Certainly it was true to the conditions of Whitman's own life, the rural-urban scenes running together as one image of the richness of life. But what catches our attention is that he retained that rural-urban image throughout a period of vast change ("a strange, unloosen'd, wondrous time," he called it), which saw American life increasingly urbanized, and Long Island increasingly swallowed up by New York City. Could it be possible that after the Civil War the image became a form of covert resistance, or rebellion, or sheer rejection of a major current? If this is true, it is so on a less than conscious level, for Whitman's proclamations are all in favor of the unhampered growth of New York and Brooklyn and their union "in one city—city of superb democracy, amid superb surroundings."

Indeed, in the only poem in which he poses the two ways of life as alternatives, Whitman rejects the pastoral for the urban, the "garden of beautiful flowers, where I can walk undisturb'd," for "Manhattan streets," and their "phantoms incessant and endless." The poem is "Give me the splendid silent sun," published in *Drum Taps* in 1865. It is not ostensibly a war poem, though it expresses with Whitman's characteristic accuracy the underlying tensions of his age. The poem opens with a catalogue of the rural images that, "tired with ceaseless excitement, and rack'd by the war-strife," the poet yearns for. The chief features of the rural scene are its quiet and its solitude; there are trellised grapes, grass unmowed, "serene-moving animals," a "sweet-breath'd woman," a "perfect child." Instead of the noise of the city and the burden of national life, the poet wants "to warble spontaneous songs, reliev'd, recluse by myself, for my ears only." The catalogue with its refrain of "Give me," is the cry of the poet's soul—a most familiar romantic cry, it will be noted. The Wordsworthian theme is suddenly reversed, however, as the poet "adheres" to his city, which holds him "enchain'd," refusing to give him up. What holds him are "faces," and stanza one ends on the reversal: "I see my own soul trampling down what it ask'd for."

The cry in stanza two is now, "Keep your splendid, silent sun; Keep your woods, O Nature." Now Whitman catalogues the "shows" of Manhattan, the "interminable eyes" and the "powerful throbs," the "endless and noisy chorus." Threaded among the common city images, the wharves and theaters, are many images of the war, parades of recruits and of returning veterans, drums and pageants, a "turbulent musical chorus." It is in favor of all this, the variety of crowds, the promiscuous mingling of peoples, that Whitman rejects the womblike content of the country; as, indeed, America as a whole seemed to be doing at that very moment. The poem's best achievement is its musical tonality, and the contrast between the rich and placid lines of stanza one with the harsh, nervous and pulsing beats of stanza two suggests that the poem comes out of an intense personal conflict. In spite of the line of argument, the poem seems to me less of a choice between two ways of life than a plain confrontation, and one that poses in personal terms a historical conflict of an entire culture. The choice is convincing neither in the poem nor in Whitman's later life, which remained, as I have shown, divided between city and country. What matters is, however, that the catalogue of rural images effuses an unmistakable aura of a dream, of a life always intended but never realized. It is the dream generated precisely by those tensions which come from modern city life (and, significantly, modern war)—a dream which needs to be stated in order to be rejected by the conscious, realistic mind.

In 1861-62, shortly before his departure for the battlefront at Fredericksburg, Whitman had written a series of twenty-five articles for the Brooklyn *Standard,* which provide an important glimpse of this same conflict on the eve of his Civil War experiences. He had just published the famous 1860 Third Edition of *Leaves of Grass,* and was in a period of cautious relaxation. Whitman's prose rarely expresses as affectively as his poetry his sense of crisis and tension, and this series of historical and personal reminiscences of Brooklyn is no exception. But "Brooklyniana" [14] does reveal that certain things were brewing in him, and these things help us see the connection between the rural-urban conflict of "Give me the splendid silent sun" with the rainbow-grid conflict of New York.

The articles were not written as formal history, but as an informal account of local traditions, obscure events, prominent families, old houses and so on. Whitman wrote not as a scholar but as a popular journalist; as a native of Brooklyn, he frequently referred to stories he had heard from old-timers like General Jeremiah Johnson, and to his own childhood memories. He also described some of his favorite rambles and outings on Long Island. The entire series has the flavor of a relaxed, easygoing, whimsical excursion. There is small literary merit to these newspaper articles, and Whitman himself did not try to preserve them. Nevertheless, it is apparent that the series had at the time a significance for him beyond their value as popular newspaper pieces. The articles were an attempt, he wrote in the opening paragraph of No. 1, to

[14] *The Uncollected Poetry and Prose of Walt Whitman,* ed. Emory Holloway (New York, 1932), II, 222-325. All page references are to this edition.

preserve the traditions of the locale. Agreeing with a New York journal which had remarked "that the whole spirit of a floating and changing population like ours is antagonistic to the recording and preserving of what traditions we have of the American Past," Whitman pointed out that this antihistorical tendency was especially true "in the huge cities of our Atlantic seaboard." Brooklyn and New York, for example, are "filled with a comparatively fresh population, *not* descendents of the old residenters, and without hereditary interest in the locations and their surroundings" (pp. 222-23). Still, he felt sure, "there will come a time, here in Brooklyn, and all over America, when nothing will be of more interest than authentic reminiscences of the past. Much of it will be made up of subordinate 'memoirs,' and of personal chronicles and gossip" (p. 223). With their gossip and personal memories, his own articles are obviously a response to the changing conditions of American life. They will try to "preserve" what General Johnson tried to defend, the consciousness of a regional uniqueness.

It is significant that Whitman does not oppose Brooklyn to Manhattan; in fact, he encourages closer ties between the two cities. In several of his articles, he makes the point that Brooklyn is a healthier place to live than New York, and hopes more New Yorkers will take advantage of the "city of homes." He points out that the earliest Dutch settlers selected Manhattan only for their outpost, while Brooklyn was their residence. Manhattan was "sterile and sandy, on a foundation of rock . . . bleak, sterile and rough," while the "aboriginal Island of Paumanock," was a "beautifully rich country, sufficiently diversified with slopes and hills, well wooded, yet with open ground enough" (p. 224). The agricultural settlers chose Brooklyn, the traders chose Manhattan. And although Manhattan has the best commercial situation in the world, nothing recommends the city as a *place to live*. In Brooklyn, the natural terrain has been preserved, he pointed out, making it a beautiful as well as healthy city.

Whitman did not foresee any conflict between the local pride and regionalism he wished to preserve, and the large urban center of "a great million inhabitants" he prophesied for Brooklyn. In one article he pointed out that the greater attractions of Brooklyn were already "steadily drawing hither the best portion of the business population of the great adjacent metropolis" (p. 252). He described the advantages of Brooklyn; the best and cheapest gas, "the best water in the world," moderate taxes and honest city authorities (Boss Tweed was at this time rising to power in New York). He boasted of the "architectural greatness" of Brooklyn, consisting of "hundreds and thousands of superb private dwellings for the comfort and luxury of the great body of middle class people" (p. 253). His outlook was, in short, cheerful and optimistic; he betrays no uneasiness about a city of a million inhabitants, in fact encourages it.

But the very existence of "Brooklyniana," and its stated purposes in No. 1 clearly enough demonstrates that Whitman sensed a loss in such numbers. Part of the time he sounds like a local booster, urging more and more growth, closer ties with Manhattan, and over-all progress; but other times his tone is nostalgic and backward-looking. This is not a conflict Whitman admits; that must wait until "Give me the splendid silent sun." But it is implicit nonetheless. Written just five years before John Roebling was to lay his plans for an East River bridge before a group of enterprising New York and Brooklyn businessmen, "Brooklyniana" fails to mention a bridge, but Whitman's explicit argument is very close to that which wanted a convenient highway for all those millions who would live in Brooklyn, own Brooklyn property, pay Brooklyn taxes, and work in Manhattan. Whitman's own logic leads one to see the inefficiency of the ferry as a means of passage. Yet the loss of the ferry, a direct consequence of Brooklyn Bridge, meant the loss at the very least of one means of making a slow and meaningful transition between the "beautiful hills of Brooklyn" and the "tall masts of Manhattan." Writing in the early 1860s Whitman faced a watershed in the history of his city; he looked back to the rural past, and ahead to "a great million inhabitants," only faintly suspecting that the difference would be much more than one of numbers.

In 1829 the New York *Gazette* reported a proposal for a chain suspension bridge, optimistically figured at 2,100 feet from toll station to toll station, and 160 feet above the East River. The proposer had two arguments: such a bridge would supply a monument to rank Brooklyn and New York with Westminister and London, and, "the rise of property in Brooklyn alone would defray the expense of the project." He also suggested that "pure" water from Brooklyn could be conveyed to Manhattan in pipes under the bridge floor, implying that such a bridge would practically fuse city and country.

A more feasible proposal came in 1835 from a civil engineer and architect, W. Lake, in a letter to the *American Railroad Journal.* He referred to the common inconvenience suffered by all ferry users, especially those in a hurry. A solution to the daily interruptions of business, he wrote, would be a suspension bridge, which would not interfere with river traffic (although his plan was for a five-span bridge, which would have rather crowded the river with supporting piers). Such a bridge, he pointed out, was not only practical from the engineering point of view, but also profitable from the commercial point of view; it would be a good speculation for an ambitious company. It would also add beauty to the city.

> The rapidly increasing intercourse between New York and Long Island will, probably, soon require the formation of a wide street leading from Broadway. What a beautiful connection would such a bridge, as it is here described, form between this supposed new street and Fulton Street, Brooklyn! It would altogether be one of the most magnificent suspension bridges in the world.[15]

In a subsequent issue of the journal, Mr. Lake reinforced his proposal by describing the theory and history of suspension bridges, referring frequently to Thomas Pope's *Treatise on Bridge Architecture,* thus demonstrating a continuity in proposals for a "magnificent" bridge across the East River.

There were yet other plans and projects. In 1836, someone suggested a dike across the river; in the 1840s, there was talk of a stupendous bridge one hundred feet wide. One projector blandly proposed to fill in the East River, giving the city more land and more profit, and settling for all time the matter of bridges. In these years a street in Brooklyn running down to the river was named Bridge Street. In the 1870s this street received the abutment of John A. Roebling's rainbow, Brooklyn Bridge. And sixty years later another poet, Hart Crane, recognized in Roebling's bridge a "steeled Cognizance," a "mystical synthesis of America," that united, however unstably, the values of both rainbow and grid. His poem *The Bridge* (1930) thereby fulfilled more than a century of aspiration.

15 *American Railroad Journal,* Vol. IX, No. I (January 10, 1835), pp. 4-5.

Afternote

An altered version of this essay appears as Chapter 2 of *Brooklyn Bridge: Fact and Symbol* (New York: Oxford University Press, 1965).

Alan Trachtenberg is an Associate Professor of English at Pennsylvania State University. [This article appeared in Vol. XVI, No. 1 (Spring, 1964).]

John William Ward

The Meaning of Lindbergh's Flight

ON FRIDAY, MAY 20, 1927, at 7:52 a.m., Charles A. Lindbergh took off in a silver-winged monoplane and flew from the United States to France. With this flight Lindbergh became the first man to fly alone across the Atlantic Ocean. The log of flight 33 of "The Spirit of St. Louis" reads: "Roosevelt Field, Long Island, New York, to Le Bourget Aerodrome, Paris, France. 33 hrs. 30 min." Thus was the fact of Lindbergh's achievement easily put down. But the meaning of Lindbergh's flight lay hidden in the next sentence of the log: "(Fuselage fabric badly torn by souvenir hunters.)"

When Lindbergh landed at Le Bourget he is supposed to have said, "Well, we've done it." A contemporary writer asked "Did what?" Lindbergh "had no idea of what he had done. He thought he had simply flown from New York to Paris. What he had really done was something far greater. He had fired the imagination of mankind." From the moment of Lindbergh's flight people recognized that something more was involved than the mere fact of the physical leap from New York to Paris. "Lindbergh," wrote John Erskine, "served as a metaphor." But what the metaphor stood for was not easy to say. The *New York Times* remarked then that "there has been no complete and satisfactory explanation of the enthusiasm and acclaim for Captain Lindbergh." Looking back on the celebration of Lindbergh, one can see now that the American people were trying to understand Lindbergh's flight, to grasp its meaning, and through it, perhaps, to grasp the meaning of their own experience. Was the flight the achievement of a heroic, solitary, unaided individual? Or did the flight represent the triumph of the machine, the success of an industrially organized society? These questions were central to the meaning of Lindbergh's flight. They were also central to the lives of the people who made Lindbergh their hero.

The flight demanded attention in its own right, of course, quite apart from whatever significance it might have. Lindbergh's story had all the makings of great drama. Since 1919 there had been a standing prize of $25,000 to be awarded to the first aviator who could cross the Atlantic in either direction between the United States and France in a heavier-than-air craft. In the spring of 1927 there promised to be what the *New York Times* called "the most spectacular race ever held—3,600 miles over the open sea to Paris." The scene was dominated by veteran pilots. On the European side were the French aces, Nungesser and Coli; on the American side, Commander Richard E. Byrd, in a big tri-motored Fokker monoplane, led a group of contestants. Besides Byrd, who had already flown over the North Pole, there were Commander Davis, flying a ship named in honor of the American Legion which had put up $100,000 to finance his attempt, Clarence Chamberlin, who had already set a world's endurance record of more than fifty-one hours in the air in a Bellanca tri-motored plane, and Captain René Fonck, the French war ace, who had come to America to fly a Sikorsky aircraft. The hero was unheard of and unknown. He was on the West Coast supervising the construction of a single-engined plane to cost only ten thousand dollars.

Then fate played its part. It seemed impossible that Lindbergh could get his plane built and east to New York in time to challenge his better equipped and more famous rivals. But in quick succession a series of disasters cleared his path. On April 16, Commander Byrd's "America" crashed on its test flight, crushing the leg of Floyd Bennett who was one of the crew and injuring Byrd's hand and wrist. On April 24, Clarence Chamberlin cracked up in his Bellanca, not seriously, but enough to delay his plans. Then on April 26, Commander Davis and his co-pilot lost their lives as the "American Legion" crashed on its final test flight. In ten days, accidents had stopped all of Lindbergh's American rivals. Nungesser and Coli, however, took off in their romantically named ship, "The White Bird," from Le Bourget on May 8. The world waited and Lindbergh, still on the West Coast, decided to try to fly the Pacific. But Nungesser and Coli were never seen again. As rumors filled the newspapers, as reports came in that the "White Bird" was seen over Newfoundland, over Boston, over the Atlantic, it soon became apparent that Nungesser and Coli had failed, dropping to their death in some unknown grave. Disaster had touched every ship entered in the trans-Atlantic race.

Now, with the stage cleared, Lindbergh entered. He swooped across the continent in two great strides, landing only at St. Louis. The first leg of his flight established a new distance record but all eyes were on the Atlantic and the feat received little notice. Curiously, the first time Lindbergh appeared in the headlines of the New York papers was Friday, the thirteenth. By this time Byrd and Chamberlin were ready once again but the weather had closed in and kept all planes on the ground. Then, after a week of fretful waiting, on the night of May 19, on the way into New York to see "Rio Rita," Lindbergh received a report that the weather was breaking over the ocean. He hurried back to Roosevelt Field to haul his plane out onto a wet, dripping runway. After mechanics painfully loaded the plane's gas by hand, the wind shifted, as fate played its last trick. A muddy runway and an adverse wind. Whatever the elements, whatever the fates, the decisive act is the hero's, and Lindbergh made his choice. Providing a chorus to the action, the *Herald Tribune* reported that Lindbergh lifted the overloaded plane into the sky "by his indomitable will alone."

The parabola of the action was as clean as the arc of Lindbergh's flight. The drama should have ended with the landing of "The Spirit of St. Louis" at Le Bourget. That is where Lindbergh wanted it to end. In *"WE,"* written immediately after the flight, and in *The Spirit of St. Louis,* written twenty-six years later, Lindbergh chose to end his accounts there. But the flight turned out to be only the first act in the part Lindbergh was to play.

Lindbergh was so innocent of his future that on his flight he carried letters of introduction. The hysterical response, first of the French and then of his own countrymen, had been no part of his careful plans. In *"WE,"* after Lindbergh's narrative of the flight, the publisher wrote: "When Lindbergh came to tell the story of his welcome at Paris, London, Brussels, Washington, New York, and St. Louis he found himself up against a tougher problem than flying the Atlantic." So another writer completed the account in the third person. He suggested that "the reason Lindbergh's story is different is that when his plane came to a halt on Le Bourget field that black night in Paris, Lindbergh the man kept on going. The phenomenon of Lindbergh took its start with his flight across the ocean; but in its entirety it was almost as distinct from that flight as though he had never flown at all."

Lindbergh's private life ended with his flight to Paris. The drama was no longer his, it was the public's. "The outburst of unanimous acclaim was at once personal and symbolic," said the *American Review of Reviews.* From the moment of success there were two Lindberghs, the private Lindbergh and the public Lindbergh. The latter was the construction of the imagination of Lindbergh's time, fastened on to an unwilling person. The tragedy of Lindbergh's career is that he could never accept the role assigned him. He always believed he might keep his two lives separate. But from the moment he landed at Le Bourget, Lindbergh became, as the *New Republic* noted, *"ours* . . . . He is no longer permitted to be himself. He is US personified. He is the United States." Ambassador Herrick introduced Lindbergh to the French, saying, "This young man from out of the West brings you better than anything else the spirit of America," and wired to President Coolidge, "Had we searched all America we could not have found a better type than young Lindbergh to represent the spirit and high purpose of our people." This was Lindbergh's fate, to be a type. A writer in the *North American Review* felt that Lindbergh represented "the dominant American character," he "images the best" about the United States. And an ecstatic female in the *American Magazine,* who began by saying that Lindbergh "is a sort of symbol. . . . He is the dream that is in our hearts," concluded that the American public responded so wildly to Lindbergh because of "the thrill of possessing, in him, our dream of what *we* really and truly want to be." The act of possession was so complete that articles since have attempted to discover the "real" Lindbergh, that enigmatic and taciturn figure behind the public mask. But it is no less difficult to discern the features of the public Lindbergh, that symbolic figure who presented to the imagination of his time all the yearnings and buried desires of its dream for itself.

Lindbergh's flight came at the end of a decade marked by social and political corruption and by a sense of moral loss. The heady idealism of the First World War had been succeeded by a deep cynicism as to the war's real purpose. The naïve belief that virtue could be legislated was violated by the vast discrepancy between the law and the social habits of prohibition. A philosophy of relativism had become the uneasy rationale of a nation which had formerly believed in moral absolutes. The newspapers agreed that Lindbergh's chief worth was his spiritual and moral value. His story was held to be "in striking contrast with the sordid unhallowed themes that have for months steeped the imaginations and thinking of the people." Or, as another had it, "there is good reason why people should hail Lindbergh and give him honor. He stands out in a grubby world as an inspiration."

Lindbergh gave the American people a glimpse of what they liked to think themselves to be at a time when they feared they had deserted their own vision of themselves. The grubbiness of the twenties had a good deal to do with the shining quality of Lindbergh's success, especially when one remembers that Lindbergh's flight was not as unexampled as our national memory would have it. The Atlantic was not unconquered when Lindbergh flew. A British dirigible had twice crossed the Atlantic before 1919 and on May 8 of that year three naval seaplanes left Rockaway, New York, and one, the NC-4 manned by a crew of five, got through to Plymouth, England. A month later, Captain John Alcock, an Englishman, with Arthur W. Browne, an American, flew the first heavier-than-air land plane across the Atlantic nonstop, from Newfoundland to Ireland, to win twice the money Lindbergh did, a prize of $50,000 offered by the London *Daily Mail.* Alcock's and Browne's misfortune was to land in a soft and somnolent Irish peat bog instead of before the cheering thousands of London or Paris. Or perhaps they should have flown in 1927.

The wild medley of public acclaim and the homeric strivings of editors make one realize that the response to Lindbergh involved a mass ritual in which America celebrated itself more than it celebrated Lindbergh. Lindbergh's flight was the occasion of a public act of regeneration in which the nation momentarily rededicated itself to something, the loss of which was keenly felt. It was said again and again that "Lindy" taught America "to lift its eyes up to Heaven." Heywood Broun, in his column in the *New York World,* wrote that this "tall young man raised up and let us see the potentialities of the human spirit." Broun felt that the flight proved that, though "we are small and fragile," it "isn't true that there is no health in us." Lindbergh's flight provided the moment, but the meaning of the flight is to be found in the deep and pervasive need for renewal which the flight brought to the surface of public feeling. When Lindbergh appeared at the nation's capital, the *Washington Post* observed, "He was given that frenzied acclaim which comes from the depths of the people." In New York, where 4,000,000 people saw him, a reporter wrote that the dense and vociferous crowds were swept, as Lindbergh passed, "with an emotion tense and inflammable." The *Literary Digest* suggested that the answer to the hero-worship of Lindbergh would "throw an interesting light on the psychology of our times and of the American people."

The *Nation* noted about Lindbergh that "there was something lyric as well as heroic about the apparition of this young Lochinvar who suddenly came out of the West and who flew all unarmed and all alone. It is the kind of stuff which the ancient Greeks would have worked into a myth and the medieval Scots into a border ballad. . . . But what we have in the case of Lindbergh is an actual, an heroic and an exhaustively exposed experience which exists by suggestion in the form of poetry." The *Nation* quickly qualified its statement by observing that reporters were as far as possible from being poets and concluded that the discrepancy between the fact and the celebration of it was not poetry, perhaps, but "magic on a vast scale." Yet the *Nation* might have clung to its insight that the public meaning of Lindbergh's flight was somehow poetic. The vast publicity about Lindbergh corresponds in one vital particular with the poetic vision. Poetry, said William Butler Yeats, contains opposites; so did Lindbergh. Lindbergh did not mean one thing, he meant many things. The image of itself which America contemplated in the public person of Lindbergh was full of conflict; it was, in a word, dramatic.

To heighten the drama, Lindbergh did it alone. He was the "lone eagle" and a full exploration of that fact takes one deep into the emotional meaning of his success. Not only the *Nation* found Sir Walter Scott's lines on Lochinvar appropriate: "he rode all unarmed and he rode all alone." Newspapers and magazines were deluged with amateur poems that vindicated one rhymester's wry comment, "Go conquer the perils / That lurk in the skies - - / And you'll get bum poems / Right up to your eyes." The *New York Times,* that alone received more than two hundred poems, observed in trying to summarize the poetic deluge that "the fact that he flew alone made the strongest impression." Another favorite tribute was Kipling's "The Winners," with its refrain, "He travels the fastest who travels alone." The others who had conquered the Atlantic and those like Byrd and Chamberlin who were trying at the same time were not traveling alone and they hardly rode unarmed. Other than Lindbergh, all the contestants in the trans-Atlantic race had unlimited backing, access to the best planes, and all were working in teams, carrying at least one co-pilot to share the long burden of flying the plane. So a writer in the New York *Sun,* in a poem called "The Flying Fool," a nickname that Lindbergh despised, celebrated Lindbergh's flight: ". . . no kingly plane for him; / No endless data, comrades, moneyed chums; / No boards, no councils, no directors grim— / He plans ALONE . . . and takes luck as it comes."

Upon second thought, it must seem strange that the long distance flight of an airplane, the achievement of a highly advanced and organized technology, should be the occasion for hymns of praise to the solitary unaided man. Yet the National Geographic Society, when it presented a medal to Lindbergh, wrote on the presentation scroll, "Courage, when it goes alone, has ever caught men's imaginations," and compared Lindbergh to Robinson Crusoe and the trailmakers in our own West. But Lindbergh and Robinson Crusoe, the one in his helmet and fur-lined flying coat and the other in his wild goatskins, do not easily co-exist. Even if Robinson Crusoe did have a tidy capital investment in the form of a well-stocked shipwreck, he still did not have a ten thousand dollar machine under him.

Lindbergh, in nearly every remark about his flight and in his own writings about it, resisted the tendency to exploit the flight as the achievement of an individual. He never said "I," he always said "We." The plane was not to go unrecognized. Nevertheless, there persisted a tendency to seize upon the flight as a way of celebrating the self-sufficient individual, so that among many others an Ohio newspaper could describe Lindbergh as this "self-contained, self-reliant, courageous young man [who] ranks among the great pioneers of history." The strategy here was a common one, to make Lindbergh a "pioneer" and thus to link him with a long and vital tradition of individualism in the American experience. Colonel Theodore Roosevelt, himself the son of a famous exponent of self-reliance, said to reporters at his home in Oyster Bay that "Captain Lindbergh personifies the daring of youth. Daniel Boone, David Crocket [*sic*], and men of that type played a lone hand and made America. Lindbergh is their lineal descendant." In *Outlook* magazine, immediately below an enthusiastic endorsement of Lindbergh's own remarks on the importance of his machine and his scientific instruments, there was the statement, "Charles Lindbergh is the heir of all that we like to think is best in America. He is of the stuff out of which have been made the pioneers that opened up the wilderness, first on the Atlantic coast, and then in our great West. His are the qualities which we, as a people, must nourish." It is in this mood that one suspects it was important that Lindbergh came out of the West and rode all alone.

Another common metaphor in the attempt to place Lindbergh's exploit was to say that he had opened a new "frontier." To speak of the air as a "frontier" was to invoke an interpretation of the meaning of American history which had sources deep in American experience, but the frontier of the airplane is hardly the frontier of the trailmakers of the old West. Rather than an escape into the self-sufficient simplicity of the American past, the machine which made Lindbergh's flight possible represented an advance into a complex industrial present. The difficulty lay in using an instance of modern life to celebrate the virtues of the past, to use an extreme development of an urban industrial society to insist upon the significance of the frontier in American life.

A little more than a month after Lindbergh's flight, Joseph K. Hart in *Survey* magazine reached back to Walt Whitman's poem for the title of an article on Lindbergh: "O Pioneer." A school had made Lindbergh an honorary alumnus but Hart protested there was little available evidence "that he was educated in *schools.*" "We must look elsewhere for our explanation," Hart wrote and he looked to the experience of Lindbergh's youth when "everything that he ever did . . . he did by himself. He lived more to himself than most boys." And, of course, Lindbergh lived to himself in the only place conceivably possible, in the world of nature, on a Minnesota farm. "There he developed in the companionship of woods and fields, animals and machines, his audaciously natural and simple personality." The word, "machines," jars as it intrudes into Hart's idyllic pastoral landscape and betrays Hart's difficulty in relating the setting of nature upon which he wishes to insist with the fact that its product spent his whole life tinkering with machines, from motorcycles to airplanes. But except for that one word, Hart proceeds in uncritical nostalgia to show that "a lone trip across the Atlantic was not impossible for a boy who had grown up in the solitude of the woods and waters." If Lindbergh was "clear-headed, naif, untrained in the ways of cities," it was because he had "that 'natural simplicity' which Fenimore Cooper used to attribute to the pioneer hero of his Leatherstocking Tales." Hart rejected the notion that any student "bent to all the conformities" of formal training could have done what Lindbergh did. "Must we not admit," he asked, "that this pioneering urge remained to this audacious youth because he had never submitted completely to the repressions of the world and its jealous institutions?"

Only those who insist on reason will find it strange that Hart should use the industrial achievement of the airplane to reject the urban, institutionalized world of industrialism. Hart was dealing with something other than reason; he was dealing with the emotion evoked by Lindbergh's solitude. He recognized that people wished to call Lindbergh a "genius" because that "would release him from the ordinary rules of existence." That way, "we could rejoice with him in his triumph, and then go back to the contracted routines of our institutional ways [because] ninety-nine percent of us must be content to be shaped and moulded by the routine ways and forms of the world to the routine tasks of life." It is in the word, "must," that the pathos of this interpretation of the phenomenon of Lindbergh lies. The world had changed from the open society of the pioneer to the close-knit, interdependent world of a modern machine-oriented civilization. The institutions of a highly corporate industrial society existed as a constant reproach to a people who liked to believe that the meaning of its experience was embodied in the formless, independent life of the frontier. Like Thomas Jefferson who identified American virtue with nature and saw the city as a "great sore" on the public body, Hart concluded that "certainly, in the response that the world—especially the world of great cities—has made to the performance of this midwestern boy, we can read of the homesickness of the human soul, immured in city canyons and routine tasks, for the freer world of youth, for the open spaces of the pioneer, for the joy of battling with nature and clean storms once more on the frontiers of the earth."

The social actuality which made the adulation of Lindbergh possible had its own irony for the notion that America's strength lay in its simple uncomplicated beginnings. For the public response to Lindbergh to have reached the proportions it did, the world had by necessity to be the intricately developed world of modern mass communications. But more than irony was involved. Ultimately, the emotion attached to Lindbergh's flight involved no less than a whole theory about American history. By singling out the fact that Lindbergh rode alone, and by naming him a pioneer of the frontier, the public projected its sense that the source of America's strength lay somewhere in the past and that Lindbergh somehow meant that America must look backward in time to rediscover some lost virtue. The mood was nostalgic and American history was read as a decline, a decline measured in terms of America's advance into an urban, institutionalized way of life which made solitary achievement increasingly beyond the reach of ninety-nine per cent of the people. Because Lindbergh's ancestors were Norse, it was easy to call him a "Viking" and extend the emotion far into the past when all frontiers were open. He became the "Columbus" of another new world to conquer as well as the "Lochinvar" who rode all alone. But there was always the brute, irreducible fact that Lindbergh's exploit was a victory of the machine over the barriers of nature. If the only response to Lindbergh had been a retreat to the past, we would be involved with a mass cultural neurosis, the inability of America to accept reality, the reality of the world in which it lived. But there was another aspect, one in which the public celebrated the machine and the highly organized society of which it was a product. The response to Lindbergh reveals that the American people were deeply torn between conflicting interpretations of their own experience. By calling Lindbergh a pioneer, the people could read into American history the necessity of turning back to the frontier past. Yet the people could also read American history in terms of progress into the industrial future. They could do this by emphasizing the machine which was involved in Lindbergh's flight.

Lindbergh came back from Europe in an American man-of-war, the cruiser *Memphis*. It seems he had contemplated flying on, around the whole world perhaps, but less adventurous heads prevailed and dictated a surer mode of travel for so valuable a piece of public property. The *New Republic* protested against bringing America's hero of romance home in a warship. If he had returned on a great liner, that would have been one thing. "One's first trip on an oceanliner is a great adventure—the novelty of it, the many people of all kinds and conditions, floating for a week in a tiny compact world of their own." But to return on the *Memphis,* "to be put on a gray battleship with a collection of people all of the same stripe, in a kind of ship that has as much relation to the life of the sea as a Ford factory has! We might as well have put him in a pneumatic tube and shot him across the Atlantic." The interesting thing about the *New Republic's* protest against the unromantic, regimented life of a battleship is that the image it found appropriate was the Ford assembly line. It was this reaction against the discipline of a mechanized society that probably led to the nostalgic image of Lindbergh as a remnant of a past when romance was possible for the individual, when life held novelty and society was variegated rather than uniform. But what the Ford Assembly Line represents, a society committed to the path of full mechanization, was what lay behind Lindbergh's romantic success. A long piece in the Sunday *New York Times,* "Lindbergh Symbolizes the Genius of America," reminded its readers of the too obvious fact that "without an airplane he could not have flown at all." Lindbergh "is, indeed, the Icarus of the twentieth century; not himself an inventor of his own wings, but a son of that omnipotent Daedalus whose ingenuity has created the modern world." The point was that modern America was the creation of modern industry. Lindbergh "reveres his 'ship' as a noble expression of mechanical wisdom. . . . Yet in this reverence . . . Lindbergh is not an exception. What he means by the Spirit of St. Louis is really the spirit of America. The mechanical genius, which is discerned in Henry Ford as well as in Charles A. Lindbergh, is in the very atmosphere of [the] country." In contrast to a sentiment that feared the enforced discipline of the machine there existed an attitude of reverence for its power.

Lindbergh led the way in the celebration of the machine, not only implicitly by including his plane when he said "we," but by direct statement. In Paris he told newspapermen, "You fellows have not said enough about that wonderful motor." Rarely have two more taciturn figures confronted one another than when Lindbergh returned to Washington and Calvin Coolidge pinned the Distinguished Flying Cross on him, but in his brief remarks Coolidge found room to express his particular delight that Lindbergh should have given equal credit to the airplane. "For we are proud," said the President, "that in every particular this silent partner represented American genius and industry. I am told that more than 100 separate companies furnished materials, parts or service in its construction."

The flight was not the heroic lone success of a single daring individual, but the climax of the co-operative effort of an elaborately interlocked technology. The day after Coolidge's speech, Lindbergh said at another ceremony in Washington that the honor should "not go to the pilot alone but to American science and genius which had given years of study to the advancement of aeronautics." "Some things," he said, "should be taken into due consideration in connection with our flight that have not heretofore been given due weight. That is just what made this flight possible. It was not the act of a single pilot. It was the culmination of twenty years of aeronautical research and the assembling together of all that was practicable and best in American aviation." The flight, concluded Lindbergh, "represented American industry."

The worship of the machine which was embodied in the public's response to Lindbergh exalted those very aspects which were denigrated in the celebration of the flight as the work of a heroic individual. Organization and careful method were what lay behind the flight, not individual self-sufficiency and daring romance. One magazine hailed the flight as a "triumph of mechanical engineering." "It is not to be forgotten that this era is the work not so much of brave aviators as of engineers, who have through patient and protracted effort been steadily improving the construction of airplanes." The lesson to be learned from Lindbergh's flight, thought a writer in the *Independent,* "is that the splendid human and material aspects of America need to be organized for the ordinary, matter of fact service of society." The machine meant organization, the careful rationalization of activity of a Ford assembly line, it meant planning, and, if it meant the loss of spontaneous individual action, it meant the material betterment of society. Lindbergh meant not a retreat to the free life of the frontier past but an emergence into the time when "the machine began to take first place in the public mind—the machine and the organization that made its operation possible on a large scale." A poet on this side of the matter wrote, "All day I felt the pull / Of the steel miracle." The machine was not a devilish engine which would enthrall mankind, it was the instrument which would lead to a new paradise. But the direction of history implicit in the machine was toward the future, not the past; the meaning of history was progress, not decline, and America should not lose faith in the future betterment of society. An address by a Harvard professor, picked up by the *Magazine of Business,* made all this explicit. "We commonly take Social Progress for granted," said Edwin F. Gay, "but the doctrine of Social Progress is one of the great revolutionary ideas which have powerfully affected our modern world." There was a danger, however, that the idea "may be in danger of becoming a commonplace or a butt of criticism." The speaker recognized why this might be. America was "worn and disillusioned after the Great War." Logically, contentment should have gone with so optimistic a creed, yet the American people were losing faith. So Lindbergh filled an emotional need even where a need should have been lacking. "He has come like a shining vision to revive the hope of mankind." The high ideals of faith in progress "had almost come to seem like hollow words to us—but now here he is, emblematic of heroes yet to inhabit this world. Our belief in Social Progress is justified symbolically in him."

It is a long flight from New York to Paris; it is a still longer flight from the fact of Lindbergh's achievement to the burden imposed upon it by the imagination of his time. But it is in that further flight that lies the full meaning of Lindbergh. His role was finally a double one. His flight provided an opportunity for the people to project their own emotions into his act and their emotions involved finally two attitudes toward the meaning of their own experience. One view had it that America represented a brief escape from the course of history, an emergence into a new and open world with the self-sufficient individual at its center. The other said that America represented a stage in historical evolution and that its fulfillment lay in the development of society. For one, the meaning of America lay in the past; for the other in the future. For one, the American ideal was an escape from institutions, from the forms of society, and from limitations put upon the free individual; for the other, the American ideal was the elaboration of the complex institutions which made modern society possible, an acceptance of the discipline of the machine, and the achievement of the individual within a context of which he was only a part. The two views were contradictory but both were possible and both were present in the public's reaction to Lindbergh's flight.

The Sunday newspapers announced that Lindbergh had reached Paris and in the very issue whose front pages were covered with Lindbergh's story the magazine section of the *New York Times* featured an article by the British philosopher, Bertrand Russell. The magazine had, of course, been made up too far in advance to take advantage of the news about Lindbergh. Yet, in a prophetic way, Russell's article was about Lindbergh. Russell hailed the rise to power of the United States because he felt that in the "new life that is America's" in the twentieth century "the new outlook appropriate to machinery [would] become more completely dominant than in the old world." Russell sensed that some might be unwilling to accept the machine, but "whether we like this new outlook or not," he wrote, "is of little importance." Why one might not was obvious. A society built on the machine, said Russell, meant "the diminution in the value and independence of the individual. Great enterprises tend more and more to be collective, and in an industrialized world the interference of the community with the individual must be more intense." Russell realized that while the co-operative effort involved in machine technology makes man collectively more lordly, it makes the individual more submissive. "I do not see how it is to be avoided," he concluded.

People are not philosophers. They did not see how the conflict between a machine society and the free individual was to be avoided either. But neither were they ready to accept the philosopher's statement of the problem. In Lindbergh, the people celebrated both the self-sufficient individual and the machine. Americans still celebrate both. We cherish the individualism of the American creed at the same time that we worship the machine which increasingly enforces collectivized behavior. Whether we can have both, the freedom of the individual and the power of an organized society, is a question that still haunts our minds. To resolve the conflict that is present in America's celebration of Lindbergh in 1927 is still the task of America.

Afternote

The essay on Lindbergh seems to be the most popular piece I have written. At least, it has appeared in four collections of articles on American history by other students. So, counting its first appearance in *American Quarterly*, this marks the sixth time it has been printed which, as much as I still like it myself, seems to me a bit excessive. But, as Ben Franklin would say, I defer to better judgments.

Those who read it now may find further interest in another article, "Lindbergh, Dos Passos and History," *Carleton Miscellany*, VI (Summer, 1965), 20–41. Among other things it describes how I happened to do the essay on Lindbergh in the first place but, perhaps more interesting for students of American culture, also tries to explore the difficult matter of the relation between literature and history.

John William Ward is Professor of History and American Studies at Amherst College. [This article appeared in Vol. X, No. 1 (Spring, 1958).]

Robert L. Tyler

The I. W. W. and the West

THE INDUSTRIAL WORKERS OF THE WORLD HAS WON A PLACE FOR ITSELF IN American folklore and literature although, as an organization with more precise ends, it was ineffectual and short-lived. This radical labor union, remembered primarily as a fraternity of Western migratory workers in lumber, mining and agriculture, preached its gospel of "One Big Union" and the "General Strike" from corner soap boxes, led exasperating wildcat strikes, badgered local law enforcement officials, bore the brunt of anti-radical sentiment during the First World War, and then quietly withered on the radical vine without leaving many tangible fruits. On its guerrilla skirmishes with the "master class" it seemed to build only an exaggerated, fearsome reputation. Such a discrepancy between accomplishments and reputation invites study, if for no other reason than the possibility of exploring one facet of a durable American myth. The argument here presented is that the I.W.W. of legend derives from a tendency, only partly sustained by evidence, of stressing its "Western" character and habitat, thus making it another symbol within the complex myth of the West, that migrating American region of primitive vitality that serves as heroic age and seedbed of our national *virtu* and *pietas.*

An aura of romance certainly surrounds the I.W.W. Wobblies figure, for example, in a wide assortment of American novels, and such different writers as Zane Grey and John Dos Passos have used them in their fiction. Zane Grey made them imps of Satan compounding the troubles of an honest and patriotic wheat farmer,[1] but he nevertheless drew them as villains somewhat outside tame reality. Dos Passos sprinkles his ambitious trilogy, *U.S.A.,* with Wobblies, like Mac in the first narrative thread or Joe Hill, William D. Haywood and Wesley Everest in the inserted

[1] Zane Grey, *The Desert of Wheat* (New York: Harper & Bros., 1919).

biographical sketches.[2] Besides the obvious function they serve as radical martyrs in Dos Passos' leftish criticism of American society, they also serve as mythic symbols, as spiky individualists setting off the dreary conformism and money-grubbing of a decaying American capitalism. Consciously or unconsciously, Dos Passos chose Western Wobblies to serve these purposes, thus associating them implicitly with a traditional view of the West.

Other writers have placed the I.W.W. in the same kind of symbolic context that Dos Passos did in *U.S.A.* In a recent biographical novel by Wallace Stegner, the Wobbly protagonist, Joe Hill, is presented as the very type of the creative primitive, both frustrated and stimulated by his rude Western environment, seeking dimly a higher culture and esthetic.[3] The central conflict of the novel, in a sense, is the personalization of a dilemma that Henry Nash Smith and others have found inherent in the "frontier hypothesis," the dilemma of a seminal and vital frontier that can only "progress" to the effete civilization that it nourishes.[4] Even in a contemporary and sophisticated satire like Mary McCarthy's *The Groves of Academe,* a Wobbly briefly appears—in the wings, so to speak—in his mythic Western role, weaning an absurd "poet of the people" from the cant and sterility of Communism to a more elemental and vital anarchism.[5] A repentant American Communist in his memoirs also strikes these particular strings of romance in describing a famous Wobbly exile, William D. Haywood, in Moscow. Benjamin Gitlow found Haywood a sick and lonely old man living out his expatriation in Russia, homesick amid the scholastic Bolsheviks, the noble savage from Utah expiring in a strange cage.[6]

As the I.W.W. withered and died after the First World War, its peculiarly "Western" character became fixed in the minds of many writers, journalists and scholars. Almost imperceptibly over the last generation the I.W.W. has been incorporated into the corpus of Western folklore, along with earlier mountain men, cowboys and sodbusters. Its heroes and exploits receive space in most of the compilations of American and regional folklore.[7] In the Pacific Northwest alone Stewart Holbrook,

2 John Dos Passos, *U. S. A.* (New York: The Modern Library, 1939).

3 Wallace Stegner, *The Preacher and the Slave* (Boston: Houghton Mifflin Co., 1950).

4 Henry Nash Smith, *Virgin Land: The American West as Symbol and Myth* (Cambridge: Harvard University Press, 1950), pp. 250-51.

5 Mary McCarthy, *The Groves of Academe* (New York: Harcourt, Brace & Co., 1951).

6 Benjamin Gitlow, *I Confess: The Truth About American Communism* (New York: E. P. Dutton & Co., 1940), pp. 467-69.

7 B. A. Botkin (ed.), *A Treasury of Western Folklore* (New York: Crown, 1951), pp. 627-30, 730; B. A. Botkin (ed.), *A Treasury of American Folklore* (New York: Crown, 1944), pp. 882-83, 886-87.

Archie Binns, Nard Jones and others have staked out a kind of regional claim on the I.W.W., using its violent and bumptious history for their local color purposes. Nothing much of historical analysis remains in most of these regional works. The I.W.W. *cause célèbre,* apparently, is to be understood as only another instance of frontier exuberance, like the shooting up of a saloon. In describing the I.W.W. disturbances at Everett and Centralia, Washington, Nard Jones wrote, "This was the frontier and a man spoke out, with his voice or with his gun."[8] Archie Binns devotes many pages in a recently published book to twice-told tales about the I.W.W., presenting the Wobbly as some kind of frontier relic challenging the urbanization and capitalistic development of the Puget Sound region.[9]

By 1926 Stewart Holbrook had claimed the I.W.W.'s distinctive slang for the West, although admitting that much of it derived from general underworld and hobo argot.[10] Twenty years later, in describing an old Wobbly of Portland, Oregon, a kind of Burnside Street landmark, Holbrook makes the Pacific Northwest the "real home of the Wobs," and ends his description with a hyperbolic coda that reveals in sharp relief the I.W.W. legend as it had developed by 1946:

> . . . Boose will put away his colors and brushes, and talk of the great days when the Wobbly brand of revolution ran like fire through the wheat, the mines, the woods of the West; when the West fairly reeked of Wobblies, and the Wob organizers hung stiffly from bridges and trestles by their necks, or died on the bloody decks of the *Verona* in Everett harbor, or went down in the choking dust of Wheatland or Bisbee. . . . Aye, my lads, those were the great days when working stiffs had nothing to lose but their chains, unless on occasion their lives. . . .[11]

The Wobblies themselves, in large measure, helped to start this identification of their organization with the myth of the West. The internal history of the I.W.W.—as is the case apparently with most radical movements—is a history of schisms and purges. Begun in 1905 in Chicago by a heterogeneous group of socialists and industrial unionists as a corrective to the stodgy and conservative American Federation of Labor, the I.W.W. almost immediately fell apart in internecine quarreling. By 1908 most of the founding fathers from the Socialist Party and the Socialist Labor Party and all of the really functioning constituent unions had

[8] Nard Jones, *Evergreen Land: A Portrait of the State of Washington* (New York: Dodd, Mead & Co., 1947), p. 81.

[9] Archie Binns, *Sea in the Forest* (New York: Doubleday & Co., 1953).

[10] S. H. Holbrook, "Wobbly Talk," *American Mercury*, VII (January, 1926), 62.

[11] S. H. Holbrook, "The Last of the Wobblies," *American Mercury*, LXII (April, 1946), 467-68.

deserted or had been purged. The I.W.W. that remained after 1908 became more and more a splinter group of intellectuals, impatient activists and fanatic professional union leaders manning a few barely skeletal unions. The most durable source of friction within the organization was a conflict between two groups calling themselves the "Centralizers" and the "Decentralizers." In 1913 the organization barely escaped a fourth schism because of this dispute, the anarchical Decentralizers advocating an abolition of the Chicago headquarters and of all central authority in the I.W.W.. In 1924 the I.W.W., by this time moribund, did finally split over this dispute, the Decentralizers establishing their own "Emergency Program" in excommunication in Portland, Oregon. The Decentralizers drew support largely from the hobo membership and could perhaps be called a "Western" faction, although the leaders of the opposing Centralizers were also Westerners. At any rate, the I.W.W. press tended to identify the anarchists as Westerners.[12] Wobblies discussed at great length in their press the respective merits of the "Western" hobo worker, or "bindle stiff," and the more sedentary Eastern factory worker, or "home guard." The General Executive Board of the I.W.W. in 1913 attacked this typically "Western" hobo Wobbly, this anarchical Decentralizer, for his excessive contentiousness and, strangely enough, for his inaction:

> We find a situation in the West that if continued means the complete disruption of the only industrial organization in the world. In time of strike they sit around the hall talking of what ought to be done or devising means to do away with General Headquarters. It is impossible, however, to get them out on the picket line to fight the boss. They will talk of sabotage and direct action but leave it to the boss to use on the few who take up the fight. If this condition continues the I.W.W. will die of dry rot. . . .[13]

Other I.W.W. writers, however, defended the Western migrant worker as a source of great revolutionary strength, describing him in phrases foretelling the Wobbly of more recent popular legend. He was less a wage slave, less servile, than the Eastern industrial worker. He was, indeed, a "vagabond adventurer," "the scout of the labor army," "the franc tireur of the class struggle."[14] Western Decentralizers, in their own defense, harped upon the dangers of autocracy, corruption, the scholastic ideology-mongering that emanated from the Chicago headquarters, traits, of

12 Frank Bohn, "Is the I. W. W. to Grow?" *International Socialist Review*, XII (July, 1911), 42-44.
13 *Proceedings of the Eighth Annual Convention of the I. W. W., 1913*, p. 34.
14 *Solidarity*, November 21, 1914, p. 3.

course, of an effete East. This emerging portrait of the "Western" Wobbly, drawn by both sympathetic and unsympathetic I.W.W. publicists, resembles in many features the picture of Frederick Jackson Turner's frontiersman with his "coarseness and strength," his "restless, nervous energy," his "buoyancy and exuberance."[15]

The legendary Wobbly from the logging camps, the non-ferrous mines and the wheat fields has, of course, a considerable basis in fact, but the legend tends to obscure other significant facts of I.W.W. history. At the first convention in 1905 the individual delegates, the founding fathers, were more apt to be Easterners than Westerners. The impetus for the constituent convention came as much from William Trautman of the brewers' union as it did from the Western Federation of Miners. Though the strongest functioning union that joined the new I.W.W. was the Western Federation of Miners, much of the program, ideology and initial prestige derived from such delegates as William Trautman, Daniel De Leon of the doctrinaire Socialist Labor Party, Eugene V. Debs of the newer Socialist Party, "Mother" Jones of the coal fields and from other prominent radicals and industrial unionists with few if any ties to the "frontier." Furthermore, the I.W.W. scored its first successes in the industrial East, in the steel and textile industries, where it attracted during brief crises great numbers of unskilled, immigrant workers. The stories of these mass strikes of the I.W.W. before the First World War have been told often. Indeed the pamphlet, newspaper, magazine and documentary literature on the early I.W.W. in the East is voluminous. But to correct the notion that the Wobbly was uniquely a frontiersman, some features of these strikes deserve to be reviewed and underscored.

Early in 1909 the Pressed Steel Car Company of McKee's Rocks, Pennsylvania, announced a new wage system that confused and irritated the predominantly immigrant labor force. The new rates were not to be posted, and the worker's wages were to be dependent upon the output of his "gang." The new system broke a camel's back already loaded with many grievances, and in July forty men formed an *ad hoc* committee to request the posting and explanation of the new wage rates. The company peremptorily discharged the forty men. The strike followed immediately. McKee's Rocks became an armed camp with special deputies and two hundred state constables on patrol. Violence inevitably occurred. When, in one riot, a striker was killed, the "Unknown Committee" directing the strike issued a bloodthirsty "life for a life" ultimatum to the authorities. The funeral procession for the dead striker became a

[15] Frederick Jackson Turner, *The Frontier in American History* (New York: Henry Holt & Co., 1920), p. 37.

grim demonstration with eulogies delivered at the grave in fifteen languages. The I.W.W. did not appear upon the scene—at least openly—until August. William Trautman conducted a public meeting for the strikers and organized an I.W.W. local. A week later strikers fought a pitched battle with state troopers in which eleven persons were killed. The strikers arrested after this fray were dragged down the streets behind troopers'—or Cossacks', as they were called by the Slavic strikers—horses. Finally as public sentiment in the Pittsburgh area swung around in support of the strikers, the Pressed Steel Car Company surrendered and granted the I.W.W.'s demands.[16]

Less than three years later the I.W.W. again attracted national attention when prominent Wobblies became leaders of a strike of textile workers in Lawrence, Massachusetts. On January 1, 1912, a newly enacted state law took effect, reducing the hours of work for women and minors from 56 hours, or more, to 54 hours a week. At the first pay day in January, 1912, it became obvious that the American Woolen Company mills in Lawrence had obeyed the letter of the law but had given a pro rata reduction in wages as well. The wage reduction was a serious crisis for many families living on the margins of their small budgets. When mill operators refused to see a committee from the small existing I.W.W. local, a strike spread quickly through most of the mills in Lawrence. On January 13, Joseph Ettor of the I.W.W. General Headquarters arrived to take up the reins of the strike. He became chairman of a strike committee composed of three delegates from each foreign language group in Lawrence. Militia companies also arrived, bringing in their wake sporadic violence. In the last week of January troops fired into the ranks of an I.W.W. parade and one woman striker was killed. Ten more companies of troops hurried to Lawrence. Ettor and Artur Giovannitti, a Wobbly poet and intellectual, were arrested as accessories to the murder of the woman striker. The I.W.W. thereupon sent William D. Haywood to succeed Ettor, and under Haywood's direction, the strike committee began to send children of strikers out of Lawrence to sanctuary in the homes of sympathizers in New York and other cities. A national outcry of sympathy for the strikers arose from this propaganda tactic that the I.W.W. borrowed from European Syndicalist practice, particularly after the Lawrence police on one occasion used violence and brutality to stop the children's exodus at the railroad station. A dynamite plot was uncovered and laid at the doorstep of the I.W.W., but the plot backfired

16 R. D. Smith, "Phases of the McKee's Rocks Strike," *Survey*, XXIII (October 2, 1909), 38. The *Survey* published a number of other articles and news items on the McKee's Rocks strike.

when evidence pointed not to the I.W.W. but to a local undertaker with ties to the operators. In March the operators gave up the fight, and the I.W.W. celebrated another victory.[17]

The Lawrence strike attracted widespread attention, leading to a Congressional investigation and thousands upon thousands of words of comment in the press. Progressives saw it as proof of the dangers of the high tariff and of "invisible government" by the "interests" supporting the Payne-Aldrich Tariff. Socialists, of course, gloated. The strike proved, if proof was necessary for them, that capitalists were behaving exactly as they were supposed to behave and creating in their wake a really disciplined and revolutionary working class. Conservatives trembled. Nativists saw the strike as a typical plot of "foreign radicals" that should convince even the blind of the need for immigration restriction.

In 1913 a silk strike in Paterson, New Jersey, stirred up almost as much excitement as had the Lawrence strike. Greenwich Village intellectuals at this point began their flirtation with the I.W.W. The Bohemian Left organized a great "strike pageant" in New York City, and real strikers were imported from the Paterson picket lines to move through the various *tableaux* created by John Reed and others.[18] These bitter industrial conflicts in the East—and there were others—appeared as ominous thunder clouds over American society. Besides newspaper comment and Congressional inquiry, they stimulated a great deal of "sociological" explanation.[19] At this high point of its effectiveness, the I.W.W. did not strike most Americans as a band of frontier individualists but rather as a cabal of dangerous "new immigrants" insinuating Syndicalism and other outlandish and un-American doctrines into a mythically classless America.

As late as 1917, the first scholarly historian of the I.W.W. interpreted the movement as the American reflection of a world tendency in radical labor unionism and not as a frontier phenomenon.[20] Another scholar viewed the I.W.W. as the response to the needs of two groups of submerged American workers, the Western migrants of legend *and* the unskilled immigrants of Eastern industry. The author of this latter study cited membership figures sent him by Vincent St. John of the I.W.W. General Executive Board, figures showing that over half of the Wobblies

[17] The Congressional investigation of the Lawrence strike was conducted by the Rules Committee of the House of Representatives and published as *The Strike at Lawrence, Massachusetts* (Washington, D. C.: Government Printing Office, 1912).

[18] New York *Times,* May 22, 1913, p. 4; June 8, 1913, II, p. 2; June 9, 1913, p. 8.

[19] For example: John Graham Brooks, *American Syndicalism: The I. W. W.* (New York: Macmillan Co., 1913); Andre Tridon, *The New Unionism* (New York: Huebsch, 1913).

[20] Paul Frederick Brissenden, *The I. W. W.: A Study of American Syndicalism* (New York: Columbia University Press, 1920).

at that date came from the Eastern steel and textile industries.[21] By 1935, however, two historians of the American labor movement presented the Wobbly as a kind of Lochinvar from the West: "In 1909 these neglected and despised workers [Eastern unskilled, immigrant workers] found a champion which saw in their degradation and weakness a justification for its intervention. This champion came from the West."[22] Haywood, of course, and several other Wobblies who rushed to the Eastern strikes to take over the leadership were indeed Westerners, trained for their jobs in the burly class wars fought by the Western Federation of Miners, but many other agitators and leaders were Easterners, such as Elizabeth Gurley Flynn, Carlo Tresca, Artur Giovannitti or George Andreytchine. Furthermore, the I.W.W. at this crest of its career published newspapers in a half-dozen foreign languages. The organization obviously could command literate editorial talent in various immigrant groups and apparently expected to recruit most of its members from among Eastern immigrant workers. The thesis that the I.W.W. was a champion from the West requires some explanation if not defense.

Many Wobbly tactics, presumed to be so typically "Western" in the minds of regional authors, had their exact counterparts in as un-Western a place as New York City. "Free-speech Fights," and similar guerrilla combat devices, were not in fact limited to the West. While Wobbly "bindle stiffs" in Portland, Oregon, were entering expensive restaurants and ordering meals for which they had no intention of paying,[23] New York Wobblies were up to the same kind of pranks. Under the leadership of Frank Tannenbaum Wobblies exasperated the authorities of New York City by seeking refuge from the winter in exclusive middle-class churches.[24] It was an Italian Wobbly of the urban and Eastern "New Immigration," Joseph Ettor, who organized and helped direct the 1907 lumber mill strike in Portland, Oregon, that introduced the I.W.W. to the whole Pacific Northwest.[25] Other Eastern Wobblies played important parts in the sanguinary "Everett Massacre" of 1916 in the state of Washington.

The romance of the West that has come to encrust the I.W.W. undoubtedly began during the First World War when the organization did indeed conduct its last and noisiest efforts in the West. Wobblies

21 Louis Levine, "Development of Syndicalism in America," *Political Science Quarterly*, XXVIII (September, 1913), 478.

22 Selig Perlman and Philip Taft, *Labor Movements, 1896-1932* (John R. Commons, *et al.*, *History of Labor in the United States*, Vol. IV [4 vols.; New York: Macmillan Co., 1926-35]), 262.

23 Portland *Oregonian*, December 23, 1913, p. 13.

24 New York *Times*, March 5, 1914, p. 1.

25 Portland *Oregonian*, March 10, 1907, p. 1.

led wartime strikes in the non-ferrous mining regions of the West, and, in particular, they directed a general strike in the lumber industry of the Pacific Northwest. The public viewed this latter strike as little better than deliberate sabotage of the war effort, especially the production of Sitka spruce for airplane construction. In the lumber strike Wobblies hit upon tactics that writers have since cited as evidence of sorts for placing the Wobblies among the folk heroes of the frontier. As the suppression of the strike became more and more effective, Wobblies by the hundreds were put away in jails or in specially constructed "bull pens." Many stayed in jail for weeks, or even months, as the authorities searched for charges to bring against them, perhaps for draft evasion, perhaps for violations of the 1917 Espionage Act, perhaps, at last, for only vagrancy. At this point in the strike, the Wobblies "took the strike to the job," as they called it. Strikers went back to work but continued their harassments with slowdowns, sabotage and psychological attrition. For example, Wobblies acted as if their eight-hour-day strike demand had been won, and they quit work regularly after an eight-hour stint. When apoplectic foremen fired them, they merely packed their "bindles" and moved to another job to repeat the tactic. On the job they might also lose all initiative and know-how and wait helplessly for foremen's orders when even the most simple and obvious decisions had to be made. The I.W.W. claimed advantages for these exasperating tactics. The authorities, obviously, could no longer arrest strikers because everybody "worked" after a fashion. The companies' payrolls also unwittingly financed the "commissary" of the strike.[26]

These disturbances in the West, coming as they did in the embattled years of 1917 and 1918, aroused more fear and indignation throughout the nation than had the earlier strikes in Lawrence or Paterson. City, county, state and federal governments, as well as extralegal vigilantes, turned their full wrath upon the I.W.W. The image of the Wobbly as a kind of backwoods bomb-thrower, as a buckskin Bolshevik, became current. It is this picture of the Wobbly that appears in Zane Grey's popular wartime novel, *The Sea of Wheat*. The riot in Centralia, Washington, on Armistice Day, 1919, in which Wobblies defended their hall against marchers in an American Legion parade, produced a postwar *cause célèbre* and also helped to fix this special Western image of the Wobbly.

As liberals and radicals regrouped after the debacle of the war, they found only a decaying and doctrinaire I.W.W. still surviving. The

[26] James Rowan, *The I. W. W. in the Lumber Industry* (Seattle, Wash.: I. W. W. Lumber Workers Industrial Union No. 500, n.d.).

organization had been bludgeoned by the Department of Justice, raided by the new Communist movement, broken by reviving internal squabbles of Centralizers and Decentralizers and it had already begun to ossify around its anarcho-syndicalist fundamentalism that was fast becoming irrelevant to the changing America of the 1920's and, before long, of the Great Depression. Perhaps naturally the American Left looked back to the irrepressible Wobblies as the expended shock troops of an old-style radicalism. Because the West had seen the last agony of the I.W.W., it was also perhaps natural to see the Wobblies as latter-day frontiersmen defending the fort of American liberty against the mounting forces of reaction and "fascism," forces which many intellectuals by the 1930's feared were on the point of winning the day. For the Left, the I.W.W. fitted very comfortably into the framework of Bacon's Rebellion, Jacksonian Democracy, Free-Soilism and Populism. From this perspective it was only a short step for popular writers to begin to blur all the ideological considerations and to begin to sentimentalize the "Western" Wobbly, stressing his zest for fighting, his unquenchable individualism, his crude humor, his "style." For John Dos Passos the Wobblies apparently had stood for ideological Paul Bunyans; for subsequent writers they came to be only Paul Bunyans.[27]

That the Wobbly passed from the scene while struggling in Western mining towns and logging camps against the behemoth of modern capitalism does not suffice by itself to explain the I.W.W. legend. A crucial link between the "real" I.W.W. of intellectuals, immigrant wage workers, hoboes and labor union functionaries and the I.W.W. of sentimentalists is to be found in the radical intelligentsia of the early twentieth century, whose capital was Greenwich Village and whose journals were the "little magazines" and, especially, the *Masses.*

In perspective the I.W.W. appears as only one unusually militant rebellion within a more general disaffection with American society during the early 1900's. This discontent, summarized in textbooks under the name "Progressive Movement," touched politics, religion, education, academic philosophy and the arts as well as the labor movement. Perhaps the winning and the "closing" of the last frontier after the Civil War occasioned this pervasive urge for reform and change, but certainly just as basic was the maturation of American capitalism, bringing vague but unmistakable anxieties, fears that America had shifted gears into a new era with strange new problems and frustrations. Nowhere in the web of American culture is this change of temper more recognizable than in the literature of the period, a change analyzed and charted by critics

27 The biographical sketch of Wesley Everest in *U. S. A.* is even entitled "Paul Bunyan."

of all schools. Serious young writers united in an assault upon the "Genteel Tradition," eagerly importing Naturalism, Symbolism, Decadence, Primitivism and other exotic literary postures from abroad. With the self-conscious literary revival came not so much a joy or *élan* as a heightened feeling of "alienation," endlessly discussed in the literary journals and memoirs, and a bitter and militant phase of *bourgeoisie*-baiting. The young writer avidly shopped for ideologies. Some chose anti-Puritanism, basing their position on an easy historical ignorance and a confusion of hard-headed Calvinism with the newly repudiated "Victorianism." America, they preached, too much stifled the id. Others, like Jack London, embraced Marx or Spencer, or became apostates from the whole liberal tradition and adopted the myth of the superman and the blond beast. One impresario of highbrow dissenters, Mabel Dodge, satisfied her longings by cultivating all the fashionable ideologies from Marx to Freud.

It is not surprising that some young intellectuals should soon "discover" the I.W.W. Wobblies by 1912 began to impress many intellectuals as kinds of noble primitives, enlisted to be sure under their own peculiar banners, but allies nonetheless in the common struggle against bourgeois philistinism. Greenwich Village could not fail to adumbrate a connection between the awesome I.W.W. leaders and primitivism, which in the American experience usually means the West. The connection, however, was never clearly made at this early date before the First World War because most of the Wobblies known to Greenwich Villagers of the *Masses* staff and the Liberal Club were themselves Easterners, brought to light by the textile strikes in Lawrence and Paterson. But "Big Bill" Haywood, an indubitable Westerner, early bemused the New York literary radicals. Mabel Dodge made him a popular attraction at some of her famous "evenings" in the Village. Though Mabel Dodge herself was something less than idolatrous—reporting that Haywood talked "as though he were wading blindfolded through sand"—most of her guests paid more than respectful attention.[28] To Max Eastman, Haywood was the "arch rebel, the one-eyed gigantic satan who scorned even to answer except with an oath the Socialist Party's excommunication of him."[29] When Haywood asked if he might have an article of his published in the *Masses,* Eastman, the editor, felt as though he were being admitted into an "heroic order."[30] Malcolm Cowley, a late-comer to the Village, knew of the prewar golden days only by hearsay; he described Haywood

[28] Mabel Dodge Luhan, *Movers and Shakers* (New York: Harcourt, Brace & Co., 1936), p. 89.

[29] Max Eastman, *Enjoyment of Living* (New York: Harper & Bros., 1948), p. 445.

[30] *Ibid.*

as the "one-eyed man-mountain, the cyclops of the I.W.W.," who brought to his rapt listeners at Mabel Dodge's salons a feeling of participation in the lusty class wars of the mining camps of Idaho.[31]

Without too much strain, the idea of primitive strength and virtue that at one time or another attracted such intellectuals as Sherwood Anderson, Eugene O'Neill or Carl Van Vechten was projected by some of the lusty I.W.W. There was frequently more than a hint that this primitive vitality, enlisted in the fight against effete American capitalism, was really the latter-day expression of the traditional equalitarianism and individualism of the West. Floyd Dell, novelist and onetime editor and book reviewer of the *Masses,* dealt with the Wobblies in just this ideological framework even though he was not a particular devotee of the I.W.W. In one novel, for example, a middle-aged and somewhat inhibited Bostonian moves to California and begins the rediscovery of his youth after he is thrown by circumstances into a group of young, rowdy Wobblies at a "free-speech fight."[32]

Other intellectuals of a less strenuous radicalism early tended to remake the Wobbly into a homely, one hundred per cent American, undoubtedly to distinguish him from the newer and more exotic Communists. The Wobblies themselves co-operated in this retouching job, and the emerging portrait of a rebellious, sturdy primitive, a Westerner and typical American, is virtually the finished picture. John Spargo, the leading theorist—or "theoretician"—of the American Socialist Party before the war, delineated the "typical" Wobbly for a national magazine, drawing him quite unlike the repulsive wartime portraits of the newspaper cartoonists. He was no bearded bomb-thrower. He was instead a "very attractive sort of man," sturdy, robust, virile, roughly dressed, to be sure, but with a bold and intelligent manner.[33] A few years later another writer for a national magazine continued the Americanization of the Wobbly. "The Wobs were a merry and rowdy lot, and the latter-day saints of Moscow were by way of contrast a blue-nosed and often sniveling congregation."[34] Even the Wobblies in their unhappy competition with the vaunting Communists came more and more to advertise the essential Western "Americanism" of their brand of radicalism.[35]

31 Malcolm Cowley, *Exile's Return: A Literary Odyssey of the 1920's* (New York: Viking Press, 1951), p. 66.

32 Floyd Dell, *An Old Man's Folly* (New York: George H. Doran, 1926), pp. 102-21.

33 John Spargo, "Why the I. W. W. Flourishes," *World's Work,* XXXIX (January, 1920), 244.

34 S. Putnam, "Red Days in Chicago," *American Mercury,* XXX (September, 1933), 70.

35 Abner Woodruff, "A Letter to the Professor," *One Big Union Monthly,* I (August, 1919), 25-27; *Chicago Replies to Moscow* (Chicago: I. W. W. circular, 1945).

Thus the reflection of the I.W.W. in popular legend and historiography has followed a traceable path, from an organization of dangerous, foreign "Syndicalists," to an organization of wartime saboteurs and traitors, to an organization of manly primitives fighting the good fight for freedom, to a jolly band of rogues ushering out the last frontier. Each succeeding image, of course, has served some special use, to supply evidence for nativists of the dangers of unrestricted immigration, to rally the community for a great war effort, to differentiate "American" from "Bolshevik" radicalism and to supply a colorful, boisterous tradition for writers of regional "local color." Apparently the destiny of the I.W.W. was not to bring in the "Cooperative Commonwealth" or the "Industrial Democracy" advocated so vociferously from its soap boxes but rather to stand as an exemplar of a hoary American ideology in a day of growing technological and psychological automation. In this case, the would-be Wobbly expropriators have been themselves expropriated.

Robert L. Tyler is an Associate Professor of History at Wagner College, Staten Island, N.Y. [This article appeared in Vol. XII, No. 2, Pt. 1 (Summer, 1960).]

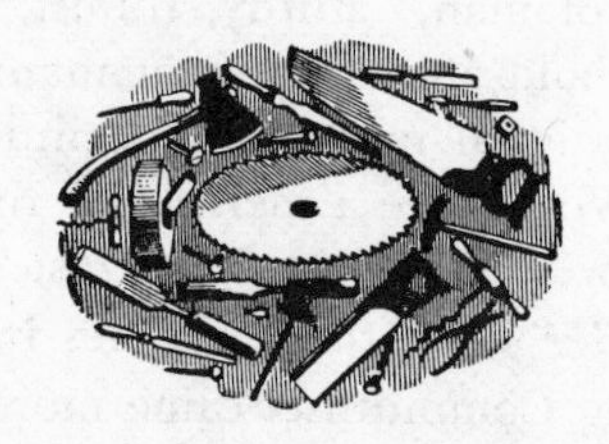

Irving Howe

The Southern Myth and William Faulkner

UNTIL very recently, regional consciousness has remained stronger in the South than in any other part of the United States. This "historical lag" is the source of whatever is most distinctive in Southern thought and feeling. After its defeat in the Civil War, the South could not participate fully and freely in the "normal" development of American society—that is, industrialism and large-scale capitalism arrived there later and with far less force than in the North or West. By the Reconstruction period New England regional consciousness was in decline and by the turn of the century the same was probably true for the Midwest; but the South, because it was a pariah region or because its recalcitrance in defeat forced the rest of the nation to treat it as such, felt its sectional identity most acutely during the very decades when the United States was becoming a self-conscious nation. While the other regions meekly submitted to dissolution, the South worked desperately to keep itself intact. Through an exercise of the will, it insisted that the regional memory be the main shaper of its life.

Perhaps because it had so little else to give its people, the South nurtured in them a generous and often obsessive sense of the past. The rest of the country might be committed to commercial expansion or addicted to the notion of progressive optimism, but the South, even if it cared to, was unable to accept these dominant American values; it had been left behind, it was living on the margin of history—a position that often provides the sharpest perspective on history. During the decades that followed the defeat of the South, its writers could maintain a relation to American life comparable, in miniature, to the relation in the nineteenth century between Russian writers and European life. For while nineteenth-century Russia was the most backward country on the continent, its writers managed to use that backwardness as a vantage-point from which to observe west-European life and thereby to arrive at a profound and withering criticism of bourgeois morality. Precisely because Russia was trailing the capitalist West, the Russian writers could examine the bourgeois code without hesitation or illusion. It was this crucial advantage of distance, this perspective from the social rear, that was the major dispensation the South could offer its writers.

And it gave them something else: a compact and inescapable subject. The Southern writer did not have to cast about for his materials, he hardly enjoyed a spontaneous choice in his use of them, for they welled within him like a dream recurrent since childhood. Faulkner has given a vivid if somewhat romantic description of this subject in *Intruder in the Dust:*

> . . . For every Southern boy fourteen years old, not once but whenever he wants it, there is the instance when it's still not two o'clock on that July afternoon in 1863, the brigades are in position behind the rail fence, the guns are laid and ready in the woods and the furled flags are already loosened to break out and Pickett himself with his long oiled ringlets and his hat in one hand probably and his sword in the other looking up the hill waiting for Longstreet to give the word and it's all in the balance, it hasn't happened yet, it hasn't even begun . . .

But of course it has happened, it must begin. The basic Southern subject is the defeat of the homeland, though its presentation can vary from the magnolia romancing of *The White Rose of Memphis* to the despairing estimate of social loss in *The Sound and the Fury.* Nor does it matter, for the moment, whether one defines the Southern subject, in Allen Tate's words, as "the destruction by war and the later degradation by carpetbaggers and scalawags, and a consequent lack of moral force and imagination in the cynical materialism of the New South," or as the defeat of a reactionary slaveowning class followed by its partial recapture of power through humiliating alliances with Northern capital and a new scrofulous commercial class of local origin. Regardless of which interpretation one accepts, the important point is that this subject, like a thick cloud of memory, has been insistently and implacably *there.* The Southern writer could romanticize it, reject it, enlarge it into an image of the general human situation; he could not escape it. And precisely this ubiquity of subject matter provided him with some very considerable advantages. Not so long before the Civil War, Hawthorne had remarked that "No author can conceive of the difficulty of writing a romance about a country where there is no shadow, no antiquity, no picturesque and gloomy wrong, not anything but a commonplace prosperity." But now the War and Reconstruction gave the Southern writers all that Hawthorne had found lacking: all but antiquity. And there were ruins to take the place of that.

It was not until the First World War, however, that serious Southern writing began to appear—that is, not until Southern regional consciousness began to decay. One reason for this lag was simply that before the 1910's and 1920's there had not been enough money in the South to send many young people to college or to encourage them in such social luxuries as literary careers. A land bent by defeat was not likely to turn to letters with an urgent passion or enthusiasm. Nor could the South look back upon a serious literary tradition of its own, certainly none comparable to that of New England; ante-bellum Southern writing had for the most part been sentimental, genteel, and insipid. Its talented men had given themselves to politics and oratory, and had looked upon literature as a minor pastime hardly sufficient to engage their intellectual capacities. Only some decades later, when the most sensitive minds of the South would be appalled by the Snopesian vulgarity of its politics, would they turn to the arts half in hope, half in desperation.

For it was the reality of twentieth-century life, in all its coarse provocation, which drove so many Southern writers to a regional past that in happier circumstances they might have peaceably neglected. The mottoes of Southern agrarianism were hardly to be taken seriously as social proposals for the most industrialized country in the world, but as signs of a fundamental quarrel with modern life, an often brilliant criticism of urban anonymity, they deserved very much to be taken seriously.

Before the Southern writers could make imaginative statements about their own past, they had to be exposed to intellectual drafts from beyond their regional horizon. Southern literature at its best—the work of Faulkner, Caldwell, Ransom, Tate, Warren—was conceived in an explosive mixture of provincialism and cosmopolitanism, tradition and modernity. To measure the stature of their ancestor Poe, the Southern writers had first to understand what he had meant to Baudelaire, and for that they had to possess a sophisticated awareness of the European literary past. For the Southern imagination to burst into high flame it had to be stimulated, or irritated, by the pressures of European and Northern ideas and literary modes. Left to itself, a regional consciousness is not likely to result in anything but a tiresome romanticizing of the past and thereby a failure to understand the present. Once, however, the South reached that point where it still remained a distinct region but was already cracking under alien influences, it could begin to produce serious works of art. As Allen Tate has shrewdly remarked, the distinctive Southern "consciousness is quite temporary. It has made possible the curious burst of intelligence that we get at the crossing of the ways, not unlike, on an infinitesimal scale, the outburst of poetic genius at the end of the sixteenth century when commercial England had already begun to crush feudal England." What Tate seems to be saying here is that Southern literature assumed a dimension of seriousness and grandeur only when the South as a region began to die, when its writers were forced to look back upon a past that was irretrievable and forward to a future that seemed intolerable.

It is therefore insufficient to say, as many critics do, that Faulkner is a traditional moralist drawing his creative strength from the Southern myth; the truth is that he writes in opposition to his tradition as well as in acceptance, that he struggles with the Southern myth even as he acknowledges and celebrates it. His relation to his own beliefs is far more ambivalent and difficult than was the case for most nineteenth-century American writers. We may safely assume that Melville and Whitman, in their major work, were moved by the democratic yearnings of nineteenth-century America; one feels of *Moby Dick* and *Leaves of Grass* that they are books written with the resources of an entire age behind them. Melville's epic conceptions and Whitman's rolling declamations follow, in part, from their adherence to a myth that is still viable and therefore likely to stir men to dedicated action. Faulkner, however, is working with the decayed fragments of a myth, the somewhat soured pieties of regional memory, and that is why his language is so often tortured, forced, and even incoherent. Unquestionably Faulkner has been influenced by Melville, but in their uses of language one can see reflected the difference between a belief still vigorous and a belief picking at its own bones. Yeats's definition of rhetoric as the will doing the work of the imagination is pertinent to both Melville and Faulkner, but particularly to Faulkner. For what is the soft shapeless rhetoric of *Sartoris* but the sign of a strained will floundering in sentimentality, and what is the agonized rhetoric of *Absalom, Absalom* but the sign of a strained will confronted with its own intolerably acute awareness?

What then *is* the Southern myth? Like any other myth, it is a story or cluster of stories that expresses the deepest attitudes and reflects the most fundamental experiences of a people. And its subject, in this case, is the fate of a ruined homeland. The homeland—so the story goes—had proudly insisted that it alone should determine its destiny; provoked into a war impossible to win, its had nevertheless fought to its last strength; and it had fought this war with a reckless gallantry and a superb heroism that, as Faulkner might say, made of its defeat not a shame but almost a vindication. But the homeland fell, and from this fall came misery and squalor: the ravaging by the conquerors, the loss of faith among the descendants of the defeated, and the rise of a new breed of faceless men who would batten on their neighbors' humiliation.

From these stories there follows that pride in ancestral glory and that mourning over the decline of the homeland which comprise the psychology of the "lost cause." Thus, for one intermittently Southern writer, John Peale Bishop, the South found its highest distinction in "a manner of living somewhat more amiable than any other that has ever been known on the continent." And for another Southern writer, Allen Tate, the South is the one place that "clings blindly to forms of European feeling and conduct that were crushed by the French Revolution." Where else, he asks, "outside of the South, is there a society that believes even covertly in the Code of Honor?"

A myth which pervades a people's imagination is hardly open to rational attack or defense, particularly when it is considered as part of a work of literature. The historian, no doubt, would have to compare the claims of the Southern myth with the actual course of Southern history. He would evaluate the tradition and order so often ascribed to the old South; inquire exactly for whom its way of living could be somewhat more amiable; speculate on the extent to which the Southern emphasis on honor and heroism may often have been a means of salvaging pride from defeat or a token of uncertainty about the moral value of its cause. And if our historian were inclined to moral reflection he might ask the one question that by its very nature the myth cannot tolerate: granted heroism, granted honor, was the homeland defending a just cause? For the critic these questions, while important, are not the crux of the matter, since it is hardly necessary to take at face value or even give substantial credence to the claims of the Southern myth—I certainly do not—in order to acknowledge the powerful uses to which it can be put by a sympathetic imagination. The Southern myth, like any other myth, is less an attempt at historical description than a voicing of the collective imagination, perhaps of the collective will. The old South over which it chants in threnody is an ideal image—a buried city, Allen Tate has called it. Both the violence and the poignancy with which this ideal image has been employed suggest an awareness that the buried city can never be found.

Such myths form the raw material of literature. The writer often comes to a myth eager for acquiescence, but after articulating its assumptions he may begin to wonder about its meaning, its value. During the past few decades Northern writers have been engaged in a large-scale examination of the myths of industrial capitalism, of enterprise, accumulation, and success; the rejection of these myths has motivated a great many contemporary writers. Somewhat similarly,

Faulkner in his stories and novels has been conducting a long, sometimes painful and at other times heroic examination of the Southern myth. He has set his pride in the past against his despair over the present, and from this counterposition has come much of the tension in his work. He has investigated the myth itself; wondered about the relation between the Southern tradition he admires and that memory of Southern slavery to which he is compelled to return; tested not only the present by the past, but also the past by the myth and finally the myth by that morality which has slowly emerged from this entire process of exploration. This testing of the myth, though by no means the only important activity in Faulkner's work, is basic to the Yoknapatawpha novels and stories; and from it comes his growing vision as an artist.

Afternote

This little essay was written in preparation for my book, *William Faulkner: A Critical Study* (New York: Random House, 1952). I was trying to understand, from the considerable distance of my own kind of experience, what were the sources of Faulkner's historical — that is, regional — involvement. In the dozen or so years that have since gone by, the process of regional dissolution which I noted has become accelerated. Can one still speak today of a Southern literature based on a firm regional identity? I doubt it, even though remains of such a literature can be seen. In Faulkner's own work, one of the reasons for the crisis in material and drop in quality which characterize his late novels is that the "Southern myth" had pretty much exhausted itself for him. He was forced to enter the commonplace world of twentieth-century American experience, and as a writer he was not prepared for that. I suspect that a somewhat similar process will soon be occurring among the Northern writers who work from the experience of Jewish urban life — and later (though given our deeply-ingrained racism, a good deal later) it will also take place among the Negro writers. For better or worse, the process of social homogenization seems irrevocable.

Irving Howe is Professor of English at Hunter College of the City University of New York and editor of Dissent. [This article appeared in Vol. III, No. 4 (Winter, 1951).]

Marvin Meyers

The Jacksonian Persuasion[1]

AN artful editor of the works of eminent Jacksonians might arrange one volume to portray the revolt of the urban masses against a business aristocracy; a second in which simple farming folk rise against the chicanery of capitalist slickers; a third volume tense with the struggle of the fresh forest democracy for liberation from an effete East; and still another book of men on the make invading the entrenched positions of chartered monopoly. With no undue demand upon editorial resourcefulness, the Jacksonian series might turn next to the party machine, managing a newly made mass electorate through the exploitation of some of the preceding themes. The terminal volume might well rest in the shadow of Jefferson: the patriotic friends of wise and frugal government, equal rights and equal laws, strict construction and dispersed power, resisting the eternally scheming tory, monocrat, and rag-baron.[2]

[1]In this article I mean to suggest a rather free and wide-ranging commentary resting immediately upon a limited selection of documents. Precise references and quotations are designed to be illustrative or suggestive, not conclusive evidence for my interpretations of Jacksonian Democracy. Some of the necessary elaborations, refinements, and documentary supports will I hope be found in my larger study of the Jacksonian ethos, now in progress, from which these notes have been drawn.

[2]The historical interpretations of Jacksonian Democracy are not, of course, so flat and monolithic as I make them out here. I have abstracted what seem to me central thesis-lines and deployed them for my own purposes. The variety of interpretations may be represented by such works as Arthur M. Schlesinger, Jr., *The Age of Jackson* (Boston: Little, Brown, 1945); Joseph Dorfman, *The Economic Mind in American Civilization*, Vol. II (New York: Viking, 1946); Frederick Jackson Turner, *The United States, 1830-1850* (New York: Holt, 1935); Alexis de Tocqueville, *Democracy in America*, 2 vols. (New York: Knopf, 1948. Bradley edition); M. Ostrogorski, *Democracy and the Party System in the United States* (New York: Macmillan, 1926); Thomas P. Abernethy, *From Frontier to Plantation in Tennessee* (Chapel Hill, N. C.: University of North Carolina, 1932); Louis Hartz, *Economic Policy and Democratic Thought* (Cambridge: Harvard, 1948); and the excellent chapter III in Richard Hofstadter, *The American Political Tradition* (New York: Knopf, 1948), together with the bibliographical essay in *ibid.*, pp. 353-57.

This partial list of possible uses of Jacksonian thought does not quite suggest that Jacksonian Democracy may mean all things to all men. Some omissions have been made with a point: for example, it is not suggested that any plausible editorial selection could identify Jacksonian Democracy with the rise of abolitionism; or (in an exclusive sense) with the temperance movement, school reform, religious enthusiasm or theological liberalism; or (in any sense) with Utopian community building. Yet the variety of meanings which can command some documentary support is too wide for easy assimilation in a coherent interpretation of Jacksonian Democracy. Here there is, I think, a fair field for the critical examination of the major contending theses and, of greater importance, for a fresh reading of the most obvious Jacksonian sources.

The present approach takes its departure from the debunking theses of recent writers like Dorfman and Abernethy, who in their separate ways have corrected a number of major and minor errors by an exemplary regard for original sources viewed carefully in historical context. Yet their very suspicions of such things as campaign appeals and public messages lead them to discount as meaningless a large part of the sustenance of the Jacksonian public, in order to pursue the "real thing"—i.e., the objective import of legal and institutional changes. If, for example, in Dorfman's terms, the major economic consequences of Jacksonian reform politics in New York were to establish free banking and incorporation laws and constitutional limits upon credit undertakings of the state—then what is the meaning of the highly-charged polemical jargon, the vague class appeals, the invocation of grand principles? Why, in short, did the language go so far beyond the practical object?

Simply to say "propaganda" does not tell why a particular lingo makes good propaganda and another kind does not. Nor is there obvious reason for regarding the traffic in "propaganda" as less significant intrinsically than the traffic in harder goods. And so these notes return to a staple of pre- or non-revisionist historians, the popular political discourse, in an attempt to identify the social values expressed or implied by opinion leaders of the Jacksonian persuasion.

The difficulties in such an enterprise are no doubt abundant and serious: the subject matter is in its nature elusive; the temptation is powerful indeed—as the debunking writers have been quick to note—to select passages from selected spokesmen, with considerable neglect of textual and situational context, in order to find some grand motif establishing the spirit of Jacksonian Democracy; and always one faces the relatively easy out of fabricating some systematic theory of Jacksonian Democrats from fragmentary words and acts, with results which tend to be laborious, intellectually arid, and unrevealing of the qualities of the Jacksonian movement.

There is nevertheless a commanding case for examining the sort of values offered to and preferred by the Jacksonian public; the popular political statement would seem a prime example of such communication; and the first spokesman must be Andrew Jackson. His presidential papers taken in all their dimensions, theory, policy, and rhetoric, and searched for certain constant, elementary moral postures, provide a revealing and somewhat unexpected commentary upon the character of Jacksonian Democracy.

The Old Hero and the Restoration

Andrew Jackson, most students agree, rose to national leadership on the strength of reputed personal qualities: the blunt, tough, courageous "Old Hero" of New Orleans—honest and plain "Old Hickory." "Old" refers to age, of course, but perhaps more to "old-style." Again, not so much to old-style ideas as to the old *ways* of our fathers. He could be—and was in a boy's capacity—a fit companion for the Revolutionary heroes. Jackson never figured as the speculative statesman. In his own estimate and the public's, he was executor of a republican tradition which required not elaboration or revision but right action, taken from a firm moral stance.

It is no novelty to say that the world revealed in Andrew Jackson's public statements appears, like the public image of the man, strikingly personal and dramatic, built upon the great struggle of people *vs.* aristocracy for mastery of the republic. In relation to such issues as the Bank War, the view offers a sharp pattern: on one side, the great body of citizens, demanding only an equal chance; on the other, their temptors and adversaries, the small greedy aristocracy, full of tricks and frauds, absorbing power and privilege. Yet the grand conflict, as it emerges from Jackson's public statements, has its ambiguities—*viz.*, the variant interpretations of Jacksonian Democracy. Within the gross polemical image of social drama much remains for further explication and explanation.

On the side of virtue, in Jackson's world, one finds the plain republican—direct descendant of Jefferson's yeoman hero—along with Poor Richard and such other, lesser friends. The presence of the sturdy, independent citizen-toiler has been no secret to historians—yet some interesting possibilities have been missed. In creating the character and rôle of the plain republican Jackson has provided, I think, an important clue for the interpretation of Jacksonian values.

"Keep clear of Banks and indebtedness," Jackson wrote to his adopted son after settling the boy's debts, "and you live a freeman, and die in independence and leave your family so . . . and remember, my son, . . . that we should always live within our means, and not on those of others."[3] Read this little paternal homily against the familiar public statements. Can it be that Jacksonian Democracy appeals not to some workingman's yearning for a brave new world; not to the possibilities of a fresh creation at the Western limits of civilization; not to the ambitions of a rising laissez-faire capitalism—not to any of these so much as to a *restoration* of old virtues and a (perhaps imaginary) old republican way of life?

It will be my contention that the Jacksonian appeal evokes the image of a calm and stable order of republican simplicity, content with the modest rewards of useful toil; and menacing the rustic peace, an alien spirit of risk and novelty, greed and extravagance, rapid motion and complex dealings. In short, we may discover in the political discourse of Jacksonian Democracy a powerful strain of restorationism, a stiffening of republican backs *against* the busy tinkerings, the restless projects of innovation and reform—against qualities so often set down as defining characteristics of Jacksonian America.

Of course this is not to say that the Jacksonians—master politicos and responsible rulers—designed to whisk away the given world, nor that their public actions yielded such a result. In practice they met issues as they came out of the play of current politics, adapting skillfully to the requirements of local conditions, special interests, and party rule. If the plain-republican theme is a substantial component of the Jacksonian persuasion, it need not dictate the precise policy line or control the objective consequences of party action in order to qualify as significant. The degree of coincidence or divergence is another (most important) question which cannot be approached until one knows what appeared in that dimension of political life which consists in the effective communication of value-charged language.

The Real People

Jackson's contemporary rivals damned him for appealing to class against class; some modern writers praise him for it. Beyond question, his public statements address a society divided into classes invidiously distinguished and profoundly antagonistic. But to understand the meaning of such cleavage and clash, one must see them within a controlling context. There is for Jackson a whole body, the sovereign people, beset with aristocratic sores.

[3]Quoted in John Spencer Bassett, *The Life of Andrew Jackson*, II (New York: Macmillan, 1916), 707-8.

The relentless and apparently irresistible use of "the people" in Jacksonian rhetoric is reflected in the diary of a wealthy New York City Whig, Philip Hone, who daily grinds the phrase through his teeth; or, with accumulated effect, in the growling humor of a Whig delegate to the New York Constitutional Convention of 1846—"The love of the people, the dear people was all that the gentlemen said influenced them. How very considerate. The love of the people—the dear people—was generally on men's tongues when they wanted to gain some particular end of their own. . . ."[4]

In the opposition view Jackson—and Jacksonians generally—were the worst sort of demagogues who could appropriate with galling effectiveness both the dignity of the sovereign people and the passion of embattled classes. That is just the point for Jackson: nasty imputations about demagoguery aside, there are the whole people and the alien aristocracy, and the political advantages which result from the use of this distinction further confirm its validity. Jackson's notion of the-class-of-the-people is grounded first in the political order, more precisely in the republican order. From this fixed base, and with this fixed idea of the double character of the people, Jackson's representation of the group composition of society may be analyzed first in the standard terms of Jacksonian scholarship, and then, by what seems to me a necessary extension, in the context of the restoration theme.

In the most inclusive and high-toned usage, the people would comprise "all classes of the community" and "all portions of the Union." From their midst arises a general "will of the American people" which is something considerably more than a fluctuating majority vote (though the vote for Jackson is acknowledged as a fair index). There are interests of a class and sectional character, legitimate and often illegitimate; but also a pervasive common interest (which corresponds neatly with the main items of the Democratic platform). The general will is originally pure—("Never for a moment believe that the great body of the citizens of any State or States can deliberately intend to do wrong . . ."); liable to temporary error through weakness—(corruptionists will sometimes succeed in "sinister appeals to selfish feelings" and to "personal ambition"); and in the end, straight and true—("but in a community so enlightened and patriotic as the people of the United States argument will soon make them sensible of their errors").[5]

[4]Allan Nevins (ed.), *The Diary of Philip Hone, 1828-1851*, 2 vols. (New York: Dodd, Mead, 1927), *passim. Report of the Debates . . . of the Convention for the Revision of the Constitution of the State of New-York. 1846* (Albany: Evening Atlas, 1846), p. 179.

[5]James D. Richardson (ed.), *Messages and Papers of the Presidents, 1789-1897* (Washington: Government Printing Office, 1896), III, 5, 296, 118-19, 296.

A brief, sharp exemplification of this view occurs in Jackson's argument for direct election of the president. The extent of American territory—Madison's chief reliance for controlling the threat of majority faction—suggests to Jackson the dangerous prospect of sectional parties, which in turn will present sectional candidates and, in the zeal for party and selfish objects, "generate influences unmindful of the general good." Evil comes from the official apparatus, the mechanical contrivances of the complex electoral system. However, "the great body of the people" armed with a direct presidential vote which can express the general "will" must always defeat "antirepublican" [sic.] tendencies and secure the common good.[6]

These "antirepublican" forces are identified as the "intriguers and politicians" and their tools, who thrive on political consolidation, chartered privilege, and speculative gain. Jackson sums up in relation to the bank war:

The bank is, in fact, but one of the fruits of a system at war with the genius of all our institutions—a system founded upon a political creed the fundamental principle of which is a distrust of the popular will as a safe regulator of political power, and whose ultimate object and inevitable result, should it prevail, is the consolidation of all power in our system in one central government. Lavish public disbursements and corporations with exclusive privileges would be its substitutes for the original and as yet sound checks and balances of the Constitution—the means by whose silent and secret operation a control would be exercised by the few over the political conduct of the many by first acquiring that control over the labor and earnings of the great body of the people. Wherever this spirit has effected an alliance with political power, tyranny and despotism have been the fruit.[7]

In these rough outlines there is enough to reconstruct what there is of a Jacksonian theory concerning the people and the classes. I doubt that the job is worth doing in any elaborate way. The Jacksonian persuasion is both more and much less than a theoretic structure; and Jackson's "people" are not reducible to a lump-quantity in a formal democratic scheme. What is missing is a sense of the nurture, character, and worth of the people as they are represented in Jackson's public papers. In Jackson's revealing phrase, there are still "*the real people*" to be considered.

When Jackson speaks of the people—the real people—he regularly specifies: planters and farmers, mechanics and laborers, "the bone and sinew of the country." Thus a composite class of industrious folk is marked off within society. It appears to be a narrower group than "the sovereign people" of democratic doctrine—though it would

[6]*Ibid.*, pp. 147-48, 176-77.
[7]*Ibid.*, p. 165.

surely encompass the mass of enumerated inhabitants of the Jacksonian era. Historians who identify the favored Jacksonian class simply as the common man tell too little. Others, who make the separation upon wage-earner lines, or by rich/poor, town/country, East/West, or North/South, accept what seem to me variable secondary traits. Jackson's real people are essentially those four specified occupational groups, whose "success depends upon their own industry and economy," who know "that they must not expect to become suddenly rich by the fruits of their toil." The lines are fixed by the moral aspects of occupation.[8]

Morals, habits, character are key terms in Jackson's discussion of the people—and almost every other subject. Major policies, for instance, are warranted by their capacity to "preserve the morals of the people," or "to revive and perpetuate those habits of economy and simplicity which are so congenial to the character of republicans." And so with the differentiation of classes according to worth: the American "laboring classes" are "so proudly distinguished" from their foreign counterparts by their "independent spirit, their love of liberty, their intelligence, and their high tone of moral character." At a still higher level within the bloc of favored classes, those who work the land—"the first and most important occupation of man"—contribute to society "that enduring wealth which is composed of flocks and herds and cultivated farms" and themselves constitute "a hardy race of free citizens."[9]

The positive definition of the real people significantly excludes pursuits which are primarily promotional, financial, or commercial. This does not mean that Jackson raises a class war against mere occupational categories. (He was himself lawyer, office-holder, land-speculator, and merchant at various times.) The point seems to be that virtue naturally attaches to, and in fact takes much of its definition from, callings which involve some immediate engagement in the production of goods. Vice enters most readily through the excluded pursuits, though it may infect all classes and "withdraw their attention from the sober pursuits of honest industry." As indicated before, vice is to be understood largely in terms of certain occupational ways, the morals, habits, and character imputed to the trades which seek wealth without labor, employing the stratagems of speculative maneuver, privilege-grabbing, and monetary manipulation.[10]

Like the Jeffersonians, Jackson regularly identifies the class enemy as the money power, the moneyed aristocracy, etc. There is in this

[8]*Ibid.*, p. 305.
[9]*Ibid.*, pp. 19, 67-69, 166, 162.
[10]*Ibid.*, p. 302.

undoubtedly some direct appeal against the rich. The mere words call up the income line as an immediate source of invidious distinction. Yet I would maintain that this is a secondary usage. First, Jackson's bone-and-sinew occupational classes clearly allow for a considerable income range—it would be fair to say that upper-upper and lower-lower could enter only exceptionally, while there would be a heavy concentration at the middling-independent point. Income as such does not become a ground for class preference in the usual terms of differential economic or power interest. Instead, Jackson links income with good and evil ways. The real people cannot expect sudden riches from their honest, useful work. And surplus wealth would in any case prove a temptation to the anti-republican habits of idleness and extravagance, as well as an engine of corruption. Briefly, a stable income of middling proportions is generally associated with the occupations, and with the habits, morals, and character of the real people.[11]

More important, however, is the meaning given to phrases like "money power"—and note that Jackson typically uses this expression and not "the rich." The term occurs invariably in discussions of corporations and, particularly, of banking corporations; it signifies the *paper* money power, the *corporate* money power—i.e., concentrations of wealth arising suddenly from financial manipulation and special privilege, ill-gotten gains. If the suggestion persists in Jackson's public statements that such is the common road to wealth—and certainly the only quick way—then it is still the mode and tempo of acquisition and not the fact of possession which is made to damn the rich before Jackson's public.

Further, the money power—as I have defined it—is damned precisely as a *power*, a user of ill-gotten gains to corrupt and dominate the plain republican order. Any concentration of wealth may be a potential source of evil; but the real danger arises when the concentration falls into hands which require grants of special privilege for economic success. So a wealthy planter (and Jackson was this, too) should need no editorial or legislative hired hands; a wealthy banker cannot do without them.

Thus, Jackson's representation of the real people in the plain republican order supplies at least tentative ground for an interpretation of Jacksonian Democracy as, in vital respects, an appeal to an idealized ancestral way. Beneath the gross polemical image of people *vs.* aristocracy, though not at all in conflict with it, one finds the steady note of praise for simplicity and stability, self-reliance and independence, economy and useful toil, honesty and plain dealing. These ways are

[11] *Ibid.*, p. 305.

in themselves good, and take on the highest value when they breed a hardy race of free citizens, the plain republicans of America.[12]

Hard Coin and the Web of Credit

As a national political phenomenon, Jacksonian Democracy drew heavily upon the Bank War for its strength and its distinctive character. The basic position Andrew Jackson established for the Democratic party in relation to money and banking continued to operate as a source of political strength through the eighteen-forties. So powerful, in fact, was the Jacksonian appeal that large sections of the rival Whig party finally capitulated on this issue explicitly for the purpose of saving the party's life. First, shrewd Whig party managers like Weed of New York, and later the generality of Whig spokesmen were forced to plead in effect: a correct (Old Whig) position on banking is incompatible with political survival in America.

The standard outlines of Jackson's case against banking and currency abuses have already been sketched above. Within the matrix of his Bank War, the crucial class split is discovered and the general principles of Jacksonian Democracy take shape. However, the Bank War—viewed as a struggle for possession of men's minds and loyalties—does not simply offer a self-evident display of its own meaning. Out of the polemical language there emerges a basic moral posture much like the one which fixes Jackson's representation of the republican order.

Jackson's appeal for economic reform projects, at bottom, a dismantling operation: to pull down the menacing constructions of federal and corporate power, and restore the wholesome rule of "public opinion and the interests of trade." This has the sound of laissez faire, it is laissez faire with a difference suggested by the previous discussion of the real people and their natural, legitimate economic interests. Poor Richard and economic man may be given a common enemy with the plain republican; surmounting serious difficulties, the forest democrat, poor man, and workingman might be recruited for the same cause. Indeed the sweeping effect of Jackson's negative case may be explained in part by his touching off a common hatred of an all-purpose villain. Yet, if the dismantling operation gives promise of catching several particular enemies in the broad aristocracy trap, does it not

[12]The familiar identification of Jacksonian Democracy and its favored folk with the West has its points, but not when it blends into the image of the Wild West. Jackson shows little sympathy for the rural adventurer, the marginal mover and jumper. Nor does the moral restoration projected in his public papers bear any resemblance to American primitivism in the Davey Crockett mode. Neither the forest shadows, nor the half-man, half-alligator tone, nor a wild-woods democracy lies at the heart of the Jacksonian persuasion. Rather, it sees a countryside of flocks and herds and cultivated farms, worked in seasonal rhythm and linked in republican community.

promise still more winningly a *dismantling*, and a restoration of pure and simple ways?

Tocqueville, though he reaches an opposite conclusion, suggests very effectively this unmaking spirit:

> The bank is a great establishment, which has an independent existence; and the people, accustomed to make and unmake whatsoever they please, are startled to meet with this obstacle to their authority. In the midst of the perpetual fluctuation of society, the community is irritated by so permanent an institution and is led to attack it, in order to see whether it can be shaken, like everything else.[13]

But what is it about the great establishment which provokes hostility and a passion for dismantling? How can the permanence of the Bank, set over against the perpetual fluctuation of society, explain the ceaseless Jacksonian complaint against the tendency of the Bank to introduce perpetual fluctuation in the economic affairs of society? There is, I think, another and better explanation of the symbolic import of the Bank War.

The Bank of the United States, veritable incarnation of evil in Jackson's argument, assumes the shape of "the monster," which is to say, the unnatural creature of greed for wealth and power. Its managers, supporters, and beneficiaries form the first rank of the aristocracy, i.e., the artificial product of legislative prestidigitation. The monster thrives in a medium of paper money, the mere specter of palpable value. The bank system suspends the real world of solid goods, honestly exchanged, upon a mysterious, swaying web of speculative credit. The natural distributive mechanism, which proportions rewards to "industry, economy, and virtue," is fixed to pay off the insider and the gambler.

To knock down this institution, then, and with it a false, rotten, insubstantial world, becomes the compelling object of Jackson's case. He removed the public deposits, so he said, "to preserve the morals of the people, the freedom of the press, and the purity of the elective franchise." Final victory over the Bank and its paper spawn "will form an era in the history of our country which will be dwelt upon with delight by every true friend of its liberty and independence," not least because the dismantling operation will "do more to revive and perpetuate those habits of economy and simplicity which are so congenial to the character of republicans than all the legislation which has yet been attempted."[14]

The Jacksonian appeal for a dismantling operation and the restora-

[13]Tocqueville, *Democracy in America*, I, 178-79.
[14]Richardson, *Messages and Papers*, III, 19, 166.

tion of old republican ways flows easily into the course of the hard coin argument. Hard coin, I have already suggested, stands for palpable value as against the spectral issue of the printing press. In plainer terms, Jackson argues before the Congress: "The great desideratum in modern times is an efficient check upon the power of banks, preventing that excessive issue of paper whence arise those fluctuations in the standard of value which render uncertain the rewards of labor." Addressing a later Congress, Jackson pursues the point: Bank paper lacks the stability provided by hard coin; thus circulation varies with the tide of bank issue; thus the value of property and the whole price level are at the mercy of these banking institutions; thus the laboring classes especially, and the real people generally, are victimized, while the few conniving speculators add to their riches.[15]

A related appeal to the attractions of stability, of sure rewards and steady values and hard coins, can be found in Jackson's warnings against the accumulation and distribution of the revenue surplus: an overflowing federal treasury, spilling into the states, would produce ruinous expansions and contractions of credit, arbitrary fluctuations in the price of property, "rash speculation, idleness, extravagance, and a deterioration of morals." But above all it is the banks and their paper system which "engender a spirit of speculation injurious to the habits and character of the people," which inspire "this eager desire to amass wealth without labor," which turn even good men from "the sober pursuits of honest industry." To restore hard coin is to restore the ways of the plain republican order. Dismantling of the unnatural and unjust bank and paper system is the necessary first step.

The Sum of Good Government

The one essential credential of public or private worth—whether of individual, or class, or trade—is conveyed by Jackson through the term "republican"; that which is anti-republican is the heart of evil. With all valuations referred to the republican standard, and that standard apparently a category of politics, one might expect some final revelation of the Jacksonian persuasion in Jackson's representation of the good state. The truth is, on my reading, somewhat different: Jackson rather defines republican by ways of living and working, than refers those ways to republicanism in the strict political sense. The good republic he projects—and remembers from the Revolutionary days of '76 and 1800—is on the political side the ornament, the glory, and the final security of the worthy community, not its creator.

Jackson's sketch of a political system congenial to old republican

[15]*Ibid.*, pp. 164, 247-48.

ways uses nothing beyond the memorable summation in Jefferson's First Inaugural Address: "a wise and frugal government, which shall restrain men from injuring one another, shall leave them otherwise free to regulate their own pursuits of industry and improvement, and shall not take from the mouth of labor the bread it has earned. This is the sum of good government, and this is necessary to close the circle of our felicities." The literal Jacksonian translation prescribes: the Constitution strictly construed; strict observance of the "fundamental and sacred" rules of simplicity and economy; separation of the political power from the conduct of economic affairs.[16]

His political appeal both parallels and supports the general themes discussed in previous sections. This is no government of projects and ambitions. It does its simple, largely negative business in a simple, self-denying way. Firm and strong, it trims drastically the apparatus of power. The hardy race of independent republicans, engaged in plain and useful toil, require no more than a stable government of equal laws to secure them in their equal rights. In Jacksonian discourse, government becomes a fighting issue only when it grows too fat and meddlesome. Again, the republic is defined and judged positively by its republicans and only negatively by its government.

The Bank War once more provides the crucial case. Jackson mobilized the powers of government for what was essentially a dismantling operation. His cure avoids with terror any transference of the powers of the Bank to another agency: to give to the president the currency controls and the power over individuals now held by the Bank "would be as objectionable and as dangerous as to leave it as it is." Control of banks and currency—apart from the strictly constitutional functions of coinage and regulation of value—should be "entirely separated from the political power of the country." Any device is wicked and dangerous which would "concentrate the whole moneyed power of the Republic in any form whatsoever." We must, above all, ignore petty, expediential considerations, and "look to the honor and preservation of the republican system."[17]

Paradox

And so the circuit of Jackson's public appeal may be closed. Plain, honest men; simple, stable economy; wise and frugal government. It reads less as the herald of modern times and a grand project of reform than as a reaction against the spirit and body of the changing world. Jacksonian Democracy, viewed through Jackson's public statements, wants to undo far more than it wishes to do; and not for the purpose

[16]*Ibid.*, pp. 18, 108, 161-62.
[17]*Ibid.*, pp. 7, 18, 111.

of a fresh creation, but for the restoration of an old republican idyl. The tremendous popularity of Andrew Jackson and his undoubted public influence suggest that this theme can be ignored only at great peril in any general interpretation of Jacksonian Democracy. We must prepare for a paradox: the movement which in many ways cleared the path for the triumph of laissez-faire capitalism and its culture in America, and the public which in its daily life acted out that victory, held nevertheless in their conscience an image of a chaste republican order, resisting the seductions of risk and novelty, greed and extravagance, rapid motion and complex dealings.

Afternote

The readiness of some critics to place this approach to American political thought unequivocally in the new "myth and symbol" school of historiography has led the author to re-emphasize his distinction between the methods appropriate to the analysis of "persuasion"—"a half-formulated moral perspective involving emotional commitment"—and the more formal techniques suited to the study of political ideas proper. In brief, texts in different forms expressing different purposes in different contexts require different modes of reading and understanding. Neglect of this truism leads to arid schematizations of revealing "loose talk," on one side, and to arbitrary reductions of complex thought, on the other.

As to the particular interpretation of Jacksonian Democracy: the author has been neither surprised nor shaken (though often enlightened) by more recent writings that argue the pervasive egalitarian tendency of the age (he had aggressively acknowledged his profound debt to Tocqueville); that emphasize the diversity of interests and motives within the broad and loose Jacksonian array (he had proposed to search for the distinctive, salient elements that gave some common public definition to the movement led and symbolized nationally by Jackson, not to impose a uniform identity on all Democrats); or that focus upon the tensions and contrarieties of rhetoric and practice (he had taken exactly that as the key problem of interpretation). The new wave of behavioral research on voting and other countable things is still far from offering clear, precise portraits of party constituencies; at best it will leave a very wide range for qualitative analysis, including the sensitive study of political expression, if we are to understand the significant transactions between politicians and people in the Jacksonian age.

A revised version of this article was incorporated into *The Jacksonian Persuasion* (Stanford, Cal.: Stanford University Press, 1957) of which a paperback with a new preface was published by Vintage Books in 1960.

Marvin Meyers is the Harry S. Truman Professor of History at Brandeis University. [This article appeared in Vol. V, No. 1 (Spring, 1953).]

William H. Goetzmann

The Mountain Man as Jacksonian Man*

ONE OF THE MOST OFTEN STUDIED AND LEAST UNDERSTOOD FIGURES IN AMERICAN history has been the Mountain Man. Remote, so it would seem, as Neanderthal, and according to some almost as inarticulate, the Mountain Man exists as a figure of American mythology rather than history. As such he has presented at least two vivid stereotypes to the public imagination. From the first he has been the very symbol for the romantic banditti of the forest, freed of the artificial restrictions of civilization—a picturesque wanderer in the wilderness whose very life is a constant and direct association with Nature.

> "There is perhaps, no class of men on the face of the earth," said Captain Bonneville [and through him Washington Irving], "who lead a life of more continued exertion, peril, and excitement, and who are more enamoured of their occupations, than the free trappers of the west. No toil, no danger, no privation can turn the trapper from his pursuit. His passionate excitement at times resembles a mania. In vain may the most vigilant and cruel savages beset his path; in vain may rocks, and precipices, and wintry torrents oppose his progress; let but a single track of a beaver meet his eye, and he forgets all dangers and defies all difficulties. At times, he may be seen with his traps on his shoulder, buffeting his way across rapid streams amidst floating blocks of ice: at

* The term "Jacksonian Man" is used throughout this essay in a general rather than a particular sense. It is intended to describe a fictional composite, the average man of the period under consideration regardless of whether or not he was a follower of Andrew Jackson and his party. Those qualities which I take to be general enough to characterize the average man are defined in my quotations from Richard Hofstadter, Marvin Meyers and Alexis de Tocqueville. It should not be inferred from this that I seek to portray the Mountain Men as members of Andrew Jackson's political party nor that I mean to suggest that the particular objectives of the Democratic Party were necessarily those described by Hofstadter, Meyers and Tocqueville. Rather their terms seem to characterize to some extent men of all political persuasions in this period. Lee

other times, he is to be found with his traps on his back clambering the most rugged mountains, scaling or descending the most frightening precipices, searching by routes inaccessible to the horse, and never before trodden by white man, for springs and lakes unknown to his comrades, and where he may meet with his favorite game. Such is the mountaineer, the hardy trapper of the west; and such as we have slightly sketched it, is the wild, Robin Hood kind of life, with all its strange and motley populace, now existing in full vigor among the Rocky mountains."[1]

To Irving in the nineteenth century the Mountain Man was Robin Hood, a European literary convention. By the twentieth century the image was still literary and romantic but somewhat less precise. According to Bernard De Voto, "For a few years Odysseus Jed Smith and Siegfried Carson and the wing-shod Fitzpatrick actually drew breath in this province of fable," and Jim Beckwourth "went among the Rockies as Theseus dared the wine-dark seas. Skirting the rise of a hill, he saw the willows stirring; he charged down upon them, while despairing Blackfeet sang the death-song—and lo, to the clear music of a horn, Roland had met the pagan hordes. . . ."[2]

On the other hand, to perhaps more discerning eyes in his own day and down through the years, the Mountain Man presented another image —one that was far less exalted. Set off from the ordinary man by his costume of greasy buckskins, coonskin cap and Indian finery, not to mention the distinctive odor that went with bear grease and the habitual failure to bathe between one yearly rendezvous and the next, the Mountain Man seemed a forlorn and pathetic primitive out of the past. "They are stared at as though they were bears," wrote Rudolph F. Kurz, a Swiss artist who traveled the Upper Missouri.[3]

The Mountain Man, so it was said, was out of touch with conventional

---

Benson in his recent book, *The Concept of Jacksonian Democracy,* has shown that in New York State, at least, the Jackson party had no particular monopoly on such terms as "egalitarianism" and "democracy," and that indeed most parties in the state including the Whigs actually preceded the Jackson men in their advocacy of these views. He thus demonstrates that there were certain values and goals common to all men of the day. Benson then concludes that instead of calling the period "The Age of Jackson," it should properly be called "The Age of Egalitarianism." His evidence indicates to me, however, that a still more precise term for the period might well be "The Age of Expectant Capitalism," and following Hofstadter and Meyers, and before them Frederick Jackson Turner, I have seen this as the most generally applicable descriptive concept for the period. Thus it forms the basis for my definition of "Jacksonian Man," or *Genus Homo Americanus* during the years of the presidency of Andrew Jackson and his successor Martin Van Buren.

1 Washington Irving, *The Rocky Mountains: or, Scenes, Incidents, and Adventures in the Far West* (2 vols.; Philadelphia, 1837), I, 27.

2 Bernard De Voto, "Introduction," *The Life and Adventures of James P. Beckwourth,* ed. T. D. Bonner (New York, 1931), p. xxvii.

3 Quoted in Dorothey O. Johansen, "Introduction," *Robert Newell's Memoranda* (Portland, Ore., 1959), p. 2.

civilization and hence not quite acceptable.[4] Instead in his own time and even more today he has been viewed as a purely hedonistic character who lived for the year's end rendezvous where he got gloriously drunk on diluted rot-gut company alcohol, gave his beaver away for wildly inflated company trade goods and crawled off into the underbrush for a delirious orgy with some unenthusiastic Indian squaw. In this view the romantic rendezvous was nothing more than a modern company picnic, the object of which was to keep the employees docile, happy and ready for the coming year's task.

Pacified, satisfied, cheated, impoverished and probably mortified the next day, the Mountain Man, be he free trapper or not, went back to his dangerous work when the rendezvous was over. He was thus to many shrewd observers not a hero at all but a docile and obedient slave of the company. By a stretch of the imagination he might have seemed heroic, but because of the contrast between his daring deeds and his degraded status he seemed one of the saddest heroes in all history. Out of date before his time was up, he was a wild free spirit who after all was not free. He was instead an adventurer who was bringing about his own destruction even as he succeeded in his quest to search out the beaver in all of the secret places of the mountain West. A dependent of the London dandy and his foppish taste in hats, the Mountain Man was Caliban. He was a member of a picturesque lower class fast vanishing from the face of America. Like the Mohican Indian and quaint old Leatherstocking he was a vanishing breed, forlorn and permanently class-bound in spite of all his heroics.[5]

Both of these steretoypes embody, as do most effective stereotypes, more than a measure of reality. The Mountain Man traveled far out ahead of the march of conventional civilization, and the job he did required him to be as tough, primitive and close to nature as an Indian. Moreover, it was an out-of-doors life of the hunt and the chase that he often grew to like. By the same token because he spent much of his time in primitive isolation in the mountains, he very often proved to be a poor businessman ignorant of current prices and sharp company practices. Even if aware of his disadvantageous position he could do nothing to free himself until he had made his stake.

The fact is, however, that many Mountain Men lived for the chance to exchange their dangerous mountain careers for an advantageous start in civilized life. If one examines their lives and their stated aspirations one

[4] *Ibid.*, pp. 2-3; see also Ray A. Billington, *The Far Western Frontier* (New York, 1956), p. 44.

[5] Billington, pp. 46-47; Robert Glass Cleland, *This Reckless Breed of Men* (New York, 1952), pp. 24-25; Bernard De Voto, *Across the Wide Missouri* (Boston, 1947), pp. 96-104. See also Henry Nash Smith, *Virgin Land* (Boston, 1950), pp. 59-70, 81-89. My portrait is a composite derived, but not quoted from the above sources.

discovers that the Mountain Men, for all their apparent eccentricities, were astonishingly similar to the common men of their time—plain republican citizens of the Jacksonian era.

Jacksonian Man, according to Richard Hofstadter, "was an expectant capitalist, a hardworking ambitious person for whom enterprise was a kind of religion." [6] He was "the master mechanic who aspired to open his own shop, the planter, or farmer who speculated in land, the lawyer who hoped to be a judge, the local politician who wanted to go to Congress, the grocer who would be a merchant. . . ." [7] To this list one might well add, the trapper who hoped some day, if he hit it lucky and avoided the scalping knife, to be one or all of these, or perhaps better still, a landed gentleman of wealth and prestige.

"Everywhere," writes Hofstadter, the Jacksonian expectant capitalist "found conditions that encouraged him to extend himself." [8] And there were many like William Ashley or Thomas James who out of encouragement or desperation looked away to the Rocky Mountains, teeming with beaver and other hidden resources, and saw a path to economic success and rapid upward mobility. In short, when he went out West and became a Mountain Man the Jacksonian Man did so as a prospector. He too was an expectant capitalist.

Marvin Meyers has added a further characterization of Jacksonian Man. He was, according to Meyers, the "venturous conservative," [9] the man who desired relative freedom from restraint so that he might risk his life and his fortune, if not his sacred honor, on what appeared to be a long-term, continent-wide boom. Yet at the same time he wished to pyramid his fortune within the limits of the familiar American social and economic system, and likewise to derive his status therefrom. Wherever he went, and especially on the frontier, Jacksonian Man did not wish to change the system. He merely wished to throw it open as much as possible to opportunity, with the hope that by so doing he could place himself at the top instead of at the bottom of the conventional social and economic ladder. "They love change," wrote Tocqueville, "but they dread revolutions." [10] Instead of a new world the Jacksonian Man wished to restore the old where the greatest man was the independent man—yeoman or mechanic, trader or ranchero—the man who basked in comfort and sturdy security under his own "vine and fig tree."

The structure of the Rocky Mountain fur trade itself, the life stories of the trappers and on rare occasions their stated or implied aspirations all make it clear that if he was not precisely the Meyers-Hofstadter Jack-

6 Richard Hofstadter, *The American Political Tradition* (New York, 1955), p. 57.
7 *Ibid.*, p. 59. 8 *Ibid.*, p. 57.
9 Marvin Meyers, *The Jacksonian Persuasion* (New York, 1960), pp. 33-56.
10 Quoted in *ibid.*, p. 43.

sonian Man, the Mountain Man was most certainly his cousin once removed, and a clearly recognizable member of the family.

It is a truism, of course, to state that the Rocky Mountain fur trade was a business, though writers in the Mountain Man's day and since have sometimes made it seem more like a sporting event. The Mountain Man himself often put such an ambiguous face on what he was doing.

> "Westward! Ho!" wrote Warren Ferris, an American Fur Company trapper. "It is the sixteenth of the second month A.D. 1830, and I have joined a trapping, trading, hunting expedition to the Rocky Mountains. Why, I scarcely know, for the motives that induced me to this step were of a mixed complexion,—something like the pepper and salt population of this city of St. Louis. Curiosity, a love of wild adventure, and perhaps also a hope of profit,—for times *are* hard, and my best coat has a sort of sheepish hang-dog hesitation to encounter fashionable folk—combined to make me look upon the project with an eye of favor. The party consists of some thirty men, mostly Canadian; but a few there are, like myself, from various parts of the Union. Each has some plausible excuse for joining, and the aggregate of disinterestedness would delight the most ghostly saint in the Roman calendar. Engage for money! no, not they;—health, and the strong desire of seeing strange lands, of beholding nature in the savage grandeur of her primeval state,—these are the only arguments that *could* have persuaded such independent and high-minded young fellows to adventure with the American Fur Company in a trip to the mountain wilds of the great west." [11]

Ambiguous though the Mountain Man's approach to it may have been, it is abundantly clear that the Rocky Mountain fur trade was indeed a *business,* and not an invariably individualistic enterprise at that. The unit of operation was the company, usually a partnership for the sake of capital, risk and year-round efficiency. Examples of the company are The Missouri Fur Company, Gantt and Blackwell, Stone and Bostwick, Bean and Sinclair, and most famous of all, the Rocky Mountain Fur Company and its successors, Smith, Jackson, and Sublette, Sublette & Campbell, and Sublette, Fitzpatrick, Bridger, Gervais and Fraeb. These were the average company units in the Rocky Mountain trade and much of the story of their existence is analogous to Jackson's war on the "Monster Bank" for they were all forced to contend against John Jacob Astor's "Monster Monopoly," the American Fur Co., which was controlled and financed by eastern capitalists.

[11] W. A. Ferris, *Life in the Rocky Mountains,* ed. Paul C. Phillips (Denver, Colo., 1940), p. 1.

Perhaps the most interesting aspect of the independent fur companies was their fluid structure of leadership. There was indeed, "a baton in every knapsack" or more accurately, perhaps, in every "possibles" bag. William Ashley, owner of a gun powder factory and Andrew Henry, a former Lisa lieutenant, and lead miner, founded the Rocky Mountain Fur Company.[12] After a few years of overwhelming success, first Henry, and then Ashley, retired, and they were succeeded by their lieutenants, Jedediah Smith, David Jackson and William Sublette, three of the "enterprising young men" who had answered Ashley's advertisement in the St. Louis *Gazette and Public Advertiser* in 1823. When Smith and Jackson moved on to more attractive endeavors first William Sublette and Robert Campbell, then Tom "Broken Hand" Fitzpatrick, James "Old Gabe" Bridger, Henry Fraeb, Milton "Thunderbolt" Sublette and Jean Baptiste Gervais moved up to fill their entrepreneurial role.

In another example Etienne Provost was successively an employee of Auguste Chouteau, partner with LeClair and leader of his own Green River brigade, and servant of American Fur.[13] Sylvestre Pattie became a Santa Fe trader, then an independent trapper, then manager of the Santa Rita (New Mexico) Copper Mines and ultimately leader of an independent trapping venture into the Gila River country of the far Southwest—a venture that ended in disaster when he was thrown into a Mexican prison in California and there left to die.[14] Most significant is the fact that few of the trappers declined the responsibility of entrepreneurial leadership when it was offered them. On the contrary, the usual practice was to indenture oneself to an established company for a period of time, during which it was possible to acquire the limited capital in the way of traps, rifle, trade goods, etc., that was needed to become independent and a potential brigade leader. Referring to his arrangement with the old Missouri Fur Company in 1809, Thomas James wrote,

> We Americans were all private adventurers, each on his own hook, and were led into the enterprise by the promises of the Company, who agreed to subsist us to the trapping grounds, we helping to navigate the boats, and on our arrival there they were to furnish us each with a rifle and sufficient ammunition, six good beaver traps and also four men of their hired French, to be under our individual commands for a period of three years.

[12] Harrison C. Dale, *The Ashley-Smith Explorations and the Discovery of a Central Route to the Pacific, 1822-1829,* rev. ed. (Glendale, Calif., 1941), pp. 57-61.

[13] Dale L. Morgan, *Jedediah Smith* (Indianapolis and New York, 1953), pp. 145-48; Ferris, pp. 150, 156, 158.

[14] James Ohio Pattie, *Personal Narrative,* ed. Timothey Flint (Cincinnati, 1831), *passim.*

> By the terms of the contract each of us was to divide one-fourth of the profits of our joint labor with the four men thus to be appointed to us.[15]

James himself retired when he could from the upper Missouri trade and eventually became an unsuccessful storekeeper in Harrisonville, Illinois.[16]

In addition to the fact of rapid entrepreneurial succession within the structure of the independent fur companies, a study of 446 Mountain Men (perhaps 45 per cent of the total engaged in this pursuit between 1805 and 1845) indicates that their life-patterns could be extremely varied. One hundred seventeen Mountain Men definitely turned to occupations other than trapping subsequent to their entering the mountain trade. Of this number 39 followed more than one pursuit. As such they often worked at as many as four or five different callings.[17]

[15] Thomas James, *Three Years Among the Indians and Mexicans*, ed. Milo M. Quaife (Chicago, 1953), pp. 9-10.

[16] *Ibid.*, p. 100. When his store failed, Thomas James set out in May 1821 on a trading venture to Santa Fe. By July of 1822 he had returned to his home in Illinois.

[17] This study is based upon the lives of the Mountain Men whose entrance into the Rocky Mountain fur trade during the period 1805-45 can be proven, and who fit the criteria listed below. As anyone who has worked in the field will undoubtedly understand, the estimated one-thousand-man total given for those who would possibly qualify for consideration under these criteria represents merely an informed guess, since it is impossible with present-day evidence to determine with accuracy *all* of the Mountain Men who entered the West during this period. The data upon which this study is based is the sum total of men and careers that the extensive investigation described below has yielded. The author believes this to be the most extensive such investigation undertaken to date and also the largest number of such Mountain Men and careers located as of this time. However, in presenting this statistical analysis, the author wishes to stress the tentativeness of the conclusions herein reached. Further study of those whose "other occupations were indeterminable," and those "whose other occupations are probable" quite obviously might alter the present statistical results to a significant degree, and though the attempt was made to determine the occupations of as many men as possible, the author wishes specifically to acknowledge this possibility.

The basic sources for this sample study were: 1) General histories of the western states. In this respect the pioneer register in H. H. Bancroft's *History of California* proved to be particularly useful. 2) Original and modern editions of the relevant fur trade classics listed in Henry Raup Wagner and Charles Camp, *Plains and Rockies*. 3) The many available monographs and biographies relating to the fur trade such as those by Hiram M. Chittenden, Paul C. Phillips, Dale L. Morgan and John E. Sunder. 4) The files of historical journals containing materials on the fur trade of the Far West. 5) Reports submitted to the United States Government and published in the House and Senate document series. 6) Newspapers and periodicals for the fur trade period. In this latter category the author's research was by no means complete, nor was it possible to carry out the research project to the extent of consulting the multitude of local and county histories that almost certainly would have yielded further information. Enough research was conducted in these latter two categories of materials, however, to indicate the probable extent of their utility, which the author deemed insufficient for the present purposes.

The criteria for selecting the men to be included in the study are relatively simple. 1) They must have been associated with the fur trapping enterprise during the period 1805-45. 2) They must have pursued their trapping activities in the Rocky Mountains,

Moreover beyond the 117 definite cases of alternative callings, 32 others were found to have indeterminate occupations that were almost certainly not connected with the fur trade,[18] making a total of 149 out of 154 men for whom some occupational data exists who had turned away from the trapping fraternity before 1845. Of the remaining men in the study, 110 men yielded nothing to investigation beyond the fact that they had once been trappers, 182 can be listed as killed in the line of duty and only five men out of the total stayed with the great out-of-doors life of the free trapper that according to the myth they were all supposed to love.

TABLE 1

Total Number of Cases	446
Persons whose other occupations are known	117
Persons whose other occupations are probable	32
Persons with more than one other occupation	39
Persons who stayed on as trappers	5
Persons whose status is unknown	110
Persons killed in the fur trade	182

The list of alternative callings pursued by the trappers is also revealing. Twenty-one became ranchers, fifteen farmers, seventeen traders (at stationary trading posts), eight miners, seven politicians, six distillers, five each storekeepers and army scouts, four United States Indian agents, three carpenters, two each bankers, drovers and hatters and at least one pursued each of the following occupations, sheepherder, postman, miller, medium, ice dealer, vintner, fancy fruit grower, baker, saloon keeper, clockmaker, cattle buyer, real estate speculator, newspaper editor, lawyer, lumberman, superintendent of schools, tailor, blacksmith, and supercargo of a trading schooner. Moreover many of these same individuals pursued secondary occupations such as that of hotel keeper, gambler, soldier, health resort proprietor, coal mine owner, tanner, sea captain, horse thief and opera house impresario.

northern or southern; hence the term Mountain Man. 3) They could not be employees of the American Fur Company, nor engagées at any of the Missouri River trading posts. The American Fur Company men are excluded from this study for two reasons: first, because the majority of them were river traders, not Mountain Men and they have never been classified under the old stereotyped images; secondly, of those few American Fur men who did go into the mountains in this period a large percentage were killed. Further study of the survivors, however, indicates that they too changed occupations much as did the Mountain Men. (See for example the career of Warren A. Ferris.)

18 This conclusion is deduced by the author primarily upon the basis of their residence during this period in places far removed from fur trapping or trading activities.

TABLE 2

List of Occupations

A. *Primary*

1. Farmer	15		17. Blacksmith	1
2. Rancher	21		18. Tailor	1
3. Politician	7		19. Supercargo	1
4. Sheepherder	1		20. Superintendent of Schools	1
5. Scout [For Govt.]	5		21. Lumberman	2
6. Trader	17		22. Newspaper Editor	1
7. Miner	8		23. Carpenter	3
8. Postman	1		24. Cattle Buyer	1
9. Distiller	6		25. Clockmaker	1
10. Miller	1		26. Saloon Keeper	1
11. Storekeeper	5		27. Baker	1
12. Medium	1		28. Fruit Grower	1
13. Banker	2		29. Vintner	1
14. Drover	2		30. Ice Dealer	1
15. Hatter	2		31. Real Estate Speculator	1
16. Indian Agent	4		32. Lawyer	1

B. *Secondary*

1. Trader	4		12. Lumberman	2
2. Transportation	2		13. Gambler	3
3. Scout	5		14. Blacksmith	1
4. Hotel Keeper	1		15. Soldier	1
5. Miner	2		16. Spa Keeper	1
6. Farmer	5		17. Coal Mine Operator	1
7. Politician	3		18. Tanner	1
8. Rancher	5		19. Opera House Impresario	1
9. Storekeeper	4		20. Sea Captain	1
10. Miller	3		21. Carpenter	1
11. Real Estate	3		22. Horse Thief	1

From this it seems clear that statistically at least the Mountain Man was hardly the simple-minded primitive that mythology has made him out to be. Indeed it appears that whenever he had the chance, he exchanged the joys of the rendezvous and the wilderness life for the more civilized excitement of "getting ahead." In many cases he achieved this aim, and on a frontier where able men were scarce he very often became a pillar of the community, and even of the nation. From the beginning, as Ashley's famous advertisement implied, the Mountain Men were men of "enterprise" who risked their lives for something more than pure romance and a misanthropic desire to evade civilization. The picturesqueness and the quaintness were largely the creation of what was the literary mentality of an age of artistic romanticism. For every "Cannibal Phil" or Robert Meldrum or "Peg-Leg" Smith there was a Sarchel Wolfskill (vintner), a George Yount (rancher) and a William Sublette (banker-politician).

Two further facts emerge in part from this data. First, it is clear that though the Jeffersonian agrarian dream of "Arcadia" bulked large in the Mountain Man's choice of occupations, it by no means obscured the whole range of "mechanical" or mercantile pursuits that offered the chance for success on the frontier. Indeed, if it suggests anything a statistical view of the Mountain Man's "other life" suggests that almost from the beginning the Far Western frontier took on the decided aspect of an urban or semi-urban "industrial" civilization. Secondly, though it is not immediately apparent from the above statistics, a closer look indicates that a surprising number of the Mountain Men succeeded at their "other" tasks to the extent that they became regionally and even nationally prominent.

William H. Ashley became Congressman from Missouri and a spokesman for the West, Charles Bent an ill-fated though famed governor of New Mexico. "Doc" Newell was a prominent figure in the organization of Oregon Territory. Elbridge Gerry, William McGaa and John Simpson Smith were the founders and incorporators of Denver. Lucien Maxwell held the largest land grant in the whole history of the United States.

Joshua Pilcher was a famous superintendent of Indian Affairs. William Sublette, pursuing a hard money policy, saved the Bank of Missouri in the panic of 1837 and went on to be a Democratic elector for "young hickory" James K. Polk in 1844. Benjamin Wilson was elected first mayor of Los Angeles. James Clyman and his Napa Valley estate were famous in California as were the ranches of George Yount and J. J. Warner, while Sarchel Wolfskill was a co-founder of the modern California wine industry. James Waters built the first opera house in Southern California, and Kit Carson, in his later years a silver miner, received the supreme tribute of finding a dime novel dedicated to his exploits in plunder captured from marauding Apache Indians who had recently attacked and massacred a wagon train.[19]

Many of the Mountain Men achieved fame and national status through works that they published themselves, or, as in the case of Carson, through works that immortalized correctly, or as was more usual, incorrectly, their exploits. Here one need only mention Kit Carson's *Autobiography* and his

19 Kit Carson, *Autobiography*, ed. Milo M. Quaife (Chicago, 1935), p. 135.

favorable treatment at the hands of Jessie Benton Frémont, T. D. Bonner's *Life and Adventures of James Beckwourth,* Francis Fuller Victor's *River of the West* (about Joe Meek), James Ohio Pattie's *Personal Narrative,* Thomas James' *Three Years Among the Indians and Mexicans,* H. L. Conard's *Uncle Dick Wooton,* David Coyner's *The Lost Trappers* (about Ezekial Williams), Irving's portrait of Joseph Reddeford Walker in *The Adventures of Captain Bonneville,* Zenas Leonard's *Narrative,* Peg-Leg Smith's "as told to" exploits in *Hutchings' California Magazine,* Stephen Meek's *Autobiography,* Warren Ferris' letters to the Buffalo, New York, *Western Literary Messenger,* John Hatcher's yarns in Lewis H. Garrard's *Wah To Yah and The Taos Trail* and perhaps most interesting of all, trapper John Brown's pseudo-scientific *Mediumistic Experiences,* to realize the extent and range of the Mountain Man's communication with the outside world in his own day. Not only was he a typical man of his time, he was often a conspicuous success and not bashful about communicating the fact in somewhat exaggerated terms to his fellow countrymen.

Direct evidence of the Mountain Men's motives is scarce, but it is clear their intentions were complex.

"Tell them that I have no heirs and that I hope to make a fortune," wrote Louis Vasquez ("Old Vaskiss" to Bernard De Voto) in 1834 from "Fort Convenience" somewhere in the Rockies.[20] Later as he set out on one last expedition in 1842 he added somewhat melodramatically, "I leave to make money or die." [21] And finally Colonel A. G. Brackett, who visited Fort Bridger (jointly owned by Bridger and Vasquez), described him as "a Mexican, who put on a great deal of style, and used to ride about the country in a coach and four." [22]

"It is, that I may be able to help those who stand in need, that I face every danger," wrote Jedediah Smith from the Wind River Mountains in 1829, "most of all, it is for this, that I deprive myself of the privilege of Society and the satisfaction of the Converse of My Friends! but I shall count all this pleasure, if I am allowed by the Alwise Ruler the privilege of Joining my Friends. . . ." And he added "let it be the greatest pleasure that we can enjoy, the height of our ambition, now, when our Parents are in the decline of Life, to smooth the Pillow of their age, and as much as in us lies, take from them all cause of Trouble." [23] So spoke Jedediah Smith of his hopes and ambitions upon pursuing the fur trade. No sooner had he left the mountains, however, than he was killed by Plains Indians

[20] Quoted in Leroy Hafen, "Louis Vasquez," *The Colorado Magazine,* X (1933), 17. De Voto's nickname for Vasquez appears in *Across the Wide Missouri,* p. xxvi.

[21] *Ibid.,* p. 19. [22] *Ibid.,* p. 20.

[23] Jedediah Smith to Ralph Smith, Wind River, East Side of the Rocky Mountains, December 24, 1829. MS. Kansas State Historical Society. Also reproduced in Morgan, *Jedediah Smith,* pp. 351-54.

before he could settle down in business with his brothers as he had intended.[24] Noble and ignoble were the motives of the Mountain Men. Colonel John Shaw, starting across the southern plains and into the Rockies in search of gold; Thomas James, desperate to recoup his failing fortunes; the Little Rock *Gazette* of 1829 "confidently" believing "that this enterprise affords a prospect of great profit to all who may engage in it"; the St. Louis *Enquirer* in 1822 labeling the Rocky Mountains "the Shining Mountains," and innocently declaring, "A hunter pursuing his game found the silver mines of Potosi, and many others have been discovered by the like accidents, and there is no reason to suppose that other valuable discoveries may not be made";[25] Ashley calling clearly and unmistakably for men of "enterprise," all added up to the fact that the Mountain Man when he went West was a complex character. But in his complexity was a clearly discernible pattern—the pattern of Jacksonian Man in search of respectability and success in terms recognized by the society he had left behind. His goal was, of course, the pursuit of happiness. But happiness, contrary to Rousseauistic expectations, was not found in the wilderness; it was an integral product of society and civilization.

If the Mountain Man was indeed Jacksonian Man, then there are at least three senses in which this concept has importance. First, more clearly than anything else a statistical and occupational view of the various callings of the Mountain Man tentatively indicates the incredible rate and the surprising *nature* of social and economic change in the West. In little more than two decades most of the surviving enterprising men had left the fur trade for more lucrative and presumably more useful occupations. And by their choice of occupations it is clear that in the Far West a whole step in the settlement process had been virtually skipped. They may have dreamed of "Arcadia," but when they turned to the task of settling the West as fast as possible, the former Mountain Men and perhaps others like them brought with them all the aspects of an "industrial," mercantile and quasi-urban society. The opera house went up almost simultaneously with the ranch, and the Bank of Missouri was secured before the land was properly put into hay.

24 Jedediah S. Smith to Ralph Smith, Blue River, fork of Kansas, 30 miles from the Ponnee Villages, September 10, 1830. MS. Kansas State Historical Society. Also reproduced in Morgan, *Jedediah Smith,* pp. 355-56.

25 St. Louis *Enquirer* quoted in Donald McKay Frost, *Notes on General Ashley* (Barre, Mass., 1960), p. 67. Little Rock *Gazette* quoted in Leroy R. Hafen, "The Bean-Sinclair Party of Rocky Mountain Trappers, 1830-32," *The Colorado Magazine,* XXXI (1954), 163.

Secondly, as explorers—men who searched out the hidden places in the western wilderness—the Mountain Men as Jacksonian Men looked with a flexible eye upon the new land. Unlike the Hudson's Bay explorer who looked only for beaver and immediate profit, the Mountain Man looked to the future and the development of the West, not as a vast game preserve, but as a land like the one he had known back home.

> "Much of this vast waste of territory belongs to the Republic of the United States," wrote Zenas Leonard from San Francisco Bay in 1833. "What a theme to contemplate its settlement and civilization. Will the jurisdiction of the federal government ever succeed in civilizing the thousands of savages now roaming over these plains, and her hardy freeborn population here plant their homes, build their towns and cities, and say here shall the arts and sciences of civilization take root and flourish? Yes, here, even in this remote part of the Great West before many years will these hills and valleys be greeted with the enlivening sound of the workman's hammer, and the merry whistle of the ploughboy . . . we have good reason to suppose that the territory *west* of the mountains will some day be equally as important to the nation as that on the east." [26]

In 1830 in a famous letter to John H. Eaton, the Secretary of War, Jedediah S. Smith, David E. Jackson and William L. Sublette aired their views on the possibilities of the West. Smith made clear that a wagon road route suitable for settlers existed all the way to Oregon, and Sublette dramatized the point when he brought ten wagons and two dearborns and even a milch cow over the mountains as far as the Wind River rendezvous. Their report made abundantly clear that in their opinion the future of the West lay with settlers rather than trappers. Indeed they were worried that the English at Fort Vancouver might grasp this fact before the American government.[27] In short, as explorers and trappers theirs was a broad-ranging, flexible, settler-oriented, public view of the Far West.

Tied in with this and of the greatest significance is a third and final point. Not only did they *see* a settler's future in the West, but at least some of the Mountain Men were most eager to see to it that such a future was *guaranteed* by the institutions of the United States Government which must be brought West and extended over all the wild new land to protect the settler in the enjoyment of his own "vine and fig tree." The Mexican Government, unstable, and blown by whim or caprice, could not secure the future, and the British Government, at least in North America, was under the heel of monopoly. France was frivolous and decadent. Russia

[26] Zenas Leonard, *Narrative of the Adventures of Zenas Leonard,* ed. John C. Ewers (Norman, Okla., 1959), pp. 94-95.

[27] Reproduced in Morgan, *Jedediah Smith,* pp. 343-48.

was a sinister and backward despotism. Only the free institutions of Jacksonian America would make the West safe for enterprise. So strongly did he feel about this that in 1841 the Mountain Man Moses "Black" Harris sent a letter to one Thornton Grimsley offering him the command of 700 men, of which he was one, who were eager to "join the standard of their country, and make a clean sweep of what is called the Origon [*sic*] Territory; that is clear it of British and Indians." Outraged not only at British encroachments, he was also prepared to "march through to California" as well.[28] It may well have been this spirit that settled the Oregon question and brought on the Mexican War.[29]

Settlement, security, stability, enterprise, free enterprise, a government of laws which, in the words of Jackson himself, confines "itself to equal *protection,* and as Heaven does its rains, showers its favors alike on the high and the low, the rich and the poor," [30] all of these shaped the Mountain Man's vision of the West and his role in its development. It was called Manifest Destiny. But long before John L. O'Sullivan nicely turned the phrase in the *Democratic Review,*[31] the Mountain Man as Jacksonian Man—a "venturous conservative"—was out in the West doing his utmost to lend the Almighty a helping hand. James Clyman perhaps put it most simply:

> Here lies the bones of old Black Harris
> who often traveled beyond the far west
> and for the freedom of Equal rights
> He crossed the snowy mountain Hights
> was free and easy kind of soul
> Especially with a Belly full.[32]

28 Quoted in Charles L. Camp, ed. *James Clyman Frontiersman* (Portland, Ore., 1960), pp. 61-62.

29 Ray Allen Billington, *The Far Western Frontier,* pp. 154-73. See also Frederick Merk, *Manifest Destiny and Mission in American History* (New York, 1963).

30 James D. Richardson, ed. *A Compilation of the Messages and Papers of the Presidents 1789-1897* (1900), II, 590-91. Italics mine.

31 John L. O'Sullivan, "Annexation," unsigned article, *United States Magazine and Democratic Review,* XVII (July-August 1845), 797-98. See also his more popular statement in the New York *Morning News,* December 27, 1845.

32 Camp, *James Clyman Frontiersman,* p. 64.

Afternote

Since writing the above article I have had an opportunity to consider the Mountain Man in the larger context of his role as explorer and harbinger of civilization. See "L'Exploration des Régions de L'Ouest en Rétrospective," *Journal of World History*, VIII (1965), 707–31, and my recently published history of American exploration in the nineteenth century, *Exploration and Empire* (New York: Alfred A. Knopf, 1966). These further researches lend a greater significance to the role of the Mountain Man as Jacksonian Man in two senses. First, in contrast to the French, Spanish, and English explorers, the American Mountain Man had a much greater freedom of choice in terms of his economic occupation. He was mobile and flexible in what he could do. All explorers are, to a degree, "programmed" by the civilized centers from which they depart. The American Mountain Man had a variety of alternatives or possible "programs" which he might follow due to the various and almost multi-origined nature of the civilized center (*e.g.*, St. Louis) from which he departed. As the above article indicates, the result was that in contrast to his Spanish, French, and English counterparts he looked for more kinds of economic and social possibilities in the West, and thus more effectively facilitated the coming of permanent settlement and civilization to the West. Therefore the Mountain Man explorer can, with caution, be made to serve as an index to the American character which was itself shaped by the unique circumstance of being able to draw upon a variety of European models and experiences rather than a single national experience and tradition.

A second point is the degree to which even the supposedly most primitive of explorers *were* in fact "programmed" by civilized centers in some way. In *Exploration and Empire* I have, in addition to the study of the explorers themselves, also used the western art of the times to support this thesis. Lewis O. Saum's "The Fur Trader and the Noble Savage," XV (Winter, 1963), 554–71, adds further confirmation. He concludes that very often even the rude fur traders (Jacksonian men in my view) saw the Indian as "noble savage" although this did not square with their actual experience. He declares, "In either case, first-hand experience in the crude realities of wilderness existence provided no absolute immunity from that intriguing and perennial passion, the ennobling of the savage." In other words, the fur trader or Mountain Man was, in part, absorbing his view of the West not from experience but from European stereotypes and images passed along to him out on the Rocky Mountain and Missouri River frontiers. Thus the newest of "that new man," the frontier American, circa 1820–1840, in one sense held values and concepts that were very old (at least rooted in the eighteenth century), but what made him new was the freedom to select from all of these older values, images and traditions to form a new combination that was flexible, unique, characteristic of his time and American.

William H. Goetzmann is a Professor of History and Director of the American Studies Program at the University of Texas. [This article appeared in Vol. XV, No. 3 (Fall, 1963).]

Charles L. Sanford

An American *Pilgrim's Progress*

A CONVENTIONAL rhetoric of spirit antedating Columbus' voyages of discovery helped to invest the new Western world and the way West with a magnetic attraction over European imaginations. It functioned to give the otherwise sordid pursuit of material riches moral and spiritual sanction, without which most men seem disinclined to dare and do. This rhetoric revolved on the spiritual voyage or quest for personal salvation and reached its fullest literary expression in Dante's *Divine Comedy* and Bunyan's *Pilgrim's Progress.*

In the journey patterns of Scripture as well as in the language of medieval church symbolism, the spiritual quest had traditionally been known as a "journey toward light."[1] According to this interpretation, if the bower of light was Paradise or the Celestial City, the original source of the bright beam was God, symbolized by the life-giving sun. The sun in medieval popular thought represented God's truth and righteousness, illuminating the dark corners of sin with His saving radiance in its solar cycle from East to West. Medieval fable with its strange wonders and miraculous beings had the kingdom of earthly desire located vaguely and variously in Abyssinia, in Cathay and Ophir, somewhere in the Far East, beyond the western seas. Medieval explorers sought out the warmest climes of the sun.[2] But Christians, for the most part, looked

[1]This is expounded in Helen F. Dunbar, *Symbolism in Medieval Thought and its Consummation in the Divine Comedy* (New Haven: Yale University Press, 1929), *passim*, and in Dorothy Donnelly, *The Golden Well: An Anatomy of Symbols* (London: Sheed and Ward, 1950), pp. 115-53.

[2]For the relationship between medieval legend and early exploration see Don Cameron Allen, *The Legend of Noah* (Urbana: University of Illinois Press, 1949); A. R. Anderson, *Alexander's Gate, Gog and Magog and the Inclosed Nations* (Cambridge: The Medieval Academy of America, 1932); Washington Irving, *Life and Voyages of Christopher Columbus* (New York: Thomas Y. Crowell, n.d.), Appendices XIX-XXVI; Leonard Olschki,

for the promised land in the other world of life-after-death while they huddled in misery in this world. Anticipating the future importance of the direction West, Dante, in a famous passage from the *Divine Comedy*, has Ulysses sailing through the straits of Gibraltar to reach the West, seeking, "the new experience/ Of the uninhabited world behind the sun."[3] Shouldering the dawn in the unknown western seas, Ulysses comes upon Mount Purgatory, where one begins the ascent to the Celestial City. Columbus, too, was saturated with medieval legend and thought literally that he had discovered "the terrestrial paradise."[4]

But God's divine light did not shine everywhere with equal brilliance. "Wheresoever the children of Israel dwelt," Genesis maintained, "*there* was light." In other words, His brightest beams were reserved for God's elect, the chosen people. The Reformed Churches of Europe, under the leadership of Martin Luther, in effect revived the old Hebraic conception of a chosen people and claimed that the light of the true gospel dwelt in their house.[5] Since the Reformation rose first in the west of Europe and spread westward from Germany to France, the Netherlands, and thus to England, it became almost commonplace for the favored ones to suppose that the succession to the moral and spiritual leadership of the world followed the solar cycle of the sun from East to West. Settlement of the New World by militant Protestants completed the identification of geographical westering with moral and spiritual progress and, with the secularization of millennial hopes, contributed to the eighteenth and nineteenth-century idea of progress.

Before and during the settlement of America, the English considered themselves the custodians of the apostolic succession.[6] Shakespeare's England was not only "this blessed plot, this earth, this realm"; it was also a bower of light, "this other Eden, demi-paradise, this fortress built by Nature" for a chosen people. On the eve of settlement, as Louis B. Wright has pointed out, Protestant theologians were frantically transferring the Ark of the Covenant from Abraham to the English. There were, undoubtedly, many laymen who cried with the Baptist Henry Nicholas, "We have it, we are the Congregation of Christ, we are Israel, lo here it is!" or with the Anglican William Crashaw, "The

"Ponce de Leon's Fountain of Youth: History of a Geographical Myth," *Hisp.-Am. Hist. Rev.*, XXI, no. 3 (August 1941), 361-85.

[3]Dante, *The Divine Comedy, I, Hell*, trans. Dorothy L. Sayers (Penguin Classics), p. 236.

[4]Hakluyt Society, *Select Documents Illustrating the Four Voyages of Columbus* (London: Hakluyt Society, 1933), II, 42, 30-50, *passim*.

[5]Ernest Tuveson, *Millennium and Utopia* (Berkeley: University of California Press, 1950), pp. 27, 39.

[6]Louis B. Wright, *Religion and Empire* (Chapel Hill: University of North Carolina Press, 1943), p. 91, *et sequitur*.

God of Israel is . . . the God of England."[7] But there were also many Englishmen who were not loath to see the succession pass westward to America, so long as it redounded to the power and glory of England. Indeed, the English were divinely appointed to establish themselves in the promised lands of the New World! Thus, Richard Hakluyt urged in his *Discourse of Western Planting* that the western discoveries had provided England a heaven-sent opportunity for the spread of the gospel, "whereunto the Princes of the refourmed Relligion are chefely bounde."[8] John White of Dorchester, author of *The Planters Plea*, considered England to be singled out for that work, "being of all the States that enjoy the libertie of the Religion Reformed" the most orthodox and sincere.[9] As early as 1583 Sir Humphrey Gilbert thought England's "full possession of those so ample and pleasant countreys . . . very probable by the revolution and course of Gods word and religion, which from the beginning hath moved from the East, towards, and at last unto the West, where it is like to end. . . ."[10]

The belief that the bounties of God followed the course of the sun westward brought numerous prophecies of a bright future for America and contributed, in part, to their fulfillment.[11] Sir William Alexander, who was to become proprietor of Nova Scotia, wrote in 1616:

> America to Europe may succeed;
> God may stones raise up to Abram's seed.

The poet John Donne predicted in 1622 that the Virginia Company would make England a bridge between the Old World and the New "to join all to that world that shall never grow old, the kingdom of Heaven." A few years later another Anglican poet, George Herbert, noted in his *Church Militant* that

> Religion stands tip-toe in our land
> Ready to pass to the American strand.

Whereupon, Dr. Twiss, "considering our English Plantations of late, and the opinion of many grave divines concerning the Gospel's fleeing

[7]See especially the promotional sermons and colonizing tracts calendared in Alexander Brown, *The Genesis of the United States*, 2 vols. (Boston, 1890), and many similar rhetorical pronouncements quoted in William Haller, *The Rise of Puritanism* (New York: Columbia University Press, 1938).

[8]Quoted in Wright, *Religion and Empire*, p. 45.

[9]Peter Force, comp., *Tracts and Other Papers, Relating principally to the Origin, Settlement, and Progress of the Colonies in North America* . . ., 4 vols. (Washington, 1836-46), II, 3, 12.

[10]Original Narratives Series, *Early English and French Voyages* . . ., ed. Henry S. Burrage (New York: Charles Scribner's Sons, 1906), p. 183.

[11]Quotations in this paragraph are from Edward D. Neill, *The English Colonization of America* . . . (London, 1871), 177-178n.

westward," asked his fellow clergyman, Mede—"Why may not that be the place of the new Jerusalem?" His question was later echoed by American colonists who founded cities in the wilderness and led periodic religious revivals on the frontier.[12]

The image of a new Jerusalem in the western world accompanied dreams of empire and a higher civilization. Among the blessings which God had bestowed upon fallen reason, and whose great revival, according to seventeenth-century Chiliasts, was to usher in the last stage before the millennium, was culture and learning. "Learning, like the Sun," Thomas Burnet wrote in his *Archaeologiae* in 1692,[13]

> began to take its Course from the *East*, then turned *Westward*, where we have long rejoiced in its Light. Who knows whether, leaving these Seats, it may not yet take a further Progress? Or whether it will not be universally diffused, and enlighten all the World with its Rays?

The English Puritan divine, John Edwards, also traced the advance of culture and religion as a westward movement. In 1725 Jeremy Dummer, Massachusetts' agent in London, hoped, apropos of his collection of books for the new Yale library, that religion and polite learning would not rest in their westward progress until they took up their chief residence in America.[14] Two years later Bishop Berkeley summed up for posterity ideas which had been in circulation for more than a century. His famous poem beginning, "Westward the course of empire takes its way," restated the familiar solar analogy to conform to the imperial vision of eighteenth-century Englishmen.

Although Englishmen transplanted in America shared this dream of imperial grandeur, they assumed a rôle for themselves which eclipsed that of the mother country and unconsciously hastened the separation of the colonies. They believed that they were the chosen instruments of God appointed to carry out the Protestant mission in the New World, which was to set up a "city on the hill" as an example to Europe and the rest of the world of the true Reformation.[15] In this mission they regarded themselves as the heirs of all history, curiously unappreciated

[12]See, for instance, the *Letter-Book of Samuel Sewall* in *Coll. Mass. Hist. Soc.*, 6th ser., 2 vols. (Boston, 1886-88), I, 177; II, 156, 201. Sewall quoted both Twiss and Mede on this point and for many years sought to elucidate it by biblical prophecies.

[13]Quoted by Tuveson, *Millennium and Utopia*, p. 166.

[14]In his letter to Timothy Woodbridge, *Trans. Col. Soc. Mass.* (Boston, 1895-present), VI, 201-02.

[15]Perry Miller, *The New England Mind: From Colony to Province* (Cambridge: Harvard University Press, 1953), pp. 4-5; also his "Errand into the Wilderness," *Wm. and Mary Qtly*, 3rd ser., X (1953), 3-19. This belief was by no means confined to New England Puritans, however. For the importance of the religious impulse in the colonizing of Virginia see Perry Miller, "The Religious Impulse in the Founding of Virginia," *ibid.*, 3rd ser., V (1948), 492-522; VI (1949), 24-41; and the promotional sermons and tracts calendared in Alexander Brown, *The Genesis of the United States*.

by Englishmen at home, for whose salvation they prayed. Their preëminence on the stage of history seemed guaranteed not only by the westward progression of religion and culture, but also by God's Providence in concealing America from European eyes until the time of the Reformation.[16] There was little doubt in their minds that the final drama of moral regeneration and universal salvation was to begin here, with them.

This sense of unique destiny bred a religious patriotism which unwittingly started the colonists down the long road to political independence. The inner logic of their position was revealed by Thomas Paine, who on the eve of the American Revolution acknowledged the design of Heaven, adding, "The Reformation was preceded by the discovery of America, as if the Almighty graciously meant to open a sanctuary to the persecuted in future years. . . ."[17] An incipient patriotism was also reflected, unconsciously to be sure, in the change in emphasis which many colonists, particularly New Englanders, gave to the conventional sun rhetoric. In the symbolic language of spirit they sometimes denied the sun its regular transit from East to West, and, instead, had it hovering or rising for the first time over them. As early as 1647 John Eliot, missionary to the Indians, was announcing "The Daybreaking if not the Sunrising of the Gospel . . . in New England."[18] "O New-England," Samuel Willard hymned in a sermon of 1704, "thou art a Land of Vision; and has been so for a long time. The Sun for one day stood over Gibeon, so has the Sun of the Gospel been standing over us for Fourscore years together."[19] The Sun of Righteousness, according to Jonathan Edwards, "shall *rise in the west*, contrary to the course of this world, or the course of things in the old heavens and earth."[20] Such language implied a break with the European past. It is not surprising that Thomas Jefferson proposed as a Seal of State for the new nation a representation of the children of Israel led by a pillar of light, or that the goddess of liberty on our coins is flanked by a rising sun.

The chosen people of the American colonies looked upon their mission in the wilderness not merely as the continuation of something old, but as the beginning of something new: they were to usher in the final stage of history. They had inherited a new world in a physical sense, and in order "to vindicate the most rigorous ideal of the Reformation" they

[16]This idea recurs frequently in colonial writing, but see especially Cotton Mather, *Magnalia Christi Americana* . . ., 2 vols. (Hartford, 1820), I, 40-41; Jonathan Edwards, *Works*, 4 vols. (Boston, 1843), III, 314-15.

[17]In his *Common Sense* (1776).

[18]John Eliot, *The Daybreaking if not the Sunrising of the Gospel with the Indians in New England* (London, 1647).

[19]Quoted by Perry Miller, *The New England Mind; From Colony to Province*, p. 178.

[20]Jonathan Edwards, *op. cit.*, III, 316, 314-17. Italics are mine.

felt it necessary, as Jonathan Edwards said, "to begin a new world in a spiritual respect." Moreover, they associated their drama of moral and spiritual regeneration with a special plot of virgin land untouched by mistakes of the past and where failure was inexcusable. By national covenant with the children of Israel, God had appointed a promised land in Canaan. John Cotton told his people that they were the heirs of the covenant promise and that New England was the appointed place.[21] Up and down the colonies, from Maine to Virginia, with a frequency suggesting that most colonists were, to a greater or less degree, touched by a sense of mission, colonists likened themselves to the tribes of Israel and called their country the "new Canaan," the "second Paradise," the "promised land," the "new heaven on earth." Not a few colonists, especially in New England, lived daily in agonized expectation of the Second Coming of Christ to America to inaugurate the millennium.[22] What the colonists did not realize was that, in tying their spiritual hopes to a plot of earth, they had already begun the process of what Carl Becker has called dismantling the celestial heaven in favor of an earthly one.

By the eighteenth century, piety had largely given way to moralism. But moralism continued to express a sense of mission and was intimately connected with the land. Just as the early frontier hardships had been held to be a test of the fitness of an Elect people in their incessant warfare against sin, so success in subduing the wilderness was tantamount to entering the kingdom of Heaven and seemed to demonstrate a direct causal relationship between moral effort and material reward. The opportunity for advancement afforded by the free lands of promise was contrasted to the static caste system of a Europe still fettered by feudalism. America's answer to Europe was now to rise in the economic scale by the application of industry, sobriety, and frugality, to improve upon the brutish state of nature, to carve out of the wilderness a pleasant land of rural villages, small shops, churches, and tilled fields—in short, to establish a superior civilization in which prosperity was the mark of special virtue. The process of moral regeneration was indeed a civilizing process, but, as opposed to the corrupt urban culture of Europe, the new American civilization was to have an agrarian basis, celebrating the simple virtues of the saw and the axe. The ultimate effect of the discovery of the new world was thus to substitute for the spiritual pilgrimage of Dante and Bunyan the "way West" as the way of salvation. It re-

[21]John Cotton, *God's Promise to his Plantations* (London, 1630), reprinted in *Old South Leaflets*, no. 53, pp. 1-15.

[22]Ira V. Brown, "Watchers for the Second Coming: The Millenarian Tradition in America," *Miss. Valley Hist. Rev.*, XXXIX (1952), 441-58. Millennialism was more widespread in colonial America than Perry Miller is willing to grant.

mained for an American Bunyan, Benjamin Franklin, to express the sense of this transformation in a moral fable which has gripped the imaginations of Americans ever since.

II

It would be rather easy to show that Benjamin Franklin was the product of eighteenth-century urban culture extending from Europe to colonial Boston and Philadelphia, that Franklin's "Poor Richard" had an affinity with the *Compleat Tradesman* of Daniel Defoe's England, and that therefore Franklin's moral virtues were broadly middle-class rather than peculiarly American.[23] But such a view, whatever its merits, would overlook the fact that Americans, in response to a frontier environment and to a cyclical theory of history, have tended to emphasize the theme of moral regeneration in connection with the supposedly superior virtues of an agrarian civilization. The two most perceptive foreign observers of the nineteenth century, Alexis de Tocqueville and James Bryce, agreed in calling Americans as a whole the most moralistic and religious people in the world. The philosopher George Santayana once remarked that to be an American "is of itself almost a moral condition, an education, and a career," and in a similar tenor the expatriate Logan Pearsall Smith complained that Americans acted as if "America were more than a country, were a sort of cause."[24]

A. Whitney Griswold has shown that Franklin's thirst for moral perfection was a distillation of the Protestant business ethic taught by Puritan ministers in Franklin's hometown of Boston. Franklin himself acknowledged the influence of Cotton Mather's "Essays to Do Good." Though the colonial urban culture opened to Franklin the opportunities for advancement, gave him access to the scientific and philosophic ideas of the Enlightenment, and enlisted him in projects for civic improvement, his moral vision was colored by the presence of the frontier. The colonial city, after all, rested on rural foundations. Cosmopolitan though he was, Franklin dreamed of a great agrarian utopia in which to preserve America's "glorious public virtue."

As early as 1753, when he was preoccupied with problems of Indian defense, he proposed, as a means both of enriching himself and strengthening the British empire, to settle a wilderness colony on the banks of

[23]This view is suggested by Stuart P. Sherman, "Franklin and the Age of Enlightenment," in *Americans* (New York: Charles Scribner's Sons, 1922), pp. 28-62; Carl and Jessica Bridenbaugh, *Rebels and Gentlemen: Philadelphia in the Age of Franklin* (New York: Reynal and Hitchcock, 1942), Ch. I; Gladys Meyer, *Free Trade in Ideas* (Morningside Heights: King's Crown Press, 1941); Vernon L. Parrington, *Main Currents in American Thought* (New York: Harcourt, Brace and Company, 1927), I, 166.

[24]George Santayana, *Character and Opinion in the United States* (New York: Charles Scribner's Sons, 1920), p. 168; Logan Pearsall Smith, *Unforgotten Years* (Boston: Little, Brown and Company, 1939), p. 280.

the Ohio. "What a glorious Thing it would be," he wrote on that occasion, "to settle in that fine Country a large strong Body of Religious and Industrious People!"[25] But his imperialistic vision of a greater England in the West reserved a special destiny for Americans which overshadowed the rôle of the mother country. He expressed this incipient patriotism in the sun and light imagery common to the rhetoric of westward expansion. " 'Tis said the Arts delight to travel Westward," he once remarked.[26] He was long of the opinion "that the *foundations of the future grandeur and stability of the British empire lie in America.*"[27] He playfully attributed a cosmic significance to the work of spiritual pioneering: "by *clearing America* of Woods" Americans were "*Scouring* our Planet, . . . and so making this Side of our Globe reflect a brighter Light to the Eyes of the Inhabitants in *Mars* or *Venus*. . . ."[28] Franklin early identified the frontier with opportunity and tended to measure spiritual progress by progress in converting the wilderness into a paradise of material plenty.

A city-dweller, by profession a printer and tradesman, Franklin nevertheless located the true source of virtue in agricultural pursuits. "There seem to be but three ways for a nation to acquire wealth," he wrote, with an eye to the widening breach between England and the colonies. "The first is by *war*, as the Romans did, in plundering their conquered neighbors. This is *robbery*. The second by *commerce*, which is generally *cheating*. The third by *agriculture*, the only *honest way*, wherein man receives a real increase of the seed thrown into the ground, in a kind of continual miracle. . . ."[29] This was more than physiocratic doctrine; it was a program to keep a chosen people on the path of righteousness and prepare them for the moral and spiritual leadership of the earth. He made it clear that public morality was his special concern when he wrote after independence had been secured: "The vast Quantity of Forest Lands we have yet to clear, and put in order for Cultivation, will for a long time keep the Body of our Nation laborious and frugal."[30] He repeatedly contrasted the vices of Europe and England with the "glorious public virtue" of America and habitually bestowed upon American farmers the ennobling title of "Cultivators of the Earth." By an outstanding example of good works, by his *Almanacks* and *Autobiography*, by his proposed *Art of Virtue* and by other writings, Franklin constituted himself chief guardian of the national conscience.

[25] *The Writings of Benjamin Franklin*, ed. Albert H. Smyth, 10 vols. (New York: MacMillan Company, 1905-07), III, 339.
[26] *Ibid.*, IV, 194.
[27] *Ibid.*, IV, 4.
[28] *Writings*, III, 72-73.
[29] *Writings*, V, 202.
[30] *Ibid.*, IX, 245.

It has been said that Franklin's ethics were those of a tradesman and that the eighteenth-century concept of tradesman was English in origin. Yet an English writer, D. H. Lawrence, has found Franklin's archetypal new-world quality essentially in his moralism, and Herbert Schneider has written that, as a moralist, Franklin was "a child of the New England frontier."[31] The truth is that the individualistic virtues of industry, frugality and sobriety taught, if not always practiced, by Franklin, were adaptable to both the tradesman and farmer. Like the middle-class tradesman, the pioneer farmer was a small entrepreneur and capitalist, a speculator in land, a "cultivator," as Veblen has said, "of the main chance as well as of the fertile soil." The career of Daniel Defoe, who died in obscurity and poverty, shows that Defoe spoke for a single class which was not yet able to break through the cramping restrictions of class and caste. Franklin spoke for a whole nation of middle-class *arrivistes*, but addressed himself particularly to the "Cultivators of the Earth" in opposition to the urban dwellers of the colonial city and of the European metropolis.

The American mission of moral regeneration derived its dynamism from the tension generated by the polarity between what the colonists considered an over-ripe stage of civilization in a Europe corrupted by feudal institutions and a simpler, agrarian society which more than made up in morals what it lacked in sophistication. American moralism implied a repudiation of European culture and of urbanism, though not a denial of the civilizing process. As the Revolution drew near, Franklin exaggerated the differences. From England he wrote to Joseph Galloway, who longed for a reconciliation, "When I consider the extream Corruption prevalent among all Orders of Men in this old rotten State, and the glorious publick Virtue so predominant in our rising Country, I cannot but apprehend nore Mischief than Benefit from a closer Union."[32] Political and military necessity demanded a smiling compliance with the ways of the world in Paris, where, among the powdered heads, he wore his fur cap as a native emblem; but he also had private reservations about the state of French culture. Occasionally his moral obsessions led him to flirt with a primitivism akin to the sentimental cult of the noble savage. Returning from a tour of Ireland and Scotland, he wrote:[33]

> . . . if my Countrymen should ever wish for the honour of having among them a gentry enormously wealthy, let them sell their Farms and pay rack'd Rents; the Scale of the Landlords will rise, as that of the Tenants

[31] D. H. Lawrence, *Studies in Classic American Literature* (New York: Thomas A. Seltzer, 1923), pp. 13-31; Herbert W. Schneider, *The Puritan Mind* (New York: Henry Holt and Company, 1930), p. 256.

[32] *Writings*, VI, 311-12.

[33] *Ibid.*, V, 362-63.

is depress'd, who will soon become poor, tattered, dirty, and abject in Spirit. Had I never been in the American colonies, but was to form my Judgment of Civil Society by what I have lately seen, I should never advise a Nation of Savages to admit of Civilization: For I assure you, that, in the Possession and Enjoyment of the various Comforts of Life, compar'd to these People every Indian is a Gentleman. . . .

In his identification of prosperity with virtue Franklin remembered that the covenant promise was with a whole people, not merely the few, and he wanted, as he said, "a general happy Mediocrity of fortune."

To be an American was to be a backtrailer to a more sophisticated society, in itself a moral condition. An aristocracy of wealth based on commerce and land speculation blossomed in the larger seaport towns of America. Rich Boston merchants thirsted after London, much as London aspired to Paris. Like Jefferson and many other Americans imbued with a sense of mission, Franklin did not want to see colonial urban centers emulate the class patterns of European society, and he, too, sometimes wished for an "ocean of fire" between the old world and the new. He transferred some of his animus against Europe to the coastal towns. "The People of the Trading Towns," he wrote at the end of the Revolution, "may be rich and luxurious, while the Country possesses all the Virtues, that tend to private Happiness and publick Prosperity. Those Towns are not much regarded by the Country; they are hardly considered as an essential Part of the States . . . we may hope the Luxury of a few Merchants on the Seacoast will not be the Ruin of America."[34] Franklin viewed with some alarm the social dislocations and misery caused by the new factory system in Europe. No more than Jefferson did he want to see Americans "twirling a distaff" in factories. Though he was the prophet of American technological efficiency, he did not anticipate industrialism. It may be supposed that his response to such urban problems as fire-fighting, poor street-lighting, pauperism, and improper sanitation was unconsciously motivated by a patriotic desire to avoid or mitigate the worst evils of urbanization.

Franklin's whole moral fiber was geared to raising a new man and a new society in the world of nations. Viewed in this light, his *Autobiography* is a great moral fable pursuing on a secular level the theme of John Bunyan's *Pilgrim's Progress.* There is little doubt of the serious intent underlying either the *Autobiography* or the creation of "Poor Richard," to impart moral instruction to the public. He wrote the *Autobiography*, as he said, to acquaint his posterity with the means of his success, "as they may find some of them suitable to their own situations,

[34] *Writings*, IX, 245-46, 248.

and therefore fit to be imitated."[35] After breaking off the work, a friend persuaded him to continue it on the grounds that it would be useful to millions and would "lead the youth to equal the industry and temperance of thy early youth."[36] Another friend urged its continuation "in conjunction with your Art of Virtue (which you design to publish) of improving the features of private character, and consequently of aiding all happiness, both public and domestic."[37] Franklin originated *Poor Richard's Almanack* to make money, but, more importantly, to convey "instruction among the common people." He filled the calendar spaces "with proverbial sentences, chiefly such as inculcated industry and frugality, as the means of procuring wealth, and thereby securing virtue."[38] Of late it has been popular to say with Robert Spiller that "Poor Richard" was a humorous creation, never intended to be taken seriously. But Franklin's very humor was a vehicle for serious moral instruction and also expressed his sense of special destiny. Thus, his tall tales of sheep with tails so heavily laden with wool that they needed trailer-carts to carry them and of the whale which chased salmon up Niagara Falls, tales which anticipated the characteristic humor of the American frontier, were Franklin's way of whittling the urban sophisticate and European down to size and telling him, in effect, that things grew bigger and better in God's country.

The *Autobiography* is not simply a formless record of personal experience, or just a charming success story. Consciously or unconsciously, it is a work of imagination which, by incorporating the "race" consciousness of a people, achieves the level of folk myth. Franklin's biographer, Carl Van Doren, tells us that Franklin had no model for his kind of autobiography.[39] This is not quite true. As a report on Franklin's spiritual progress in the new heaven on earth, the *Autobiography* in its basic dramatic form parallels Bunyan's great allegory. Franklin merely substituted, to use the phrase of Carl Becker, the secular story with a happy ending for the Christian story with the happy ending. *Pilgrim's Progress* was a best seller in New England during the latter part of the seventeenth century.[40] It admirably fitted the situation of a people whose feet were planted on the path to worldly success, but whose heads were still filled with visions of the Celestial City. Franklin's first book was *Pilgrim's Progress*, and his favorite author was John Bunyan.[41]

[35]Benjamin Franklin, *Autobiography*, ed. Dixon Wecter (Rinehart Edn., 1948), p. 1.
[36]*Autobiography*, p. 71.
[37]*Ibid.*, p. 73.
[38]*Ibid.*, pp. 97-98.
[39]Carl Van Doren, *Benjamin Franklin* (New York: Viking Press, 1938), pp. 414-15.
[40]See the book lists in Daniel Henchman's ms. account book in the Boston Public Library. Also Thomas G. Wright, *Literary Culture in Early New England, 1620-1730* (New Haven: Yale University Press, 1920), p. 123.
[41]*Autobiography*, pp. 10, 21.

Franklin absorbed from the pages of *Pilgrim's Progress* lessons in artistry as well as confirmations for the new-world theme of moral regeneration. According to Franklin, Honest John was the first author whom he had met "who mixed narration and dialogue, a method of writing very engaging to the reader, who in the most interesting parts finds himself, as it were, brought into the company and present at the discourse."[42] Franklin regarded Defoe's works as imitations of Bunyan in this respect. Franklin also combined narrative and dialogue in his *Autobiography* in order to convey the felt immediacy of his experience, but in relating Bunyan's theme to the details of his new environment, he created an allegory of American middle-class superiority.

Franklin states his central organizing theme at the outset: his emergence "from the poverty and obscurity" in which he was born and bred "to a state of affluence and some degree of reputation in the world."[43] He gives to this secular "rise" a moral and spiritual meaning discoverable in the special blessings of God. The boy entering Philadelphia with three loaves under his arm is obviously the prototype of Bunyan's Christian beginning his toilsome ascent to the Heavenly City. Franklin heightens the drama of his struggle upward against odds in his more worldly pilgrimage by reiterating the contrast between his humble beginnings and his improved station in life. Three times he halts his narrative at conspicuous points in order to recall to his readers the pathetic picture of his first arrival in Philadelphia. He frames the Philadelphia anecdote as carefully as if he were deliberately setting out to create an immortal legend. "I have been the more particular," he writes, "in this description of my journey, and shall be so of my first entry into the city, that you may in your mind compare such unlikely beginnings with the figure I have since made there."[44] He would have the reader believe that his future wife, Deborah Read, happened also to be present on that occasion to observe his unlikely beginnings.

Since his marriage is a marriage of convenience contributing to his rise in life, he associates the episode of the rolls with his courtship of Miss Read. Once established as an up-and-coming printer, he notes for the reader's convenience that he "made rather a more respectable appearance in the eyes of Miss Read than I had done when she first happened to see me *eating my roll* in the street."[45] Though his success story is a triumph of moral individualism and personal salvation, he identifies it with the rise of a whole people. His rise in life thus parallels the growth of Philadelphia. After he has bought out his partner Meredith,

[42] *Autobiography*, p. 21.
[43] *Ibid.*, p. 1.
[44] *Autobiography*, p. 23.
[45] *Ibid.*, p. 27. Italics are mine.

there is a building boom: "whereas I remembered well, that when I first walked about the streets of Philadelphia, *eating my roll*, I saw most of the houses in Walnut Street . . . with bills on to be let. . . ."[46] When, finally, he achieves world-wide fame by his electrical experiments, he confesses to being flattered by the honors heaped upon him: "for, *considering my low beginning*, they were great things to me."[47] By now he has no need to mention the symbolic rolls.

Franklin's confessed *errata* are analogous to Christian's bundle of sins and to the giant Despair, over which he must prevail in order to gain the Heavenly City. Carl Van Doren has said that Franklin owed his success to "natural gifts of which Poor Richard could not tell the secret."[48] But Franklin was not altogether without a sense of sin, and he believed that good works were the necessary means to personal salvation, or success. Obversely, as his attitude towards charity in the *Autobiography* indicates, he felt that failure to rise in life was the result of moral turpitude. Accordingly, in one of the most famous passages of the *Autobiography*, about the year 1728, Franklin "conceived the bold and arduous project of arriving at moral perfection."[49] The important point is not that he failed, but that he tried and that the program of good works which he outlined here and elsewhere, in effect, completed the long process of dismantling the Celestial City. A tale by Nathaniel Hawthorne, "The Celestial Railroad," suggests an ironic inversion of Bunyan's original allegory. Franklin, in his pilgrimage towards the heavenly city, sends his baggage ahead by postal service and sets up signposts for other travelers. He fills the Slough of Despond with Philadelphia cobblestones and almanacs. He lights the Valley of the Shadow of Death with street lamps. He smites Apollyon with a thunderbolt. He throws a bridge over the River Styx.

In the spiritual drama of a chosen people lay the source of that economic romanticism, so frequently confused with materialism, by which so many Americans have assumed a God-given right to the fruits of an Edenic tree. As Franklin said, "The Divine Being seems to have manifested his Approbation . . . by the remarkable Prosperity with which He has been pleased to favour the whole Country."[50] Americans after Franklin would merely inherit the earth by presumption and without waiting for Divine Approbation. Franklin's motives for land speculation were not sordidly pecuniary, but included, as did his enthusiasm for science, a poetic conception of national destiny. Thus, he called his

[46]*Ibid.*, p. 65. Italics are mine.
[47]*Autobiography*. p. 123. Italics are mine.
[48]Carl Van Doren, *Franklin*, p. 118.
[49]*Autobiography*, p. 83.
[50]*Writings*, VIII, 614.

proposed colony on the Ohio the future "paradise on earth."[51] The outbreak of the Revolution ended his petition to the Crown for western lands, but Americans came into a larger inheritance. To a great degree the American passion for liberty was an extension of the passion to possess the earthly inheritance. This passion was not essentially economic, for Americans felt that they were enacting a spiritual pilgrimage in their westward trek towards light.

The spiritual longing of the colonists prepared the psychological foundations of the nineteenth-century concept of Manifest Destiny, which sanctioned American imperialism. Thus, Nathaniel Ames, Franklin's competitor in almanacs, predicted in 1758 that "As the celestial light of the gospel was directed here by the finger of God, . . . So arts and sciences will change the face of nature in their tour from hence over the Appalachian Mountains to the Western Ocean."[52] After Franklin's death Americans who were disappointed with the results of coastal civilization pursued their special destiny inland, continuing to read the promise of American life in the westward cycle of the sun. At the height of westward expansion in the nineteenth century, Fourth of July orators often recaptured the old millennial fervor and were typically lyrical in sun worship:[53]

> Christianity, rational philosophy, and constitutional liberty, like an ocean of light are rolling their resistless tide over the earth. . . . Doubtless there may be partial revulsions. But the great movement will . . . be progressive, till the millennial sun shall rise in all the effulgence of universal day.

Americans refashioned for their own use a conventional rhetoric of spirit which had antedated the voyages of Columbus. For the millions who went west in their new-world version of "Pilgrim's Progress," the classic anecdote was the story of the poor boy who came to Philadelphia with three rolls under his arms and rose to fame and fortune.

[51]Quoted by Carl Van Doren, *Franklin*, p. 592.

[52]In Moses Coit Tyler, *A History of American Literature, 1607-1765* (Ithaca: Cornell University Press, 1949), p. 372.

[53]The following quotation, typical of a great many in the literature of nineteenth-century westward expansion, is taken from Ralph H. Gabriel, *The Course of American Democratic Thought* (New York: Ronald Press, 1940), p. 36.

Afternote

This article was expanded to form Chapters 3 and 7 of my book, *The Quest for Paradise: Europe and the American Moral Imagination* (Urbana: University of Illinois Press, 1961).

Charles L. Sanford is an Associate Professor of Language and Literature at Rensselaer Polytechnic Institute. [This article appeared in Vol. VI, No. 4 (Winter, 1954).]

William C. Spengemann · L. R. Lundquist

Autobiography and the American Myth

LIKE ALL OF OUR IMAGINATIVE WRITERS, AMERICAN AUTOBIOGRAPHERS HAVE traditionally drawn their materials from the fund of metaphors which grow out of our shared experiences, assumptions and beliefs—the American myth. The main difference between American autobiographers and writers of fiction is that the autobiographers have employed these metaphors in self-scrutiny and self-portrayal rather than in the presentation of fictional characters, but the resulting creation lends itself to cultural analysis as readily as purely fictional characters do. The created character in both cases represents values that are recognized by the reading audience at large. A consideration of several American autobiographers as cultural types may provide some new ways of viewing this special genre in our literature and suggest that autobiography in general is, in Georg Misch's words, "not only a special kind of literature but also an instrument of knowledge." [1] By regarding the creation of autobiographical character in America as a cultural act, we may suggest some of the ways in which Americans shape their views of themselves by attending closely to the dominant patterns of our culture. In addition, by noting the similarities between the fictional and autobiographical processes, we may offer an explanation of the striking coalition which these two genres have formed in our own time.

Before going on to examine specific cases, we should understand what we mean by "autobiography" and by "the American myth." We must recognize, first of all, that the term "autobiography" implies only that the author is writing specifically about himself; it has nothing to do with factual truth. Autobiography does not communicate raw experience, for

[1] *A History of Autobiography in Antiquity* (2 vols.: Cambridge, 1951), I, 10.

that is uncommunicable. It presents, rather, a metaphor for the raw experience. The language of autobiography stands in symbolic relation to both author and subject. As an author translates his life into language he creates for himself a symbolic identity and sees himself through the focusing glass of language. Since the language of the autobiographer is the common possession of his culture, it is not only subject to his personal manipulation, but it is filled with the assumed values of his society. The act of writing about oneself brings together the personal, unassimilated experiences of the writer and the shared values of his culture. The act of recollection becomes an act of creation and an act of self-evaluation at the same time.

When a man writes his autobiography he translates a unique view of himself into the language of his culture, subjecting some part of his private self to public evaluation. In doing so, he creates a fictive character who undergoes adventures drawn from the author's memory and a narrative persona who reports these experiences and evaluates them according to their place in the cultural pattern. The narrative persona stands between the created character and the body of cultural value that the author recognizes and describes an evaluative relationship between the two. Any autobiography, then, may be described according to the attitude of the narrative persona toward the behavior of the created character, in relation to the evaluated beliefs of the society as the author sees them. As Georg Misch puts it, "The spirit brooding over the recollected material is the truest and most real element in autobiography." [2]

As for the meaning of "the American myth," it is almost impossible to talk about *the* myth of any culture, since cultural values will undergo continual change as long as individuals have experiences and translate them into social belief. Even when communal assumptions take the form of a concrete story, that tale must remain sufficiently flexible and suggestive to allow for repeated interpretation. When it can no longer be reinterpreted to depict contemporary belief and to explain present problems it must fall into disuse and interest only the antiquarian. It is doubly difficult, furthermore, to define the myth of a democratic society such as ours, which at least purports to allow free competition among its individuals and its institutions for the allegiance of the people. In the United States, institutions rise to power and fall into impotence, and each describes national or cultural value in its own voice and its own terms. For the very reason that no single institution ever enjoys complete power, however, our cultural beliefs must be larger than their formulation by any one voice.

[2] *Ibid.*

The more or less orderly shift in dominant institutions in America suggests that the entire process occurs within a single system of values, which, compared to the forms it takes at different times, remains relatively constant. Social change in the United States is never more than apparently radical, it seems. An abiding and slowly shifting cultural pattern bridges all gaps and softens all shocks, no matter how deep or severe. Each new aspirant to social dominion must capitalize on values already a part of the tradition, even though he may intend to change them once he is in power. Indeed, the necessity to subscribe to these traditions at the outset limits his ability to change them in the long run. Our broadest values and traditions, then, either remain intact through all subsidiary change, or they alter so gradually that their movement may be charted and explained. Dissidence and competition do not deny the existence or power of a cultural myth; on the contrary, they serve to define it.

The American myth, in its most general form, describes human history as a pilgrimage from imperfection to perfection; from a dimly remembered union with the Divine to a re-establishment of that union. Within these very broad outlines, Americans have continually reinterpreted the several terms of the myth. For the Puritans, imperfection meant the natural depravity of human nature as exemplified by Adam; perfection referred to ultimate salvation through God's grace. For the Rationalists of our eighteenth century, the two terms meant, respectively, intellectual backwardness and worldly happiness through reason. For the Transcendentalists, they meant separation from and union with the spirit that is alive in Nature. For some later nineteenth-century reformers they denoted predatory individualism and collective Utopian harmony. For all of these groups the two terms were absolutely inseparable from the belief in America as a moral idea.

Whatever the particular form in which the myth has presented itself, it remains, as Charles Sanford has shown,[3] an adaptation of Christian mythology to the particular problems of American life, for which it has been both a source and a means of solution. As a Christian myth, it has concerned itself mainly with reconciling human life with divine law; as an American myth it has combined, and often confused, the religious ideas of sin and atonement with the political issues of democracy. Just as the religious life attends to the task of reconciling the finite many with the infinite one, the political life works to reconcile the particular individual with the general group.

[3] *The Quest for Paradise: Europe and the American Moral Imagination* (Urbana, Ill., 1961), esp. chaps. i-v.

Like all myths, this one directs individual energies toward a common goal, by evaluating forms of behavior, delineating appropriate roles, and making it generally possible for individuals to relate their lives to a larger pattern of value and purpose, to transcend their existential limitations and to extend beyond their proper selves their sphere of influence. Acts are evaluated in this case primarily according to how well they contribute to "progress," however that term is defined at any time. The primary roles described by the myth, similarly, arise out of this notion of progress. They receive their specific lineaments from previous objectifications of the myth, in sacred scripture and in secular literature. Every myth has its heroes and its villains, its victors and its victims.

This function of myth is particularly important for our purposes, since in autobiography the writer explains his life by depicting himself according to culturally evaluated images of character. As he turns his private experiences into language he assumes one of the many identities outlined in the myth and so asserts his connection with his culture. Given the millennial cast and the pervading futuristic spirit of the myth, we are not surprised to find the main character types to be the Prophets (those who interpret the complex relationship between present and future), the Heroes (those who successfully enact the prophecies), the Villains (those who throw up obstacles to fulfillment) and the Outcasts (those who fail to make a place for themselves in the great cultural program). There are, in short, a whole range of stances available to autobiographers, whether they choose to affirm the values stated in the myth or to deny the "truth" of the myth and define themselves by an act of negation. A very brief look at some characteristic American autobiographers in the act of portraying themselves should serve to illustrate a few of the available stances and some of the specific images and ideas that the myth has encompassed as it has influenced the lives of individual Americans.

Properly enough, the first man to relate his personal experience to the American myth was Columbus, who by grounding Christian prophecy in the New World soil became our first Prophet. "God made me the messenger of the new heaven and the new earth," he said, "of which He spoke in the Apocalypse by St. John, after having spoken of it by the mouth of Isaiah; and He showed me the spot where to find it." [4] Columbus learned to see himself as a Prophet—spiritually descended from Isaiah and John—after absorbing the Medieval and Renaissance

[4] *Four Voyages to the New World: Letters and Selected Documents,* trans. and ed. R. H. Major (New York, 1961), p. 148.

mythology of the western paradise.[5] Considered as a part of European intellectual history, this self-image has wide and complex significances; considered as a part of American mythology, it is a crude beginning. Five centuries of American life have carried the myth in many directions from this starting point. Yet, this short passage marks the first autobiography to explain the life of the writer by relating it to a body of belief which may be called American.

The right to connect personal experience with great destinies is not vouchsafed to discoverers of continents alone. The true Prophet must work constantly to find a place in history for *all* his acts. His job, after all, is to teach the faithful how they may make their lives part of the great program, and he learns from his own life the wisdom he gives them. Cotton Mather judged all things according to their place in the divine plan. In the following passage from his diary he attempts to elevate the meanest concerns to that high degree of significance he elsewhere assigned to the New England settlements.

> There are with me, in common with all the Children of Men, the usual Evacuations of Nature, to be daily attended. I would not only improve the Time which these call for, to form some Thoughts of Piety, wherein I may differ from the Brutes, (which in the Actions themselves I do vary little) and this I have usually already done; but I would now more particularly study that the Thoughts I form on these Occasions, may be of some abasing Tendency. The Actions themselves carry Humiliations in them; and a Christian ought alwayes to think humble of himself, and be full of self-abasing and self-abhorring Reflections. By loathing of himself continually, and being very sensible of what are his own loathsome Circumstances, a Christian does what is very pleasing to Heaven. My Life (above any Man's) ought to be filled with such Things: and now I contrive certain Spotts of Time, in which I shall be by Nature itself invited unto them.[6]

This hierophantic voice descends from Augustine by way of Luther, proclaiming, as it does, that human nature impedes the progress of divine history and delays the journey to the Heavenly City.

A more sanguine Prophet, Walt Whitman, indicates how humanized the divine plan had become in a century and a half. Celebrating his transcendent self, he wrote:

> I do not press my fingers across my mouth,
> I keep as delicate around the bowels as around the head and heart,

[5] See Sanford, chap. iv.

[6] *The Diary*, "Collections of the Massachusetts Historical Society" (2 vols.; Boston, 1911), I, 357.

Copulation is not more rank to me than death is.

I believe in the flesh and the appetites,
Seeing, hearing, feeling, are miracles, and each part and tag of me is a miracle.[7]

Even while these vaunts mark an important change in the American self-image since Edward Taylor wrote the humbly supplicatory *Sacramental Meditations,* the prophetic aim—to define the mythic significance of daily activity—has not altered. A century after Whitman, we detect the same tone in Norman Mailer: "A phallic narcissist she called me. Well, I was phallic enough, a Village stickman who could muster on the head of his will enough of the divine It to call forth more than one becoming out of the womb of feminine Time."[8] Mather debased himself in order to be exalted; Whitman sought to exalt the base; Mailer seems to enjoy debasing the exalted. All three saw that men must discover some way to align secular life with a fundamentally religious idea of destiny.

Because these passages illustrate so clearly how an individual may assimilate mythical themes in forming his autobiographical personality, they may seem to be extreme cases. When we compare these self-portraits to those of such beloved culture-heroes as Thomas Paine and Theodore Roosevelt, however, we see that Americans often employ rather crude, although effective, metaphors in defining themselves and their world. What is more, these men display considerably more sophistication in distinguishing rhetorical metaphor from observable fact than do men like James J. Strang, who was king of the Mormon settlement at Beaver Island; Lorenzo Dow, the great revivalist; and John Humphrey Noyes, founder of the Utopian colony at Oneida. These men were as little able to separate metaphor from fact as were Coronado and the seekers for the Seven Cities of Cibola. Noyes, for instance, recounting past prophecy, present torment and future hope, shows how absolutely he identified American expectation with the Biblical images which had conventionally expressed it. "Between the present time and the establishment of God's kingdom over the earth," he said, "lies a chaos of confusion, tribulation and war such as must attend the destruction of the fashion of the world and the introduction of the will of God as it is done in heaven. God has set me to cast up a highway across this chaos, and I am gathering out the stones and grading the track as fast as possible."[9]

7 "Song of Myself," in *Walt Whitman, Representative Selections* rev. ed. Floyd Stovall, "The American Writers Series" (New York, 1961), pp. 26-27 (11. 519-23).

8 *Advertisements for Myself* (New York, 1959), p. 496.

9 G. Wallingford Noyes, *Religious Experience of John Humphrey Noyes* (New York, 1923), p. 308. Columbus never considered it irrational to look in the Western Hemisphere for the Earthly Paradise of Christian mythology. In his letter from the

Similarly possessed by the myth was Bronson Alcott. Instead of looking for a material enactment of spiritual prophecy, however, he propelled himself entirely into the world of spirit and passed off the physical world as a snare and an imperfect delusion. He was possessed by a millennial strain in American mythology which traces its ancestry back through Protestant history to the Gnostics and the Pelagians, and forward to Mary Baker Eddy. In the never-never land of his imaginings, evidences of imperfection and trouble passed away, and all his hopes became imminent possibilities. Walking in his garden on the Fourth of July 1846, he mused on the meaning of true freedom:

> I cast my silent vote for the emancipation of the human soul, amidst the plants I love. The aroma of the buckwheat, eloquently humming with the winged freemen of the hives, disturbed now and then by the gunner's crack aiming death to the joyous songsters of the air and groves. They ventured not, these monstrous boys, into my coppice of protecting boughs, not into my peaceful glebes. Ah me! War rages near me, and the fields of this my Concord are beleaguered round with armed ruffians. Happy for myself if I am as yet a freeman, and a soul at peace . . . Alone in my benefice, why should I not rejoice in that freeness that cheapens all conventions, and makes me, in thought if not in deed, independent of the States and times, an honest and upright man in the midst of my age.[10]

The more obsessed of these prophetic figures usually undergo a violent self-transformation of some sort. This experience creates the intensified self-consciousness which prompts them to write autobiography in the first place, and it usually appears in the narrative itself as a "calling." The subject may feel himself wrenched out of an unsatisfactory, commonplace or misguided existence and swept up in the rush of divine history, as do so many of the converts who described their experiences in our great revival movements. One of these, an obscure and uncommonly endearing zealot from Kentucky named John Hinkle, explains that, after several uncertain inklings that God wanted him to give up farming and become a preacher, he went through long torment ("The flames of hell pierced my mouth and nose"), then transfiguration: "I fell

New World written during his third voyage, he said, regarding a river he had seen, "I hold that if this river does not issue from the Earthly Paradise, it must come from an immense country that lies to the S., of which there has been no knowledge until now: but I am well assured in my own mind that there, where I have declared, lies the Earthly Paradise, and I rest my opinion on the arguments and authorities which I have given above." *Narratives of the Discovery of America,* eds. A. W. Lawrence and Jean Young (New York, 1931), p. 300.

[10] *The Journals of Bronson Alcott,* ed. Odell Shepard (Boston, 1938), p. 183.

asleep for a short time and when I awoke I was happier than I ever was in all my life. All my troubles were gone, and I felt as helpless as a little child; did not think I could move my hands or feet, but soon I moved, and saw that I had physical strength . . . I felt that I never would commit another sin and that I could soar in the air shouting and praising God for the great love He had made manifest to me. I think that was January 1, 1886."[11] Elder Hinkle, as he calls himself, also shows how the autobiography of the assumed stems from the experience of assumption, when he says in his first sentence, "I have had a desire to tell the dealings of the Lord with me."[12]

Political callings may dictate a similarly religious expression, particularly when the assumed one's party embodies the utopian or millennial aspirations peculiar to religious prophecy. John Reed's metamorphosis from aristocrat to proletarian follows the pattern and employs the language of religious conversion at times, as does this account of Emma Goldman's response to the death of the Chicago anarchists:

> I was in a stupor; a feeling of numbness came over me, something too horrible even for tears . . . I was entirely absorbed in what I felt was my own loss . . . I was put to bed, and soon I fell into a deep sleep. The next morning I awoke as from a long illness, but free from the numbness and the depression of the final shock. I had a distinct sensation that something new and wonderful had been born in my soul. A great ideal, a burning faith, a determination to dedicate myself to the memory of my martyred comrades, to make their cause my own, to make known to the world their beautiful lives and heroic deaths.[13]

Once again, we seem to be concerned with extreme cases; and it is true that not all autobiographers who describe self-transformation become Prophets in their reincarnations. Many have simply undergone some experience that has changed their cultural status, and, consequently, their self-image. These write autobiographies to assess the mythical significance of their new selves, to re-establish the cultural contact which the change interrupted. They may have risen from relative anonymity to national importance, as did U. S. Grant because of his part in the Civil War. They may have abandoned a troublesome identity for one culturally even more precarious, like the controversial jazz musician Mez Mezzrow, when he decided to become a Negro. Or, they may have had their culture forcibly stripped from them and been hurled by accident into a new life, as was Cabeza de Vaca when, cut off from his countrymen

11 *I Saw My Savior* (New York, 1953), p. 15.
12 Hinkle, p. 1.
13 *Living My Life* (New York, 1931), p. 10.

in the primitive Southwest, he found himself becoming more an Indian than a Conquistador. In each case, the autobiography serves, among other ends,[14] to articulate the experience of transformation and so make sense of it.

This first group of autobiographers is comprised of restless types, searching for truth, undergoing personal metamorphosis, interpreting the holy mysteries of their tribe, forecasting the collective destiny. A second variety of autobiographer has seen the elephant; he has taken the journey prescribed by the myth; and he looks back with some satisfaction on events which seem to have fulfilled his initial expectations. His real life, he says, corresponds significantly to the mythical ideal; it has enacted the values his society holds sacred. Benjamin Franklin introduces his autobiography with these words: "Having emerged from the poverty and obscurity in which I was born and bred, to a state of affluence and some degree of reputation in the world, and having gone so far through life with a considerable share of felicity, the conducing means I made use of, which with the blessing of God so well succeeded, my posterity may like to know, as they may find some of them suitable to their own situations, and therefore fit to be imitated."[15]

The mythical elements are all here: the progress from penury to wealth, the religious overtones of secular success, the identification of affluence and worldly reputation with happiness. Furthermore, the sense of personal fulfillment, characteristically, makes the subject feel that he has the right to teach and so to perpetuate a viable tradition. His teaching was well heeded, as we know; a whole nation of entrepreneurs has found him a model of success, perfectly "fit to be imitated."

Franklin's optimism is legendary; it caused him to view his personal past as the fulfillment of earlier prophecy and the foreshadowing of greater things to come in the general history of mankind. A somewhat similar figure, Andrew Carnegie, concerned himself more with his personal career and less with universal history, but he worked equally hard to depict his past as an enactment of divine commandment. God spoke to Carnegie, as He did to Franklin, through natural law, but the law had become more severe in one hundred and fifty years. At one period in his life, Carnegie tells us, he was "all at sea":

> All was chaos. I had outgrown the old [religion] and had found no substitute . . . Here came to me Spencer and Darwin, whom I read with absorbing interest, until laying down a volume one day I was

[14] Grant wrote his memoirs to be sure that his family would be solvent after his death; Cabeza de Vaca's recollections appear in an official report to his king.

[15] *Autobiography*, ed. Dixon Wecter (New York, 1948), p. 1. For a very important analysis of this work as a social myth, see Charles Sanford, chap. vii.

> able to say, "That settles the question." I had found at last the guides which led me to the temple of man's real knowledge upon the earth. These works were revelations to me: here was the truth which reconciled all things as far as the finite mind can grasp them, the alembic which harmonized hitherto conflicting ideas and brought order out of chaos . . . I was on firm ground, and with every year of my life since there has come less dogmatism, less theology, but greater reverence.[16]

The similarity between Franklin and Carnegie has not gone unnoticed; D. H. Lawrence read back into Franklin the excesses, the selfishness and meanness which his ideals bred in the nineteenth century. In Carnegie's autobiography, a shrill note of protestation seems to replace the natural optimism sounded by Franklin, and that work marks a mid-point between eighteenth-century hope and twentieth-century nostalgia. Latter-day Heroes who write these autobiographies of fulfillment are apt to locate the golden age in the past rather than in the future. The past offered grand opportunities for successes like mine, they tell us, but those days will never come again. Striking an unusually docile pose, H. L. Mencken recalls the "gaudy life that young newspaper reporters led in the major American cities at the turn of the century. I believed then," he goes on, "and still believe today, that it was the maddest, gladdest, damndest existence ever enjoyed by mortal youth." [17] The nostalgia evident here resembles that which tints all American writing in the local-color tradition. But the mood is less pervasive in this urban piece than it is in its pastoral counterparts—Mark Twain's *Roughing It,* for example. The city, after all, was to move steadily into the thematic center of American mythology and to push the farm and the frontier farther and farther onto the periphery. By the twentieth century, the autobiographer who wished to characterize his life as a fulfillment of agrarian values and still sound optimistic about the future of those values, had to perform some startling gymnastics to do so. Leland Cutler, in *America is Good to a Country Boy,* portrays Henry Kaiser (and, by strong implication, himself) as a man who has succeeded in commerce and industry because he possesses the rustic virtue of a love for nature.[18] De-

16 *Miscellaneous Writings,* ed. Burton J. Hendrick (2 vols.; Garden City, N. Y., 1933), II, 297. How little the specific matter under consideration by the writer in any autobiography may dictate the stance may be illustrated by a comparison of the widely divergent metaphorical uses of Darwin in the autobiographies of Carnegie, Henry Adams and Hamlin Garland.

17 *Newspaper Days* (New York, 1941), p. ix.

18 About Kaiser, Cutler says, "Great builder that he is, I think he has not ever crushed a flower half hidden in the grass that he did not wish he might have walked some other way." *America is Good to a Country Boy* (Stanford, Calif., 1954), p. 156.

spite specific changes in the meaning of optimism we see, a single stance unites all the autobiographers who choose to explain their lives as fulfilling cultural and personal expectation. Each merely adapts the general characteristic of the stance to his particular purposes.

So far, we have looked at several Prophets and some autobiographers whom we call Heroes. The third main group includes all those who, for some reason, find themselves outside the limits of culturally approved behavior. They may be distinguished by the way they react to the realization that their lives have failed to assert and demonstrate the established values and beliefs of their world. To review the several stances included in this group, we may pass from the most contrite to the most unregenerate, looking first at the man who writes his autobiography to confess his sins and to make an example of himself, to get back into the social family.

One of the most typical, and least lovable, of these confessions to appear in recent years is Whittaker Chambers' *Witness,* which chronicles a life of political sin followed by an awakening to grace. "What I had been," Chambers writes, "fell from me like dirty rags. The rags that fell from me were not only Communism. What fell was the whole web of the materialist modern mind—the luminous shroud which it has spun about the spirit of man, paralyzing in the name of rationalism the instinct of his soul for God, denying in the name of knowledge the reality of the soul and its birthright in that mystery on which mere knowledge shatters and falters at every step."[19] Chambers elects here to describe his passage in the language of evangelical anti-intellectualism, which has been an integral part of American mythology since the eighteenth century, at least. Such a tone was guaranteed to reunite him with those from whom he felt most exiled.

Our next type adopts a considerably different tactic as he works to insinuate himself into a state of social grace. Instead of repenting his past misdeeds, P. T. Barnum argues that they were not misdeeds at all, but virtues in disguise. Dedicating his autobiography to the "Universal Yankee Nation of which I Am Proud to Be One," Barnum refutes charge after charge that he is a humbug, a cheat and a thief. What have been called his avarice and guile, he insists, are the Yankee virtues of thrift and ingenuity—all of which he learned from Ben Franklin.[20] Indeed, by the time he has finished reporting his life in the jargon of American commerce, it is hard to distinguish between his career and that of any respectable entrepreneur. Of his early genius for business, he tells us:

[19] *Witness* (New York, 1952), p. 83.
[20] *Barnum's Own Story* (New York, 1961), p. 8.

"Always looking for the main chance . . . I had sheep of my own, a calf of which I was the sole proprietor, and other individual property which made me feel, at twelve years of age, that I was a man of substance."[21] Such a career would have to please even so secure an insider as Leland Cutler, who suggested that great men in America succeeded because they learned at an early age "what money meant."[22]

Moving farther along a scale marked off in degrees of commitment to established belief, we come to the socially condemned autobiographer who feels that his apparent social failures are actually insignificant, since he was following a higher and truer law than that espoused by his society. Such men portray themselves as condemned by a blind or unregenerate society, and they use their autobiographies to show that *they* know the true way. Mary Austin, criticized for her feminist agitation and her oddly emancipated ways, explains, "Since the pattern of my adult behavior was in no sense a made-up pattern, but one that rose through the surface index of Mary, myself, out of a deeper self, of which the umbilical cord which bound it to the source of selfness had not been cut, it in a measure justified all its behaviors, rid me of the onus of responsibility for those which failed to coincide with the current standards of success."[23] No apologetic tone marks this stance, only a certain lingering pity for the uninitiated multitude.

More rational and less subjective is the self-exiled critic who has found a high ground on which to stand and survey the inconsistencies, hypocrisies and injustices of the myth. Whittaker Chambers denigrated his intellect to make himself morally acceptable to the American public; the critic will often assert his intellect in order to emphasize the degree of his detachment from popular belief. After excoriating all the minions of American know-nothingness—"the prohibitionists of Kansas, the lynchers of Georgia, the hardheaded businessmen in the chambers of commerce in a thousand cities, the members of the National Security League, The American Legion, the Loyal American League . . . all these self-appointed inquisitors and Black Hundreds"—Ludwig Lewisohn underscores his position by refusing to adopt one of his country's most cherished attitudes: "Shall I say now, in order to end agreeably: It is always

21 Barnum, p. 6.

22 In explanation of the success of certain construction magnates, Cutler says, "The mothers and fathers of these boys . . . did the best they could, unconsciously training them for their later roles: to work unceasingly . . . to know what money meant . . . to love the land of their birth. . . . Because these boys grew to manhood honoring their fathers and their mothers, their days were many in the land and the name of the Six Companies is a name to reckon with." *America is Good to a Country Boy*, pp. 154-55.

23 *Earth Horizon* (New York, 1932), p. viii.

darkest before the dawn? No; for that kind of professional optimism is precisely one of our national vices. The hour is dark."[24]

Interestingly enough, both Chambers and Lewisohn regard their lives as morally symbolic and, like Franklin's, "fit to be imitated." Lewisohn says, "There are thousands of people among us who can find in my adventures a living symbol of their own and in whom, as in me, this moment in history has burned away delusion to the last shred."[25] And Chambers, seeking an altogether different end, intones, "On a scale personal enough to be felt by all, but big enough to be symbolic, the two irreconcilable faiths of our time—Communism and Freedom—came to grips in the persons of two conscious and resolute men . . . The Great Case would end in the destruction of one or both of the contending figures, just as the history of our times . . . can end only in the destruction of one or both of the contending forces."[26] Whether he agonizes over his exile or seeks to ensure it, it seems, the Outsider is often moved to enlist a following by capitalizing on the myth which defines his stance. As he cleanses his soul, Chambers becomes another Cotton Mather, struggling with the devil and purifying the Commonwealth; Lewisohn assumes the guise of Tom Paine, ridiculing superstition and preaching the true, enlightened freedom.

The reason that these two men betray this similarity despite their obvious differences, of course, is that, Outcasts or not, they both care deeply about American life and its future. Our next type, however—the last of those whom we call the Outsiders—deserves that name most of all. While Chambers, Barnum, Lewisohn and Mary Austin adopt attitudes actually provided for by American mythology, and so are, in a sense, acceptable Outsiders, the most abandoned type cares nothing for acknowledged American values. Like Mae West, who attacks American sexual hypocrisy in *Goodness Had Nothing to Do With It,* this autobiographer mentions our values only to expose what he considers their idiocies, and he does so with unmistakable detachment, finding some sort of unique, individual balance. As Miss West says, "I have held firmly to my ideas and my values . . . I have made a peace, or at least an armed truce, with myself and with the universe. I am in key with my world as I know it and have seen it."[27]

Very few of these renegades manage to maintain their defiant attitudes throughout their autobiographies, however. Even Mae West felt impelled by the public nature of the form to intone, irrelevantly, "I have done

[24] *Up Stream: An American Chronicle* (New York, 1922), pp. 236, 248.
[25] Lewisohn, p. 10.
[26] Chambers, p. 4.
[27] *Goodness Had Nothing to Do With It* (Englewood Cliffs, N. J., 1959), p. 257.

what I set out to do, which was to review . . . a life that goes down deeply into the human enigma, the problems of man (and woman) in relation to the godhead and the yet unopened secrets of the universe,"[28] and to mention the importance of religion (unspecified) in sexual education. Caryl Chessman, although he operated all his life well outside the bounds of acceptable behavior, offers his life as a constructive criticism of his society, which he hopes will make the necessary legal alterations and prosper. An autobiographical statement like William Burroughs' introduction to *Naked Lunch,* which depicts the writer's total withdrawal from the forms of belief which Americans cherish, is rare, even in this age of dissident memoirs. No American autobiographer, Henry Miller included, has assumed the stature and notoriety of Sade.

All these stances, with the possible exception of the last, derive partly from the traits of character and forms of behavior prescribed by the American myth and partly from the subject's knowledge of previous autobiographies. Misch has discussed how much any autobiographer may learn from his predecessors, revising earlier modes of self portrayal to suit his own needs. Columbus learned to see himself and to interpret his experience by following the lead of St. John. Cotton Mather modeled his self-image on Luther, just as Luther seems to have emulated Augustine. Franklin tells us that Bunyan and Mather were his teachers; but since he aimed to represent his life as an earthly pilgrimage, we see how earlier forms may be adapted to present demands. Barnum shows us still another application of the basic form when he legitimizes otherwise reprehensible conduct by reporting it in the manner of Franklin. Autobiography does not merely follow the cultural pattern, it is clear; it contributes to that pattern by developing and formulating the very structure of individuality.

We must always remember that these stances are forms of self-knowledge and self-portrayal assumed for literary and cultural purposes. Obviously, no man maintains the same stance throughout his life, nor does he usually take the same attitude toward all problems at any one time in his life. His journals and his letters may show him taking on a number of these personae over time. But when he comes to write his autobiography—whether he seeks to discover himself through it or to publicize what he has already found out—he must adopt some consistent, overriding view of himself and his past. He must identify the "I" which unites all his past experiences. If he does not, his life will seem to him fragmented and incoherent, and its story will appear to us pointless and confused. Mencken, for example, presents himself throughout his long

28 Mae West, p. 256.

career in a variety of guises—irascible critic, learned scholar, champion of human dignity, irresponsible bad boy. But when he was faced with the task of organizing his recollections into a single volume, he recognized the need to come to some decision about what they all amounted to. He says of his life:

> My days of work have been spent . . . in recording the current scene, usually in a far from acquiescent spirit. But I must confess, with sixty only around the corner, that I have found existence on this meanest of planets extremely amusing, and taking one day with another, perfectly satisfactory. . . . The Gaseous Vertebrata who own, operate and afflict the universe have treated me with excessive politeness, and when I mount the gallows at last I may well say with the Psalmist (putting it, of course, in the prudent past tense): The lines have fallen to me in pleasant places.[29]

Any stance, then, is a cultural convention, formulated first by a particularly daring and imaginative analyst of the self, like Augustine or Rousseau, and then imitated by a host of autobiographical followers. But what happens when none of the conventions satisfies an autobiographer's need to order the details of his life? What happens to the man whose faith in the myth has led him to ruin? The autobiographer in this predicament either invents some new way of giving meaning to his experience or records his *anomie* in what we may call the autobiography of the Disenchanted. This man no longer draws strength from his culture, and having nothing to substitute for it, he can neither criticize it nor flout its mandates with any satisfaction. When F. Scott Fitzgerald realized that his life was not leading to paradise, he described his sense of loss:

> This was something I could neither accept nor struggle against, something which tended to make my efforts obsolescent, as the chain stores have crippled the small merchant, an exterior force, unbeatable. . . . There was not an "I" any more—not a basis on which I could organize my self-respect. . . . It was strange to have no self—to be like a little boy left alone in a big house, who knew that now he could do anything he wanted to do, but found that there was nothing that he wanted to do.[30]

Fitzgerald strikes here at some of the fundamental tenets of American faith which have gone to define many of the stances we examined earlier: the efficacy of the individual will, the infinite resources of the

[29] H. L. Mencken, *Happy Days* (New York, 1940), p. ix.
[30] *The Crack Up*, ed. Edmund Wilson (New York, 1956), pp. 78, 79.

spirit, the joys of freedom. This stance, among all those we have discussed so far, seems to have the most to tell us about those autobiographical forms which we recognize as being distinctly modern.

We have seen that autobiographical form is inextricably bound up with cultural belief, that civilization prescribes fairly specific roles for its citizens to adopt when portraying themselves in writing. In Western civilization, these roles share a common quality: they all express an integrated, continuing personality which transcends the limitations and irregularities of time and space and unites all of one's apparently contradictory experiences into an identifiable whole. This notion of individual identity, in fact, may well be the central belief of our culture. With all its ramifications—personal responsibility, individual destiny, dissent, vocation and so forth—it forms the core of our being and the fabric of our history. Ever since St. Augustine wrote his *Confessions* and turned autobiography into a literary act of spiritual self-consciousness, it has retained an unswerving belief in the individual as a definable entity, linked to the divine, which reveals itself through self-analysis.

Although this belief in the integrated consciousness continues to inform large areas of public activity at the present time, it has become the object of increasing critical examination during the past century—especially in those places where social and institutional forms which express and support it have been disrupted by ideological upheaval, revolution and war. Self-consciousness, it seems, will recommend itself only as long as the world allows some fruitful occupation for the liberated individual. When it only thwarts and dismays him, he may seek to escape from identity, into selflessness, anonymity and rest. Or, on the other hand, the anxieties which attend purposeless and corrosive self-awareness may prompt the subject to go back and find some new basis upon which to establish his being, and so create a new order of life. Although the impulse to escape from being is antithetical to the very meaning of autobiography, we should expect to find written records of those individuals who are searching for new forms of identity.

And so we do, but not in conventional autobiography, which grew out of a very special idea of individuality and so is unfit in its traditional form to examine new possibilities of being. The ideals of spiritual identity gave autobiography its subject and its form; new ideals must seek new forms appropriate to them. The modern autobiographer needs an especially flexible form, one that can always outrun attempts to define it, one notably amenable to innovation and experiment. Unable to identify himself within the conventional framework, the modern autobiographer seems to have taken to the novel to find the freedom he needs to conduct his experiments with self.

Traditional autobiography can satisfy only those self-analysts whose identities are clear enough and whose lives seem coherent enough to be expressed in conventional form. The teleology implied in the convention of a narrator surveying his past in terms of the present, rules out all autobiographers who perceive no such purposeful progression or continuity in the events of their lives. Although he wrote no formal autobiography, Emerson exhibited the frame of mind most amenable to it. In a letter to Margaret Fuller, F. O. Matthiessen tells us, he stated that "he could discern no essential difference between the experience of his boyhood and that of his maturity . . . 'A little more excitement now [Emerson said] but the fact identical, both in my consciousness and in my relations.' "[31] The inviolable, transcendent self provided him with a sense of identity, apparently, which survived all temporal change.

Wright Morris, on the other hand, feeling no such assurance about his identity, describes how he has sought other forms to chronicle his conceptions of self. "Before coming of age," Mr. Morris writes,

> . . . I had led, or rather been led by, half a dozen separate lives. Each life had its own scene, its own milieu; it frequently appeared to have its own beginning and ending, the only connecting tissue being the narrow thread of my *self*. I had been there, but that, indeed, explained nothing. In an effort to come to terms with the experience, I processed it in fragments, collecting pieces of the puzzle. In time, a certain overall pattern *appeared* to be there. But this appearance was essentially a process—an imaginative act of apprehension—rather than a research into the artifacts of my life.[32]

Unable to adopt one unifying attitude, the autobiographer in this uncertain condition substitutes for exposition an examination of the details of experience. The process of review takes the place of the consistent, evaluative point of view as a unifying principle. Since that process may adopt such non-narrative modes of unification as symbolism and imagery, the surface of the work may appear discontinuous and fragmented. The writer speaks here as an individual, whose unwillingness to assume one of the identities prescribed by his culture prevents him from speaking as a public figure and from employing the extended, continuous forms appropriate to those roles.

When the novel abandoned its original function of evaluating social behavior from an increasingly clear point of view and began to devise

[31] F. O. Matthiessen, *American Renaissance* (New York, 1941), p. 58.
[32] *The Territory Ahead* (New York, 1963), p. 15.

ways to escape the moral smugness which its bourgeois origins had thrust upon it, it turned away from history to the lyric for less explicit, more symbolic modes of expression. In so doing, it recoiled from society and directed its gaze inward, searching for some surer experiential basis for reality and judgment. This, it seems, is that point where autobiography and the novel begin to merge. Under the pressures and anxieties of social dislocation, the novel became increasingly autobiographical. Disenchanted with the conventional roles which society offered, the autobiographer found in the new novel the chance to examine personal experience without having to assume some ill-fitting social guise. Although conventional autobiographies and novels continue to be written by people who have no quarrel with tradition, those works which we recognize as being significantly of our time have made the terms "novel" and "autobiography" very often indistinguishable.

This entire problem of the purpose and limits of the organizing judgment has generated some of the most important critical studies of the twentieth century. And yet we too often assume that the heavily subjective novel has been restricted to Europe, at least until the twentieth century. We concentrate on the German line of development from Goethe to Hesse, or the even more popular English evolution of Joyce out of Butler, forgetting that nineteenth-century America produced a group of writers who experimented continually with autobiographical forms to solve their problems of spiritual alienation from a society whose myths failed to satisfy their personal demands. Poe's *Narrative of Arthur Gordon Pym* adopts the conventions of autobiographical travel narrative to explore the labyrinths of the disoriented psyche. Herman Melville and Mark Twain arrived at their respective masterpieces by way of the same autobiographical form, the exactly opposite narrative modes of *Moby-Dick* and *Huckleberry Finn* reflecting their respective authors' very similar conclusions about the value of personal experience. Furthermore, the works which follow these two great novels—that is, *Pierre* and *The Mysterious Stranger*—examine the psychic disintegration which results when the self recoils altogether from established norms of judgment.

Wherever we choose to study it, however, the fact remains that autobiography can elucidate for us those central issues which have brought literature to its present state, inform its present concerns and chart its future course. Certainly, modern writers must find their way out of the apparent impasse into which attention to the self has brought them; but just as certainly, they cannot go back to the older forms. Regarding the formal problems of his own autobiography, Henry Adams said in his "Editor's Preface" that "his great ambition was to complete St. Augustine's 'Confessions,' but that St. Augustine, like a great artist, had worked from multiplicity to unity, while he, like a small one, had to reverse the method." [33] The way back to unity is closed off, obstructed by the wreckage of a hundred philosophies. The new directions can come only from present attempts to find in experience new forms, new myths, new roles for the self, which the writer can adopt to speak once again as an integral part of his culture.

Afternote

This essay is part of a work in progress on American autobiography, which will include discussion of such innovative American autobiographers as Benjamin Franklin, Mark Twain and Henry Adams as well as a study of the autobiographical impulse in American fiction and poetry.

William C. Spengemann is an Associate Professor of English at the Claremont Graduate School, Claremont, California. L. R. Lundquist is a member of the staff of the San Francisco Art Commission. [This article appeared in Vol. XVII, No. 3 (Fall, 1965).]

[33] *The Education of Henry Adams* (New York, 1931), pp. vii-viii.

Ideas

Stow Persons

The Cyclical Theory of History in Eighteenth Century America[1]

A CONCISE statement of the cyclical view of history was set forth by Bolingbroke in *The Patriot King* of 1738, as follows:

> Absolute stability is not to be expected in any thing human; for that which exists immutably exists alone necessarily, and this attribute of the Supreme Being can neither belong to man, nor to the works of man. The best instituted governments, like the best constituted animal bodies, carry in them the seeds of their destruction: and though they grow and improve for a time, they will soon tend visibly to their dissolution. Every hour they live is an hour the less that they have to live. All that can be done therefore to prolong the duration of a good government, is to draw it back, on every favorable occasion, to the *first good principles* on which it was founded. When these occasions happen often, and are well improved, such governments are prosperous and durable. When they happen seldom, or are ill improved, these political bodies live in pain or in languor, and die soon.[2]

My purpose is to indicate the general currency of such a cyclical theory of history in late eighteenth century America, and to explore its relationship to the idea of progress, which has generally been regarded as the characteristic outlook on history of enlightened thinkers, both in Europe and in America.

[1]An earlier version of this paper was presented at the Newberry Library Conference on American Studies, October 13, 1951.

[2]Henry Saint-John Bolingbroke, *Letters on the Spirit of Patriotism: on the Idea of a Patriot King: and on the State of Parties, at the Accession of King George the First* (New ed., London: Cadell, 1783), p. 128.

As an epoch in the history of thought the American Enlightenment may be taken to have commenced with the reaction to the great religious revival of the 1740's and to have ended with the War of 1812. The function of the revival was to precipitate issues and crystallize parties. Conflicts of interest helped to sharpen objectives and straighten the lines of thought. The Great Awakening presented the first common intellectual issues for Anglo-Americans widely scattered along the continental seaboard, and from it radiate the intellectual traditions that are properly to be called American rather than provincial. Three distinct theories of history were to be found in the thought of the time, with one of which, the cyclical theory, I am particularly concerned.

The investigation involves an approach to the mind of the Enlightenment in America that may seem heretical on at least two counts. On the one hand, it was a complex of ideas which stemmed from the interests of a particular group. We should not be misled by the cosmopolitan content of enlightened thought—its emphasis upon natural law, reason, universal benevolence, and the rights of man. Here was perhaps the first instance of those ambiguous relationships between interest and profession which have given the history of our national ideology its elusive character. To force enthusiastic believers in immediate revelation and special providences to recognize the primacy of natural law and submit to the rule of reason was at the outset precisely the point at issue. On the other hand, by emphasizing the utility of enlightened ideas as weapons in the hands of a class of men in America, I am also risking the charge of ignoring the fact that these ideas were current throughout most of Western civilization in the eighteenth century, with the implication that their analysis in the purely local context must be inadequate. While there is much truth in this, I would nevertheless suggest that the relationship between enlightened thinkers in Europe and in America is one of descent from a common parentage, the English latitudinarians of the previous century, and that the differences between the eighteenth century offspring are to be understood in part at least as the consequence of local controversies. In short, the mind of the American Enlightenment was not a mass mind, but the creed of a party, several of whose doctrines are fully understood only as planks in a party platform.

I

The first of the three conceptions of history was that of the revivalists of the Great Awakening. It was a frankly supernaturalist interpretation of history as the unfolding revelation of divine purpose. Human history was conceived to be, in Jonathan Edwards' phrase, the work of redemption, a work which would be completed with the second coming of Christ and the establishment of his millennial kingdom. Many were convinced that the wholesale conversions accomplished by the revival entailed that purification of spirit and morals presumably characteristic of the "latter day" foretold by the prophets. Edwards himself believed that the new world had been reserved for recent discovery and the conversion of the heathen aborigines, in order that a seat might be prepared for the imminent establishment of Christ's kingdom.[3] Night after night expectant revivalists "flew as doves to their windows" to witness the coming of the Lord in clouds of glory.

The relevance of this quaint excitement to our exploration of the moderate and empirical temper of the enlightened mind was suggested twenty years ago by Carl Becker in his study of the French *philosophes*. The idea of progress, Becker observed, is to be understood as a secularization of the millennialist interpretation of history. The conception of the progress of the human race from the earliest primitive horde postulated by Condorcet to its estimable condition in the eighteenth century with its infinitely enticing prospects for the future, is nothing but the pious Christian's account of the work of redemption, with somewhat different characters and emphases, to be sure, but with essentially the same form of plot. Becker's thesis has been employed in a similar analysis of the origins of the idea of progress in America by Professor Rutherford Delmage,[4] who has assembled some interesting evidence tracing the transformation of the one view into the other. One may well be reluctant, however, to accept an historical connection established in terms of the similarity of idea-form alone, when in other crucial respects the millennial expectation and the idea of progress represent such sharply contrasting interests and temperaments. The cyclical theory seems to have performed a mediating function in accommodating these theories of history to each other.

II

A central issue in the controversies arising out of the Great Awakening concerned the method of God's governance of the world. Did he intervene by means of special providences and direct inspiration for the guidance of men and the historical process, or was he content to achieve his ends through those "general and steady laws" known to men through Scripture, experience, and the observation of nature? The revivalists held the former view and their opponents the latter. The millennial expectation

[3]Jonathan Edwards, *A History of the Work of Redemption* (3rd. Amer. ed., Worcester: Thomas, 1792), pp. 280-81, 310-11.

[4]Rutherford E. Delmage, "The American Idea of Progress, 1750-1800," *Proceedings of the American Philosophical Society*, XCI (1947), pp. 307-14.

was the culminating affirmation of men prepared to commit human history to a transcendent purpose which would in the end give history its meaning. The millennial hope itself, however, could not become a major issue in the conflict because either party insisted upon its Protestant orthodoxy, and all acknowledged the testimony of Scripture that Christ would ultimately return to judge the quick and the dead.[5] The work of the anti-revivalists was less to reject the millennial hope than to reformulate the issues in such a way that the expectation of the second coming would eventually become a radically different concept.

The intellectual spokesmen for the opponents of the revival were the Anglican Alexander Garden, John Thomson the Presbyterian, and Charles Chauncy the Congregationalist.[6] In the controversial tracts of these men, published between 1740 and 1743, and aimed at Whitefield, Tennent, Edwards, and their followers, one finds dressed in religious garb several of the characteristic ideas and attitudes more commonly associated with the secular thinkers of the following generation. As the expression of a group conscious of its interests and of the identity of its foe enlightened ideas in America find their source here.

Fear of the social chaos anticipated in the revivalists' attack upon the privileged position of the established churches was the prime consideration which motivated the counter-attack of the anti-revivalists. All of their doctrinal argument points to this conclusion. Its essence was expressed in Chauncy's dictum that in the work of conversion the divine spirit operates upon the reason, bringing about a change in the temper of mind, and disciplining the unruly passions in accordance with the new and clearer insight into the nature of divine truth.[7] The consequence was to submerge the operation of divine grace within the human process of striving measured in moral terms, to be detected in conduct. By the use of reason and Scripture men were to discover and do God's will, confident that God would not withhold his grace from the truly penitent. This of course implied a merciful and benevolent deity.[8] The evidence of regeneration was not to be found in subjective impressions, ecstatic impulses, or "heightened affections," but in an enrichment of Christian graces, the chief of which was love. Nothing illustrates more clearly the social affiliations of the anti-revivalists than their enumeration of the

[5]Charles Chauncy, *Seasonable Thoughts on the State of Religion in New England* (Boston: Eliot, 1743), pp. 370-73.

[6]Alexander Garden, *Regeneration, and the Testimony of the Spirit* (Charlestown: Timothy, 1740); *Six Letters to the Rev. Mr. George Whitefield* (2nd ed., Boston: Fleet, 1740). John Thomson, *The Doctrine of Convictions Set in a Clear Light* (Philadelphia: Bradford, 1741); *The Government of the Church of Christ* (Philadelphia: Bradford, 1741). Charles Chauncy, *Enthusiasm Describ'd and Caution'd Against* (Boston, 1742); *Seasonable Thoughts.*

[7]Chauncy, *Seasonable Thoughts*, pp. 108-19.

[8]Stephen Williams to Eleazer Wheelock, July 18, 1740. Wheelock MSS. *Boston Evening-Post*, April 19, 1742.

qualities of the gracious Christian convert. According to Chauncy, believers should display "a spiritual *Likeness* to the LORD JESUS CHRIST, in *Faith;* in *Purity;* in *Lowliness* and *Humility;* in *Love* to GOD, and our *Neighbors;* in *Patience, Meekness,* and *Gentleness;* in *Contempt* of the *World*, Contentedness with their Condition, Resignation to God; and in a Word, a *Zeal* to *honor him*, and *do all the good they can* in the World."[9] The worst that could be said of enthusiasts was that they were "Porters, Cobblers, Barbers, etc. . . . ignorant and impudent wretches," whose restiveness under the disciplined religious leadership of an educated clergy caused them to abandon their proper stations and flock to the revivalists. As the *Boston Evening-Post* observed: "It is one of the main Disorders and Infelicities of the present Age, that many of the *meanest Rank*, and of *Inferior Capacities*, are puffed up with a Pride that is become almost past dealing with. Some of the most contemptible Creatures among us yet think themselves sufficient to direct *Statesmen*, dictate to *Legislators*, and teach *Doctors* and *Divines*."[10]

The function of reason as the monitor of the moral law is understood in this context. As Chauncy put it, "One of the most *essential* Things necessary in the *new-forming* Men, is the reduction of their *Passions* to a proper Regimen, i.e., the Government of a *sanctified Understanding*. . . . The plain Truth is, an *enlightened Mind*, and not *raised Affections*, ought always to be the Guide of those who call themselves Men."[11] Enlightened thinkers commenced by glorifying reason as a disciplinary agency, and only gradually did the course of events suggest its use as a revolutionary solvent.

I have emphasized the circumstances under which the constellation of enlightened ideas was composed because they underline the originally conservative character of the movement. The theory of history which began to emerge from this line of thought I propose to designate the theory of organic cycles. Opponents of the revival acknowledged the biblical authority upon which the millennial hope rested, but they rejected as an enthusiastic delusion the expectation that the revival itself heralded the second coming. Direct inspiration in either of its forms, as subjective impression or as overt historical event, was decisively repudiated, and with it the possibility or relevance of interpreting history as the special revelation of God's will.[12] For the opponents of the revival a pertinent interpretation of history must concern itself with the issues

[9]Chauncy, *Enthusiasm Describ'd*, pp. 8-14. Cf. Thomson, *Doctrine of Convictions*, pp. 21-25.

[10]*Boston Evening-Post*, April 5, 1742. For similar allusions to the class character of the revival see the issues of September 29, October 6, 1740; February 8, 22, 1742; January 24, 1743.

[11]Chauncy, *Seasonable Thoughts*, pp. 324-27.

[12]*Ibid.*, pp. 183-84, 370-73.

deemed of paramount importance, namely, the reasoned and moderate disciplining of the mind and appetites consistently with what had been vouchsafed men to know of the intentions of deity and of their obligations to their fellows.

The new view of history which came into vogue among conservative thinkers in the years following the revival found the source of historical dynamics in the operation of the universal moral law, the effect of which upon history was an endless cyclical movement analogous to the life cycle of the individual organism. Societies and nations rise and fall in endless sequence according as they observe or disregard those universal moral laws ordained of God and graven upon men's consciences for their governance and happiness. Suggestions of the cyclical theme were to be found both in the writers of classical antiquity, especially the historians and moralists, and more recently in the popular English literature of the early eighteenth century. It was subsequently to become a familiar theme in romantic thought. Both John Adams and Jefferson were familiar with the *Patriot King*, where they would have found the passage quoted at the opening of this paper. It is also perhaps pertinent to call attention to the prevalence in contemporary thought of two ideas easily related to the cyclical theme. One was the physiographic notion of primitive corruption and aged refinement, as popularized in the natural histories of Buffon and Raynal. The other was the historical idea of the westward transit of culture. In any event, the universal relevance of the cyclical theory appealed mightily to an age coming to pride itself upon its cosmopolitanism and to view with increasing embarrassment the sectarian limitations of the Christian pretensions. It was held by men many of whom had no immediate interest in the party battles of the revival, but who were at least united with the anti-revivalists in opposition to the emotionalism and democratic inclinations of the religious enthusiasts. The cyclical theory of history was to become for a brief period one of the distinctive historical conceptions of the dominant social group in America.

The following passage from a sermon of the Rev. David Tappan, Hollis Professor of Divinity at Harvard College, preached in 1798, will serve to illustrate the cyclical view in its most literal form.

> Experience proves that political bodies, like the animal economy, have their periods of infancy, youth, maturity, decay, and dissolution. In the early stages of their existence their members are usually industrious and frugal, simple in their manners, just and kind in their intercourse, active and hardy, united and brave. Their feeble, exposed, and necessitous condition in some sort forces upon them this conduct and these habits. The practice of these virtues gradually nourishes them to

a state of manly vigor. They became mature and flourishing in wealth and population, in arts and arms, in almost every kind of national prosperity. But when they have reached a certain point of greatness, their taste and manners begin to be infected. Their prosperity inflates and debauches their minds. It betrays them into pride and avarice, luxury and dissipation, idleness and sensuality, and too often into practical and scornful impiety. These, with other kindred vices, hasten their downfall and ruin. [History shows that] virtue is the soul of republican freedom; that luxury tends to extinguish both sound morality and piety; and that the loss of these renders men incapable of estimating and relishing, of preserving or even bearing the blessings of equal liberty.[13]

The special function of the clerical adherents to the cyclical view was to relate it to the divine government of the world. The moral law establishes an irrevocable connection between virtue and happiness on the one hand, and between vice and misery on the other. "The benevolent Ruler of the universe delights in the happiness of his subjects," and while his judgments are for their transgressions, they are also for their instruction.[14] In this most rational and equably governed of worlds sin does not always provoke speedy and sufficient retribution, for if it did there would be no scope for that testing and development of individual character which is necessary to prepare men for the future state.

The actual measures, therefore, of the divine government towards communities and particular persons appear full of wisdom and beauty. While the former receive such a recompense of their conduct, as gives a general, though incomplete display of the governing justice of God; the latter have sufficient advantages and motives to prepare for and confidently expect the ultimate triumph of virtue in the unmixed and endless happiness of its friends, and the final destruction of its obdurate enemies.[15]

Thus it appears that history is virtue teaching by example; and the decline and fall of empires represents a divine judgment upon the corruption of men.

Perhaps because it performed a didactic function in the exhortations of the clergy, we find more explicit expression of the cyclical theme in their writings. But it was widely presupposed by lay thinkers as well, at least before the French Revolution. John Adams, for instance, held it

[13]David Tappan, *A Discourse, Delivered to the Religious Society in Brattle-Street, Boston . . . on April 5, 1798* (Boston: Hall, 1798), pp. 18-19. For similar views of clerics, see Charles Backus, *A Sermon, Preached in Long-Meadow, at the Public Fast, April 17, 1788* (Springfield: Weld and Thomas, 1788), p. 9; Thomas Barnard, *A Sermon, Delivered on the Day of National Thanksgiving, February 19, 1795* (Salem: Cushing, 1795), pp. 21-22; Samuel Stanhope Smith, *The Divine Goodness to the United States of America. A Discourse . . . February 19, 1795* (Philadelphia: W. Young, 1795), pp. 20-21.

[14]Joseph Lathrop, *National Happiness, Illustrated in a Sermon, Delivered at West-Springfield, on February 19, 1795* (Springfield: Hooker and Stebbins, 1795), p. 13.

[15]Tappan, *Discourse, April 5, 1798*, pp. 24-25.

for more than half a century. As early as 1755, he attributed the rise and fall of nations to "some minute and unsuspected cause," a cause which, judging by his reflections upon the fall of Rome, the rise of America, and other great historical events, he assumed to be invariably moral in character.[16] Sixty-four years later he was still harping upon the same theme, challenging Jefferson to cite a single illustration of a nation once corrupted that had been able to cleanse itself and restore political liberty. "Will you tell me," he asked, "how to prevent riches from becoming the effects of temperance and industry? Will you tell me how to prevent riches from producing luxury? Will you tell me how to prevent luxury from producing effeminacy, intoxication, extravagance, vice and folly?"[17] This plaintive cry reminds us of John Wesley's inexorable cycle of piety, virtue, riches, and corruption before which the great evangelical for all his zeal for souls stood helpless. In fact, the thoroughly moralistic character of enlightened social theory is so striking that it is remarkable that in an age as remote from this concern as is our own it has been so seldom commented upon.

If the cyclical view of history was as widely entertained as I have assumed, we are provided with a possible explanation of why it was that the enlightened mind in America did not express itself in any more important measure in the historiographical form. In the final analysis history can only reiterate its great theme; the same yesterday, today, and forever. There was nothing to be learned from it that could not be found in one's personal experience, or in the life of one's own time. In his treatise devoted specifically to the philosophy of history, the *Discourses on Davila*, John Adams tells us that the "key . . . to the rise and fall of empires" is found in the universal operation of the human passion for distinction, in its various forms of emulation, ambition, jealousy, envy and vanity.[18] This was the psychological source and motivation of those dynamic cycles which constitute the course of history. It appears to have been assumed that the connection ordained of God between nature, personality, and history was so tight as to deprive history of that range of possibilities which alone is capable of endowing it with more than passing interest. "Such is our unalterable moral constitution," wrote Adams, "that an internal inclination to do wrong is criminal; and a wicked thought stains the mind with guilt, and makes it tingle with pain." Hence of necessity history unfolds the perennial struggle between "the cause of liberty, truth, virtue, and humanity," on the one hand, and slavery, ignorance, misery, and despotism on the other; virtue pre-

[16]Adams to Nathan Webb, October 12, 1755. *Works* (C. F. Adams, ed.), I, 23.

[17]Paul Wilstach, ed., *Correspondence of John Adams and Thomas Jefferson* (Indianapolis: Bobbs-Merrill, 1925), pp. 169-70 (December 18, 1819).

[18]Adams, *Works*, VI, 239, 232-34.

vailing during the great days of Roman culture, darkness and misery from the fourth to the fourteenth century. Once we have grasped the principle further study will merely substantiate the thesis.[19]

Jefferson also conceived of history as a series of cyclical fluctuations within a larger static framework, at least until his last years. Like Adams he also found the source of historical change to reside in the moral nature. Reflecting upon the revolutionary experiences of his own state, he expressed the opinion in the *Notes on Virginia* that when a state of public virtue prevails it is high time to erect safeguards for the protection of liberty, since "the spirit of the times may alter, will alter," and corrupt men will arise to persecute their fellows.[20] Anticipating Lord Acton's dictum that power corrupts, he appealed to history for proof that even the best governments are eventually perverted into tyrannies by those entrusted with power. To forestall this sad fate in Virginia he drafted the celebrated Bill for the More General Diffusion of Knowledge (1778), the preamble of which expresses the conviction that education aids the citizen in recognizing "ambition" and thus defeating its aims.[21] It was, in other words, the constant uniformities or repetitions of history, not its unique occurrences, that impressed Jefferson as being of value.[22] He was still of the same opinion many years later when he wrote to Adams that "in fact, the terms of whig and tory belong to natural as well as civil history. They denote the temper and constitution of mind of different individuals."[23] Such a point of view was well adapted to nurture a distinguished political science—as indeed it did—but it was not conducive to a fruitful investigation of history.

It would not do, however, to leave the reader with the impression that the cyclical conception of history was merely a convenient device whereby enlightened thinkers were enabled to concentrate their attention elsewhere. It had an integral part in the conception which the age entertained of itself, and its projection into the future suggested an attitude towards human and social possibilities that was one of the most distinctive features of the enlightened mind. Those who employed the cyclical idea were uniformly agreed that the America of their day belonged in the youthful stage of growth approaching maturity. The Rev. Thomas Barnard of Salem, for instance, comparing the prospects of the new United States with those of older European countries which had nothing to look forward to except "decline and mortification, according to the course of human affairs," remarked upon the opportunities

[19] *Ibid.*, IV (*Novanglus and Massachusettensis*), 44, 17-18.
[20] Adrienne Koch and William Peden, eds., *The Life and Selected Writings of Thomas Jefferson* (New York: Modern Library, 1944), p. 277.
[21] Jefferson, *Papers* (Boyd, ed.), II, 526-27.
[22] Koch and Peden, p. 265.
[23] Wilstach, p. 59.

for growth and progress which lay before her. "I should prefer youth and early manhood, ever employed, lively, and full of hope, to complete manhood and old age, when we every day become less active, and less pleased. I should prefer the present period of our nation, for my life, to the more perfect state to which it will gradually advance."[24] Sometimes the cyclical idea is employed in the appraisal of specific issues, as when President Samuel Stanhope Smith of the College of New Jersey warns the country against involvement in the French revolutionary wars on the ground that peace is especially important to a "young and growing country not yet enervated by luxury, nor sunk into effeminacy and sloth. These vices indeed sometimes require the purifying flame of war to purge them off; and the state emerges from its fires regenerated, as it were, and new created."[25] Or it is used to justify the spirit and form of political institutions in America, as when the Rev. Samuel Williams opined that "on all accounts, a *free and equal government* is best suited to our infant and rising state."[26]

The self-consciousness with which the Enlightened age identified itself was in part at least the consequence of a theory of history which presupposed a series of epochs alternating in character. General Washington's letter to the state governors at the end of the Revolution is characteristic of this spirit. "The foundation of our empire," he wrote, "was not laid in the gloomy age of ignorance and superstition; but at an epocha when the rights of mankind were better understood and more clearly defined, than at any former period."[27] Similar sentiments are frequently encountered, and if taken out of the cyclical context may be misunderstood to indicate a belief in unlimited progress. Actually, most enlightened thinkers had a keen sense of the precariousness of the felicity which they enjoyed, of the moral and social conditions which would make its continuation possible, and of the ultimate likelihood of its dissipation. The cyclical conception of history was the crystallization of their hopes and fears. By reading back into their thought ideas which more commonly belong to their descendants we may seriously misunderstand their point of view.

The function of the cyclical idea can perhaps be most briefly and effectively illustrated from the field of thought in which the enlightened mind achieved its supreme expression, political theory. The conservative, defensive character of that theory is now pretty generally recognized. Liberty, the supreme good, could be achieved only if men exer-

[24]Barnard, *Sermon, February 19, 1795*, pp. 21-22.
[25]Smith, *Divine Goodness*, pp. 20-21.
[26]Samuel Williams, *A Discourse on the Love of Our Country; Delivered on a Day of Thanksgiving, December 15, 1774* (Salem: S. & E. Hall, 1775), p. 18.
[27]Washington, *Writings* (Ford ed.), X, 256.

cised those moral virtues enjoined by the anti-revivalists, the practical fruit of which was the accumulation of property. The economic basis of enlightened political theory is aptly illustrated in the famous syllogism of President John Augustine Smith of William and Mary college, an ardent Jeffersonian Republican: since ninety-nine per cent of all legislation relates to property; and since it is the essence of republicanism that laws should emanate from those upon whom they bear; then restriction of the franchise to men of property is good republicanism. But property was more than an arbitrary qualification for political participation; it was an index of the moral health of the community. Unfortunately, property as we have seen was presumed to entail its own peculiar corruptions, the avoidance of which constituted a major preoccupation of political theorists. Jefferson pinned his faith to agriculture, writing to Madison in 1787 that Americans could be expected to preserve their liberties "as long as we remain virtuous, and I think we shall be so, as long as agriculture is our principal object, which will be the case, while there remain vacant lands in any part of America. When we get piled upon one another in large cities, as in Europe, we shall become corrupt as in Europe, and go to eating one another, as they do there."[28] These rural loyalties of the republican political theorists are not to be understood entirely in economic or regional terms, but perhaps primarily in moral terms. Even Benjamin Franklin, incorrigible cosmopolite, shared this sentimental agrarianism. The American counterpart of the European myth of the noble savage, living under the full light of nature, and uncorrupted by the vices of urban life, was of course the freehold farmer, whose virtuous life was the one sure foundation of national felicity.

Sound social and political institutions were, however, but temporary bulwarks against the inexorable processes of nature and history. The cyclical theory was perfectly compatible with the anticipated transformation of sturdy farmers into a landless proletariat, and with the degeneration of republican liberty into democratic license and ultimately to the tyranny of dictatorship. In his old age, John Adams looked back upon the eighteenth century and pronounced it to be, on the whole, the century "most honorable to human nature;" but he had no inclination to assume that the nineteenth century would be even more so. "My duties in my little infinitesimal circle," he wrote, "I can understand and feel. The duties of a son, a brother, a father, a neighbor, a citizen, I can see and feel, but I trust the ruler with his skies."[29]

In view of the typical emphasis upon moral conditions as the agents of cyclical change one might well question the appropriateness or sig-

[28]Jefferson, *Writings* (1903 ed.), VI, 392-93.
[29]Adams to Jefferson, November 13, 1815; September 15, 1813. Wilstach, pp. 118, 86.

nificance of the use of the organic analogy. But I think the association is worth preserving in our descriptive terminology if only because it serves to illustrate the intimate connection between nature and value, which was perhaps the most distinctive feature of enlightened thought. The transmutation of natural law into natural right was the neatest trick of the age, and although we in our time can understand it with difficulty and may even suspect fraud, we cannot fail to admire the assurance and virtuosity with which the trick was performed. The inexorable rise and fall of nations might well be ordained of God after the pattern of the life cycle of organisms, but from the creature's point of view the Deity in his beneficent wisdom has provided that our own vices and virtues, wisdom and folly, shall register a proximate if not immediate effect upon the course of human events. This we can understand, and we trust the ruler with his skies.

III

The third conception of history to be found in the thought of eighteenth century America was embodied in the idea of progress. I shall not attempt to document the rise of this idea in America, but will merely indicate what I understand to be its impact upon the revolutionary generation. To put it bluntly: the notion of progress was repugnant to the characteristic convictions and temper of the class of men who in the generation prior to the Revolution had synthesized enlightened ideas in America. But at the same time it held a fatal fascination for them. Much of their practical experience recommended its validity. With diminishing reluctance they accommodated themselves to the idea, and in the end those of them who lived long enough, like Adams and Jefferson, embraced it heartily. But in so doing they signed, as it were, articles of intellectual abdication, and the enlightened mind thus became something else.

From a genetic point of view the idea of progress as it appeared in America was the offspring of a union of the millennial hope with the moralism of the cyclical view of history. The womb in which the progeny was nurtured was the excitement of the revolutionary struggle. The respects in which the Revolution involved a domestic class struggle have been familiar to students of American history for a generation, and it is possible that the competition between these attitudes towards history might be fruitfully related to the social class struggle. In any event, certain modifications in either theory of history looking towards a rapprochement may be indicated.

As contemplated by the revivalists of the seventeen-forties, the imminent coming of the Lord represented the divine will imposed upon history. It was that not-so-far-off divine event towards which the whole creation moved; and the events of the revival, including the saving or hardening of sinners, were to be understood as but reflex actions of that mighty upheaval. But as revival enthusiasm within the Reformed churches rapidly ebbed after 1745 its proponents were placed on the defensive by a changing mood and by the extravagances of fanatics. Leading evangelicals now realized that their millennial expectations had been at best premature, and that if the hope were to be kept alive it must not disregard historical possibilities. The survival of the millennial vision was made possible, among the more intellectually respectable of the clergy at least, by measuring progress towards the final event in moral terms.[30]

To illustrate this significant tendency, again in its most literal form, I have chosen a sermon of the Rev. Ebenezer Baldwin of Danbury, Connecticut, preached in 1775 on the eve of hostilities with Britain. Baldwin looked hopefully beyond the dark days immediately ahead to a glorious future. He anticipated that the colonies were to be the "foundation of a great and mighty Empire; the largest the World ever saw, to be founded on such Principles of Liberty and Freedom, both civil and religious, as never before took place in the World; which shall be the principal Seat of that glorious Kingdom, which Christ shall erect upon Earth in the latter Days." When Baldwin delivered his sermon to the printer he appended a long footnote in amplification of this prediction in which he observed that the American population, then numbering some three million souls, was doubling every twenty-five years. This rate of increase could be expected to continue for about a century, with a somewhat lesser rate of increase for a second century, at the end of which time (i. e. 1975) a unified North American empire would contain a population of some 192 millions, a curiously accurate prediction. Because this late twentieth century empire would be the product of natural growth rather than of conquest its original principles of civil and religious liberty would have survived intact. Baldwin then reminded his readers of the common Christian conviction that Christ would establish his millennial kingdom on earth before the end of the world, and that calculations based on the prophecies in Daniel and Revelation fixed the date of the second advent at about 2000 A.D., when America would be at the height of its glory, and Europe sunk beneath tyranny, corruption, and luxury. Christ's kingdom must of course be established upon a system of civil liberty; it could not be compatible with despotism or tyranny. Since by the end of the twentieth century it would be highly improbable that liberty would prevail anywhere but in America was it "chimerical to suppose America will largely share in the Happiness of

[30]See the sermon by Samuel Langdon, *Joy and Gratitude to God for the Long Life of a Good King, and the Conquest of Quebec. A Sermon Preached . . . November 10, 1759* (Portsmouth: Fowle, 1760).

this glorious Day, and that the present Scenes are remotely preparing the Way for it?"[31] The significant features of this revised form of millennial hope are first the deferment of the great event to the remote future; but more important, the estimation of conditions under which its consummation would occur in moral terms. One could now measure the advance of mankind towards the millennium in terms of the state of civil and religious liberty.

Essentially similar sentiments were expressed a few months later in more succinct and secular terms in the greatest of revolutionary tracts, Tom Paine's *Common Sense*. "We [Americans]," cried Paine, "have it in our power to begin the world over again. A situation, similar to the present, hath not happened since the days of Noah until now. The birth day of a new world is at hand."[32] Whether Baldwin or Paine entertained the more extravagant hopes we are not required to determine. Our attention is directed to the lengthened historical perspective in which thinkers were beginning to frame their judgments. The life cycle of empires, or the "Revolution of Ages," in the phrase of the pre-revolutionary historian William Douglass, gave way to *the* revolution which marks off all history since Noah, or to the cumulative effect of specified factors pointing towards the millennium in 2000 A.D.

The "poet of the Revolution," Philip Freneau, in a Princeton commencement poem of 1771, paid his respects to the intellectual conventions of the age with an even more comprehensive synthesis. He succeeded in combining the ideas of the cyclical rise and fall of states, the westward passage of empire from Asia across Europe to the new world, and the final establishment of the millennial kingdom in America.[33]

Passages from the correspondence of Adams and Jefferson, chiefly during the second decade of the nineteenth century, both illustrate the weakening of the cyclical theory, and suggest the character of the new point of view. In their discussion of the sources of political power, Adams was inclined to stress such Machiavellian forces as selfishness, physical or psychological energy, or economic power. Jefferson, on the other hand, influenced perhaps in his later years by the French thinkers, pointed out that certain innovations of an apparently permanent character were rendering Adams' analysis obsolete. The invention of gun powder had deprived the physically strong of their primordial advantage. In the United States at least, where labor was properly rewarded, economic power was more widely distributed than ever before, with consequent equalization of political power. Even in Europe, which was

[31]Ebenezer Baldwin, *The Duty of Rejoicing under Calamities and Afflictions* (New York: Hugh Gaine, 1776), pp. 38-40 and note.

[32]Thomas Paine, *Writings* (Conway ed.), I, 118-19.

[33]"The Rising Glory of America," in F. L. Pattee, ed., *The Poems of Philip Freneau* (3 vols. Princeton: University Library, 1902), I, 49-84.

lagging behind America in these respects, a sensible change was occurring. "Science," Jefferson reported, "has liberated the ideas of those who read and reflect, and the American example has kindled feelings of right in the people. An insurrection has consequently begun, of science, talents, and courage, against rank and birth, which have fallen into contempt. . . . Science is progressive, and talents and enterprise on the alert."[34] In similar vein, he was now prepared to redefine republicanism as the conviction of those who believe in the "improvability of the condition of man, and who have acted on that behalf, in opposition to those who consider man as a beast of burden made to be rode by him who has genius enough to get a bridle into his mouth."[35] We readily recognize these ideas—the cumulative character of technology, the liberating power of science, the kindling of feelings of right, and the improvement of the condition of mankind—to be authentic features of the new faith in human progress.

Franklin was perhaps the first American to use these doctrines in such a way as to suggest a unilinear conception of history. The invention of printing, the accumulation and dissemination of knowledge, and the consequent strengthening of the spirit of liberty were coming to be regarded as unique occurrences which could not be properly evaluated within a pattern of cyclical repetition. We find these views frequently recurring in Franklin's correspondence during the 1780's.[36] In later years, the aged Jefferson agreed with Adams' favorable judgment of the eighteenth century, but he pointed out that the operation of those characteristics which rendered it notable could be traced back at least as far as the fifteenth century.[37] The age of enlightenment was not therefore to be regarded as a cyclical episode, but as a phase of a secular trend extending far back in history, and one which would conceivably project indefinitely into the future.

It is worth noting that in these early expressions of the idea of progress the moral element is strongly emphasized, and that there is nothing of the note of complacent inevitability which Ekirch, in his study of the use of the idea after 1815, finds to be one of its most prominent features. I am inclined to suspect that the enlightened theory of divine benevolence, with its associated conviction that this is the best of all possible worlds, was itself paradoxically the strongest barrier against the idea of human progress. The idea of progress was to be the fighting faith of men with a mission to perform, whether to feed the hungry, convert the heathen, or accumulate one's pile. It connoted a certain discontent with the prevail-

[34]Wilstach, pp. 93-94.

[35]Jefferson to Joel Barlow, January 24, 1810. *Writings* (Ford ed.), IX, 269.

[36]Writings (Smyth ed.), IX, 102, 657; X, 66-67. I am obliged to Professor Delmage for these references, *op. cit.*, note 4 above.

[37]Wilstach, pp. 119-20.

ing state of affairs. Its inevitability in the minds of its nineteenth-century disciples was no more incompatible with energetic effort than were the similar features of inevitability in Puritan or Marxist thinking. But such a temper of mind was largely alien to the American Enlightenment, and certain changes had to occur before the new point of view could recommend itself with any force.

We can see one such change occurring in the increasing discontent of John Adams towards the end of his life with the hedonic calculus which was a characteristic feature of the thought of his generation. The preponderance of pleasure over pain, he concluded, is not in itself sufficient to make life endurable, even for the most fortunate. Only from the hope of a future heavenly life free from pain could he draw the strength to face the ills of earthly existence. "Without the supposition of a future state," he remarked, "mankind and this globe appear to me the most sublime and beautiful bubble and bauble that imagination can conceive."[38] For Adams the future state had become what it has been to most Christian Americans ever since: an otherworldly heaven eternally removed from earth to which souls repair after death, and where the ultimate balance of pleasure over pain is assured by divine benevolence. The "heaven" of modern Christianity thus came to the rescue of a faltering hedonism, which was not quite sure after all whether the balance of earthly pleasure over pain was worth the candle.

But what had all of this to do with attitudes towards history? It simply indicated that for at least one representative of the age the idea that the creation was infinitely good and that evil or pain had a sufficient function in displaying that goodness was no longer convincing. Human experience, individually and collectively, was both incomplete and imperfect, and while for personal fulfillment one looked to heaven beyond the grave, for social fulfillment one anticipated the steady advance of morals and intellect. These matters were rather elaborately developed in the famous deistic tract, *Reason the Only Oracle of Man* (1784), traditionally ascribed to Ethan Allen. But to find the argument in the last letters of John Adams, who in earlier life had been such a staunch representative of enlightened modes of thought, suggests the pervasiveness of the new point of view. Christians, Jews, Mohammedans, and Hindoos, Adams observed, all share a similar hope for a future state analogous to the Christian millennium. But "you and I," he wrote to Jefferson in 1821, "hope for splendid improvements in human society, and vast amelioration in the condition of mankind. Our faith may be supposed by more rational arguments than any of the former. I own I am very sanguine in the belief of them, as I hope and believe you are."[39]

[38]Wilstach, pp. 136-37. [39]Wilstach, pp. 176-77.

When he had earlier employed the cyclical view of history Adams would hardly have called it a "faith." His emotions had not then been attached to a future which would right current evils, which was incidentally one reason why his interest in history had revealed such a different quality from that found in nineteenth century romantics who searched the past for confirmation of their faith in the future.

Thus the reaction to the millennialism of enthusiastic revivalists was a theory of cyclical fluctuation within a static historical continuum. The dynamic element within the cycle was the moral factor. But the implicit conservatism of this view, and the countervailing weight of American experience, seriously limited its utility in the revolutionary environment of the seventeen-seventies and eighties. The new synthesis which began to emerge after the revolution, the idea of progress, drew from millennialism its sense of the irreversible secular trend of the historical process, and from the moralism of the cyclical theory the assumption that the rôle of the individual in history is a purposive and creative one.

Afternote

When this paper was written, fifteen years ago, I did not appreciate the relevance to my theme of the eighteenth-century idea of physical and cultural degeneration. Were I revising the paper today there would have to be another section indicating the significance of the idea of degeneration as a historical theory.

Degeneration was a transitional idea, purporting to accommodate traditional religious loyalties to the newer scientific imperatives. Although all things had originally been created perfect, some things had subsequently fallen away, or degenerated. This had occurred both in nature and in culture. The theory accounted both for racial differences and for cultural barbarism. It provided scientists with a convenient device on which to arrange the accumulating evidences of deviation from created forms. It rationalized the facts of geographical distribution; and furnished Europeans a comforting perspective in which to view the heathen barbarian world of non-Europeans.

From the days of Jefferson and Samuel Stanhope Smith to those of Arnold Guyot (more than half a century) the idea of degeneration flourished because of its practical utility. Since the same categories of data used by Darwin to support his theory of "descent with modification" had been used a century earlier by Buffon to demonstrate degeneration we might say that the idea of evolution was simply degeneration turned upside down.

Stow Persons is a Professor of History at the University of Iowa. [This article appeared in Vol. VI, No. 2 (Summer, 1954).]

Ray Ginger

The Idea of Process In American Social Thought*

"THE sciences which are in any peculiar sense modern," said Thorstein Veblen in 1908, "take as an (unavowed) postulate the fact of consecutive change. . . . This notion of process about which the researches of modern science cluster, is a notion of a sequence, or complex, of consecutive change in which the *nexus* of the sequence . . . is the relation of cause and effect. The consecution, moreover, runs in terms of persistence of quantity or of force."[1] John Dewey has urged the same point: "Since the idea of history involves cumulative continuity of movement in a given direction toward stated outcomes, the fundamental conception that controls determination of subject-matter as historical is that of a *direction* of movement."[2] And again: "In science the order of fixities has already passed irretrievably into an order of connections *in process*."[3]

The first part of this paper will discuss the ideas of social process advanced by six recent American thinkers: Dewey, Veblen, Wesley C. Mitchell, John R. Commons, Theodore Dreiser, and Clarence Darrow. Then three related criticisms are made of the idea as it was formulated and applied by these men. The final section suggests the relevance

*This article is a slightly revised version of a paper presented at a joint session of the American Studies Association and the Mississippi Valley Historical Association, Chicago, April 17, 1952.

[1]Thorstein Veblen, "The Evolution of the Scientific Point of View" (read before the Kosmos Club at the University of California, May 4, 1908), *The Place of Science in Modern Civilization* (New York: B. W. Huebsch, 1919), pp. 32-33.

[2]John Dewey, *Logic: The Theory of Inquiry* (New York: Henry Holt, 1938), p. 234.

[3]John Dewey, *Reconstruction in Philosophy*, Introduction to New Edition (New York: Mentor Books, 1950), p. 28.

of the concept for the study of American civilization.

I

American social thought has produced two important variants of this idea: the determinist one, which denies the possibility of rational choice and control (Dreiser, Darrow), and the pragmatist form, which affirms that possibility. But, recognizing this crucial distinction, it is possible to give the idea of process a basic meaning acceptable to both groups: (1) Everything is constantly changing. (2) These changes are cumulative, so that term B is a modification of term A, term C is a modification of term B, and so on. Thus Veblen ridiculed Adam Smith's assertion that events, if perchance they were diverted by "disturbing elements," would return to their "natural course" as soon as the cause of disturbance was removed.[4] (3) These cumulative changes do not eventuate in any final term. Around this central meaning arose a cluster of terms: cumulative causation, going concern, analytic description.

The idea of social processes derived largely from the acceleration of social change in the United States after the Civil War. Technological revolution, the growth of corporate monopoly, the first national labor conflicts, the tramp problem and prostitution, all seemed to threaten the perpetuation of individualism, capitalism, and the traditional shapes of political democracy. This threat was emphasized by such dramatic episodes as the Paris Commune, the railroad strike of 1877, the Haymarket affair, the Pullman boycott. In this context American thinkers turned to use an idea already used in the natural sciences by Lyell and Darwin, and in the social sciences by Marx:—the idea of process. This is of course not to argue that they accepted the Marxian formulation, but the evidence suggests that socialist theory exerted a strong influence, if only by stimulating refutations.[5]

Although Veblen, Commons, and Mitchell were all economists by title, they soon discarded the static equilibrium analysis of neoclassicism, and even denied that the concept of equilibrium had a legitimate place in economics. Instead of static equilibrium they would study cumulative economic changes, regarded as an integral part of the cultural complex.

Veblen spent his career working out the historical conflict between

[4]Veblen, "The Preconceptions of Economic Science, II" (1899), reprinted in *The Place of Science in Modern Civilization*, pp. 114-17.

[5]For instance, Richard T. Ely, *French and German Socialism in Modern Times* (New York: Harper, 1883), pp. 170-82; Commons, *Myself* (New York: Macmillan, 1934), pp. 50, 80-81, 92, 148-49; Joseph Dorfman, *Thorstein Veblen and His America* (New York: Viking, 1935), pp. 116-20, 241-45, 303-4; Clarence Darrow to Henry Demarest Lloyd, March 19, 1903, Lloyd MSS., Wisconsin Historical Society.

a "matter-of-fact" viewpoint, which focuses on material, cause-effect relations, and a "higher range of theoretical explanations of phenomena," which includes philosophy, religion, patriotism, and business. This same conflict is central to Dewey's thought.[6] In modern times, Veblen argued, the conflict grows incessantly sharper, so that industry will soon retrogress if it does not vanquish the combined forces of private profit and national glory. His analysis leads to the conclusion that the slow growth of technical knowledge, in which each advance requires as a starting point the accumulated knowledge of the past, is undermining all mystical and nonfunctional concepts.

John Commons constructed his theory of capitalist development from the related threads of technological advance, institutional changes, and legal adjustments. His early essay, "American Shoemakers, 1648 to 1895," converted a few scraps of source material into a stunning account of the modes of action by which changes in market organization and productive methods had stimulated trade unionism.[7] In his theory of the common law, he emphasizes the development of habitual modes of action, the more beneficial of which are then selected for investiture with legal sanctions. Without social custom, there would be no common law, and the growth is gradual and endless.[8]

Wesley Mitchell, after studying with Veblen at Chicago and doing early research in monetary history, began his intensive study of business cycles, which were widely regarded as the chief threat to the perpetuation of capitalism. In this task he was able to turn to account two recent statistical innovations which are themselves evidence of the growing concern with processes: index numbers and correlation theory. Mitchell disavowed any intention of stating "the cause" of economic fluctuations. He would try rather to give "an analytic description of interrelated processes." In this account "the causal relationships will appear most complicated," because each item in the sequence is both an effect and a cause. Moreover, it is impossible to trace "single chains of causal influence," because each effect has more than one cause.[9]

In literature the idea of process became a new schema for plot construction. We may note the impact of this idea on American humor. Ring Lardner's short story, "Haircut," is concerned with a practical

[6]Compare Veblen, "The Evolution of the Scientific Point of View," pp. 32-55, to John Dewey, *Reconstruction in Philosophy* (New York: Henry Holt, 1920), Ch. 1, "Changing Conceptions of Philosophy."

[7]John Commons, "American Shoemakers, 1648-1895," *Quarterly Journal of Economics*, XXIV (November 1909), 39-84.

[8]John R. Commons, *The Legal Foundations of Capitalism* (New York: Macmillan, 1924).

[9]Wesley C. Mitchell, *Business Cycles, The Problem and Its Setting* (New York: National Bureau of Economic Research, 1927), pp. 470-71.

joker, who anonymously alleges to married men that their wives are unfaithful. The barber-shop loungers are quite amused by such episodes, but for our purposes the important point is that they are amused exactly because they see the single event in isolation, devoid alike of antecedents and consequences. Lardner, however, was horrified by the sense of humor displayed by his own characters, and his story constantly evokes questions which run beyond its own limits: What are the likely consequences of this prank? and: What could have produced men who think this prank is funny? As a result the reader's horror is dependent upon the characters' amusement.

The same double-vision is fundamental to Charlie Chaplin's great film, *Modern Times*. In the final scene, Chaplin reels and totters pathetically down the street, with a horde of children jeering and hooting at his heels. While the child actors laugh, the audience weeps—the audience weeps because the characters laugh. The children see only a ludicrous little man; the audience has seen what made the man. This amounts to a definition of sensitivity in art. The sensitive man sees each event in context, in process; fools and children see only the isolated episode. As John Dewey has said: "There is no such thing as *judgment* about a past event, one now taking place, or one to take place in the future in its isolation."[10]

Dewey's psychological theories provide a valuable preface to consideration of Theodore Dreiser's plot structures. In Dewey's view, the structure and functioning of a specific personality at any time is linked to a chain of development beginning at birth. Since the infant is born into a complex of customs which itself is socially developed, in a sense the chain begins before the birth of the individual. Thus habits are formed which give concrete form to the wide range of native impulses. But one habit may conflict with another, or a habit may be frustrated by changes in the environment. Intelligence comes into play to resolve the problematic situation. Dewey's focus is on the continuity of interaction between individual and environment, and the resultant continuity of modifications in both.[11] This theory contrasts sharply with the tendency in psychoanalysis to posit that event X, occurring in an individual's maturity, can be understood solely by reference to event A, which occurred in the individual's infancy, and certain ineluctable psychological laws. All intervening episodes between A and X are deemed inconsequential. Although such novels as Arthur Koestler's *Arrival and Departure* (1943) have helped to give considerable currency to this mystical psychology, it is incom-

[10]John Dewey, *Logic*, p. 230.
[11]John Dewey, *Human Nature and Conduct* (New York: Henry Holt, 1922).

patible with the outlook of Dewey and of Theodore Dreiser.

Whereas some Hemingway plots show isolated occurrences and a Thomas Wolfe novel is without real direction, Dreiser meant his novels to portray the development of character, rather than merely to reveal already existent personalities. This accounts for the length and detail of his novels; they are offered as exhaustive multiple-biographies. Already in *Sister Carrie* (1900), the typical structure emerges. This novel is built around three simultaneous processes: the ascent of Carrie Meeber from callow youth to poised actress; the disintegration of Hurstwood from club manager to suicide; the onward thrust of a ruthless society containing opportunity for the energetic like Carrie, but only destruction for the incompetent like Hurstwood. Although the increase or decay of physiological powers is a major cause of these transmutations, social environment also plays a necessary rôle. Hurstwood's debacle occurs only when he leaves his routine in Chicago to flee to New York with stolen money and a deceived mistress.

Hurstwood's theft of the $10,000 from his employers' safe shows the third major element in Dreiser's view of human affairs. This is chance. The actual theft, as distinguished from Hurstwood's inclination toward theft, depends on three conditions over which Hurstwood had no control: an exceptionally large sum of money had been left in the safe; the cashier had failed to lock the safe; and Dreiser leaves it unclear whether the door closed accidentally while Hurstwood was holding the money in his hand. Chance plays the same necessary part in Roberta Alden's death in *An American Tragedy* (1925). It is crucial to the murder novel which Clarence Darrow wrote in 1904, *An Eye for an Eye*. Darrow and Dreiser both regarded chance as an existential reality, consisting in the intersection of two processes having no causal relation to each other until the moment of intersection.

Darrow, like Dreiser, was no systematic thinker, and both men were prone to contradiction and superficiality when they stated explicitly their philosophical views. But just as Dreiser achieved solid merit in the accumulation of detail to show character development, so Darrow used the same concept in his efforts to understand crime and to manipulate the judicial machinery. They agreed that a criminal act has no "cause" other than the continuous growth of habits in the personalities of the participants; the essence of the case is what Veblen called "cumulative causation." The common question: "Why did he do it?" is subtly rephrased into: "How did he come to do it?" And full-length biographies are offered in reply. This is a major clue to Darrow's endless series of victories in criminal trials. He eschewed devastating cross-examination and legal trickery. His chief device was always the summation to the jury, and these arguments set forth fully the background to the crime. Not only did they parallel Dreiser's novels in conception—as William Dean Howells suggested when he observed that Darrow's summation in the *Kidd* trial (1898) was "as interesting as a novel"[12]—but they rival them in length.

Recognition that the life of a juror as well as that of a defendant is a continuum prompted Darrow's efforts to exclude from the jury all persons whose own lives indicated that they would not respond favorably to his account of the crime.[13] Also, the frequent criticism of Darrow for trying his cases in the headlines is valid, since he always believed that judge and jury in any major case will be swayed by the newspaper accounts.[14] During the Leopold-Loeb trial (1924) he wrote to his son: "It is an awfull [*sic*] hard fight and the papers have been so rotten that feeling runs high."[15] He overcame this bias to such an extent that his summation appeared in full in the Chicago *Herald-Examiner* under the banner headline:[16]

"You May Hang These Boys, But You
Will Turn Your Faces to the Past"

Thus he created the context which made it possible for the judge to refrain from imposing a death penalty—the only point at issue in the trial.

II

Hoping that this survey suggests the rôle of the concept of process in recent American social thought, I turn now to three related criticisms of this idea, as formulated and applied by the men under review:

1. My first criticism holds that the idea of process, as advanced and used by these six men, contains elements of philosophic idealism. As used here, the word ***idealism*** points out these related beliefs: denial that an external reality exists independently of human cognition; denial that human beings can and do have knowledge of this external reality; affirmation that knowledge can rest on some ground other than its efficacy in predicting and controlling external events; affirmation that events occur outside of time, space, and causation.

[12]Quoted in *Current Literature*, XLIII (August 1907), 157.

[13]Interview with Darrow by Paul Y. Anderson, St. Louis *Post-Dispatch*, May 10, 1925, pp. 1B, 4B; Clarence Darrow, "Attorney for the Defense," *Esquire*, 1936, pp. 36-37, 211-13. The statement is based mainly on a detailed examination of Darrow's conduct of fifty or more criminal trials.

[14]For instance, C. P. Connolly, "The Saving of Clarence Darrow," *Collier's*, December 23, 1911, p. 9.

[15]Clarence Darrow to Paul Darrow, August 3, 1924, in possession of Paul Darrow.

[16]Chicago *Herald-Examiner*, August 26, 1924, pp. 1, 3, 4, 5.

Let us first consider John Dewey's notion of causation and process.[17] Doubtless it will be urged that Dewey's assertion that causation is a logical category, given his meaning of logic, is far from synonymous with an assertion that causation is a subjective category. By substituting contextualist for substantialist meanings, by stressing the reorganization of an existential situation as the ground for knowledge, Dewey seems to have broken fully with idealism.[18] The validity of Savery's statement that Dewey belongs "to the materialist tradition" can only be tested by a detailed analysis of Dewey's philosophy, particularly his logic.[19] That task cannot be undertaken here. But an expression of doubt based on Dewey's application of his theory of inquiry to specific social events escapes being *ad hominem* because it clarifies the meaning of that theory to Dewey himself. From this perspective, Dewey appears to have a very loose conception of causality in human affairs.

His appraisal of two World Wars will serve to illustrate (but of course not to prove) the point. In 1917 he supported American entry into the war, saying that it might result in "a world organization and the beginnings of a public control which crosses nationalistic boundaries and interests."[20] He then urged that the United States should not resort to "conscription of thought" in pursuit of its military objectives.[21] But it seems proper to observe that a realistic appraisal of the situation would have eliminated both of these objectives as impossible of achievement. Dewey reached his evaluation of the possibilities only by ignoring the fact that human attitudes and beliefs are also caused and that, while they are certainly mutable under certain conditions, those conditions need to be investigated and not assumed.

The point is emphasized by his contribution to a symposium in *Common Sense* in March 1939 on the question: "If War Comes Shall America Participate or Remain Neutral?" His brief reply appeared under a strangely dogmatic title for one who has advertised adaptability: "No Matter What Happens—Stay Out."[22] He predicted that American entry into "the next war" would inevitably produce "in effect if not in name a fascist government in this country" and result

[17]John Dewey, *Logic*, Ch. XXII.

[18]Morton G. White, *The Origin of Dewey's Instrumentalism* (New York: Columbia University Press, 1943).

[19]William Savery, "The Significance of Dewey's Philosophy," in Paul Arthur Schilpp, editor, *The Philosophy of John Dewey* (Evanston and Chicago: Northwestern University Press, 1939), p. 511.

[20]John Dewey, "What America Will Fight For," *New Republic*, August 18, 1917, p. 69.

[21]John Dewey, "Conscription of Thought," *New Republic*, September 1, 1917, pp. 128-30.

[22]*Common Sense*, VIII, No. 4 (March 1939), 11.

in "the suppression of all the democratic values for the sake of which we professedly went to war." Dreading a recurrence of the reactionary wave after World War I, he concluded that the United States should and could avoid entry into another war: "If we but make up our minds that it is not inevitable, and if we now set ourselves to seeing that no matter what happens we stay out, we shall save this country from the greatest social catastrophe that could overtake us, the destruction of all the foundations upon which to erect a socialized democracy." Apart from its neglect of the dynamics of fascism, apart from its appeal to the supposedly irresistible power of will, this statement is wholly ambiguous in its exhortation: "If we but make up our minds . . ." Does the "we" suggest that enough people could be mobilized in every powerful nation to force all governments to keep the peace, or does it refer merely to Dewey and the readers of *Common Sense*? Dewey himself has made a comment that applies to these prescriptions: "To profess to have an aim and then neglect the means of its execution is self-delusion of the most dangerous sort."[23]

By identifying himself with an expansive period in American culture and projecting that period to the present, by inadequate analysis of the modes of interaction and change in social affairs, Dewey has often failed to recognize the limits that any existential situation imposes on human action within that situation. Other examples of this error are noted below.

In contrast to Dewey's lapses into what Dr. M. R. Kadish has called "optimistic voluntarism," Clarence Darrow proudly declared before a Senate committee in 1935: "I may be an idiot, but I am not a cheerful idiot."[24] This professional pessimism—and its cash value Darrow understood well enough—he supported with a hodgepodge of mechanistic determinism. Like Theodore Dreiser, he was prone to speak of mankind as being "on a raft floating on a bottomless sea."[25] He wrote blandly to Fremont Older: "Of course I know . . . that one's thoughts and philosophy have nothing whatever to do with his conduct. His reactions are purely mechanistic and cannot be changed."[26] But Darrow was unable to hold to this view, and it easily slopped over into idealism: "It may be that only the ideal really is," he wrote.

[23]John Dewey, *Reconstruction in Philosophy* (New York: Henry Holt, 1920), pp. 72-73.

[24]*Investigation of the National Recovery Administration.* Hearings before the Senate Committee on Finance, U. S. Senate, 74th Cong., 1st Session, pursuant to S.R. 79 (Washington: Government Printing Office, 1935), p. 300.

[25]Clarence Darrow in a speech on "The Universe," at Northwestern University, May 25, 1927, *The Daily Northwestern*, May 26, 1927, pp. 1, 3; see also F. O. Matthiessen, *Theodore Dreiser* (New York: Sloane, 1951), pp. 84, 122.

[26]Clarence Darrow to Fremont Older, July 14, 1923; a typewritten copy of this letter was included by Older in his letter to Theodore Dreiser, January 3, 1924, Dreiser MSS., University of Pennsylvania.

"All the facts of life are not what are, but what seems to us to be."[27] Nor is it surprising that Darrow held simultaneously these two seemingly contradictory philosophies, since both removed the test of practice from epistemology and thus negated any possibility of knowledge of the external world. What man cannot predict or manipulate, he cannot know. So Darrow's formal philosophy comes to a passive contemplation of the *Ding an sich.* Small wonder that he was never sure he found it.

The idealism of Veblen and Mitchell appears clearly in their treatment of causation. Dr. S. M. Daugert has recently shown the lasting influence on Veblen of Kant,[28] and it seems equally clear that Veblen was strongly indebted to Hume. He argued that, while such concepts as "cause" and "process" were essential "imputations" into the facts, they remained merely "unproven and unprovable" and "metaphysical" postulates,[29]—an argument that can be sustained just so long as theory remains immune from the test of practice. Mitchell went even further to deny that the idea of "cause" was needed at all. "The more complete the theory of any subject becomes in content, the more mathematical in form," he said, "the less it invokes causation."[30]

2. My second criticism applies chiefly to the pragmatists, Dewey and Commons. The theory of social process advanced by these men has proved incompetent to predict or interpret the nodal points in human affairs, when the typical situations and typical modes of action alter, and the direction of history changes. Dewey has denied the validity of any distinction between "the critical" and "the gradual."[31] Commons, describing in detail the transition of English law from the "rent-bargain" of feudalism to the "price-bargain" of capitalism, attached no significance to the seventeenth-century revolutions, although the conquest of political power by men whose interests lay with the "price-bargain" was central to the process he was tracing.[32] And again, the American Civil War is not mentioned in his account of the changing meanings of liberty, property, and due process of law, in American jurisprudence.[33]

The writings before 1929 of Commons and Selig Perlman, his closest associate, imply that the AFL was an almost perfect adaptation to

[27]Clarence Darrow, "Conduct and Profession," *The Rubric*, II, No. 2 (Chicago, [1901?]), 42.

[28]Stanley M. Daugert, *The Philosophy of Thorstein Veblen* (New York: King's Crown Press, 1950).

[29]Veblen, "The Evolution of the Scientific Point of View," *loc. cit.*, pp. 33, 33-36*n*.

[30]Wesley C. Mitchell, *Business Cycles, the Problem and Its Setting*, pp. 54-55.

[31]John Dewey, "Experience, Knowledge, and Value: A Rejoinder," in Paul Arthur Schilpp, editor, *The Philosophy of John Dewey*, pp. 593-94.

[32]John R. Commons, *Legal Foundations of Capitalism*, pp. 214-35.

[33]*Ibid.*, pp. 11-21.

American conditions, and fail to consider the likelihood of rapid and sweeping changes in those conditions. Even more striking is a statement made by Perlman in 1928: ". . . the Germany after 1918 has demonstrated how a 'normally' developed Western community might achieve a self stabilization when thrown out of equilibrium by war and revolution."[34] He went on to praise the German labor movement for its adaptation to this stabilized capitalism. The following events seem almost a deliberate mockery of Perlman's prediction: ". . . whatever hardships or even crises the future may be holding in store for the German labor movement—its experience, both in the past and in the recent years, has amply prepared it to cope with them."[35]

When Dewey and Commons borrowed the idea of adaptation from Darwin, it became synonymous with conciliation. Conflict might occur, but it always resulted in harmonious resolution, never in the destruction of one or both contestants. Human history to them held no analogs to the dinosaur.

3. This suggests my third criticism: The pragmatists have often shown undue preoccupation with one process to the neglect of other, interacting processes. It seems probable that Dewey's educational theories underestimate the extent to which the schools are shaped by the cultural context, and therefore exaggerate their potentialities as an instrument for orderly and democratic change.[36] But let us consider here his writings on the present functions of philosophy. The happy belief that every problematic situation contains a satisfactory solution characterizes Dewey's views on this subject. Whereas past philosophy was chiefly an intellectual support of the *status quo*, today scientific inquiry can serve the entire populace. Thus runs Dewey's argument. But actually scholars today are in a dilemma, since many of the necessary conditions of their scholarship are controlled by persons who do not share the scholar's values. Inadequate salaries, overwork, administrative duties, loyalty oaths, political investigations, race and sex discrimination—these are an important part of today's world. The main channels to an audience—publishing firms, academic classrooms, radio and television, the movies and art galleries and concert halls—seldom rank free inquiry as the chief virtue. These

[34]Selig Perlman, *A Theory of the Labor Movement* (New York: Macmillan, 1928), p. 66.
[35]*Ibid.*, p. 122.
[36]For instance, John Dewey, "The School and Social Progress," *The School and Society*, 2nd edition (Chicago: University of Chicago Press, 1915), pp. 3-28; Morton G. White, *Social Thought in America: The Revolt against Formalism* (New York: Viking, 1949), pp. 94-100; Thorstein Veblen, *The Higher Learning in America, A Memorandum on the Conduct of Universities by Business Men* (New York: B. W. Huebsch, 1918); Harold J. Laski, *The American Democracy* (New York: Viking, 1948), Ch. VIII; Howard K. Beale, *Are American Teachers Free?* (New York: Scribner, 1936).

considerations raise questions regarding freedom of thought: What has it actually meant in this country? Who could think freely, and about what? How wide an audience could he reach with his conclusions? On what necessary conditions did free inquiry depend in the past? To what extent are those conditions present today? Given existing conditions and their discernible course, can we establish a set of sub-conditions which will make free inquiry possible and also effective in shaping the practical conduct of social affairs? By giving inadequate attention to such problems of the sociology of knowledge, Dewey has seemed to argue that everything will be all right if we only maintain free inquiry. But the question remains: How can we?

III

In thus criticizing the idea of process as formulated and applied by these men, there is no intention of derogating their achievement or implying that the idea is worthless. On the contrary, the idea can serve as a guiding principle for historical investigations: namely, No event can be understood except in terms of those necessary conditions and those consequences relevant to the problem under investigation. And the subject matter for investigation must be delimited in such a way as to facilitate this objective; i.e., a historical subject matter must be a relatively isolated system.

This argument may seem so obvious as to forbid mention, but recent historiography is replete with contrary examples, as, for instance, the current controversy regarding the causes of the Civil War. Professors Craven and Randall have asserted that the Civil War was caused by irresponsible demagogy and a breakdown of statesmanship. Schlesinger and DeVoto have replied that the real cause was moral revulsion in the North against Negro slavery in the South.[37] No matter which of these views one accepts, the problem is not solved, it has merely shifted. Now we must ask what caused the breakdown of statesmanship; why did so many people listen to the demagogs; why did this moral revulsion break forth so strongly in the 1850's? Only when we have first understood how the Civil War came about will we be able to ask meaningfully what caused the Civil War. And then the question will be redundant. This is not to advocate a retreat into the eclecticism of Albert J. Beveridge, with its catalog of causes.

[37]Avery Craven, *The Coming of the Civil War* (New York: Scribner, 1942); J. G. Randall, *Lincoln the Liberal Statesman* (New York: Dodd Mead, 1947); Arthur M. Schlesinger, Jr., "The Causes of the Civil War: A Note on Historical Sentimentalism," *Partisan Review*, XVI, No. 10 (October 1949), 969-81; Bernard DeVoto, "Slavery and the Civil War," reprinted in Edwin C. Rozwenc, editor, *Slavery as a Cause of the Civil War* (New York: D. C. Heath, 1949), pp. 98-102.

But Beveridge's fault was not in perceiving economic causes, political causes, moral causes, and so on—his fault was a failure to find developmental interaction between these various spheres.[38] The subject matters of history are isolated relatively, not absolutely.

This problem of the causes of the Civil War could be reformulated in the terms advanced in this paper somewhat as follows: The North and the South in 1800 were characterized by different institutions and beliefs. In each section the economic and political institutions, the moral and social beliefs, were bound together by causal interactions into a culture, and some of these spheres exerted greater influence than others in the movement of the total culture. Between 1800 and 1860 these cultures developed along discrepant paths, coming into ever sharper conflict at an increasing number of points. These emergent conflicts eventuated in secession, and secession in war. Although these propositions are at best hypotheses, and are barren of specific content, the problem when stated in this way is meaningful and is susceptible of solution. But it is hard to see how insistence on this or that single cause of the Civil War, ripped out of the developmental pattern, is going to help us understand how that mighty conflict came about.

This idea of process also implies that an understanding of the social trends operative in the present, of their past development and their modes of interaction, justifies projection of their general course in the future. The objection will be made that this is risky, that it will result in error when applied to individual cases. The objection is, in brief, that prediction in the social sciences can deal at best in probabilities, whereas the natural sciences deal in certainties. But this view of the natural sciences is imperfect. To quote Einstein and Infeld: "Quantum physics formulates law governing crowds and not individuals. Not properties but probabilities are described, not laws disclosing the future of systems are formulated, but laws governing the changes in time of the probabilities and relating to great crowds of individuals."[39]

The belief that social development consists in the interaction of all spheres of a culture was doubtless basic to the formation of the American Studies Association, and this same perception has guided several outstanding pieces of recent scholarship. Oliver Larkin has shown by example that the history of American art must be studied in its cultural context,[40] and Dirk Struik has demonstrated the same

[38]Albert J. Beveridge, *Abraham Lincoln, 1809-1858* (Boston: Houghton Mifflin, 1928, two volumes), II, 2 ff.

[39]Albert Einstein and Leopold Infeld, *The Evolution of Physics* (New York: Simon and Schuster, 1938), p. 313.

[40]Oliver Larkin, *Art and Life in America* (New York: Rinehart, 1949).

proposition for the history of science.[41] C. Vann Woodward has revealed that a key to the Compromise of 1877 was the industrial development of preceding decades and the concomitant shifts in economic and political power.[42] C. Wright Mills has written a brilliant analytic description of the changing composition and status of the American middle classes.[43] While Woodward has taken his central thesis of the Civil War as a second American Revolution from Charles A. Beard,[44] the same thesis was advanced by Karl Marx, and Struik and Mills have by-passed two generations of American social thought to find their guiding principles in the writing of Marx and Max Weber. Mills, indeed, has complained that today Marx's work is "on the one side ignored and vulgarized, and on the other ignored and maligned."[45] The researches of these four contemporaries, to cite no others, indicate the crucial importance of the view that history has direction, that it is cumulative, that it is a complex of processes, since this idea offers a guiding principle for the selection and organization of factual data that is not subjective or arbitrary.

Such is the burden of this paper. As John Dewey said, following Bacon: "Knowledge is power and knowledge is achieved by sending the mind to school to nature to learn her processes of change."[46]

Afternote

Major essays embodying the idea of process are to be found in my collection, *American Social Thought* (New York: Hill & Wang, 1961). Some of the ideas discussed in the present paper are treated from other angles in my *Altgeld's America* (Chicago: Quadrangle Books, 1965). Also pertinent is Cynthia Eagle Russett's *The Concept of Equilibrium in American Social Thought* (New Haven: Yale University Press, 1966). It would be useful if someone would undertake a study of the companion idea — that of context.

Ray Ginger is Professor of History at Wayne State University. [This article appeared in Vol. IV, No. 3 (Fall, 1952).]

[41]Dirk J. Struik, *Yankee Science in the Making* (Boston: Little, Brown, 1947).
[42]C. Vann Woodward, *Reunion and Reaction: The Compromise of 1877 and the End of Reconstruction* (Boston: Little, Brown, 1951).
[43]C. Wright Mills, *White Collar: The American Middle Classes* (New York: Oxford University Press, 1951).
[44]Woodward, *Reunion and Reaction*, p. ix.
[45]Mills, *White Collar*, p. 357.
[46]John Dewey, *Reconstruction in Philosophy* (New York: Henry Holt, 1920), p. 49.

Louis J. Budd

Altruism Arrives in America

SACRIFICING self for the sake of mankind is an ancient, protean idea. Yet the word "altruism" is barely a hundred years old. Although, from the first, its meanings varied somewhat, it proved useful to many who tried again to assess human nature and to reshape human goals. It left its track in the fields of religion and ethical theory, economics, sociology, and literature. Tracing its career in the United States will clarify the chronicle of thought and event during the more than usually crucial 1890's and will point up a crisis in our native reform tradition. Just a neat synonym in our time, altruism once served as a banner in the continuing campaign to persuade man to submerge himself in the welfare of others.

Its origin is quite simple. Altruism by name sprang up in Western Europe. Adapting it from Latin, Auguste Comte coined the word for his *System of Positive Polity* (1851-1854) to denote the supreme virtue in his religion of humanity. George Henry Lewes, Harriet Martineau, and other admirers naturally spread the Frenchman's precepts in England. Altruism was borrowed also by many British and Americans who could not go all the way with Comte. Most influential among those who cared less for his hierarchy of sciences than his ethical doctrines was John Stuart Mill. For some, altruism became the "social-regarding branch" of utilitarianism, and Leslie Stephen devoted an approving chapter to it in his *Science of Ethics* (1882). Whatever its chords were, by 1879 the "Italian sweet sounds of altruism" had enough volume in England to draw the ridicule of *Fraser's Magazine.*[1]

With Herbert Spencer's help the sweet sounds swelled into a steady hum that usually drowned out any Comtean overtones. In his 1870-1872

[1]Henry Calderwood, *Handbook of Moral Philosophy* (London: Macmillan, 1902), pp. 108-15; Richmond L. Hawkins, *Positivism in the United States* (1853-1861) (Cambridge: Harvard University Press, 1938), pp. vi-vii; Morris Hillquit, *Loose Leaves from a Busy Life* (New York: Macmillan Co., 1934), pp. 1-6; "The Failure of Altruism," *Fraser's Magazine,* C (October, 1879), 497.

edition of *Principles of Psychology* Spencer had adopted the word because it contrasted so neatly with egoism. His *Data of Ethics* (1879) devoted more than three chapters to doling out praise for altruism as an evolving private motive that would weigh heavily in the eventual equilibrium between self and society. And this was the book that won a wide audience for his moral theory. The audience was not solely British, for his vogue in the United States was rising toward the peak of his triumphal visit here in 1882. By February 12 of that year the New York *Daily Tribune* could casually refer to altruism even though a Rutgers professor of mathematics had to ask about its meaning.[2] Before much longer, few intelligent readers did not know, if only because of the attacks it aroused. Yet altruism's repute was so sound that Spencer anxiously claimed most of the credit.[3] He did serve as godfather to Comte's neologism. He could not, however, control its many marriages.

Many who burned to instruct mankind pounced upon altruism as a rhetorical asset. One despairs of finding them all. Most numerous were religious thinkers like Henry Drummond, the famous British evangelist. His *Ascent of Man* (1894), which reprinted his extremely popular Lowell lectures for 1893, preached that "Progress was the object of Nature, and that Altruism was the object of Progress." Reconciling science and ethics, he propounded altruism as a natural law, the highest one in the evolutionary process. Among the more secular pundits, Benjamin Kidd in his *Social Evolution* (1894) extolled it as the force that had equalized and thus intensified the competitive struggle. Obviously, altruism had taken hold in England, and also in the United States where, said some, it threatened to become a "fad."[4] Just as obviously, different groups were bending it into such varied shapes that the standard "influence" approach is blocked. One on-the-scene analyst saw by 1897 three species of it: the appeal to the ethics of Jesus, the socialists' drive for mutual welfare, and the evolutionist concern for the social or racial unit.[5] This analyst did not allow for hybrids and did not note that Social Darwinists ranged from "soft" to "hard," but he detected altruism's swift mutations, which were most erratic in our country.

An array of altruisms flourished here because of major uncertainties in American thought between 1865 and 1900. Pressed by the higher criticism

[2]New York *Daily Tribune,* February 12, 1882, p. 6; February 20, 1882, p. 5.

[3]George S. Layard, *Mrs. Lynn Linton* (London: Methuen, 1901), pp. 310-12. Some complaints about altruism's popularity are "Altruism and Prodigality," *Spectator,* LVII (March 22, 1884), 375; Charles W. Smiley, "Altruism Economically Considered," *Popular Science Monthly,* XXXIV (November, 1888), 53-69; W. H. Mallock, "Altruism in Economics," *Forum,* XXI (August, 1896), 690.

[4]*Altruistic Review,* I (December, 1893), 283 and II (February, 1894), 107; K. T. Takahashi, "Individualism *vs.* Altruism," *Arena,* XVIII (September, 1897), 370.

[5]Takahashi, "Individualism *vs.* Altruism," 362-73.

and the successes of scientific method, many religious leaders lightened their stress on formal doctrine to talk more about social ethics. If they were seeking for moral laws to emulate physical ones or if they looked for patterns in comparative religion, altruism could be made important. Before long, religionists of every stripe had to reckon with it.[6] Spencer's potent appeal was compounded through the success of his American apostle, John Fiske, who sprang to fame with his *Outlines of Cosmic Philosophy.* Most concerned with moral theory, Fiske argued that the "fundamental characteristic of social progress . . . is a gradual supplanting of *egoism* by *altruism.*" As his blending of current science with Christianity lured more churchmen, so did altruism. Some truly respected its modern status as a natural law while others drafted it for the timeless work of saving souls.[7] Despite Comte's wishes it won religious approval, and cleared a major bar to popular esteem.

Since the growing social disciplines still reflected religious trends, it is not surprising that by 1890 economists felt themselves split into egoistic and altruistic camps.[8] A few ministers directly encouraged the gentler outlook, and Washington Gladden assured employers that a profit sharing plan "incorporates the altruistic element into industrial society." Although the sterner school obviously ruled, dissenters complained that it depended on the axiom of selfishness; they chose to build on brotherhood and to give hearty blessing to farming and industrial cooperatives. John Bates Clark, not quite famous in 1886 but already a top economist, contended in *The Philosophy of Wealth* that society had reached an extreme degree of interdependence. "This is," he said, "economic altruism, to the future of which no limits can be assigned." He firmly predicted that competition would be lessened

[6]Noah Porter, *The Elements of Moral Science* (New York: Charles Scribner's Sons, 1885), pp. 111-12, 378, 429; Octavius B. Frothingham, *The Religion of Humanity* (New York: D. G. Francis, 1873), pp. 169, 175-77; Stow Persons, *Free Religion* (New Haven: Yale University Press, 1947), p. 73; Aaron I. Abell, *The Urban Impact on American Protestantism* (Cambridge: Harvard University Press 1943), pp. 73, 80; Washington Gladden, *Applied Christianity* (Boston: Houghton Mifflin, 1886), pp. 32, 234-35, and *Recollections* (Boston: Houghton Mifflin, 1909), pp. 298-99, 310-15; Vernon P. Bodein, *The Social Gospel of Walter Rauschenbusch* (New Haven: Yale University Press, 1944), p. 24.

[7]William F. Quillian, Jr., "Evolution and Moral Theory in America," pp. 409-12 in Stow Persons, ed., *Evolutionary Thoughts in America* (New Haven: Yale University Press, 1950); Fiske, *Outlines of Cosmic Philosophy* (Boston: Houghton Mifflin, 1874), II, 201-04; Ralph Albertson, *Christian Altruism* (reprinted from *Social Gospel* of June, 1901); George D. Boardman, *Studies in the Creative Week* (New York: Appleton-Century-Crofts, Inc., 1886), p. 112, and *The Ten Commandments* (Philadelphia, 1889), pp. 349-52, 356-57. The *Altruistic Review,* II (February, 1894), 107-08, reported on Boardman's sermons from his prominent Baptist pulpit in Philadelphia.

[8]Lewis G. Janes, "The Economic Value of Altruism," *Social Economist,* V (July, 1893), 11-20. See also Richard T. Ely, *Ground under Our Feet* (New York: Macmillan Co., 1938), pp. 166-68; Abell, *Urban Impact on American Protestantism,* pp. 68-69.

further by self-sacrificing behavior.[9] Altruism could sanction a more liberal solution to rising labor problems than Spencer had intended.

Sociology had by 1890 come up with similar attacks on the harsh kind of Social Darwinism. Some respectable authorities massed behind the "law of love" doctrine.[10] Altruism had competitors like Prince Kropotkin's "mutual aid" or Franklin Giddings' "socializing forces." But it was so frequently called for that Lester Frank Ward felt forced to quarrel with it in each of his treatises. In a practical corner of sociology, it was invoked when the warm-hearted, deciding that private largess was bumbling and insufficient, discussed firmer repairs for the human wreckage of industrialism. Amos G. Warner, chief of organized aid, stated in his definitive *American Charities* (1894) that the "economic aspects of altruism" had been studied widely in the past ten years.[11] This concern with effective social work was aptly reflected in a novel by a Wellesley instructor, Margaret Pollock Sherwood's *An Experiment in Altruism.*[12] The scientific strategists of economics and sociology soon overwhelmed any moral positions. But altruism helped fight the delaying action.

It was without doubt a separate strand of thought by the 1880's. No survey of ethics could ignore it. Still, one must grant that its appearances as cited so far were mostly in a supporting role. Some writers took it up rather carelessly as the bright name for an old idea. They at least helped it emerge as the rallying slogan in a segment of reform activities that collided with the premise of man's selfishness. Altruism attracted vitally those who felt that progress was halted until a kinder theory of human nature could prevail. Although the particular stress varied from a nicer balance between private and social motives to a rapturous surrender of self, its distinctive brand sat on periodicals, utopian romances, and colonies. The first person to adopt it as his trademark was Alcander Longley.

Born in 1832, Longley had as a boy been brought into a Fourierist phalanx by his father. He never lost his faith in communitarianism, although as a freethinker he shunned religious ventures. A printer by trade, in 1868 he started a slender news-sheet in St. Louis which he called the *Communist.* He was soon wishing to purge himelf of Marxist tinges, so he baptized his

[9]Gladden, *Applied Christianity,* pp. 34-35; Clark, *The Philosophy of Wealth* (Boston: Ginn and Co., 1892), pp. 39-41, 45. Richard T. Ely, *Social Aspects of Christianity* (New York: Thomas Y. Crowell Co., 1889), pp. 6, 59-60, agreed heartily with Clark but used altruism as a casual synonym for other words.

[10]L. L. and Jessie Bernard, *Origins of American Sociology* (New York: Thomas Y. Crowell Co., 1943), p. 380.

[11]Warner, *American Charities* (New York: Thomas Y. Crowell Co., 1894), pp. 21, 128.

[12]Elizabeth Hastings, pseud., *An Experiment in Altruism* (New York: Macmillan Co., 1895). This novel's characters have no names other than the Altruist, the Anarchist, etc.; the Altruist lives in a settlement house but shows little feeling for individuals as he "translates the infinite into finite terms."

first colony the Friendship Community. Drawn for a while to cooperatives he slowly concluded that their "rewards are insufficient to satisfy either the motive of self-interest or of generous impulses."[13] By 1880 he was trying out the lure of Liberal Communism, and he incorporated his 1883 settlement as the Mutual Aid Community. Meeting little response to his many schemes, he pardonably put part of the blame on the labeling of his wares.

After quoting for clarity the latest revision of Webster, in April, 1885 he changed the name of his life-long enterprises:

> Wishing to extend the circulation of our paper more widely and also to assist all other reforms as much as we can, we have adopted the name of ALTRUIST . . . as being not only more general in its application to all progressive and reformatory movements, but also as more explicitly expressing the fundamental principle of the common interest which we advocate . . .

This gave him permanent relief from Marxist expropriation of his first nom de guerre. His Progressive Lyceum became the Altruist Society; his communal houses in St. Louis and his projected farming colonies naturally made the change. Unfortunately, his platform did not change. Shunning political action, he kept calling for a network of groups that would abolish private property and share the labor and policy making.[14] For such views more than an apt name was needed to bring success, a joy that Longley never could claim. No startling results flowed from him or his *Altruist,* which stopped with his death in 1918. He exemplified the decline of simple utopianism. He also showed that altruism appealed to some who clung to the legacy of the Enlightenment, to the dream of man living in the light of amiable reason and sharing directly with his fellow.

Longley's crusade was crippled by dying slogans and side issues like phonetic spelling. Hazlitt Alvah Cuppy avoided these handicaps. Coming to Chicago in the early summer of 1893 with few assets except a Heidelberg Ph.D., he was "moved by some Power which up to the present I have not been able to stand against." By July he had ready the first monthly number of the *Altruistic Review,* which announced:

> If this *Review* has a mission—and it has—it is to appeal to whatever will make manhood more manly, and womanhood more womanly in their highest and broadest sense. A friend has aptly expressed the object and hope of my life in these lines: "The *Altruistic Review* is an attempt to organize the good impulses of the world."

[13]The French Communards and cooperatives were disposed of in *Communist,* II (August, 1873), 53 and V (December 19, 1879), 41.

[14]Longley's *What Is Communism* (St. Louis, 1890), pp. 413-20, reprints the articles of agreement for an Altruist Community.

This was noble but vague. In practice, Cuppy's magazine, at all times distinctly religious in its undertones, dispensed inspirational cheer. Greeting "the age of philanthropy," he set up "The Altruist's Corner" to gather news of all groups organized "for the good of mankind." Although benefiting humanity did not excuse John Altgeld's pardoning of the Haymarket anarchists or even justify Sunday openings for the Columbian Exposition, Cuppy did not oppose anything too noisily. Warm approval was his forte, and he tried to make his magazine "especially adaptable to all classes."

When the first number of the third volume came out in July, 1894 Cuppy thanked subscribers in almost every state as well as eight foreign countries. Prosperity shone through his pages. He had made altruism a blanket large and pliable enough to comfort many persons who, disturbed by current tensions, hoped that goodwill could brake the collision between economic classes. While appealing often to Christ's Sermon on the Mount, the *Altruistic Review* contented itself with a deep, shadowy aura of religion as the age moved away from sectarian rivalry. Its platform remained that of "organizing and tabulating the good impulses of the world." In practice it satisfied those who could not stand pat and yet could not choose a stern plan of reform.

For the first year at least, Cuppy's straddle, veiled by some quite adequate literary farce and skilful digesting of other magazines, clearly got by. But the bubble he stood on evaporated. In February, 1896 he drifted into a merged *Pulpit Herald and Altruistic Review* which became in October the *Twentieth Century Monthly,* a title that joined it with a group of periodicals and clubs hurrying to sound another note of newness. Although the contents of the *Twentieth Century Monthly* changed much less than its title, the altruistic label had been discarded as suggestive of "some pet theory on the social question." Cuppy huddled closer to majority views and to eventual prosperity in the publishing world.

At his outset he had felt daring enough to answer a feeler from Longley, but the *Altruistic Interchange* ignored both of them.[15] The guiders of this quarterly, begun by an Altruistic Company of New York City in January, 1893, must have thought Longley too radical and Cuppy too diffuse. They proposed to handle the "exchange of news between wide-spread philanthropic societies and . . . the diffusion of information concerning various forms of progressive, organized work for the general good." This might suggest Cuppy, but the *Interchange* was clear and efficient. Its first number carried a precise account of altruism's origins,[16] and its pages aimed

[15]*Altruist,* XXV (May, 1893), 18 and (September, 1893), 35.

[16]*Altruist Interchange,* I (January, 1893), 3. In this passage, altruism was classed as a branch of utilitarianism; credit was given to Comte, Mill and Spencer. Starting with volume five, the magazine became the *Altruist;* it ran until 1904.

soberly at middle-class women, warning them against impulsive giving which cut the "nerve of independence." Its chief topic was the improvement of day nurseries, flower missions, tenement houses, and the like. Scientific sowing was to multiply the harvest of lady bountiful's charity.

Longley spurned such patchwork reformers, warning them that "nothing short of common property is genuine altruism." Yet he could not control the word's avatars. Walter S. McLain, a lawyer and osteopath, broadcast from Cookeville, Tennessee a few numbers of *The Altruist, a Monthly Magazine of Reformative Literature* that Longley found too conservative. Also in 1894, a left-wing Populist started an *Altruian* in Iowa. A year later, a cooperative that was formed to build a huge irrigation ditch in Colorado began an *Altrurian* that ran until 1901.[17] Altruism had a vitality, mixed but genuine, that the movers and shakers tried to harness. A welter of brotherhoods, fellowships, and commonwealths fought for favor. But altruism, endorsed by some of the age's intellectual sluggers, was the favorite brand name for gradualist reforms. By contrast, the efforts of Boston's busy Frank Parsons to spread "mutualism" as an amalgam of Spencerian law and Christian ethic unspectacularly failed.[18]

Even though Kropotkin's mutual aid theory must have helped him, Parsons could not overmatch William Dean Howells. When the first part of Howells' *A Traveler from Altruria* ran in the *Cosmopolitan* for November, 1892, he towered on the literary skyline. This serial, along with his "Letters of an Altrurian Traveller," rounded out the public's knowledge of altruism. His own knowledge had come almost as recently. In his writing he first used the word only as late as 1885, while praising the deeds of the Italian monk Savonarola. Yet by September 14, 1888, Henry Mills Alden, his superior on *Harper's Monthly,* could suggest that Howells express his altruism in sketches dealing with New York City life. Showing the continued drift of his mind, his charming fantasy for the Christmas number of *Harper's* in 1890 concerned an earthly paradise called the Synthesized Sympathies of Altruria. While Twain was concluding that selfishness weighed down every man, Howells was swept up by the "spirit of altruism into which the world seemed about to enter on its orbit as it swings through clouds of star-dust" (to echo the sanguine speaker before Rose Dutcher's class of 189-).[19]

[17]I have not seen these publications. Longley described them in the *Altruist,* XXVI (April, 1894), 15 and (August, 1894), 30; XXVII (February, 1897), 7. A sketch of McLain is in his *History of Putnam County, Tennessee* (Cookeville, Tennessee: Quimby Dyer & Co., 1925), pp. 75, 152. More on the Colorado *Altrurian* can be found in William A. Hinds, *American Communities and Co-operative Colonies* (Chicago: Kerr, 1908), pp. 500-04, and Ernest S. Wooster, *Communities of the Past and Present* (Newllano, Louisiana, 1924), pp. 61-62.

[18]Parsons, "The Philosophy of Mutualism," *Arena,* IX (May 1894), 783-815. Cuppy's *Altruistic Review,* II (June, 1894), 296-97, ran a digest of Parsons' essay.

[19]Letter from Alden in Houghton Library, Harvard University; Mildred Howells, *Life in Letters of Howells* (New York: Doubleday Doran, 1928), I, 148-49; "Editor's

Where or when Howells may have come to altruism is not so crucial as why. It is well known that in 1886 or 1887 his cheerful liberalism flared into the burning belief that the United States had lost the path of justice. His novels spoke his doubts. *Annie Kilburn* (1889) repeated the prevalent distrust of private charity. In his inventory of remedies in *A Hazard of New Fortunes* (1890) he divided honors between the violent socialist Lindau and Christ-like Conrad Dryfoos. However, in *The Quality of Mercy* (1892) the capitalist appeared pitiable rather than sinister, and *The World of Chance* (1893) weighed radicalisms with more of the wariness than the bitterness which were both implicit in the title. His personal letters and essays confirmed the fact that he rested uneasily in any leftist berth. Tolstoy's Christian passivism swayed him powerfully yet not unreservedly. Edward Bellamy's Nationalism or Populism attracted him only for a while. He was constrained to make up his own formula and to stop at general, millenarian terms.

Unbaffled in literary ways, Howells found a new angle in utopian fiction. He avoided describing his perfect country directly. Rather, one of its citizens toured the United States and judged its culture by standards that emerged piecemeal. As he saw it, our land had turned into a businessman's country with a solidifying class structure while in Altruria, one gathered, glorious progress had ensued after the state gradually took over economic activity. The visitor from the ideal, whose best listeners were a Yankee farm family and a banker, credited the advance to reasonable individuals and not to unionized workers who had trusted the strike over the ballot. The motive strength of the correct way had welled from the "divine rapture of self-sacrifice." Dissolving the encrusted past, altruism lent a unifying name and spirit to Aristides Homos' happy land. Now each citizen "dedicated himself, in some special way, to the general good."[20]

A controlling influence on *A Traveler from Altruria* has been claimed for various thinkers. Howells himself slyly made an antagonist accuse Homos of borrowing widely and freely. All these hints are sound. Howells tried to blend the best of the past and the present into a modern alternative. Although more radical he was as eclectic as Cuppy. He drew upon his childhood to give his utopia the easy simplicity of pre-industrial days in Ohio. He drew upon the reading of a cultured man, even working in his shallow knowledge of Hellenic virtues.[21] He drew upon the latest news

Study," *Harper's Monthly,* LXXXII (December, 1890), 152 and LXXXIV (December, 1891), 153; Hamlin Garland, *Rose of Dutcher's Coolly* (New York: Harper and Brothers, Publishers, 1895), p. 123.

[20] *A Traveler from Altruria* (New York: Harper, 1895), pp. 87, 160, 185, 272, 310.

[21] *Ibid.,* pp. 283-84; "Letters of an Altrurian Traveller," *Cosmopolitan,* XVI (December, 1893), 232. Altrurian architecture followed the Greek simplicity which Homos admired at the Chicago Exposition of 1893. Homos was perhaps named after Aristides the Just.

about Australia and New Zealand where voters had approved economic controls: both in location and public policy the two Pacific democracies were closest to Altruria.[22] These varied debts betray that Howells, like others, made altruism the carryall for a wide assortment of notions on improving man's lot.

Yet his philosophy had a base. It rested on the teachings of Christ, learned in Howells' boyhood and revitalized for him by Tolstoy's touch. Many times Homos pointed out, ". . . we believe ourselves the true followers of Christ, whose doctrines we seek to make our life as He made it His." When the Altrurians of California hailed Howells as the new prophet, he protested that his principles "were all read out of the New Testament." Somewhat unresponsive for his day to talk about natural law, he helped to lift altruism out of the grasp of Comte and Spencer and into the arms of ethical religion. Revealingly, he wrote in 1890 to his father, "The Christian Socialists are more to my mind than the Nationalists; but . . . have loaded up with the creed of the church, the very terms of which revolt me."[23] Deeply devout but chary of theology, receptive to economic determinism but too gentle to advise class war, encouraged by ballotbox victories but cynical about our major parties, alive to democratic rationalism in man's past but baffled by the choices of his own day, Howells arrived at altruism. It stood for his faith and his plight.

With his help, altruism became a banner for anti-Marxist dreamers. John Brisben Walker, who had lured Howells to the *Cosmopolitan* for a while, described in his magazine an Altruria at the headwaters of the Congo. Here too the issue had been drawn between selfishness and Christ's teachings; industrialists had led in seeing that politics and religion should conjoin, "that the highest political economy was to take care of one's neighbour."[24] Although much less prominent than Howells' and Walker's writings for the bustling *Cosmopolitan,* businessman Titus K. Smith's efforts showed even

[22]"Letters of an Altrurian Traveller," *Cosmopolitan,* XVII (September, 1894), 612; *Through the Eye of the Needle* (New York: Harper and Brothers, Publishers, 1907), pp. 132-33, 196; "The Worst of Being Poor," *Harper's Weekly,* XLVI (March 1, 1902), 261; "Editor's Easy Chair," *Harper's Monthly,* CXIV (January, 1907), 320. For American interest in Australia after 1890 see Josiah Royce, "Impressions of Australia," *Scribner's,* IX (January, 1891), 75-87, and George R. Parkin, "The Anglo-Saxon in the Southern Hemisphere," *Century*, n.s., XIX (February, 1891), 607-13. Interest of reformers in the Pacific democracies continued, as in "Happy New Zealand," *American Fabian,* II (May, 1896), 2-4, and IV (May, 1898), 7. The *Nation,* LXIII (September 17, 1896), 206-07, sneeringly declared that American Populists were "politically Australians." It is hard to believe that the similarity between the names of Altruria and Australia was a chance one.

[23]*Altrurian* (Calif.), I (January 21, 1895), 4; *Life in Letters of Howells,* II, 3; *A Traveler from Altruria,* pp. 48, 160-61, 256-57, 294-99, 302-04.

[24]Sir Robert Harton, pseud., "The Discovery of Altruria," *Cosmopolitan,* XX (November 1895), 85-93. The next month "A Brief History of Altruria" began and ran until March, 1896. That the author was Walker was shown in his letter to Howells dated October 29, 1895, now in Houghton Library, Harvard University.

more neatly altruism's catchiness. In a pamphlet of 1889 Smith had settled on Brotherhood Co-Partnership as the motto for a mixed program, but in 1895 he called his ideal community Altruria. This mythical Iowa town had tied municipal ownership of utilities to producer and consumer cooperatives. While it respected technology, its spiritual dynamos ran on social Christianity.[25] Alcanoan Grigsby, a leader of the Kansas cooperative movement, let a still stronger delight in gadgets almost turn his *Nequa* (1900) into science fiction. However, his mechanized Altruria lived by an ethereal code—the summit of moral evolution—that matched the message of Jesus.[26] If none of these later Altrurias was as famous as Howells' none was as ably done. Besides, patterns of reform were changing.

Meanwhile, during the final wave of radical colonies, some real-life tries imitated these dreamings. Longley, who never gave up himself, reported on faint stirrings in Grand Blanc, Michigan and Madison, Wisconsin.[27] Much more dramatic was the founding in October, 1894 of Altruria near Santa Rosa, California. This small settlement and its newspaper openly borrowed their name from Howells. Although guided by a Unitarian minister, the venture essayed a practical movement in fraternity and placed social gains ahead of dogma. It expressly ignored "all petty sectarian issues in religion." Its weekly *Altrurian* echoed the expansive tone of the group in a subhead of "New Thoughts, New Motives, New Aims, New Deeds." The colonists, sanguine and uneccentric, had support from labor groups as well as a string of local clubs. Nevertheless, in the summer of 1895 they succumbed to the usual difficulties of such experiments.[28] Howells had sent a generous check but had frankly advised "the long way, the way through a change in the thinking and feeling of the whole community."[29] He sensed rightly the strength of the laissez-faire rationale.

Yet he had helped make altruism an attractive front for reform groups trying to set a practical example. It covered forays more cautious than those of Bellamy's Nationalist crusade, which pretty well collapsed after the 1892 election. There was an Altruria Co-Operative Union of Oakland, California which, while opposing separate settlements, hoped to dot the

[25]Smith, *Altruria* (New York: Altruria Publishing Company, 1895). Smith had printed privately earlier his *The Allegion, or New World Religion;* it mixed eighteenth-century rationalism with "allegiance to God and fellowman."

[26]Jack Adams, pseud., *Nequa, or The Problem of the Ages* (Topeka, Kansas: Equity Publishing Co.), pp. 125-26, 359.

[27]*Altruist,* XXVI (April, June 1894), 14, 22, and XXVIII (December 1896), 46.

[28]*Altrurian,* I (March 11, 1895), 1 and (March 25, 1895), 1; Edward B. Payne, "Altruria," *American Magazine of Civics,* VI (February 1895), 168-71; Morrison I. Swift, "Altruria in California," *Overland Monthly,* n.s., XXIX (June 1897), 643-45; "Failure of the Altrurian Colony," New York *Times,* March 3, 1896, p. 6. Robert V. Hine's *California's Utopian Colonies* (San Marino: Huntington Library, 1953), pp. 101-13, is very useful.

[29]*Altrurian,* I (January 21, 1895), 4.

west coast with economic combines dedicated to justice and mutual action. Likewise, a cooperative in Pennsylvania adopted almost in full the articles of the abortive colony. In the east was an Altrurian League of New York City that joined the American Fabians before long and an Altrurian Society in Boston that followed the pastor of a labor church.[30] Finally, in 1900 an Association of Altruists organized in Moorstown, New Jersey to work toward starting industrial and farming communities that would drop competitive methods for a more orderly system.[31] We must suspect that other such projects flickered up. All of them have disappeared, for they built on shifting ground. The main cooperative movement shed any larger radicalism long ago.

After 1900 Progressives and Debs' Socialists played down the appeal to ethical schemes. Attention shifted from the nature of man's motives to rattles in the social engine. This switch was slow and incomplete, however. The legions who read Jack London's *The Sea-Wolf* heard Larsen and an intellectual debate altruism with Spencer's *Data of Ethics* as the text. A "sanely" radical magazine that searched for readers willing to mull over such departures as abolishing prisons or liberalizing the marriage ties thought *Altruria* a promising title.[32] The two years of its career partly coincided with Howells' patching together of *Through the Eye of the Needle* (1907). This volume of letters from Altruria by Homos' American bride stressed again the shunning of class hatred and repeated that utopia "literally" followed Christ's self-sacrificing love.[33] In ethical debates, amateur and professional, altruism still had defenders.[34] The Altrui Club of Jefferson Park, near Chicago, was buzzing between 1898 and 1916 with spiritual uplift for women of leisure. It merged in 1917 with the national Altrusa, whose code says that "Altrusa in the very derivation of her name is committed to the philosophy of unselfishness." From Jack London to women's clubs is a shaky span, but we can see why, as late as 1909, someone could single out altruism as the "word at present pronounced with most reverence among most intelli-

[30]*Altrurian,* I (March 18, 1895; June 1895), 1; *American Fabian,* I (April-June 1895), 5 and III (June 1897), 10; letter to New York *Daily Tribune,* June 7, 1895, p. 6.

[31]Alexander Kent, *Cooperative Communities in the United States,* p. 635, in *Bulletin of the Department of Labor,* No. 35 (July 1901).

[32]London, *The Sea-Wolf* (New York: Macmillan Co., 1904), pp. 80-81. In *An Altruist* (1897) Louise de la Ramée ("Ouida") let her British protagonist win a desirable girl and some of the reader's respect. The magazine *Altruria* (1906-08) was edited by W. J. Robinson, an M.D., and was presented as a successor to the free-thinking *Twentieth Century,* which had last appeared in June, 1898.

[33]Howells, *Through the Eye of the Needle,* pp. 151, 176, 186, 205.

[34]Anna M. McGinley, *The Profit of Love* (New York: Longmans, Green and Co., 1907); Ray M. McConnell, *The Duty of Altruism* (New York: Macmillan Co., 1910); George Herbert Palmer, *Altruism: Its Nature and Varieties* (New York: Charles Scribner's Sons, 1919); James F. Morton, Jr., "Ethics or No Ethics—Mr. Horr's Criticisms," *Altruria,* III (February 1908), 6-8.

gent and idealistic folk."[35] The other-regarding impulse has not died since then. Altruism, used casually rather than centrally, is a familiar word today.

Still, the new century's leaders had not found it sturdy enough. From the very first of his crucial career, John Dewey scored any facile line between egoism and altruism, and others who had strongly social values, like influential Charles Cooley, concluded that altruism was too inexact for practical jobs.[36] A different sign of the times rose with the *Egoist,* started in England in 1914 by an avant garde reinforced with Americans. Although primarily passionate about experimental poetry the *Egoist,* praising Max Stirner loudly, warned that universal brotherhood really meant universal monotony. Altruism slipped from the main current. Sad to say, a fuzzily leftist faith healer in Birmingham, Alabama invented an Altrurian Society whose message went over the telephone for one dollar a treatment. More respectable was the motive behind *Altrurian Farms* (1931), an antidote for hatreds breeding in the Great Depression. Its author concocted a South American settlement where, inspired by neighborly religion, corporation methods guided giant cooperatives.[37] These altruisms won little fame. Within the past ten years the most eminent Pitirim A. Sorokin has refurbished the altruism-egoism dichotomy to preach the desperate need for Christian service. Despairing of militant and less fundamental creeds, he works to change man's basic values and has set up the Harvard Research Center in Altruistic Integration and Creativity. For those who cannot rest in any of the major certainties altruism remains a little noticed answer.

Of course, to predict that we have seen the last of altruism as a persuasive movement is no less fruitless than to try to pin down its workings too minutely. Drawing on Comte's and Spencer's prestige it spread rapidly after 1880, offering a handy name for the eternal drive to unify the heart and head. It benefited further from the growing heed to Mill's call for the greatest happiness of the greatest number. During the ferment of the 1890's it had its best days. Then it was not so much rejected as dissipated—leaving a term for experts in ethics to weigh, and to choose perhaps over sympathy or benevolence. Outside of ethics, its course for a while moved di-

[35]Anna B. McGill, "Altruism as an Ideal of Culture," *South Atlantic Quarterly,* VIII (July 1909), 260-66. Although hostile, M. Grier Kidder, "Altruism," *Overland Monthly,* n.s., LXI (February, 1913), 184-89, granted altruism's wide currency. Annual announcements of the Altrui Club are in the Chicago Public Library.

[36]Dewey, *Psychology* (New York: Harper & Brothers, Publishers, 1886), pp. 326-27; Dewey and James H. Tufts, *Ethics* (New York: Henry Holt and Co., 1908), pp. 384-91; Cooley, *Human Nature and the Social Order* (New York: Charles Scribner's Sons, 1902), p. 346.

[37]Hilliard Wilkins, *Altrurian Farms* (Washington, D. C.: Employment Extension Society). Joseph F. Stanley's book of verse, *The Altruist* (Boston: Richard Badger, 1920), is negligible. An echo of the *Egoist's* view appears in Karl Ettli .ger, *Altruism; a Satire,* pp. 68-76 in Frank Shay and Pierre Loving, eds., *Fifty Contemporary One-Act Plays* (Cincinnati: Steward & Kidd, 1920).

rectly enough until popularity brought its evils. Altruism was then racked between those who saw it as a unique force and those who seized a newfangled title to gild a hoary idea. As a wry result both of its lures faded. Today, certainly, we do not hear of altruists fighting against communists or capitalists. Nor do they appear among the biologists and anthropologists who question the Darwinian struggle within the species. Ashley Montagu, for instance, prefers to call for "cooperation." Persons who urge sacrifice for others are still around, but few feel a special urgency in altruism by name or hope for incantatory help from it.

It was too malleable. Too many of even its sincere prophets invented emphases that ranged from self-immolation to scientific almsgiving. In time the intellectual confusion was fatally clear. Yet its inconclusiveness had made altruism's popularity possible. Caught between the older idealism and onrushing industrial pains, some middle-class liberals who believed in moral uplift could also see the need for group welfare and concerted action. They of course abhorred Marxism. They could not agree, however, on any detailed challenge to concrete antagonists. Altruism was their lever for lifting the masses while ignoring classes. If it was unsteady, so were the hands of the men who wielded it. Slowly social Christianity absorbed altruism as American reform moved away from spiritual fervors toward political and economic carpentering. In its most active form, altruism marked an attempt to dose an era with a brew of utopianism, minor changes, and ethical law. Those who think they know a more cogent cure for the recurring problems will think of it as the name for good-willed bafflement.

Afternote

Gordon Mills, "The Symbolic Wilderness: James Fenimore Cooper and Jack London," *Nineteenth-Century Fiction*, XIII (March, 1959), 329–40, has argued that, to counter the "loss of the spiritual significance of the wilderness," London softened the escape to nature with a mild altruism. Otherwise I have noticed no serious commentary on altruism since 1956, though I have become aware that George Herbert Palmer exerted wide influence from his post at Harvard University and that he happened to be a cousin of Robert Herrick, who looked up to Palmer both as a personality and an intellect and went further than any other novelist toward echoing his school of altruism even while preferring to avoid the term itself. The disparity between the neglect of altruism and the still mounting analyses of individualism surely measures the effective prestige of the latter values and the hollowness of the calls to selfless generosity that inflate our public rhetoric.

Louis J. Budd is a Professor of English at Duke University. [This article appeared in Vol. VIII, No. 1 (Spring, 1956).]

Henry F. May

The Rebellion of the Intellectuals, 1912-1917

AS THE nineteen-twenties move from memory into history, a standard picture of the decade emerges from reminiscence and research into the textbooks. This picture is a puzzling one. The decade is still, as it was in the thirties, the last island of normalcy and isolation between wars and crises. Yet it is also, clearly, a period of major cultural revolution. Both the "revolt of the highbrows" and the "rebellion of youth," first sketched by F. L. Allen, are a standard part of our semiofficial self-picture. In response to current historical fashions and perhaps also to their own changing worries about their country, historians are giving more attention to the revolutionary aspect of this conservative decade.

Having dealt with other revolutions, historians should be able to appreciate both the importance and complexity of this one. For instance, they should be able to avoid taking to task the rebellious intellectuals of the twenties in the manner of some critics of the forties. The spokesmen of a revolution are not, after all, its sole cause, and a healthy regime is seldom overthrown. Yet anybody, today, must recognize that revolutions are expensive. They may release, as this one certainly did, a burst of creative vigor; but they inevitably leave behind division, hatred, and shock. In the twenties, for instance, beliefs and customs that still commanded the deepest loyalties of one part of the population became to another group a dead and repressive Genteel Tradition, to be ceremonially flouted whenever possible. Suspicions dating from this cultural cleavage still poison the air. The historian must hope that analysis of the revolution and its causes can eventually help a little to clear away some of the resentment.

Starting backward, as historians must, we arrive immediately at the First World War, and there many have stopped. It is obvious that America's first major venture into world tragedy, with its rapid cycle of national exaltation, exhaustion, and revulsion played a very large part in the emotional life of the postwar rebels. By contrast with 1918 or 1919 or even 1925, hundreds of autobiographies paint the prewar period as a time of unity, moderation, progress, and sheltered childhood.

Yet we all know that postwar reminiscence, whether of the old plantation or the old literary culture, is a dubious guide for history. Those who have looked even briefly at the social and literary criticism of the prewar years know that the period 1912-1917[1] was itself, for some, a time of doubt and fragmentation, of upheaval in ideas, of the disintegration of tradition—in other words it was a pre-revolutionary or early revolutionary period. Nearly every phenomenon of the twenties from Freudianism to expatriation or the abandonment of politics was present before the war, on a smaller scale and with certain differences. If we can recapture any of the meaning or content of this prewar ferment, we may be able to understand better in what sense the revolution of the twenties was and was not postwar. In this way we may even get a few suggestions as to the perennially baffling problem of the relation between ideas and events.

In an essay published in 1913 George Santayana made an attempt to catch and pin down on paper "The Intellectual Temper of the Age." To do this for one's own time is one of the hardest tasks a writer can undertake, yet for anybody who has been for a while immersed in the records of that period it is astonishing how well this brilliant essay seems to order and illuminate the times. To Santayana it seemed that "the civilisation characteristic of Christendom has not disappeared, yet another civilisation has begun to take its place."[2] In the resulting age of confusion and transition, men were giving up the search for lasting values and firm intellectual conclusions. Instead of these, they were placing a premium on sheer vitality, on movement, change, and emotion. According to Santayana, who sometimes enjoyed but did not admire this taste, the result was that in thought and art, his generation was "in full career toward disintegration."[3]

Whether or not one shares Santayana's cool disapproval of the tendencies of his day, the vitalist spirit he describes stares out from the sources. One

[1]Through this essay I treat this period as one instead of dividing it in August, 1914. The outbreak of the war in Europe shocked American intellectuals but did not immediately become their main preoccupation. Until about the winter of 1916, radical and progressive politics, together with the new literary and philosophical tendencies, get more space than the war in the liberal and literary periodicals.

[2]George Santayana, *Winds of Doctrine* (London and New York: Charles Scribner's Sons, 1913), p. 1.

[3]*Ibid.*, p. 10.

recognizes on all sides its gaiety, its irresponsibility, its love of change, and also its contempt for reason. And it does not take much knowledge of American intellectual history to know that this spirit meant trouble. For a century and a half the dominant ideas in the national faith had been a confidence in secure moral values and a belief in progress. These two commitments had often been in conflict and formed at best a somewhat unstable compound. Now both at once were brought under devastating attack.

If one starts, as Santayana does, with philosophy, the tendencies he describes emerge very clearly. The young intellectuals of America were still most widely influenced by pragmatism, by what Morton G. White has called the revolt against formalism. Experience and movement were reality; potentiality more important than actuality. Dewey's program for intelligence remaking both the world and itself probably attracted the largest number of conscious disciples, some of them, like Randolph Bourne, soon to break away in a more emotionally satisfying direction. But it may well be that the influence of James, with his catholic and dangerous acceptance of the irrational, personal, and mysterious went deeper in a generation nourished on idealism. Emerson, universally read though misunderstood and underrated, and Whitman, the sole American patron of some of the rebels, as well as the German idealists casually studied in college courses, must have prepared them for a philosophy of intuition. Whatever the reason, it was the destructive elements in pragmatism that were the most influential. The avant-garde of 1912-17, the aggressive young innovators, were perfectly willing to see all of life as an experiment. But their purpose in experimenting was rather to express themselves and experience emotion than to solve problems in a disciplined manner.

Those who were sensitive to Atlantic breezes felt most keenly the swelling winds of antirationalism, which had been gathering force for a long time. Nietzsche, for long known vaguely by the American public as an Anti-christ, was becoming a major prophet. The most vigorous, though not the most accurate, of his American interpreters was H. L. Mencken, who in a widely read and widely praised book published first in 1908 and again in 1913 used the German prophet to belabor religion, women, and, most roughly of all, democracy in his already familiar manner.[4] But the most fashionable of Europeans was the still living and lecturing Henri Bergson, who pushed the current tendency to an extreme, contending that reality, being in constant flux and change, is only distorted by efforts to think about it and must be apprehended through intuition. His was not the only, but it was

[4]Henry L. Mencken, *The Philosophy of Friedrich Nietzsche* (Boston: Luce and Co., 1918).

probably the dominant direction in which philosophy was moving in 1913, and there is plenty of evidence that he was extraordinarily attractive to up-to-date American intellectuals. Irving Babbitt, already an alarmed defender of traditional values, saw the rise of Bergsonism as the culmination of a long, deplorable irrationalist trend, and found it in 1912 "allied with all that is violent and extreme in contemporary life from syndicalism to 'futurist' painting."[5]

Psychology, as well as philosophy, was dealing heavy blows to dominant assumptions and beliefs. From the time of Freud's famous trip to Clark University in 1908, the Viennese theories cropped up in popular magazines and political treatises as well as learned journals. Whether or not, as his supporters claim, Freud is to be regarded as himself a brave and determined champion of reason, the first impact of his doctrines in the United States seemed to confirm and deepen the hedonism, emotionalism, and egocentricity that were beginning to spread so widely.[6] On the other hand, Behaviorism, a movement launched in its most dogmatic form by John B. Watson in 1912, had to wait for its vogue until after the war.[7] Its extreme practicalism, its rejection not only of reason but of consciousness, its suspicion of emotion, did not fit the tastes of the prewar rebels.

It does not need demonstrating that restless and vigorous innovation in the graphic arts got its American start before the war. Two major tendencies already dazzled the intellectuals and startled the public. One was apparently native, the harsh and sometimes violent Ash Can realism of Sloan, Bellows and the *Masses* cartoons. The other was imported from Paris, and consisted of a kaleidoscopic series of schools of experiment in form and technique. Commenting on "Current Impressionism," a term already well out of date but helpful as a catch-all, Louis Weinberg extended his observations from and beyond contemporary art:

Impressionism as a technique is a means of recording the transitory nature of phenomena and the fluidity of motion. As a principle it is based on a philosophy of change. . . .

[5]Irving Babbitt, "Bergson and Rousseau," *Nation,* November 14, 1912, p. 455. One of the more influential of the considerable number of books on Bergson appearing in these years was H. M. Kallen, *William James and Henri Bergson* (Chicago: University of Chicago Press, 1914). There is a very large volume of periodical discussion from 1911.

[6]For a helpful review see Frederick J. Hoffman, *Freudianism and the Literary Mind* (Baton Rouge, La.: Louisiana State University Press, 1945). The early impact of Freud and many other foreign influences is clearly recorded in the works of Floyd Dell, one of Freud's important American exponents. Dell deals most specifically with these influences in his retrospective *Intellectual Vagabondage* (New York: George H. Doran Co., 1926).

[7]See Lucille C. Birnbaum, "Behaviorism in the 1920's," *American Quarterly, VII* (1955), 15-30, esp. p. 20.

But this is not alone a description of the art of our times. It is the very essence of our lives.[8]

Wherever the impressionist or vitalist tendency arose, it was expressed most frequently and characteristically not in painting or philosophy, but in politics and literature. These are the forms in which most American cultural change has been recorded, and it is to them that we must turn for a slightly closer look at prewar tendencies. Santayana's brilliant summary suggests that in politics alone the current drift toward fragmentation and chaos may have reversed itself in the constructive and integrating (though to Santayana most uncongenial) movement towards collectivism.[9] In this one opinion, regarding an area which concerned him little, I think Santayana missed the current drift and underrated the force of his own generalization. It is true that progressivism, optimistic, gradual, and in some forms mildly collectivist, was the officially dominant ideology; and that socialism was a swelling movement on the left that seemed to many sober Americans to possess the future. Yet both these political tendencies were in the early teens already under devastating attack, and from much the same irrationalist quarter.

Progressivism in all its varieties took for granted one or both of the two fundamental assumptions which had so far underlain the whole American political tradition. One of these was that we possess secure criteria by which we can judge our political achievement, the other that human beings are able consciously to remold their environment. Now both of these basic assumptions were being seriously shaken by new doctrines that had penetrated the house of progressivism itself.

Recent studies have shown that moral standards of a highly traditional sort motivated a great many of the prewar progressives. Truth and falsehood, good and evil, stand out in nearly all the speeches of Theodore Roosevelt and Wilson and good men threw out bad in most American cities. These venerable distinctions were the first to go; the younger progressive intellectuals, nourished on Dewey and H. G. Wells, were quite willing to throw out moral categories and rely on the shaping intelligence. On a popular level Lincoln Steffens spread the picture of the good boss and the honest crook. James Harvey Robinson, speaking for the main organ of the pragmatic progressives, lumped together as obsolete the ideals of "sound doctrine, consistency, fidelity to conscience, eternal verities, immutable human nature, and the imprescriptable rights of man."[10]

With these went the state and law, the traditional locus and method of

[8]Louis Weinberg, "Current Impressionism," *New Republic,* March 6, 1915, pp. 124-25.
[9]George Santayana, *Winds of Doctrine,* p. 10.
[10]James H. Robinson, "A Journal of Opinion," *New Republic,* May 8, 1915, pp. 9-10.

American reform. Many of the ablest political theorists of various schools, led by the brilliant Harold Laski, were redefining the state almost out of existence. To some it was a congeries of associations, to others the tool of a class, to still others the expression of the wish of those at present in authority. Its acts were no more final and deserved no greater obedience than those of other human groups, and it was less likely than many to be rationally motivated. Similarly, law, to the followers of the French positivist Leon Duguit or the American Roscoe Pound was no longer either the embodiment of a principle nor the command of a sovereign, but the complex resultant of social forces, prevailing opinion, and judicial will.

There remained the conscious intelligence, remolding the goals of action together with its methods. This was a moving conception, and a sufficient loyalty for many in this generation. Yet this too was seriously menaced by ideas that were attractive to the youngest generation of progressives. From the new and flourishing disciplines of sociology, anthropology and social psychology came an increasingly fashionable emphasis on custom and group emotion. It was sometimes hard to see what function this newest tendency left for intelligence and purpose.[11]

Walter Lippmann's two prewar studies, *A Preface to Politics* (1913) and *Drift and Mastery* (1914) bring together the pragmatist attack on tradition and the implicit Freudian attack on pragmatism. Appealing for a radically instrumental state, he denounces the "routineers" who rely on political machinery, law, and conventional morality. His fellow progressives seem to draw most of his fire for their naïve adherence to literal numerical democracy and narrow utilitarian goals. What is needed in politics is passion and creative emotion, still of course somehow constructively channeled and used by the far-seeing for purposes which will transcend woman suffrage or the eight-hour day.

> . . . the goal of action is in its final analysis aesthetic and not moral—a quality of feeling instead of conformity to rule.[12]

This formulation seems to me far closer to the view of postwar literary intellectuals than to that of the progressive standard-bearers. And the sources are explicit. Lippmann's friend Graham Wallas, the British author of *Human Nature in Politics*[13] had opened the eyes of his Harvard seminar to political psychology. Steffens had helped to guide Lippmann and so, in a negative direction, had his brief experience with municipal socialism in

[11]An account of all these tendencies in prewar thought, together with a vast bibliography, can be found in two helpful summaries. These are W. Y. Elliott, *The Pragmatic Revolt in Politics* (New York: The Macmillan Company, 1928) and C. E. Merriam and H. E. Barnes, eds., *A History of Political Theories, Recent Times* (New York: The Macmillan Company, 1924).

[12]Walter Lippmann, *A Preface to Politics* (New York: M. Kennerley, 1913), p. 200.

[13]London: A. Constable and Co., 1908.

Schenectady. But beyond these immediate guides one finds recurring references to James, Nietzsche and Bergson and frequent, specific acknowledgment of the work of Freud.[14]

All these new insights enriched the social sciences, and for many they doubtless furnished in practice new sources of power and freedom. Traditional progressivism, with its facile assumptions and sometimes shallow purposes needed—and for that matter still needs—rethinking. Yet much had been accomplished under the auspices of ideas that were beginning to seem stale and boring. And the new beliefs that buzzed and swarmed through the immediate postwar years were not easy to introduce into the progressive hive. To combine Lippmann or Laski with Wilson was, and soon proved to be, as difficult as to match Bergson and Nietzsche with Lyman Abbott.

It is tempting to wonder whether the actual practical difficulties of progressivism from about 1914 to 1917 were not related in part to confusion of purposes and motives. It is true at least that the Wilsonian impetus began to bog down in these years. Already one finds in the up-to-the-minute *New Republic* troubled editorials that ask the common postwar question: what has happened to the progressives?[15]

On the far left much the same process was taking place, whether one labels it fertilization or disintegration or both. Not the Marxian dialectic, but the Bergsonian and mystical syndicalism of Sorel or the anarchism of Max Stirner or Emma Goldman seemed most exciting to the younger radical intellectuals.[16] Not the earnest socialism of Milwaukee or Schenectady, with its respectability and its reliance on the discredited machinery of the state, but the romantic activism of the I.W.W. captured the emotions of the sympathizers. One of America's waves of labor violence, running through the Northwest, Colorado, West Virginia and other centers of direct action, reflecting the primitive brutality of employers' methods in the same areas, aroused the generous emotions and seemed to some to make political action irrelevant. The climax came in 1912 at Lawrence and in 1913 at Paterson, when the I.W.W. penetrated the East and the writers and artists went to its aid, when Bill Haywood was a Greenwich Village social lion and John Reed staged an immense pageant in Madison Square Garden with the letters I.W.W. flaming from the roof in red electric signs ten feet high. Even Lippmann, viewing radicalism from the outside, approved the I.W.W. rather

[14] *e.g.*, Walter Lippmann, *Drift and Mastery* (New York: M. Kennerley, 1914), pp. 249, 274.

[15] *e.g.*, January 16, 1915, pp. 6-8; November 6, 1915, p. 1; June 17, 1916, pp. 159-61; July 1, 1916, pp. 211-13.

[16] See Daniel Bell, "Marxian Socialism in the United States," in D. D. Egbert and Stow Persons, eds., *Socialism and American Life* (Princeton, N. J.: Princeton University Press, 1952), I, 289-90.

than the Socialist Party as less formalist and more in possession of the kind of emotional force that needed only to be constructively channeled.[17]

Naturally, when Max Eastman, a young man of impeccable ministerial stock, joined the Socialist Party, he chose the left wing rather than the gradualists. Under Eastman's editorship the *Masses,* focus of so much later radical nostalgia, became perhaps even more clearly than the sober *New Republic* the organ of youth. Publishing the magnificent and not always political cartoons of Sloan and Bellows, an occasional Picasso drawing, stories by Sherwood Anderson, and reporting by Reed, it fought for the new literature and the new sexual morality as well as the social revolution. The *Masses* was rich in humor and human emotion—qualities often enough lacking on the far left—and practically negligible in social program. Smashing idols was, in these years as after the war, a flourishing business, while Socialism as a political movement was already losing momentum in 1914-16.[18]

More spectacularly than anywhere else, the new spirit of 1910 or 1912 to 1917 was reflected in a literary renaissance. The story of this sudden creative outburst has often been told, and only two points need making for our present purpose. One of these is that literary departures in the prewar years were closely related to contemporary movements in other fields of thought, the other that prewar writing contains in embryo nearly all the developments of the twenties.

Here too the stimulus came in large part from abroad. Young Americans, brought up on Matthew Arnold and Thackeray, were following before he gave it the advice of Yeats at the *Poetry* dinner in 1912 to forget London and look to Paris for all that was excellent.[19] In Kroch's bookstore in Chicago, in the translations issued by a series of daring new publishers, in the eager if undiscriminating reviews by the young critics, this generation of rebels was nourished on a whole series of movements extending over the last generation in Europe. All the writers that had for so long been belaboring the European bourgeoisie—French symbolists and decadents and naturalists, Scandinavian pessimists and social critics, Russian apostles of mysticism and emotion; even from England D. H. Lawrence as well as Shaw, suddenly began to penetrate the American barrier. What this series of reagents produced was a series of explosions, and what exploded was more than the

[17]Walter Lippmann, *Preface to Politics,* pp. 277-78.
[18]See David L. Shannon, *The Socialist Party of America, A History* (New York: The Macmillan Company, 1955). As Shannon and other historians of socialism have pointed out, the apparent revival of the Socialist Party in the big Debs vote of 1920 is misleading. It belongs in the category of protest rather than party success.
[19]Harriet Monroe, *A Poet's Life* (New York: The Macmillan Company, 1938), p. 337.

genteel tradition in literature, more than conventional moral categories. With the conventions of literary form and language went the underlying assumptions about thought and communication. Randolph Bourne perhaps described this grand explosion better than he realized in June, 1917:

> What becomes more and more apparent to the readers of Dostoevsky, however, is his superb modern healthiness. He is healthy because he has no sense of any dividing line between the normal and the abnormal, or even between the sane and the insane.[20]

When Harriet Monroe, full of civic feeling as well as poetic zeal, founded *Poetry* in 1912 she seemed to tap immediately a rich underground gusher of poetic impulse. Soon the flood of experiment became too thick and varied even for *Poetry* to contain and overflowed into *Others* and the *Little Review.* As in the visual arts, a rapid series of schools succeeded each other, but perhaps the literary movement most characteristic of the period, and most obviously related to its philosophic tendencies was that of the Imagists, with its manifestoes in favor of complete freedom, concentration on the fleeting and immediate image for its own sake, and refusal to assign an image any "external" meaning or reference. Already before the war the revolution in the use of language was under way toward its ultimate destinations; Joyce was being published in the London *Egoist* and Gertrude Stein, settled in Paris, had developed her opinions and her characteristic style.

It would be misleading to divide this literary outpouring into precise categories, yet one can find suggestions of two emergent ways of thinking and feeling among writers. One group demanded freedom from European forms, confidence in emotion and spontaneity, and in general preached democratic optimism in the Whitman tradition. The other, more disciplined but also more deeply rebellious against American culture, called for concentration, rejection of irrelevant moral and political purposes, and the development of conscious intellectual aristocracy.

Obviously the former, democratic and optimist group is more distant than the other from postwar directions. This is the tendency one associates particularly with the sudden and brief Chicago Renaissance, with Sandburg and Lindsay and Miss Monroe, though it is found also in other areas, for instance in the organized and vigorous character of what Francis Hackett labeled and dated forever as Miss Amy Lowell's "Votes for Poetry movement."[21] Yet even the most exuberant of the Chicago poets were, like contemporary political radicals, destroying for the sake of redemption, like Sandburg's personified city "Shovelling, wrecking, planning, building, breaking, rebuilding."

[20]Randolph Bourne, "The Immanence of Dostoevsky," *The Dial,* LXIII (1917), 25.
[21]In the *New Republic,* November 10, 1917, p. 52.

And even in Chicago pessimistic and sceptical tendencies were also, and had long been, at work. Dreiser's not exactly rosy picture of American city life was finally finding its audience; and the small town, from E. A. Robinson's New England Tilbury town to Masters' Middlewestern Spoon River, was preparing the way for Winesburg and Gopher Prairie. In the bosom of *Poetry* magazine, at the official heart of the Chicago movement, Ezra Pound, the magazine's foreign editor, was chafing at its cover slogan, the statement of Whitman that "to have great poets there must be great audiences too." Pound preferred Dante's pronouncement that the wisest in the city is "He whom the fools hate worst" and denied that poets have any need for the rabble.

It is true that the great artist has always a great audience, even in his lifetime; but it is not the *vulgo* but the spirits of irony and of destiny and of humor, sitting with him.[22]

In that sentence lies the germ of a dozen ponderous manifestoes of the postwar Young Intellectuals. Pound stayed on *Poetry* long enough to persuade Miss Monroe to publish Eliot's "Prufrock" in 1915 and then found a refuge from uplift and Whitmanism in the *Little Review*.

In the Eastern centers of the new literary movement the mixture of optimism and nihilism, of reform and rejection was somewhat different. Harvard, which was incubating an extraordinary number of important writers, seemed to produce a strange and special mixture of ideas.[23] The dominant note in its teaching of literature was aestheticism, worship of Europe, and contempt for the native production. Irving Babbitt's vigorous attack on democratic sentimentality was already a major influence. Yet Walter Lippmann, for one, managed to combine presidency of the Harvard Socialist Club with assisting Professor Santayana. A certain survival of Emersonian and Puritan responsibility seems to have been a part of the prevalent passionate concern for literature. America might be vulgar and materialistic and nearly hopeless; if so one's duty was to search the harder for seeds of literary springtime, and literary revival would bring social regeneration as well. Like so many writers after the war, Van Wyck Brooks went to Europe to look for these seeds. He found in London in 1913-14 Ezra Pound, T. S. Eliot, John Gould Fletcher, Conrad Aiken, Elinor Wylie, Robert Frost and Walter Lippmann.[24] Across the channel he could already have run into an equally significant group of fellow-countrymen. It was in

[22]Ezra Pound, "The Audience," *Poetry, A Magazine of Verse,* V (1914-15), 30.

[23]See the following helpful autobiographies of Harvard graduates: Malcolm Cowley, *Exile's Return* (New York: W. W. Norton & Company, 1934); Harold E. Stearns, *The Street I Know* (New York: L. Furman, 1935); Van Wyck Brooks, *Scenes and Portraits* (New York: E. P. Dutton & Co., 1954).

[24]Brooks, *op. cit.,* pp. 123-48, 210 ff.

London that Brooks began to struggle seriously with the typical problem of the expatriate of the next decade: the love of European tradition and the nostalgic turning toward American vitality. He solved this problem by writing, in London in 1914, the book that most influenced the writers of the next decade, an attack on the Genteel Tradition and an appeal for a literary renaissance that seemed then, as its title implies, to mark an arrival and not just a beginning: *America's Coming-of-Age.*

From here we can see, even more clearly than Santayana could in 1913, the unrest, the disintegration of old standards, the search for vitality and movement that already was under way at that time.[25] We know, too, that what was then unrest later became cultural revolution and angry intellectual civil war. This brings us to the compelling question, what started it all? Why did this search for novelty, this gay destruction of traditional standards, occur at just this moment in the midst of an apparently placid and contented period?

This is hardly a question that can be answered with certainty. All that we know for sure is that a movement so general and noticeable in the prewar years was not started by the war. Perhaps the most obvious forces at work in early twentieth-century civilization were technological change and urban growth, but these had been at work reshaping American culture for several generations and do not afford a direct and simple explanation for the sudden restlessness of 1912-17. Moreover, an increase of mechanistic materialism rather than a new vitalism would seem a more easily understandable product of machine civilization. It may be that the prewar rebellion was in part a protest against such a long-run tendency; in 1915 the *Nation* suggested that the rising "Bergsonian school . . . owes not a little of its popularity to its expression of revolt from the dreary materialistic determinism of the closing years of the last century."[26]

One is tempted to wonder whether the new physics was at work already disintegrating the comparatively simple universe of nineteenth-century science. It seems, however, that although the Einstein revolution was being discussed before the war by American scientists and reported in the serious periodical press, it did not directly affect as yet the literary and political intellectuals to any great extent, and it was not, as it became after the war, a newspaper sensation.[27]

[25]The same traits that one finds in the ideas of the period characterize much of its social life. Ragtime and the dance craze, the furore over alleged white slave disclosures, in 1913 seem to prefigure the feverishness and the moral divisions of the postwar decade.

[26]From a review of Croly's *Progressive Democracy,* which the *Nation* associates with the Bergson influence (April 29, 1915), pp. 469-70.

[27]This impression comes from an examination of periodicals and is confirmed by an intensive though brief examination of popular scientific literature by Robert G. Sumpter.

In part the American intellectual rebellion may be considered merely a belated phase of an European antirationalist tendency. Yet it remains puzzling that Nietzsche and Dostoevsky and Baudelaire waited for their most telling American impact until they competed with Freud and Joyce. Part of the violence of the American literary and intellectual battles of the next decade arises from the fact that influences that had gradually permeated European thought presented themselves to many Americans all at once and in their extreme forms.

The time and special character of the prewar rebellion were, I believe, determined in part by the very surface placidity of the Progressive Era. Traditional American beliefs in moral certainty and inevitable progress had for some time been subjected to inner strain and external attack, yet in the prewar decade, for the last time, the official custodians of culture were able to maintain and defend a common front. Yet these almost hereditary leaders—Roosevelt and Royce and Howells in their several spheres—were growing weaker. A new generation, full of confidence and provided with leisure and libraries, was fairly literally looking for trouble. What attracts us about the standard culture of America in the early years of the century is its confident consensus, its lack of passion and violence. Passion and violence were exactly the demand of the young intellectuals of 1913 and 1914, of Lippmann and Brooks and Bourne and Pound. This was what they wanted, and this was what they got.

The war, then, was not the cause of the cultural revolution of the twenties. It played, however, the immense part that the Civil War played in the economic and political revolution of the mid-nineteenth century, speeding, widening and altering in kind a movement already under way.

The experiences of 1917-19 darkened and soured the mood of the rebels. Even at its most iconoclastic and even in those spokesmen who adopted the most pessimistic doctrines, the prewar renaissance was always exuberant. Pound, amid his fierce negations, still found it possible to make his famous and somewhat rash prophecy that the coming American Risorgimento would "make the Italian Renaissance look like a tempest in a teapot!"[28] The rejection of easy rationalism, the spurning of dull politics were to make America better and brighter. In the war and its aftermath however the rebellious generation learned something of the price of destruction and experienced personally both tragedy and (in 1919) failure. Many who had been rebellious optimists became despairing nihilists and those who had already been preaching the futility of conscious effort preached it with different emotional corollaries.

[28] Pound to Harriet Monroe, 24 September, 1914, in D. D. Paige, ed., *The Letters of Ezra Pound 1907-1941* (New York: Harcourt, Brace and Co., 1950), p. 10.

The other effect of the war was that the disintegration of traditional ideas spread far more widely among the population. Most of the prewar rebellion was confined to a small and isolated, though articulate and potentially influential, group of intellectuals. As yet the overwhelming bulk of the people took for granted the truth of the old political and moral slogans. As long as this was so rebels could be ignored or patronized; they did not tional beliefs might perhaps have been slowly adapted to new realities have to be feared and fought. Without the political events of 1917-19 traditional beliefs might perhaps have been slowly adapted to new realities out the currents of doubt and disintegration already abroad, these political events themselves might have lacked their willing and ready Cassandras.

In 1913 *Sons and Lovers, A Preface to Politics,* and *Winds of Doctrine* were published, but *Pollyanna* and *Laddie* were the best-sellers. In 1925 the best-seller list itself had to find place for *An American Tragedy.*

Afternote

The material in this article is developed and greatly expanded in my book, *The End of American Innocence* (New York: Alfred A. Knopf, 1959) and some of it is further elaborated in my pamphlet, *The Discontent of the Intellectuals: A Problem of the Twenties* (Chicago: Rand McNally, 1963).

Henry F. May is the Margaret Byrne Professor of History at the University of California, Berkeley. [This article appeared in Vol. VIII, No. 2 (Summer, 1956).]

Mulford Q. Sibley

The Traditional American Doctrine of Freedom of Thought and Speech

A GOOD case can be made for the argument that one should speak of "American *doctrines*" of freedom of thought and speech, rather than "*the* doctrine." Americans have spoken in divers tongues. Nathaniel Ward and Fisher Ames can be regarded as in the American tradition, as well as Thoreau and Justice Holmes. Even the Supreme Court, though presumably having an important hand in shaping it and playing an important role in applying it, has shown itself uncertain about the application of the "traditional American doctrine."

But assuming there is a tendency in American thought and consciousness which can be spoken of legitimately as "the American tradition" (and I believe there is), how does one go about determining it? Here it seems to me that a word of caution is in place. There is a great danger that one will read into that tradition one's own theory of liberty, with the object of supporting one's own doctrine by the authority of great names—very much as the authors of the Pentateuch attached the name of Moses to their handiwork and as some Marxists have found in Plato's dialogues many of the cardinal tenets of Marxism (Marx for them was not enough).

On the other hand, there is an equally great danger that the American tradition will be so stated that it can be used as a convenient whipping boy for those twentieth-century critics who, distressed and disturbed by the evil state of the world, believe they have found novel and regenerative principles of liberty and authority and feel the need of a flesh and blood devil whom they can attack. This is not to say that the traditional American doctrine may not need severe censure but rather to warn that it is all too easy to state and use it as certain modern critics have used the Protestant Reformation — so to distort it as to make possible and plausible attribution of all modern evils to its pernicious influence. It will be difficult to avoid these two dangers, for any historical résumé involves selection and the problem always to keep in mind is that of selecting and emphasizing those elements of American thought which in fact seem to have been uppermost in what is called the American tradition.

How are we to distinguish between the "traditional American doctrine of freedom of thought and speech" and other facets of the problem of liberty? Freedom is protean and a theory of liberty must purport to include all its forms. Here, however, we are concerned with what might be called the American tradition of *spiritual* freedom, as contrasted, for example, with economic freedom. Although we are to emphasize the former, the latter must be kept constantly in mind; for though man is body and soul, the two are not separable in any real sense. If they were indeed separable, the problem of liberty of speech and thought could hardly arise, religion and politics could in fact be kept apart, and the seemingly eternal questions of Church and State would be with us no more.

Taking spiritual freedom, therefore, as our primary problem, our text is the First Amendment to the Constitution of the United States, whose familiar words are: "Congress shall make no law respecting an establishment of religion, or prohibiting the free exercise thereof; or abridging the freedom of speech, or of the press; or the right of the people peaceably to assemble, and to petition the Government for a redress of grievances." These words are to be taken, not as a text for a constitutional law disquisition, primarily, but rather are to be examined in the context of predominant emphases in American political philosophy.

There are, it seems to me, four major elements in the traditional American doctrine: an accent on the individual; a strong "natural law" tradition which denies any necessary equation between collective decisions and the ethically right; a distrust of external constraint in matters of belief; and an emphasis on contingency in human affairs, both individual and collective. It seems hardly necessary to point out that these elements are closely interrelated; that in discussing them one should always keep in mind the distinction and often contradiction between theory and practice; and that there are other, and presumably minor, emphases in American thought and practice.

I

American history and political thought have yet to develop (at least since the seventeenth century) any predominant comprehensive theory of life and freedom which does not place the individual at the center of things. And it is the individual conceived as one for whom society and government are at best conveniences and not related organically to him as extensions and conditions of his personality. It is the individual pitted *against* society; it is usually governmental encroachments *on* an individual liberty, which tends often to be conceived as apart from social obligation. Where social obligation *is* recognized — as it must be and has been — it is as a kind of unwilling concession to the inevitable.

"The rights of individuals," said Elbridge Gerry in opposing the ratification of the Constitution, "ought to be the primary object of all government, and cannot be too securely guarded by the most explicit declarations in their favor . . ."[1] And while his view was extreme, the essentially anarchic position of Thoreau has been a prominent thread in the American tradition. "There will never be a really free and enlightened State," he maintained, "until the State comes to recognize the individual as a higher and independent power, from which all its own power and authority are derived, and treats him accordingly."[2]

But though this quasi-anarchic position should be clearly recognized, one must not forget that there have been episodes and tendencies in American history and thought when accent on the individual seemed to give way to sweeping assertions of authority in the spiritual realm. The Alien and Sedition Laws of 1798 fall into this category, as well as many enactments during World War I and its aftermath. Others are legion: post office censorship; most motion pic-

[1] *Observations on the New Constitution* (1788).
[2] "Civil Disobedience."

ture censorship, both official and unofficial; the denial during World War II of the right to practice law to a brilliant young law graduate (a denial sustained by the Supreme Court) because he professed belief in a literal interpretation of the Sermon on the Mount; the attempt to define God (as a test of conscientious objection) in the Selective Service Act of 1948; the recent anti-Communist trials. Nongovernmental institutional restrictions on freedom have also played a large role — the denial of academic freedom, for example. These nongovernmental institutional restrictions and penalties (such as threat of dismissal from work) undoubtedly violate the spirit of the American doctrine.

Such wholesale denials of spiritual freedom, however, can be interpreted in part as an accompaniment of the rather negative individualism which is so important in the American tradition. The major accent in theory being on liberty and equality, with the assumption that fraternity would automatically follow, the tendency was to sweep away even the liberty when it was discovered that fraternity *did not* automatically follow. Abstract and atomic individualism tends often to be closely connected with sweeping denials of spiritual freedom. This explanation should not be pushed too far (after all, it is a notorious human tendency to profess one belief and then act contrary to it), but it does seem to be an element in the whole tradition. The quest for community is seriously hampered when it is assumed that fraternity is a kind of by-product of abstract and nonorganic individualism.

II

In the second place, there has been a strong "natural law" tradition. American constitutional doctrines have something in common with medieval theories in this respect; for however it may be stated, the belief in a rule — of reason, morals, or what have you — over and above majority and minority decisions alike has been a persisting element. Man, Jefferson held, had an innate "sense of right and wrong," which was "as much a part of his nature as the sense of hearing, seeing, and feeling."[3] "All positive and civil laws," said Samuel Adams, "should conform as far as possible, to the Law of natural reason and equity."[4] And J. Q. Adams, whose basic philoso-

[3] Letter to Peter Carr, August 10, 1787.

[4] H. A. Cushing, ed., *Writings of Samuel Adams,* 4 vols. (New York: Putnam, 1904–8) II, 361.

phy differed at many points from that of Samuel, added his word: "This principle, that a whole nation has a right to do whatever it pleases, cannot in any sense whatever be admitted to be true." [5]

William H. Seward, in his famous eleventh of March speech before the Civil War, continued the same theme: "The Constitution regulates our stewardship; the Constitution devotes the domain to union, to justice, to defence, to welfare, and to liberty. But there is a higher law than the Constitution, which regulates our authority over the domain, and devotes it to the same noble purposes." [6] And Theodore Parker: "Without a reverence for the Higher Law of God everything will be ruled by interest and violence. The Church will collapse into nothing, the State will go down to ruin." [7] Supreme Court opinions are certainly not wanting in enunciations of the higher law doctrine, a notable example of which was Chief Justice Hughes' discussion of the nature of religious conscience in the minority opinion in *United States v. Macintosh.*[8]

It might be observed at this point that the higher law tradition has had some connection with the well-known American doctrine of judicial review of the constitutionality of legislation: The judges interpret the higher law of the Constitution in the light of their own conception of a yet higher natural law. Thus the enactments of ordinary legislative bodies come under the critical scrutiny of the judicial minority acting as guardians both of the higher law of the Constitution and, in some measure and to a certain degree, of the law standing above the Constitution. And the difficulty of amending constitutions under the American scheme often bars formal reversal of the judicial minority by legislative and popular majorities. On the other hand, one should avoid the over-formalistic conclusion that judicial review and the difficulty of amending constitutions implies that the courts have the "final" word in interpreting constitutional rights; courts, too, are political bodies, and a sufficiently strong current of opinion will have its effect on their views and tend to force their conceptions of freedom into the main stream of American thought.

Moreover, higher law doctrines are not in the American tradition

[5] "Letters of Publicola," in W. C. Ford, ed., *Writings of J. Q. Adams,* 7 vols. (New York: Macmillan, 1913–17) I.

[6] *Congressional Globe,* vol. 22, pt. 1 (31st Congress, 1st sess.), Appendix, pp. 260ff.

[7] "The Law of God and the Statutes of Men," sermon preached on June 18, 1854.

[8] 283 U.S. 605 (1931).

inseparably bound up with the principle of judicial review. Many critics of judicial review — Jefferson, for example — have adhered, nevertheless, to natural law principles or their equivalent. Popular majorities, legislative bodies, judicial courts — all, the traditional American doctrine tends to hold, must make their particular interpretations of freedom conform to certain universal principles of liberty and justice.

The importance of higher law doctrines for freedom of thought and speech is that they afford a kind of religious sanction for unorthodox opinion and even for rebellion. Although the higher law will be interpreted differently by different men, in their attempts to discover its contents and act accordingly they have the approval of the American tradition.

III

The traditional American doctrine has questioned not only the *power* of external constraints to enforce uniform beliefs but also the *desirability* of such uniformity even if the power were available. This was not always the predominant theory, for in the middle of the seventeenth century Nathaniel Ward spoke for many when he exclaimed:

> How all Religions should enjoy their liberty, Justice its due regularity, Civil cohabitation moral honesty, in one and the same Jurisdiction, is beyond the Artique of my comprehension. If the whole conclave of Hell can so compromise, exadverse, and diametrical contradictions, as to compolitize such a multimonstrous maufrey of heteroclytes and quicquidlibets quietly; I trust I may say with all humble reverence, they can do more than the Saints of Heaven . . .[9]

But this seventeenth-century emphasis on uniformity has long ago given way to the theory (if not the practice) of diversity. Jefferson argued:

> The legitimate powers of government extend to such acts only as are injurious to others. But it does me no injury for my neighbor to say there are twenty gods, or no god. It neither picks my pocket nor breaks my leg . . . Reason and free inquiry are the only effectual agents against error . . . It is error alone which needs the support of government.[10]

Mr. Justice Jackson in our own day has observed:

[9] *The Simple Cobler of Aggawam in America* (Boston: J. Munroe, 1843).
[10] *Notes on Virginia.*

As first and moderate methods to attain unity have failed, those bent on its accomplishment resort to an ever-increasing severity. As governmental pressure toward unity becomes greater, so strife becomes more bitter as to whose unity it shall be . . . Compulsory unification of opinion achieves only the unanimity of the graveyard.[11]

There has been a large Millian element in the American tradition. Expression of eccentric opinions is good, for they may and probably do contain an element of truth. Strange cults are esthetically appealing. Man's knowledge is so limited and his insight so uncertain that any possible ray of light — even if embodied in Stalinite Communism — should be permitted free expression, whether in speech, press, assembly, or religion, by both "governmental" and "nongovernmental" institutions. This liberty of expression should extend in considerable degree even to "action." The alternative, suppression of expression on the ground that it might lead remotely to subversive action, is on the whole adjudged to be the worse of two alternatives. The American tradition would admit, I believe, that some suppressions of expression — the Albigensian heresy, for example — were undoubtedly "successful" in the sense that the heretics were wiped out; but from the long-run perspective the social cost was too great, both in material and in spiritual terms.

To the argument that some generally accepted beliefs are necessary to provide an indispensable spiritual cement for society, the American tradition would answer "of course." But it would also contend that the only way to develop common beliefs — which are admittedly necessary — is by spiritual means. Once the so-called need for widespread suppressing of expression seems to arise because certain groups question the basic postulates of the community, the use of such coercion is almost certain to exacerbate the condition, to enhance the division about basic premises. There is a risk either way, it is true; but the risk involved in using only spiritual means to combat basic spiritual disunity is far less than the hazard of attempting to check the expression of opinion by law, economic pressure, or ostracism.

IV

The last and perhaps most important element in the American tradition has been the very great emphasis which it has placed on contingency and the provisional character of all human action, both individual and collective. Generally speaking, man's spirit should

[11] West Virginia State Board of Education v. Barnette. 319 U.S. 624 (1943).

be recognized as free to utter sense or nonsense, to generate spiritual power which may be for good or evil; but, at certain points, not foreseeable far in advance, the prohibition of material restraint may have to be abrogated. Words affect action, but so fallible and limited is man that he is incompetent to say that particular words led to specific actions; however, in some circumstances it seems possible to trace specific actions which injure others or the community to specific words, and in such cases public utterance of the words can be restrained. This element of contingency in the American tradition would not deny the essential soundness of the opening statement of John's Gospel, "In the beginning was the logos"; but it *would* question whether for the most part we can discover that a particular word became a particular piece of flesh and dwelt among us.

In discussing the problem of freedom of the press, Madison long ago recognized in clear terms that the freedom which led to good might also lead to evil:

> Some degree of abuse is inseparable from the proper use of everything, and in no instance is this more true than in that of the press. It has accordingly been decided by the practice of the states, that it is better to leave a few of its noxious branches to their luxuriant growth, than, by pruning them away, to injure the vigor of those yielding the proper fruits.[12]

Obviously, Madison was familiar with Scripture: The tares are to be allowed to grow up with the wheat until the time of harvest, for any previous attempt to weed out the tares would, in the words of Holy Writ, "root up also the wheat with them."[13]

But when is the time of harvest? For the most part, the American tradition holds, we do not know exactly. But generally the theory is that Truth will in the future conquer if left free to combat Error. Truth will be forever on the scaffold only if the State and non-State coercive institutions allow it to remain there by attempting external restraint on opinion. However, in a very few instances, external restraint is essential, if not to tear down the scaffold directly, at least to make possible the free flow of workmen to engage in the task. But enough of metaphors. It is obvious that we have here the "clear and present danger" doctrine, which has come to be so closely associated with freedom of thought and speech in the United States.

[12] *Letters and Other Writings of James Madison,* 4 vols. (Philadelphia: J. B. Lippincott, 1867) IV, 544.

[13] Matthew, 23:24–30.

The essence of the doctrine is old. Roger Williams, in denying that he had antinomian tendencies, stated it, although in much less restricted form than its twentieth-century definition. He likened society to a ship at sea, in which "Papists, Protestants, Jews, and Turks" each worshipped in their own way and expressed themselves freely during the voyage. Nevertheless, Williams added,

> if any should preach or write that there ought to be no commanders or officers, because all are equal in Christ, therefore no masters nor officers, no laws of orders, nor corrections nor punishments; — I say, I never denied, but in such cases, whatever is pretended, the commander or commanders may judge, resist, compel and punish such transgressors, according to their deserts and merits.[14]

When the Supreme Court of the United States originally stated the "clear and present danger" doctrine in 1919, it attempted to formulate a more exact definition of the relationship between "logos" and flesh. "The question in every case," wrote Justice Holmes, "is whether the words used are used in such circumstances and are of such a nature as to create a clear and present danger that will bring about the substantive evils that Congress has a right to prevent. It is a question of proximity and degree."[15] Since then, the Court has attempted on many occasions to provide corollaries.

Chief Justice Hughes laid down the principle that

> The greater the importance of safeguarding the community from incitements to the overthrow of our institutions by force and violence, the more imperative is the need to preserve inviolate the constitutional rights of free speech, free press and free assembly in order to maintain the opportunity for free political discussion, to the end that government may be responsive to the will of the people and that changes, if desired, may be obtained by peaceful means.[16]

Mr. Justice Roberts has emphasized that abridgement of freedom in any concrete case must always be an exception: "The power of a state to abridge freedom of speech and of assembly is the exception rather than the rule and the penalizing even of utterances of a defined character must find its justification in a reasonable apprehension of danger to organized government."[17] Freedom of discussion is

[14] J. R. Bartlett, ed., "Letters of Roger Williams, 1632–1682," in *Publications of the Narragansett Club* (Providence: Providence Press Co., 1866–74) 274.

[15] Schenck v. United States, 249 U.S. 47 (1919).

[16] DeJonge v. Oregon, 299 U.S. 353 (1937).

[17] Herndon v. Lowry, 301 U.S. 242, 258 (1937).

a unique good, basic to the democratic process itself; and legislative enactments which in other instances would be given the presumption of constitutional validity are to be denied that presumption in cases involving spiritual freedom. Thus Mr. Justice Rutledge: "Only the gravest abuses, endangering paramount interests, give occasion for permissible limitation."[18]

The Supreme Court has recognized that the clear and present danger doctrine, as interpreted and restated, had what Justice Reed once called the "vice of uncertainty."[19] But it has felt, nevertheless, that any other formula attempting to translate the essence of spiritual freedom into the material world would be subject to the same criticism.

As indeed it probably would. The plain fact seems to be that unless one is willing to equate the will of the majority or a particular minority or an individual with the ethically right and to blot out any distinction whatsoever between the word and the act, between logos and flesh, one is left with an unsatisfied feeling about the whole problem. Previous restraints on the press are outlawed; generally one can utter what one pleases; but there is always the law of slander and libel and the possibility of legislative bodies controlling or prohibiting words which seem to lead directly to acts disruptive of good order, whatever that may mean. The minority may be right; the majority may be right; what is more likely, neither may be right. Majority rule is a practical expedient (necessary because decisions somehow have to be made) but itself is subject to the moral law and to continue, it must restrain itself in controlling words and doctrine lest its control prevent future majorities from arising, thus destroying the principle of majority rule itself. Tares are part of the price we pay for wheat; allow both to grow until the harvest; but the State, in general, is not to preside over the harvest. All this seems to be an integral part of the American tradition of freedom of speech and thought.

No one will deny that, from the viewpoint of providing a clear-cut, pat formula on the problem of freedom of expression in relation to authority and the continuity of the community, it is grossly wanting. Perhaps, however, it is so unsatisfying—or at least the defender of the American tradition would probably so hold—precisely because,

[18] Thomas v. Collins, 323 U.S. 516 (1945).
[19] Pennekamp *et al.* v. Florida, 328 U.S. 331 (1946).

while man is constantly seeking the absolutes which would seem to accord with the spiritual side of his nature, he yet finds it impossible to ignore his material condition with all the contingency and the unpredictability that it involves. In search of an absolute formula, he sometimes forgets his halfway position between the absolutes of godhood and the restrictions and contingencies of material circumstance in which he is also involved. Perhaps, the defender of the traditional American doctrine might argue, we should recall the lines of that Alexander Pope whom many of the founders of the American tradition read with profit when they considered the nature of man:

> Placed on this isthmus of a middle state,
> A being darkly wise, and rudely great:
> With too much knowledge for the sceptic side,
> With too much weakness for the stoic's pride,
> He hangs between; in doubt to act, or rest;
> In doubt to deem himself a God, or beast;
> In doubt his mind or body to prefer;
> Born but to die, and reasoning but to err . . .
> Created half to rise and half to fall;
> Great lord of all things, yet a prey to all;
> Sole judge of truth, in endless error hurled;
> The glory, jest, and riddle of the world!

Afternote

Since this article was written, American society passed through the era of "McCarthyism," during which some of the worst violations of the traditional American doctrine occurred. Thus in Dennis v. United States, 341 U.S. 494 (1951), the Supreme Court appeared to stretch the "clear and present danger" doctrine almost beyond recognition. Opinion, administrative decisions and legislative bodies ran roughshod over freedom of expression. After the late fifties, to be sure, there was a strong reaction against McCarthyism, evident both in public opinion and in the courts. But spiritual freedom continued to be in jeopardy, nevertheless. Obsessions of the "cold war" remained in a State heavily armed for "hot" war; men still lost their livelihoods because of unorthodox beliefs or associations; and some continued to be sent to prison for publishing "obscene" literature under incomprehensible judicial definitions of the term. While in stated principle most Americans probably continued to subscribe to the traditional doctrine, their actual practices were often another story.

Mulford Q. Sibley is Professor of Political Science at the University of Minnesota. [This article appeared in Vol. II, No. 2 (Summer, 1950).]

Machines

Max Lerner

Big Technology and Neutral Technicians

THE Americans did not develop modern machine technology first, but they have carried it farthest and shown the most marked affinity for it. The sway of the machine is less disputed in America than that of any other institution, including the science which made it possible and the capitalism which has organized its use. Unlike the democratic idea, which is assigned to the realm of what ought to be, the empire of Big Technology is an integral part of the daily living and thinking of Americans. They pride themselves on their "production miracles," much as the English used to call their islands the "workshop of the world."

The Big Technology has been for Americans what the Cross was for the Emperor Constantine: *in hoc signo vinces.* It set the pace for an impressively swift and thorough conquest of a new environment and of world leadership. The American has been a machine-intoxicated man. The love-affair (it has been nothing less) between the Americans and their Big Technology has been fateful, for it has joined the impersonal power of the machine to the dynamism of the American character. As by some tropism of the spirit, the Americans have followed out the logic of technology all the way. The world has seen civilizations based on very different principles: on beauty and an equipoise of living, on other-worldliness and the reality of the supernatural, on close personal allegiance, on military prowess, on ascetic control of the self. But in each case the principle was embodied mainly in the life and outlook of an elite group. Never before has the motive-principle of a civilization spread so pervasively through all strata of its population, so completely changing the lives of its ordinary people.

Veblen's ironic argument on the "merits of borrowing" is now familiar: that England, where the Industrial Revolution was first given scope, paid the "penalty for taking the lead" by falling behind in the later industrial race, and that the borrowing countries—America, Germany, Japan, Russia—won because they started on a higher technological level, without the cluttering bric-a-brac of customs and vested interests which Britain had developed.[1] Toynbee, an Englishman himself, ruefully approaches the same problem in terms of "hosts" and "parasites," quoting J. B. S. Haldane's: "A step in evolution in any animal group is followed by an evolutionary advance on the part of their parasites."[2] Yet one cannot fail to notice that aside from the Americans the other "parasites" or "borrowers," whatever they be called, have not made the same effective use of their borrowings or hosts; and that the Germans, the Japanese, even the Russians, still seem technologically like bright and enterprising younger brothers of the American, trying hard to catch up with his skills. There is more complexity in the machine achievement of America than is dreamt of in the philosophy of Veblen and Toynbee.

The American social climate favored the flowering of the borrowed seeds of technology. The resources, the separating ocean which spurred self-sufficiency, the lack of institutional hindrances, the tinkering skill of the craftsmen and the organizing skill of the managers, the lure of profit, the growing population and markets, the Promethean sense throughout of the mastery of a continent: it was in the frame of these influences that the Big Technology came into its empire in America.

More than anything else, it is what gives America its revolutionary character today. It is idle to talk of a "second" or a "third Industrial Revolution" in America. The changes in production and motive power, in transport and communications, on the farm and in the city, in the air and on the ground and under the ground, have been so unremitting as to merit somewhat Trotsky's phrase, the "Permanent Revolution," which by a curious twist the editors of *Fortune* have applied to the American technical and social scene. While the phrase is ripped out of its context of class-meaning which Trotsky had intended, the vaguer idea of a continuing dynamism with far-reaching consequences still makes sense. The technological advance, through war and peace, through prosperity and slump, has been so constant as to become an element of the surrounding American atmosphere, easily taken for granted. The American is scarcely aware of the changes in the physical

[1]Thorstein Veblen, *Imperial Germany and the Industrial Revolution* (New York: The Macmillan Co., 1915).

[2]Arnold J. Toynbee, *A Study of History* (London: Oxford University Press, 1934), IV, 430.

conditions of his living almost from day to day; he takes a longer measurement of it by the span of generations, when he compares his grandfather's daily life with his own, and that in turn with the life his grandchildren will live.

II

There have been brilliant American inventors, from the colonial craftsmen and the Yankee toolmakers, through Eli Whitney and the Wright Brothers, to De Forest and Zworykin. Yet the nature of the Big Technology cannot be understood in terms of the drama of the inventions; nor even in terms of the billions of energy units which the horsepower school of American technological greatness is fond of citing. For the transformations of power (the steam engine never played the rôle in America that water power and petroleum and electric power have played) are only one phase of the characteristic pattern of American technology.

Item two is the use of precision machine tools, which have made possible the mass-production not only of commodities but of machines themselves. Item three: the principle of interchangeable "parts," which allow the machine not only to be assembled but to be repaired with standardized ease. Item four: the "assembly-line" or "belt-line" method of processing any operation, first applied to iron and steel in the earlier foundries, and to meat-slaughtering in Cincinnati and Chicago and then made famous by Ford in automobile manufacture. This has been modernized into a system of "continuous assembly," with conveyor belts and fork trucks both to feed the parts to the assembly line itself and also to take the finished product away; and with the whole factory laid out around the central assembly line, as around the heart arteries. Item five: the related principle of "automaticity," as applied to the process industries, especially to America's newest and greatest industrial segment, the chemical industries, in the form of the "continuous flow" operation in chemical plants. In 1952 an entire napalin plant in Ohio required only four operators per shift, thus "missing 100% automaticity by a hair," as a recent article on "The Factory of the Future" put it. Item six: the vacuum-tube principle, which carries the automatic machine to its farthest reach in the "robot machines": already developed in the electronic calculators and the magnetic tape recorders, and likely to go much farther in making the assembly line automatic and in revolutionizing not only the factory but the office as well.

Obviously not all of this is American. The development of precision machine tools is largely British, the use of power sources comes from the common Western technology, and some of the elements of the "continuous flow" process were contributed by the German chemical industries. The roots of the whole mass-production process go back several centuries to the beginnings of the Industrial Revolution in Europe. American technology is the logical fulfillment of them.

One element to which the Americans have given a good deal of emphasis is the over-all principle that organizes all the technical elements—what used to be called "scientific management" and is still called the "managerial function." This has led to a high degree of resourcefulness and flexibility in both the process and the product, and the imaginative use of a technology that was available to all. Out of it has come an emphasis that would be impossible except where the principle of industrial organization is central: the focusing on productivity per man-hour. This has become for Americans the measure and common denominator of all forms of technical progress. The strides in productivity were what amazed the Europeans most in the American production record; and when under the E. C. A. the Europeans expressed a desire to know more about the methods of American technology, they were asked by Paul Hoffman to send "productivity teams" to visit American factories and study their methods. This emphasis on a rising productivity has helped give Americans the self-confident *élan* which Nietzsche saw as a possible by-product of modern technology, and which accounts for much of the optimism and bounce in their character.

But where the Americans hold their foremost position most securely is in the machine skills. Whether they be those of scientist, inventor, machine-maker, engineer, factory planner and manager, or skilled worker, it is the skills that count most in technology. In the abstraction of the "machine," we tend to forget that machines are created by human beings, organized by them, run by them. American technology is the collective possession, as it is the collective creation, of the American community. Individual inventors have been responsible for specific additions to the sum total of knowledge and tinkering and experiment, but in every case they have stood on the shoulders of all their predecessors. Giedion, in his masterly summary of western (especially American) technology, *Mechanization Takes Command* (1948), calls his book "anonymous history"—the story of what has been created by thousands of men whose names have in many cases been lost. This includes also the additional thousands whose ingeniously contrived ideas and gadgets never found practical use, and are gathering dust in the files of the Patent Office, yet left some mark on the successful ones that followed them.

III

Today the task of the American inventor has become harder. If he is a lone wolf he must find a laboratory to work in, the capital to make his invention "practical" and "marketable," the factory to produce it, and the sales organization to sell it. The days are over when a couple of bicycle fixers called Wilbur and Orville Wright got some pointers for the wing design of their plane by watching the flight of birds across the sand dunes of Kittyhawk, and then built a foot-square windbox for a couple of dollars to test the wings. But plane designers today need a wind tunnel costing millions, capable of testing the stresses on planes under conditions of supersonic speed. Most inventions today are therefore the product of corporate employees, working in corporate laboratories with corporate research funds, seeking new processes and products that can be subjected to corporate mass-production methods and marketed under a corporate patent monopoly by corporate distributive mechanisms to a vast mass market for corporate profit, with the inventor getting sometimes only his employee pay, and sometimes a small royalty payment added.

Americans call these collective skills underlying their technology, as they call technology itself, by the expressive word "know-how." More and more there has been a transfer of this "know-how" from the many workers who used to tend the machines to the many machines that now need ever fewer workers to tend them. The crucial technological skills are now located in a small elite group of engineers and technicians who design the machines and lay out the continuous-process operations, and who know what to do when the machines break down. The ultimate goal of this process is, of course, the Aldous Huxley nightmare of an assembly line in an auto factory or chemical plant with no worker on the assembly line, directed only by other machines which direct and feed themselves, and need only taping by man's hand to set them on their course. The goal of complete automaticity will never be reached, but it is always being approached more closely.

This process has not, as expected, resulted in the much mooted "technological unemployment." There have been two other results. One is the steady shifting of workers from the unskilled (the earth-lifting machines have almost wholly done away with the pick-and-shovel man) to the semiskilled, and from the semiskilled in turn to the skilled and highly skilled, or the technicians. Since the latter group remains small, the second result has been a further shift of workers out of the industrial occupations themselves into the merchandising, distributive, and white-collar groups of the corporations, the professions, and the government and Army bureaucracies.

Thus by an ironic twist of history, the American industrial mass civilization which seemed about to conscript the whole population into machine occupations is actually becoming something very different. It is emerging as a civilization with small specialized industrial groups, with a growing population of machines and a dwindling population of machine-tenders; and with an ever larger portion of the population in nonindustrial (what Veblen used to call "pecuniary") occupations. Thus the reliance of industry on the workers is growing less, and its reliance on the machines themselves is growing more.

As a consequence the competitive strategy of corporations is also shifting. It is less important now to keep wages down than to use the new machines in increasing productivity per man-hour. And it is less important to be near a supply of cheap labor power than it is to have control of a patent pool, either to keep one's competitors at a disadvantage or to control the use of the patents by them and to collect royalties for their use. At the mid-century, for example, the most dramatic development in American communications was the race for color-television patents between the Radio Corporation of America and the Columbia Broadcasting System. The Big Technology has made the strategy of patent control the crucial strategy of American business; but it has not wiped out the fact that patent pools and patent rights themselves have little meaning except as broken-off segments of the collective heritage of community know-how.

IV

Given these changes, and the changing patterns of work in America, there is a problem which has baffled students of American society, especially those who come to it from the experience of European history. Here (they argue) is a working population cut off from the soil, severed from its tools and from the idea of work as craft and calling: why does it not become the victim of revolutionary movements and demagogues? Granted that the unique conditions of American history have played hob with the idea of a self-conscious revolutionary proletariat, why has not America re-traversed the experience of the Roman Empire, whose landless, rootless, tool-less population was used by adventurist leaders? Or the similar experience of Hitler's Germany?

Behind these questions there is the running theme of alienation and its political effects. Most Americans, especially the industrial and white-collar classes, have been alienated from some crucial life experiences—from the soil, from independent enterprise, from the ownership of tools, from the sense of craft and the dignity of work, from the sense of relation to the total product. One might expect this to turn the American into the "formless" man, whom Nietzsche dreaded and whose emergence in the modern machine-world Ortega y Gasset has described, and thus easy material for either revolutionary or reactionary adventures.

The catch is in the failure to see that men uprooted from one kind of social and institutional soil can become rooted in another. The loss of some of the old life-values may affect the long-range survival of the culture, but what counts for the cohesion of a culture in the generations immediately ahead is whether people have—or think they have—what their culture has taught them to value. While the American has been alienated by the machine from his old rôle as independent farmer-artisan-entrepreneur, his culture still has a strong hold on him. The loss of a sense of independence in the productive processes has been replaced by a feeling of well-being in the realm of consumption and living standards. The pull of property, no longer in tools or productive land but in consumers' goods; the sense of power and pleasure in the means of sight and sound and movement placed at his disposal by the communications revolution; the glorying in what seems to make the world of drama and entertainment accessible; the whole range of popular culture; the feeling of access to new gradients of income and experience: these form the new soil in which the American has found new roots.

The values of income, consumption, and status and popular culture are a different set of values from those of soil and craft and small-scale productive property, and in that sense the whole ground tone of American civilization has changed under the Big Technology. But the point is that in their own way they are values, not emptiness or formlessness.

What makes the whole process even more striking is that it is the Big Technology that has raised living standards, created leisure, carried through the communications revolution, and set the conditions for the new popular culture. That is to say, it is the machine itself that has cut American industrial, white-collar, and professional workers away from the machine, and has transferred their interest and life energies from the making of goods to the making of money with which to buy and enjoy the goods.

V

In this sense Big Technology has been a conservative rather than a revolutionary political force. This runs counter to Veblen's classic theory that the "instinct of workmanship" has been left in the trusteeship of the industrial workers and engineers, and that the unremitting "discipline of the machine process" is bound to undercut the "price system," whose values are at variance both with technology and the instinct of workmanship. Veblen worked out his thesis with an impressive and subtle detail to which I cannot do justice here. He even took account of the suction force of "leisure-class" (capitalist and consumption) values on the "underlying population," while contending that it is more than counterbalanced by the daily contact with the material and tangible and the daily submission to precision techniques. He read into the machine process, however, a psychological potency for inducing political skepticism which it does not seem to possess. Russia was industrialized under a Communist regime and Japan under a militarist one, yet in neither case did the introduction of Big Technology shape minds prepared to question the bases of authoritarianism. America was industrialized under capitalism, but the minds of the machine workers have been more concerned with their place in capitalist production and their share of capitalist distribution than with questioning the power and glory of the system which carried industrialism through.

In fact, under every system of power it is not the industrial or white-collar worker—subject to precision techniques or engineering or calculating techniques—who questions the bases of power, but the intellectual dealing in ideas, values, and other intangibles. The machine process tends to make the mind more conservative by limiting the sense of personal reliance and the play of the imagination. To the worker accustomed to the tangibles of the machine, the intellectual who deals with ideas seems "up in the air," and therefore dangerous. The machine tender is likely to seek only relaxation from the machine's rigors and a larger share of the enjoyment which the machine places within his reach.

VI

The sense of craftsmanship that was spread widely through the whole of the earlier agrarian-artisan society has, under the Big Technology, been specialized with the group of technicians. From Saint-Simon in nineteenth-century France to Veblen and James Burnham in twentieth-century America, students have written about the technicians ("engineers," "managers") as the carriers of social transformations. There was a brief moment during the Great Depression when the "Technocracy" movement seemed to promise or threaten a social system run by what Veblen called a "Soviet of engineers," in terms of energy (ergs) rather than prices, profits, and wages. But Technocracy, with its hopes and fears, was only a spluttering brief candle. Of more long-range importance is what Burnham has termed the "managerial revolution" which has brought about in every industrialized society a reshuffling of class lines and a shift of power. In America it would be farfetched to say that the technicians have taken power, but they have come to represent a fairly well-defined power group with some marks of an elite.

The technicians feel themselves the creators and guardians of the community's productive skills. Once the men who made the products had this sense of guardianship. Now it is the men who design and make the machines and machine tools, and lay out the factories, and plan the industrial and plant operations. It is this monopoly of skills and sense of guardianship, rather than any special status or power, that give them the character of an elite.

They have not (despite Burnham's thesis) taken over the governing functions, nor is there any sign that they want to or can. They have concentrated on the fact of their skills rather than on the uses to which their skills are put. The question of the *cui bono* the technician regards as beyond his own technical competence. With his training in specialization and the division of labor, he is the more inclined to leave economics to the businessman, politics to the politician, war to the general, beauty to the artist, and religion and morals to the preacher. Even when you count (as you must) the business managers, the politicians, and the generals as parts of the new technical elite, the cast of mind is still the same.

VII

The rôle of the Neutral Technician thus casts its shadow over the whole present era. It becomes the rôle of the Great Withdrawal, or—as Erich Kahler puts it—a kind of nihilism of values along with an exaltation of techniques. "What is the job you want done?" asks the technician, "and I'll do it." Many worriers about American life have worried about commercialism in art and literature and thought, but often what seems a sellout for money is as likely to be surrender to the technician's sense of neutrality: the feeling that the technique carries its own ethic with it, and that the use of technics is not to be judged by a system of ethics outside of it.

One can speak, paraphrasing William James, of the varieties of technical experience in America. They have obscured the fact of a unity of outlook which cuts across them, and whose core is the overriding sense of technical assurance and neutrality. The engineers, corporate managers, government administrators and civil servants, scientists, army officers, lawyers, writers for the movies and the radio, ad-writers, public-relations men: however diverse these may be in other respects, they are all there to do a job whose shape and purposes are determined by others. Thus the federal governmental workers are required by the Hatch Act to refrain from any political activity: America has gone much farther than Britain, for example, in making political eunuchs of its civil service. A similar neutrality is coming to be expected of the growing number of state and municipal workers, and those in public utilities at the nerve centers of transport and communication. In the case of policemen, for example, even the right to join unions has been challenged. In the case of the military services the doctrine of neutrality is of great moment, since the swelling of military forces and of the war segment of the economy has given the officer class more power than ever in American history.

The episode of the dismissal of General MacArthur in 1951 lighted up the crisis of technical neutrality. On the one hand the principle of civilian control of the military had been challenged by a great soldier in an important area of policy. On the other hand, much of MacArthur's popular support came from the implicit belief in the technical division of labor: since MacArthur was a general (it was reasoned) he ought to know about war and peace; therefore President Truman's effort to control him was civilian meddling. Which is to say, again, that the technic carries its own ethic.

VIII

The situation of the scientists sets them apart from the other technicians. Given their freedom to work, American scientists have paid little heed to what is done socially with their discoveries. Scientific detachment, which began as a shield against entangling alliances which might hamper the single-minded concentration on scientific work, became an isolating barrier. Objectivity became quietism and withdrawal, *dis*interestedness turned into *un*interestedness, scientific method into social apathy. The scientist's pride of specialization buttressed the wall he had built between what was being fashioned in the realm of science and what was happening in the "unscientific" realm of human relations.

It took the atom bomb to shatter that wall, and jolt American scientists into a sense of responsibility about the world they had been so instrumental in shaping. Perhaps nothing short of the vision of atomic death—what Chancellor Hutchins called "the good news of damnation"—could have had such an effect. The American physicists became men who have known sin and cannot erase the memory. The sense of shock and guilt led some to turn their emphasis to the life sciences, led others into the cause of "world government," still others to a group vigil for civilian control of atomic energy and for the maintenance of an open society in the face of the "secrecy" demands of the new war weapons. Almost alone among the technicians, the scientists grappled with the ethical consequences of technics.

A study by Meier of the political attitudes of scientists (published in 1952 in the *Bulletin of Atomic Scientists*) showed the engineers tending on the whole toward conservatism, the chemists toward the middle of the road, and the physicists toward the liberal and radical. Allowing for the vagueness of the political terms, the study is worth noting. It suggests that where science approaches most closely to the applied sciences (mainly engineering, since chemistry is borderline) the neutral rôle of the technician asserts itself; but with theoretical science, especially in physics, the scientist asks questions about the uses to which his work is put. For the work of theoretical science is not a reflection of the machines: it precedes them. It is work involving a high degree of imaginativeness and a severe logic. Like other men of ideas, the scientists are not content (with Hamlet) "to eat the air, promise-crammed." Science and technology are revolutionary only in the sense that they have extended the realm of the socially possible. They therefore offer to men of ideas a new yardstick by which to measure social accomplishment, compelling the sense of the socially possible to keep pace—although always at some remove—with the sense of the technically possible.

But turning back to the technicians, what makes their place in America so contradictory is that, despite the stretching of social possibility by technology itself, the technicians for the most part remain a guild of neutral artificers. They have brought a universe of living standards and popular culture within reach of a population from whose choices and dilemmas they have cut themselves off.

Afternote

This essay was published, in revised form, as a section of *America As a Civilization* (New York: Simon and Schuster, 1957).

Max Lerner is a Professor of American Civilization at Brandeis University and a columnist for the New York Post. [This article appeared in Vol. IV, No. 2 (Summer, 1952).]

Hugo A. Meier

American Technology and the Nineteenth Century World

THE CHARGE of "isolationism" that so frequently has been hurled against nineteenth-century America cannot, in all justice, be ascribed also to her interest in technology. Americans, indeed, were rather vociferously proud of their achievements in engineering and invention—but that did not prevent them from taking an active interest in similar activities elsewhere in the world. That pride was based on the assumption that Americans could be as good in the fields of applied science as any civilized nation of Europe. But there was more to the matter than simply pride. From the time of the Revolution, the nature of American technology was made one important measure by which the citizens of the overseas republic might explain to Europeans the peculiarities of the American system.

As we look backward from the twentieth century such a point of view offers a new insight into the problem of evaluating the relationship of the new nation to the international scene. It sheds additional light on the development of nationalism in the United States and the struggle for prestige, as well as on the growth of ideals of international co-operation and understanding. It offers clues to how nineteenth-century Americans understood the relationship between developments in technology and the problem of maintaining adequate national security in a modern nation-state. Similarly, it reveals the links between such technological developments and the nature of progress in peace-thought. And finally, one can trace through this special approach the prevailing hope and belief that the "American Way" could best be explained and even disseminated abroad by the vehicle of American technology. The over-all story that results from such a study is that of a vigorously developing nationalism confronting the international personality of science and invention. Its sources are limitless, but are especially meaningful in the words of engineers and inventors and their spokesmen who were principally the writers in the burgeoning technological journalism of the nineteenth century. Something of the continuity as well as the changes involved in this nineteenth-century American analysis of technology's role in relating America to the world can be demonstrated by reference to each of the several broad periods of national development.

"Technology" was a word probably quite unknown to Americans of the late eighteenth century. Yet the pragmatic impulse encouraged by an environmentally enforced self-dependence already had created an awareness that doing things mechanically was rather appropriately an American characteristic. If in colonial times this propensity was not always self-consciously expanded, certainly in the period of the wars with England practical science was subjected to new demands—and a new importance. Indeed, a nationalistic point of view was imposed on it—the obligation to defend the struggling revolutionary society and its newly created nation from the military and economic might of a European power. Again, it assumed the responsibility of guaranteeing the material success of republicanism at home—and by the example of that success, encouraging its expansion abroad.

Thus the outbreak of war with England served at once to make Americans acutely conscious of their technological dependence upon Europe, and the need, if victory was to be assured, for a much greater degree of self-sufficiency. Those who in more temperate days had counseled such a condition now found their arguments bolstered by the harsh realities of war. While patriotic citizens scrabbled in the dank earth of cellars and sheds for precious saltpeter for their gunpowder, native engineers and inventors enlisted fertile imaginations in the cause of liberty.[1] Recall, for example, the efforts of men like Horace Bushnell and Colonel John Stevens who sought with their inventions to confound the all-powerful British navy. Linked with patriotism, technology commenced to play a more conscious role as a progenitor of American nationalism. Pride in the modest achievements of a native technology replaced complacency and began to find open expression. American Philosophical Society members must have listened with considerable satisfaction in 1780 to Timothy Matlack's confident assertion that "*British* tyranny restrained us from making Steel, to enrich her Merchants and Manufacturers, but we can now make it ourselves as good as theirs."[2]

In a time of deep emergency, such self-confidence was commendable. The war, it appeared, was stimulating American technological talent. Nor

[1]Numerous references to such activities, specifically and generally, are scattered throughout C. Ford *et. al.* (eds.), *The Journals of the Continental Congress, 1774-1789* (34 vols.; Washington, D. C., 1904-1937).

[2]*An Oration Delivered March 16, 1780 before the American Philosophical Society* . . . (Philadelphia, 1780), p. 4.

could there be a letdown, for with independence achieved, a new time of troubles commenced. With French armies jauntily striding over Europe and British fleets troubling the sea lanes American engineers and inventors found renewed demands on their genius. National security became a dominant pressure on Yankee technological thinking, and individuals like Robert Fulton, Oliver Evans, John Stevens and even the Patent Office's own Commissioner, Dr. William L. Thornton, added to the catalogue of weapons, real or hypothetical, to insure national integrity. But it was also a time for choosing sides, at least emotionally, and prominent American inventors and engineers joined their fellow citizens in their enthusiasms and hatreds regarding foreign belligerents. Being practical men, such technologists could enlist their know-how in the favored cause. Robert Fulton, for example, sought to peddle abroad his plans for "plunging boats" and "torpedoes," or underwater mines, wavering in sympathy between belligerents, it appears, in proportion as his prospects for employment by either one waxed or waned. The liberty-loving William L. Thornton suggested to his admired French republicans such useful refinements in weapons as cannonballs filled with molten iron, and glass grenades capable of producing grievous wounds on the persons of Englishmen. "I do not speak from Theory—but Experiment," he assured.[3] Oliver Evans, too, abandoned his patent flour mills long enough to promise the world, in rather bad rime,

> "A great gun, that has got
> The pow'r to fire an hundred shot
> Of largest size, in one short minute!!
> And kill more men than any seen yet."[4]

Such proposals, of course, did not augur well for international goodwill and understanding at the beginning of the new century. But there were those Americans who were already conscious of the paradox that war, while a stimulant to technology, might at once also be its greatest waste and perversion. Even while the muskets rattled in the cause of colonial independence Benjamin Franklin, no mean technologist himself, lamented this fear to Dr. Joseph Priestley. "As you grow older," Franklin confided, "you may . . . repent of having murdered in mephitic air so many honest, harmless mice, and wish that to prevent mischief you had used Boys and Girls instead of them."[5] The return of peace provoked Franklin to his

[3] "To the Citizen-President of France" [n.d.]. *Thornton Papers* (Library of Congress), I (Nos. 162-63).

[4] Oliver Evans [Elisha, Patrick N. Esq., Poet Laureate, pseud.], *Patent Right Oppression Exposed* . . . (Philadelphia, 1813), p. 73.

[5] To Joseph Priestley, Paris, June 7, 1782. A. H. Smyth (ed.), *The Writings of Benjamin Franklin* (10 vols.; New York: The Macmillan Co., 1905), VIII, 451-53.

famous dictum that "there never was a good War, or a bad Peace,"[6] and to point out on several occasions the great things—canals, roads, bridges—which technological know-how might have accomplished with the money and efforts squandered on war.[7]

Might not technology, then, which was proving itself so effective in making war, be converted into a means for enforcing peace? This idea intrigued Americans at the turn of the century no less than it has those of the succeeding century and a half. Benjamin Franklin watched French balloon experiments with curious interest and, in a mood less pessimistic than that with which he considered Priestley's adventures with "mephitic air," the aged inventor pondered their possibilities in the cause of peace. Might not ballons, for instance, be so effective a means of national invasion and hence so costly to repel that no sane monarch would venture the folly of war?[8] It was an early version of the argument of "the weapon too dreadful to use"—an argument that was adapted to each new technological and scientific advance which possessed potentialities for destruction. Robert Fulton, indeed, developed at greatest length the defense of unusual and even atrocious weapons of war. To European bureaucrats the submarines and torpedoes of this brash young American seemed impractical and not a little barbarous. But in his own opinion, Fulton's motives were humane and noble—the desire to destroy aggressive navies. Had not even Thomas Jefferson hailed his torpedoes as equivalent to vaccination against foreign aggression?[9] Fulton argued hotly that they were the means of producing the liberty desired by every rational soul,[10] and to charges of their barbarousness retorted, "This I admit . . . but all wars are barbarous . . . I am of opinion that the blowing up English ships of war, or French, or American, were there no other, and the men on shore, would be humane experiments of the first importance to the United States and to Mankind."[11]

By 1800, Americans generally were beginning to sense the persuasion of the new national spirit, not only in politics but in social, and indeed, technological matters. It aggravated antagonisms which earlier had been felt toward the too-able competition of foreign engineers, a condition which Washington and Madison had noticed in connection with their Potomac

[6]To Sir Joseph Banks, July 27, 1783. Smyth, *Writings of Benjamin Franklin,* IX, 74.

[7]To David Hartley, Oct. 16, 1783. Smyth, *Writings of Benjamin Franklin,* IX, 107-8.

[8]To Jan Ingenhousz, Jan. 16, 1784. Smyth, *Writings of Benjamin Franklin,* IX, 155-56.

[9]To Robert Fulton, March 17, 1810. A. A. Lipscomb (ed.), *The Writings of Thomas Jefferson* (15 vols.; Washington, D. C., 1903), XII, 380-81.

[10]"Thoughts on the Probable Effect of This Weapon" in Fulton's pamphlet on Torpedo Warfare reprinted in *American State Papers: Naval Affairs I,* No. 60, p. 221.

[11]"On the Imaginary Inhumanity of Torpedo War," *loc. cit.,* p. 223.

Canal project.[12] In 1800, John Adams felt compelled to report that the giving of appointments to visiting engineers "mortifies the honest pride of our officers, and damps their ardor and ambition."[13] Another instance finds President Monroe employing great delicacy in winning the co-operation of native engineers on the board for planning coastal defenses in 1816 with his new appointee, Simon Bernard, who—however fine an engineer—was, after all, a French import.[14]

Antagonism toward Europe and Europeans was reflected also in an evident jealousy regarding credit for invention. If Russian claims troubled a later century, there were still the British to contend with in these earlier decades. "I see by the Journal of this morning, that they are robbing us of another of our inventions to give it to the English," complained Jefferson, in Paris, to Crèvecoeur in 1787. To be sure, "it" was only a wheel of one piece, but Jersey farmers, thought Jefferson, had gotten the idea from the ancient Greeks—and, he observed optimistically, "ours are the only farmers who can read Homer."[15] If this appeared to be a circuitous method of proof, by 1816 Jefferson felt on surer ground when he praised Commissioner Thornton for his Patent Office Report which, to Jefferson, proved American supremacy in invention.[16] The question of credit for priority troubled American innovators also; personal pique was becoming more strongly blended with national pride as the nineteenth century got underway. Oliver Evans, for example, turned his acerbic pen on the British in 1813, protesting that "in the mighty and *infallible* opinion of Englishmen, no inventions, improvements, or original ideas, at least possessed of merit, can spring from any other quarter of the world, than the 'fast anchored isle.'"[17] And if most Americans might concede the artistic and literary supremacy of Europe in these early years of the nineteenth century, they were too proud of their practical sciences not to expect due recognition for their achievements in this field, at least.

But the growing national self-consciousness could not eliminate an awareness of the continuing technological debt to Europe. Thinking citizens not

[12]To Marquis de Lafayette, Feb. 15, 1785. J. C. Fitzpatrick (ed.), *The Writings of George Washington from the original manuscript sources, 1745-1799* (39 vols.; Washington, D. C.: U.S. Government Printing Office, 1931-1944), XXVIII, 73.
Madison to Jefferson, Jan. 2, 1786. G. Hunt (ed.), *The Writings of James Madison* (9 vols.; New York: G. P. Putnam's Sons, 1900-1910), II, 221.

[13]To S. Dexter, Sec. of War, July 25, 1800. C. F. Adams (ed.), *The Works of John Adams, second President of the United States* (10 vols.; Boston, 1850-1856), IX, 66.

[14]"Brvt. Major Gen. Simon Bernard." *Professional Memoirs, Corps of Engineers, U.S. Army and Engineer Department at Large* (Washington, D.C., 1913), pp. 306-14.

[15]To M. De Crèvecoeur, Paris, Jan. 15, 1787. Lipscomb, *Writings of Thomas Jefferson*, VI, 53-55.

[16]Jefferson to Thornton, May 20, 1860. *Thornton Papers,* IV (No. 730).

[17]Evans, *Patent Right Oppression Exposed,* p. 64.

only were fully aware of this alleged deficiency, but cautioned against the excessive nationalistic zeal which encouraged indifference toward European technology. "I am ashamed to own, that scarcely a branch of science can be fully investigated in America for want of books," lamented Noah Webster to Dr. Priestley in 1800.[18] Inventors' associations appealed to Congress to require the Patent Office to import the latest technical works, if only to help determine more accurately the priority of discovery and to avoid duplication of efforts.[19] John Redman Coxe in 1812 cautioned readers of his new *Emporium of Arts and Sciences* that he must borrow heavily from European publications. "To aid our researches," said Editor Coxe, "we still require that solid information arising out of extensive operations and experience, which European contemporaries are continuously affording.[20]

In these years of early national development American technology also began modestly to play the role of silent missionary of the American Way. That "Way" was embodied in the term "republicanism." The devotion of Yankee technology to the everyday uses of the ordinary citizen was looked on as additional proof of republican blessings. Yankee apple-parers which already were invading European kitchens were tacit emissaries of this new philosophy of a free republican science. The outspoken identification of American technology and American political and social forms was, to be sure, much more fully developed in subsequent decades, but there existed already a feeling that the talent for devising humble tools to serve the everyday needs of citizens was rather distinctly American—something of which to be proud and not ashamed. And the inventors themselves, like their fellow-citizens, shared the pride in their politics through an interest in the fate of republicanism elsewhere in the world. Fulton's participation in this interest was far outranked, in the matter of sincerity and enthusiasm, by that of Patent Commissioner Thornton, who became an ardent champion of republican causes the world over. He who already in the 1780's had campaigned for colonization of American slaves in Africa, after 1800 identified himself as "one who thanks Heaven that he lives in this Age of Revolution, in this Age of Light and Reason."[21] His interest in the French Revolution, and in those in Greece and South America while he was still acting as Patent Commissioner irked conservative John Quincy Adams, who suspected such enthusiasms and refused in 1820 to grant Thornton a diplo-

[18]Noah Webster, *Ten Letters to Dr. Joseph Priestley* . . . (New Haven, 1800), Letter IX, p. 23.

[19]"Application for a Revision of the Patent Laws Communicated to the House by the Mass. Assoc. for the Encouragement of Useful Inventions," in *American State Papers, Misc. Vol. II*, No. 291, pp. 149-51.

[20]"Prospectus," *The Emporium of Arts & Sciences* (Philadelphia, 1812), Series I, v-viii.

[21]"To Citizen President" [of France], June 12, 1794. *Thornton Papers*, I (Nos. 160, 161).

matic post in Latin America he desired,[22] or to allow him to dun government officials one day's pay to aid the cause of the struggling Greeks.[23] The "American Way"—the republican way—was being well served by the nation's technologists.

From the second war with England to the Civil War, American engineering and invention continued to play an ever-increasing role in the interpretation of American civilization to the world. For one thing, there was a slowly growing attention and respect abroad toward American products and know-how—even if mingled with some jocular disdain for the apple-parers and other gadgets in which the empirical spirit of the Yankee delighted. And in turn, Americans, albeit with an often ill-concealed air of apology for their materialist conception of science, a feeling which continued in varying degree to mid-century, happily recounted their achievements and contributions to the world's stock of technological devices and knowledge. A continuing sensitivity to criticism encouraged a "chip on the shoulder" attitude which grew bolder by mid-century, but practical evidence of their own achievements justified in American minds the beliefs that technological independence was being won and that world supremacy itself in practical science must be inevitable for a free and democratic people. But as before, there were those of a more restrained turn of mind who cautioned their fellow Americans against excessive nationalism in technological matters, and pointed out the need for an uninhibited reciprocity of ideas.

One encounters a sense of deep satisfaction on the part of the writers in the rapidly expanding technical and popular press after 1820 with the growing reputation abroad of American inventive abilities. European men of science, reported the *American Journal of Science* in 1822, were astonished at the rapidity of American discovery and improvement.[24] The flow of ideas now was moving in two directions, and in the 1840's a Congressional committee could report proudly that "Formerly, we borrowed and copied much that was valuable from Europe. Now, Europe is borrowing and copying with no little advantage from us."[25] By mid-century Americans were reading with immense satisfaction headlines announcing, for example, "Another American triumph in England," as Samuel Colt's revolvers,[26] and the

[22]C. F. Adams, *Memoirs of John Quincy Adams, comprising portions of his diary from 1795 to 1848* (12 vols.; Philadelphia, 1874-1877), IV (Feb. 20, 1820), 528.

[23]*Memoirs of John Quincy Adams*, VI (May 10, 1824), 324.

[24]"Extracts of a Letter from Wm. McClure to Editor—Madrid, Dec. 4, 1821: 'Progress of American Science,'" *American Journal of Science* (New York), V (1822), 197.

[25]"Report of the Select Committee Appointed to Take into Consideration the State and Condition of the Patent Office." *Mechanics Magazine and Register of Inventions and Improvements* (New York), VII (May, 1836), 330.

[26]"Colt's Revolvers," from Dover (Eng.) *Telegraph*, reprinted from *Appleton's Mechanics Magazine and Engineers' Journal*, II (Feb., 1852), 47.

variety of American farm machines stirred favorable comment overseas.[27] Meanwhile, American engineers were following American gadgets overseas, carrying with them the evidence of Yankee technical prowess. American mechanics, reported an observer in 1837, were in every Christian country. "Kings think well of them and honor them with their friendship," he pointed out. "Yankee enterprise cannot be arrested; it acknowledges no limits and seems to be advancing in every corner of the world."[28]

With Young America flexing its muscles in these years, the step from justified pride in modest achievement to boastfulness was an easy one. The older somewhat petulant apology for Yankee devotion to material things assumed a more aggressive form. If it were true that Yankee apple-parers still symbolized common-sense utilitarianism, writers, lecturers and editors warned Europeans that American tools, harvesting machines and engineers were achieving such supremacy that Mother Europe had best beware of her New World competitor. Engineering in America was on its way toward true professionalism, and the world was duly informed that, given a fulcrum, the American engineer, like his Greek predecessor, could move creation.[29] Let any European—and in particular an Englishman—deprecate by word or indifference the merits of American technology or its products and a ready retort was forthcoming from the offended. "Rivalry from America is not to be endured," sneered an annoyed American in 1847,[30] and the prevailing suspicion that, while lifting her nose, England was stealing credit for Yankee inventions drove some editors to extravagant expostulation. "If only they would purge themselves of that unfortunate way they have of claiming the merit of all inventions under the sun," sputtered one in protest in 1852. "To grapple at everything you can lay your hands on is not the *clever* thing, Uncle John, however it may square with your notions of honesty."[31] The sensitivity toward criticism and the readiness to word-whip England indicated, one suspects, the respect in which the technological opinions of that island were held.

But even in these enthusiastic and sensitive years of Yankee expansion calmer voices pleaded again for fairness and temperance. Some cautioned patent-hasty inventors to first actually perfect their creations.[32] The re-

[27] "Another American Triumph in England." *The People's Journal* (New York), I (March, 1854), 14-47.

[28] *Baltimore Monument,* cited in "American Mechanics," *The Mechanic's Register, or, Journal of the Useful Arts, Trades, Manufactures, Science* (Philadelphia, 1837), I (Feb. 22, 1837).

[29] *Syracuse Argus* cited in "The Mechanical Arts," *Mechanic's Magazine . . .,* p. 150.

[30] "The 'Unfortunate?' Steamer Washington," *Eureka: or, The National Journal of Inventions, Patents and Science,* II (Sept. 18, 1847), 11.

[31] *Appleton's Mechanics Magazine and Engineers' Journal,* II (Feb., 1852), 47-48.

[32] Joseph Tinker Buckingham, *An Address delivered before the Massachusetts Charitable Mechanic Association . . . Eighth Triennial Festival* (Boston, 1830), pp. 20-21.

spected mathematician, Benjamin Peirce, eloquently pleaded before members of the American Association for the Advancement of Science in 1853 that "It is not to be forgotten that the Temple of Science . . . belongs to no country or clime. It is the world's Temple, and all men are free of its communion. Let us not mar its beauty by writing our names upon its walls."[33] In this spirit, those who felt that the world should be a free field for invention approved the reduction by the Patent Office of its fees for foreign inventions.[34]

Until 1860, American technological interest in warfare still had largely national rather than international implications. In European caricature, the average American sauntered about carrying a Colt and a Bowie knife; but although some curious attention was given European military developments, probably most Americans agreed with the premature judgment of the *Scientific Artisan* in 1859 that America's contests were over nature, not men.[35] To Thomas Ewbank, Commissioner of the Patent Office from 1849 to 1852, war was a parasitical drain on science and the practical arts.[36] This reflection of Benjamin Franklin's earlier attitude was shared by the advocates of the Peace Movement, but from time to time patriotic citizens conjured up another weapon "too horrible to use"—and to Franklin's balloon armadas and Fulton's torpedoes "modern progress" added others. "There can be no land battle when steam cannon shall pour their torrents of shot . . . and annihilate both armies before they come within sound of their trumpets," predicted an optimist of 1839.[37] But the half century closed with American inventions for war vastly outranked by those for peace;[38] and even the Civil War, though naturally it stimulated inventions for war purposes, also produced an unprecedented flood of inventions for peace and industry.

What, finally, was American technology expected, in these prewar years, to tell the world about the American way of life? Emphasis not on republicanism, with its more nearly political connotations, but on democracy with

[33]"American Association for the Advancement of Science . . . Opening Address of 7th Regular Session, Thursday, July 28, 1853." *Annals of Science* (Cleveland), I (Aug. 1, 1853), 207-8.

[34]"Encourage Invention," *Scientific American,* III (Nov. 6, 1847), 53.

[35]"War! Horrid War!" *Scientific Artisan: A Journal Devoted to Science, Art, Discovery, and Invention* (Cincinnati), I (July 30, 1859), 398.

[36]Thomas Ewbank, *The Position of our Species in the Path of its Destiny—or, the comparative Infancy of Man and of the Earth as His Home* (New York, 1860), p. 14.

[37]James T. Austin, *An Address delivered before the Massachusetts Charitable Mechanic Association . . . Eleventh triennial Festival & Second Exhibition and Fair* (Boston, 1839), p. 35.

[38]Emerson Davis, *The First Half Century; or a History of Changes that have taken place, and events that have transpired, chiefly in the United States, between 1800 and 1850* (Boston, 1851), 270-73.

its social content now characterized the interpretation. The utilitarian American devices flooding European shops were a symbol of Jefferson's ideal of a chemistry that could be taught to brew and bake.[39] He who served his fellow man in practical ways, was the true citizen of the modern age! Perhaps no man of the century had greater faith in the engineer's ability to aid all mankind than did Commissioner Thomas Ewbank of the Patent Office whose books and pamphlets warned that "political gamblers and titled buffoons"—as he put it—had had their day. It was now the engineer's turn to lead society.[40] That viewpoint was disseminated amongst the readers of the technical press to whom, as the new *Scientific American* observed in 1848, a share was assigned in America's role of carrying freedom, science and knowledge to the ends of the earth.[41]

That mission by 1865 appeared to be getting very tangible results. Tsar Alexander had freed an estimated 23,000,000 serfs. Was this an act of enlightened magnanimity? To Simon Stern, addressing his Cooper Institute audience in 1865, not imperial charity but rather the farmer of the Far West, using American machinery, had taught the Tsar a lesson in economic progress. "Is it not a glorious result," exulted Stern, ". . . that with every cut of the McCormick reaper, . . . the shackles of a bondsman of Europe fall clanging to earth!"[42] Elsewhere in Europe, liberal movements also had been taking place, if with less sanction from ruling monarchs. Perhaps no American contribution mingled the practical and symbolic as did the boxes of Colt's Patent Repeating Fire-Arms presented by their inventor to Louis Kossuth and to Garibaldi.[43]

By the time the Civil War closed this amazing expansionary era in American history the world was coming to know a great deal about the democratic nation overseas through the frame of reference of its technology. By the 1860's, indeed, Americans had come to accept their profitable emphasis on technological change as both normal and good, and the self-conscious justification of that interest was becoming less evident. In the closing era of the nineteenth century, not apology for, but the matter-of-fact acceptance of that kind of progress predominated. The terrific "American War" had demonstrated the might and the potentialities of the United States in the manner perhaps most clearly understood by Europeans. Now, in the remain-

[39]To Thomas Cooper, July 10, 1812. Lipscomb, *Writings of Jefferson,* XIII, 176.

[40]Thomas Ewbank, *A Descriptive and Historical Account of Hydraulic and Other Machines for Raising Water* (New York, 1842), "Preface," vi.

[41]"Modern Science," *Scientific American,* III (Jan. 22, 1848), 141.

[42]"Machinery and Liberty," *American Artisan and Patent Record* (New York), n.s. I (May 10, 1865), 2.

[43]Barnard, Henry, *Armsmear: The Home, The Arm, and The Armory of Samuel Colt* (New York, 1866), pp. 138, 347.

ing years of the nineteenth century, two great dramatic circumstances even more clearly epitomized the significance of technology to the relationship of the United States with the world. The laying of the Atlantic Cable, realized in this period, challenged American imaginations in a manner almost unprecedented; and the series of great international exhibitions to which all the world flocked, colorfully illustrated the universal interdependence of science and the arts. Both circumstances served to make American citizens more conscious of their role in world civilization, and both lent prestige and significance to that role in the eyes of other nations.

Cyrus Field's Atlantic Cable was a technological venture which, more perhaps than any other factor, promised to end American isolation and to demonstrate to the world that American business acumen and technical ingenuity were equal to any task. The flickering into silence of the first short-lived cable in 1858—after all the enthusiastic celebrations, the bonfires and ringing of bells—left genuine dismay throughout the states. Had this wonderful venture, some asked, been merely a hoax, part of some scheme of stock speculation?[44] Great indeed had been the expectations for this slender strand hidden in the Atlantic depths. In the popular mind the keynote of peace and international brotherhood had dominated all considerations of commercial utility; indeed, presumably the first message transmitted was "Peace on Earth, Good Will to Men."[45] Unhealthy national isolation must now be at an end, for it seemed impossible that old prejudices and hostilities should longer exist while such an instrument had been created for an exchange of thought between all the nations of the earth.[46] Samuel Morse promised that a uniform telegraphic code now realized at last the ideal of a universal language,[47] for—as an enthusiastic clergyman described it—the cable translated equally "all the gutterals, sneezes, and labials" of every tongue as it united nations like dried apples on a string in a New England farmhouse.[48]

Thus, at long last, international co-operation in every area seemed truly possible. The rialtos of the world's commerce united together, nations could

[44]Henry M. Field, *History of the Atlantic Telegraph* (New York, 1867), p. 216.

[45]*Ocean Telegraphy: The Twenty-Fifth Anniversary of the Organization of the First Company Formed to Lay an Ocean Cable, New York, March 10, 1879* (New York, 1879), p. 31.

[46]Charles F. Briggs and Augustus Maverick, *The Story of the Telegraph and a History of the Great Atlantic Cable* (New York, 1858), pp. 21-22.

[47]Samuel F. B. Morse, "Examination of the Telegraphic Apparatus and the Processes in Telegraphy," in William P. Blake, *Reports of the United States Commissioners to the Paris Universal Exposition, 1867* (6 vols.; Washington, D. C., 1870), IV, 50.

[48]"Address of Rev. Henry W. Bellows, D.D." Chamber of Commerce of the State of New York, *The Atlantic Telegraph: Report of the Proceedings at a Banquet, Given to Mr. Cyrus W. Field, by the Chamber of Commerce of New York,* at the Metropolitan Hotel, November 15, 1866, p. 50.

join in a grand Crédit Mobilier for the fuller development of creation.[49] And after three-quarters of a century of suspicion and misunderstanding the thread that linked Great Britain with the United States must surely unite in common brotherhood the two great English-speaking peoples. The London *Times,* it is true, pointed out that a cable might generate a greater discord by too ready communication of every trifling misunderstanding,[50] but even while the failure of the first cable imposed silence during America's bitter internal war there were those who wondered if a cable might not have prevented the *Trent* and *Alabama* controversies from reaching near-fever pitch.[51]

Almost from the beginning questions of national control over cable communications troubled even the optimists. Could improved international understanding be entrusted to the care of politicians and military men? In his congratulatory message on the first cable completion, President James Buchanan urged all nations of Christendom to guarantee forever its neutrality.[52] Cyrus Field himself carefully pointed out how British co-operation had made the cable possible,[53] but fears of British domination remained.[54] And would not the need for secrecy require every government to insist on control of its own cables?[55] Such need to define cable policies resulted in 1884 in a protocol which forbade wilful injuries or interruption, and by 1900 cable policy in time of peace, at least, was believed to be reasonably well established.[56]

If the Atlantic Cable inaugurated a new era of electrical communication between Americans and the peoples of the world, international exhibitions provided a magnificent opportunity to weigh democratic practical arts and science against the achievements of the Old World. Americans were very much aware that Europe still looked upon the United States as a social and political experiment. Obliged to rely principally on private enterprise, American participation in the fairs was a wondrously naïve revelation of the technological interests of the sprawling overseas democracy. Amused European observers commented brightly on the sudden contrasts

[49]S. F. Van Choate, *Ocean Telegraphing* (Cambridge, 1865), p. 35.

[50]*Proceedings at the Banquet Given by Mr. Cyrus W. Field at the Palace Hotel, Buckingham Gate, London, on Thursday, the 28th, November, 1872 . . .* (London, 1872), pp. 34-36.

[51]Arturo de Marcoartu, *Telegraphic Submarine Lines Between Europe and America and the Atlantic and Pacific* (New York, 1863), pp. 39-40.

[52]George Grafton Wilson, *Submarine Telegraphic Cables in International Relations* (1901), p. 30.

[53]Chamber of Commerce of the State of New York, *The Atlantic Telegraph: Report of Proceedings at a Banquet . . . November 15, 1866,* p. 19.

[54]"The Atlantic Telegraph—New Communications with Europe," *American Artisan and Patent Record,* III (Sept. 12, 1866), 298.

[55]*Boston Post,* July 19, 1865. Review of S. F. Van Choate, *Adaptation of New Principles for the Successful Working of Submarine Cables* (1865).

[56]G. C. Wilson, *Submarine Telegraphic Cables . . .* pp. 12 ff.

they encountered as they passed from the voluptuous French and Viennese displays to the pyramids of soap and varieties of milk-churns, india-rubber overshoes, clothes-wringers and patent cow-milkers which dominated the American department.[57] But there was tacit appreciation also of these citizen-technologists who paid so much attention to the welfare of the many instead of the luxury of the few. The crowned heads of Europe, thought Vermont's own representative to the Paris Universal Exposition of 1867, must surely have new and enlarged ideas after contrasting their ornamental gewgaws with the simple, useful Yankee products.[58] The American reaction to European criticism, is well summed up in the defiant verses of "Brother Jonathan's Epistle," penned in 1852 after London's Crystal Palace. For, said "Jonathan"—

John Bull, you laugh in proud emotion
At our small wares sent o'er the ocean
. . . .
But to my own plain Yankee notion
We're in the right.

You laughed aloud, in high disdain
At our machine that cuts the grain;—
And swallowed down your words again,
Conceited John.

We beat you, John, at all that *pays;*
'Tis idle in these stirring days,
To fool your time, and only raise
What's old tomorrow![59]

To some Americans these glamorous exhibitions with their fine promises of understanding and peace were a fraud, a waste of effort and wealth. American motives, they argued, were pure, unselfish—but Europeans used the exhibitions as advertisements for their wares in a quest for new markets.[60] Or—worse—they were aimed at stealing technical secrets—especially American.[61] That talk of "international education" and "friendly intercourse of peoples" was rubbish, was another accusation asserted at a time when Americans, having ended their Philadelphia Centennial, were prepar-

[57]George Augustus Sala, *Paris Herself Again in 1878-9* (2 vols.; London, 1879), II, 78.

[58]Albert D. Hager, *Report of Commissioner to Attend the Universal Exposition of 1867 at Paris, France* (Rutland, Vt., 1867), p. 47.

[59]*Brother Jonathan's Epistle to His Relations Both Sides of the Atlantic, But Chiefly to His Father, John Bull, Brother Jonathan Being a Leetle Riled by the Remarks Made by John Bull at His Small Wares Displayed At the Opening of the Grand Exhibition* (Boston, 1852), pp. 4-6.

[60]William A. Drew, *Glimpses and gatherings, during a voyage and visit to London and the great exhibition, in the summer of 1851* (Augusta, Me., 1852), pp. 324-25.

[61]Joseph H. Buckingham, *An Address before the Massachusetts Charitable Mechanic Association on the occasion of their Fifteenth Triennial Festival . . .* (Boston, 1851), pp. 18-19.

ing for the Paris Fair of 1878. The alpha and omega of exhibitions was business and business only.[62] In an address in Congress in 1877 Samuel Sullivan Cox of New York argued that "The War going on in the Orient will do more for material America than all the palaces dedicated so ostentatiously to peace. Guns, drums, blunderbusses, and thunder, with a plentiful supply of breadstuffs, will open our trade and give us markets."[63]

Of course, Americans had much to gain from such exhibitions. They placed American technology and craftsmanship in better perspective against the more sophisticated European background. Exhibitions spaced every few years also provided check-points for measuring America's rate of progress. They revealed the certainty, too, of ever-continuing interdependence of the nations.

Finally, the busy years ending in 1900 found American engineers in still greater numbers gaining new experience in foreign projects, especially in Latin America and Asia, and co-operating with international technical commissions. The ending of the Civil War had channeled technical energies into new fields—"We ought," urged one technical editor in 1865, "to be doing something to keep up our reputation for running faster, flying higher, diving deeper, and coming up drier, than all other people in creation."[64] A hint of things to come was hidden in headlines such as "The March of Empire and the Mechanical Arts"; and engineering activity no longer was conceived as pausing at the Pacific shore.[65] Meanwhile, America's engineering reputation was rising, especially with such achievements behind it as the new Pacific railroads and telegraphs. Britain's Lord Mayo even made the heterodox suggestion that Yankee engineers be called upon to rectify British railroad blunders in India![66] Opportunity beckoned everywhere. A former American minister to Siam could report in 1899 that, "What I have repeatedly seen, has convinced me that the engineer is perhaps today the most essential element in the development of these unknown Asiatic countries. He will act and be successful where the diplomatist, missionary, and business man fail."[67]

[62]Charles Gindriez and James Morgan Hart, *International Exhibitions, Paris—Philadelphia—Vienna* (New York, 1878), p. 32.

[63]Hon. Samuel Sullivan Cox, *Expositions Exposed, Speech of Hon. S. S. Cox, of New York in the House of Representatives, November 19, 1877* (Washington, D. C., 1877), pp. 23-24. For an almost bitter reply, see the speech by Abram Hewitt, *Speech of Hon. Abram S. Hewitt, of New York, in the House of Representatives, November 19, 1877,* pp. 3-13.

[64]"A 'Sensation' Wanted," *American Artisan* . . . ns. II (Dec. 27, 1865), 121.

[65]"The March of Empire and the Mechanic Arts," *American Artisan* . . . ns. VII (Dec. 2, 1868), 329.

[66]"American Engineers in India," fr. *Engineering* (Br.), cited in *American Artisan* . . . ns. IX (Dec. 8, 1869), 354.

[67]"America, England, and Germany as Allies for the Open Door," by Hon. John Barrett, late U. S. Minister to Siam, *The Engineering Magazine,* XVII (September, 1899), 896.

And indirectly, at least, the American technologist also was participating in the imperialist enthusiasm, particularly where economic factors were significant. He reported back home, with mixed admiration and misgiving, the increasing competition from the technology and salesmanship of the burgeoning German Empire, and cautioned that American technical education must not fall behind in an age where technological superiority and national power were complementary.[68]

The nineteenth century drew to its close, therefore, with an American technology which once had been apologetic regarding its place in world civilization, now confidently self-assertive and eager to meet new challenges. Inventors, engineers, their spokesmen and their admirers, continued to define technology's role in the light of what they conceived to be the existing domestic needs for security from aggression and expanded national development. But they recognized also the importance of the practical arts in encouraging harmony and understanding among the nations of the world. The inventor and engineer seemed peculiarly well adapted to epitomize to the world the social goals of democracy.

When Cornell's civil engineering alumni assembled for their first annual reunion in June of 1905, guest speaker Henry Goslee Prout aptly pointed up the issue in his address on "Some Relations of the Engineer to Society." "My proposition," said Prout, "is that the engineer more than all other men will guide humanity forward until we come to some other period of a different kind. On the engineer and on those who are making engineers rests a responsibility such as men have never before been called upon to face, for it is a peculiarity of the new epoch that we are conscious of it, that we know what we are doing, which was not true in either of the six preceding epochs, and we have upon us the responsibility of conscious knowledge."[69]

Surely this was a bold and inspiring challenge. But by 1900 the record of a century of technological achievements in the interests of mankind possessed an authority which defied pessimism.

Hugo A. Meier is an Associate Professor of History at Pennsylvania State University. [This article appeared in Vol. X, No. 2, Pt. 1 (Summer, 1958).]

[68]"President's Address: A Higher Industrial and Commercial Education as an Essential Condition of our Future Material Prosperity," by Prof. John B. Johnson . . . *Proceedings of the Society for the Promotion of Engineering Education,* VI (1898), 11-36.

"America and Germany as Export Competitors and Customers," by Louis J. Magee, *The Engineering Magazine,* XVII (April, 1899), 115-21.

"The New Education," by Dean Johnson of University of Wisconsin Engineering School . . . *Wisconsin Engineer,* VI (April, 1902), 205-10.

[69]*Transactions of the Association of Civil Engineers of Cornell University,* XIV (1906), 3-14.

Lowell Tozer

A Century of Progress, 1833-1933: Technology's Triumph Over Man

IN the Hall of Science at the Chicago Century of Progress International Exposition in 1933 stood a large sculptural group containing a nearly life-sized man and woman, hands outstretched as if in fear or ignorance. Between them stood a huge angular robot nearly twice their size, bending low over them, with an angular metallic arm thrown reassuringly around each.[1]

The significance of the sculptural group was missed by most visitors, although the exposition was focused upon change. The Fair was held to celebrate Chicago's centennial, and to display the progress made since 1833. The theme was "progress through the application of science to industry," that is, through Technology. But of the many changes that had occurred between 1833 and 1933, the important one symbolized by the robot statue was not recognized. The relative positions of Man and Technology had become reversed in the American mind: in 1833 Technology was understood as one of Man's tools; by 1933 it had become his acknowledged master.

The traditional concept states that Man has an intelligence and a will, and that Technology is a tool that he uses in effecting his purposes. Most Americans before 1865 either held this view explicitly, or spoke and acted *as if* they did. Franklin's attitude, for example, is suggested by the first words of his famous prophecy of 1780:

> . . . it is impossible to imagine the Height to which may be carried, in a thousand years, the Power of Man over Matter.[2]

[1]The best single source for pictures of the exposition is Chicago Century of Progress International Exposition, *The Official Pictures of A Century of Progress Exposition, Chicago, 1933-1934* (New York: Encyclopaedia Britannica, Inc., 1933).

[2]*The Writings of Benjamin Franklin*, ed. Albert H. Smyth (New York: The Macmillan Company, 1905-7), VIII, 10.

In 1829 Jacob Bigelow said in his *Elements of Technology* that the mark of modern times is the application of science to "the arts of life."[3] And as late as 1855, even the forward-looking Thomas Ewbank was still clearly within the tradition:

The original and all-comprehending injunction, "replenish the earth and subdue it," was given before "the fall." In it, the true relationship of man to the earth, and the business of his life, are compressed in half-a-dozen words. On agriculture and the arts his powers, mental and physical, were to be concentrated. No intimation of limits to his progress in them is conveyed.[4]

The Century of Progress exposition demonstrated in two ways a radical shift from the orthodox view: attention was focused on what Technology can do rather than on what Man needs or wants, and Technology was acknowledged to be in a position to dictate to Man.

The exposition placed great emphasis on geographical mobility. The outstanding virtue of the Lama Temple was that it had been brought "halfway around the world." Most of the buildings at the Fair were mobile. They were flimsy, made mostly of plasterboard "clipped" to frameworks, so they could be easily dismantled and moved away. This was partly for economy, and for the special needs of an exposition, but other motives emerge in the following statement by the Secretary of the Architectural Commission of the Fair:

If this exposition will demonstrate that serviceable and attractive buildings can be erected without the enormous expenditure now involved in present-day building methods and that these buildings will last as long as buildings need to last in this ever-changing civilization of ours, the exposition will have proved itself vastly worth while.[5]

The Fair presented an almost overwhelming display of motion for its own sake. Practically nothing stood still. Every scientific exhibit that could possibly be made to move did so, even if it only bubbled. Most of the hundreds of vehicles on display were up on blocks with their wheels spinning. At night the Fair was alive with searchlights, and most of them were kept moving restlessly about the sky, even playing on the dirigibles and airplanes that circled overhead, and on the continuously shuttling cars of the famous Sky-Ride.

The people at the Fair were delighted by Technology's ability to produce in greater size and quantity than had been previously pos-

[3](Boston: Hilliard, Gray, Little and Wilkins), pp. 4-5.

[4]*The World a Workshop* (New York: D. Appleton and Company, 1855), pp. 183-84.

[5]F. Crissey, "Why the Century of Progress Architecture?" *Saturday Evening Post*, CCV (June 10, 1933), 63. With A. D. Albert, Secretary of the Architectural Commission.

sible. The dome of the Travel and Transport building was "bigger than the dome of St. Peter's or that of the capitol in Washington," and the twin towers of the Sky-Ride were "taller than any building in Chicago." One of the official claims of the exposition was the following:

> During the period from June 1 to November 1 of this year [1933] there will be more colored lights visible at night on the Exposition grounds than in any equal area or even in any city of the world.[6]

If there were any benefits to Man to be derived from greater size and quantity, they were not specified.

Technology was also admired for doing things in a "new way." A driverless farm tractor wandered about an enclosed field at the exposition. The desirability of a remotely controlled tractor was not questioned. Neon and other kinds of "tube" lights were a sensation at the Fair, but no one mentioned how they were *better*. Some of the "new ways" have since proved useful; others have not. The important point is that anything developed by Technology was *assumed* to be good.

The development of the artificial and the illusory was Technology's fourth achievement. Dazzling color was used to hide shoddy and ridiculous design. Human preferences were, in general, either ignored or deceived. This was Technology's day, and the only concession made was camouflage. At night, colored lights were used to "build," so that it was difficult to tell where buildings ended and sheets of light began. Vertical shafts of light were used extensively in an attempt to lift squatty buildings off the flat, filled-in land of Chicago's Lake Front by means of Arc Light Gothic. When Technology failed to satisfy, it dazzled Man into acquiescence.

Finally, Man's defeat was stated officially in plain words:

SCIENCE FINDS—INDUSTRY APPLIES—MAN CONFORMS.[7]

The triumph of Technology over Man was celebrated blatantly at the Fair. The symbols of victory were of two main types: architectural and iconographical.

The architectural style of the buildings was unmistakably dedicated to Technology. It was of two motifs: Streamlined and Machineryesque. Among the Streamlined were the Hall of Science, which seems built from parts of the superstructure of a yacht; the Federal Building, which looks like the tail of a rocket protruding from the ground; and the Electrical building, which is a jumble of Assyrian temples and airplane parts. Some examples of Machineryesque are the Administra-

[6]Chicago Century of Progress International Exposition, *Official Book of the Fair, Giving Pre-Exposition Information, 1932-1933* (Chicago: A Century of Progress, Inc., 1932), p. 21.

[7]Chicago Century of Progress International Exposition, *Official Guidebook of the Fair* (Chicago: A Century of Progress, Inc., 1933), p. 11.

tion building, whose front suggests the grille of a 1942 Buick; the Foods and Agriculture building, which resembles an inverted ore boat; and the Travel and Transport building, the rotunda of which looks like a building permanently under construction, and whose attached hall resembles an elongated generator housing. The Streamlined and Machineryesque motifs were the architectural symbols of the triumph of Technology.

The iconographic symbols of victory came close to suggesting the deification of Technology. The robot sculpture represented the first step. The progression continued. In high relief on an outside wall of Communications Hall stood a figure perhaps twenty-five feet tall; his feet rested on a geared wheel, and in his hands he held the lightning. The climax is represented by the twin figures, Science and Industry, which flanked the main entrance of the Administration building. The two herculean figures were about forty feet tall, and were coated with aluminum leaf. Arms folded across their chests, they frowned majestically down upon the people below.

These figures boldly symbolized an attitude that was expressed with varying degrees of subtlety by the whole exposition. But regardless of the form it took, the idea aroused almost no comment. It surprised no one. The Fair expressed a fact: in the American mind, Technology was now accepted as Man's master, and Man did indeed "conform." The tool had come a long way, since 1833.

Afternote

The subject is explored in the author's unpublished doctoral dissertation, "American Attitudes Toward Machine Technology, 1893–1933," University of Minnesota, 1953.

The best single book on the subject is Leo Marx, *The Machine in the Garden: Technology and Pastoral Idea in America* (New York: Oxford University Press, 1965). Clark A. Chambers, "The Belief in Progress in Twentieth-Century America," *Journal of the History of Ideas*, XIX (April, 1958), 197–224, presents in its footnotes a virtually complete bibliography of the subject. Other fruitful sources include Marvin Fisher, "The Iconology of Industrialism, 1830–1860," *American Quarterly*, XIII (Fall, 1961), 347–364; Robert Woods Kennedy, "Architecture and the New Package Style," *New Republic*, CXXXII (April 4, 1955), 12–15; Perry Miller, "The Responsibility of Mind in a Civilization of Machines," *American Scholar*, XXXI (Winter, 1961–1962), 51–69; Lewis Mumford, "Apology to Henry Adams," *Virginia Quarterly Review*, XXXVIII (Spring, 1962), 196–217; Elting E. Morison, *Men, Machines and Modern Times* (Cambridge, Mass.: M.I.T. Press, 1966).

Lowell Tozer is a Professor of English at San Diego State College. [This article appeared in Vol. IV, No. 1 (Spring, 1952).]

F. Eugene Melder

The "Tin Lizzie's" Golden Anniversary

CENTENNIAL, GOLDEN, SILVER AND OTHER ANNIVERSARY OBSERVANCES, LIKE human birthdays and national holidays, are occasions of celebration in American society as in many others. They symbolize achievement and growth. They serve as unifying and centripetal forces in a community threatened with civil conflict by the discordant and centrifugal pressures of disparate interests. They are reminders of past events which shape current culture.

Two centenaries celebrated in 1959 were the Oregon Centennial of Statehood and the observance in Titusville, Pennsylvania, of the hundredth anniversary of "Colonel" Drake's "bringing in" the world's first oil well. However, a "Golden Anniversary" of significant import which has received almost no public attention is the advent of the Model T Ford.[1]

Perhaps the most recent attention of significance the Model T Ford has received in the American press is a protest of derision. An early Model T was included in the United States exhibit in the Brussels World Exposition of 1958. The doors of the fair had barely opened when the car became the object of a complaint which was carried ultimately to the White House. It prompted the President to dispatch a special repre-

[1] It is the thesis of this paper that the central place of the automobile in the material organization and culture of American society properly began with the Model T Ford. This is in no way an original thesis. However, it has not been systematically developed or argued. Factory production of the Model T began in October, 1908, and first delivery of the cars was made in February, 1909. See: Ford Motor Company, Archives, Accession 96, Box 8, Dodge Estate Legal. Fourteen cars were manufactured in October, 1908. Charles Sorenson reported in his autobiographical *My Forty Years with Ford* (New York: W. W. Norton & Co., 1956), ". . . first delivery of [Model T] cars was made in February, 1909." p. 119.

sentative to Brussels and left the President "very irritated" about the quality of the American contribution to the Brussels fair.[2]

It may seem to many Americans who are not well along into middle age, as it seemed to the complainant, that the Model T is an anachronism in an international exhibit. However, to Americans who are in their golden years, the "tin Lizzie" may well seem to be an appropriate symbol of the American way of life in an Age of Plenty. Few would argue that American life is not largely centered around the automobile. From conception to the grave, the automobile is an ever present and powerful force. What better symbol of modern American life?

Before the advent of the Model T in 1908, the automobile was little more than an expensive plaything of the rich. An observer of the period, Stuyvesant Fish, later declared, "Nobody dreamed that automobiles would come into general use." [3] In 1907, car registrations for the entire United States were 140,300, and only 157,000 cars had been produced and sold by the hundreds of producers of the American car industry. Nineteen years later, 1926, the last full year of Model T production, the automobile had attained its present role in American life as an ubiquitous necessity. A majority of the 22,044,600 cars registered were Model T Fords.[4]

The introduction of the Model T was a marked contrast to the birth of a new name in cars recently. The Model T was developed in a small room partitioned off in one corner of the early Ford Motor Company plant on Piquette Street, in Detroit.[5] Most of the design was worked out by a Hungarian immigrant, Joe Galamb, under the watchful eye of Henry Ford, over a period of about two years.[6] Its development cost was but a few thousand dollars. In contrast, the Edsel, a recent addition to the roster of American cars, cost the Ford Motor Company a quarter of a billion dollars over a period of seven years before it was shown to the public in September, 1957.[7]

The Model T had little advance publicity and no market research to forecast its appeal or demand. It had only the inspired hunch of Henry Ford that a cheap, small, lightweight, standardized and reliable car would

2 New York *Times*, pp. 1, 3, June 18, 1958. *Wall Street Journal*, p. 1, June 18, 1958.

3 Cleveland Amory, *The Last Resorts* (New York: Harper & Bros., 1952), p. 202.

4 R. L. Polk, *Motor Vehicle Registrations in the United States*, 1926.

5 Charles E. Sorenson, *Reminiscences*, Archives Ford Motor Company, Oral History Section, MS., edited by Owen Bombard. References to *Reminiscences* which follow are from typescripts prepared by Bombard as parts of the Oral History collection of the Archives, Ford Motor Company, from 1951 to 1956.

6 C. J. Smith, *Reminiscences;* Sorenson, *Reminiscences;* George Holley, *Autobiography*, MS., Archives, Ford Motor Company.

7 *Printers Ink*, August 30, 1957, p. 16.

find a wide market,[8] and, more important, that profits would be satisfactory if a policy of price reductions were combined with the economies of mass production.

The publicity budget of the Edsel for the first five months was $12,000,000, of which $1,000,000 was spent before the date of public showing.[9] After intensive market research, the Edsel was planned with a "market personality" as "the smart car for the younger executive or professional family on its way up."[10] The Model T was first announced to the world in an obscure trade periodical, "The Horseless Age," in one sentence: "Yet other surprises—yes, a light touring car—that will be the delight of prospective buyers, the despair of competitors."[11] That was the complete statement of the Ford Motor Company—as yet the Model T was unnamed. A typical advertiser's boast, it proved to be a great understatement.

Upon reaching the market, the Model T was successively advertised as "the family car at an honest price," "the farmer's car," "the doctor's car," "the merchant's car" and finally, in sweeping terms, as the *Universal* car, which it remained.[12] Introduced with no fanfare, the Model T developed the most remarkable and widely heralded "personality" in the entire history of the automobile in the nearly twenty years of its production.

Perhaps the best-known summary of the Model T's personality is that provided in a classic epitaph by Lee Strout and E. B. White in 1936. Fact, legend and experience were woven together when they wrote: "The Fords were obviously conceived in madness: any car which was capable of going from forward into reverse without any perceptible mechanical hiatus was bound to be a mighty challenging thing to the human imagination."[13] Again in 1953, White wrote, ". . . Model T was not a fussy car. It sprang cheerfully toward any stretch of wasteland whether there

[8] C. J. Smith, *Reminiscences;* John Wandersee, Joseph Galamb and others, Archives, Ford Motor Company.

[9] *Printers Ink,* August 30, 1957, p. 16.

[10] Eric Larrabee, "The Edsel and How It Got That Way," *Harper's* Magazine, September, 1957.

[11] Advertisement of Ford Motor Company, *The Horseless Age,* a trade journal, November, 1907.

[12] See the *Ford Times,* monthly organ of the Ford Motor Company, volumes 1-5 inclusive, issues 1908 through 1912.

[13] Lee Strout and E. B. White, *Farewell to Model T* (New York: G. P. Putnam's Sons, 1936). Essentially the same essay appeared in *The New Yorker,* May 16, 1936 under the title, "Farewell, My Lovely." It also appears in *A Subtreasury of Humor,* eds. E. B. White and L. S. White (New York: Random House, 1941), pp. 747-53.

was a noticeable road under foot or not. It had clearance, it had guts, and it enjoyed wonderful health." [14]

Not only did the Model T acquire a public reception and personality that exceeded that of any other car in history, each individual of the species is reputed to have displayed peculiarities of its own. As Allan Nevins wrote: "No two cars were quite alike. Mastery of any one involved highly personal qualities of courage, skill, intuition, and luck. As of Cleopatra, it could be said that time could not wither nor custom stale the infinite variety of the flivver; with all its superior dependability and simplicity, it combined an arch and mercurial eccentricity. It was more like a human being (of feminine gender) than any other car ever known to man." [15]

In 1953, John Steinbeck remembered his first Model T, not as a female but as a neuter gender personality. He recalled:

> "I guess Model T's would run forever, if you would let them. I was well gone in adolescence before I came by one at a price I could afford to pay—fifty dollars. It was almost as old as I was, and it had been around a helluva lot more than I had and was probably smarter to begin with. . . . I think I loved that car more than any car I ever had. It understood me. It had an intelligence not exactly malicious, but it did love a practical joke. It knew, for instance, exactly how long it could keep me spinning the crank and cursing it before I would start kicking its radiator in. It ran perfectly when I was in blue jeans, but let me put on my best suit and a white shirt, and maybe a girl beside me, and that car invariably broke down in the greasiest possible manner.
>
> "I never gave it a name. I called it 'It.'
>
> "The Model T was not a car as we know them now—it was a person—crochety and mean, frolicsome and full of jokes—just when you were ready to kill yourself, it would run five miles with no gasoline whatever." [16]

If one theme runs through all of these sketches, it is that of a public image with durability and simplicity marked by a strain of humor mixed with temperamental idiosyncrasy. For millions of rural Americans, it occupied a place of affection synonymous with the horse or mule which it replaced. For urban and rural Americans alike, it was an invitation to the open road, to broader horizons, to escape from the drudgery and fatigue of the kitchen or the farm.

14 E. B. White, "From Sea to Shining Sea," *Ford Times*, XLV, No. 7, (July, 1953), 9. 34-39.

15 Allan Nevins, *Ford, The Times, The Man, The Company* (New York: Charles Scribner's Sons, 1954), p. 395.

16 John Steinbeck, "A Model Named 'It'," *Ford Times*, XLV, No. 7 (July, 1953), 34-39.

Meanwhile, the Model T ushered in the inexpensive automobile and placed individual motor transportation within reach of masses of Americans. The near-universal ownership of the motor car opened new horizons and whetted consumer appetites for a host of changes which add up to a social and cultural revolution in America more rapid than any large society had ever experienced before.

A vast body of humor and folklore grew up around the Model T which largely remains to be systematically investigated and analyzed in terms of its relations to American folk literature and value systems. For approximately a decade after 1913, dozens of editions of "Ford Joke Books" collected and spread the stories, mostly humorous, about the foibles of the car, of Henry Ford, its maker, its users, its uses and almost every imaginable feature of the machine. In one multi-volume interpretation of recent American social history, there was a chapter on the Ford joke.[17] An endless series of stories, limericks, puns, conundrums and verse attested to Model T's reputed characteristics and personality. Its noisiness, diminutiveness, tinniness ("Tin Lizzie"), cheapness, rough-riding qualities, toughness, economy of operation and many other traits were themes of the stories. It contributed new words to the dictionary, among them "flivver" and "jitney."

Legends grew up about the Model T, which are still with us. For instance, a writer in 1958 drew upon this body of legend when he likened the eighteenth-century harpsichord to the Model T Ford, "made for people with lots of time on their hands." "Every time the Model T owner took his car out, there was a contest to see who'd succeed, the car or the driver. Every driver brought a tool kit with screwdrivers, pliers, heavens knows what." [18] This is sheer legend, on a par with the 1916 story of the Ford car which broke down in front of a junk shop. The driver entered the shop, quickly picked over a pile of miscellany and paid twenty cents for a bedspring, a remnant of garden hose and various odds and ends. The junk dealer observed that on the driver's return to his car, he lifted the hood, tinkered briefly with the motor while attaching his newly acquired junk, closed the hood, cranked the motor, mounted the driver's seat and rattled away down the road. The junkshop man, after a few moments of apparent mental concentration, looked up at the sign above his shop door, stepped to the rear of his store, returned with brush and paint, painted out "Junk of all Kinds," and replaced it with "Ford Parts and Accessories." [19]

[17] Mark Sullivan, *Our Times, The United States, 1900-1925* (New York: Charles Scribner's Sons, 1932), IV, 61-72.

[18] Bernard Asbell, "After Hours," *Harper's Magazine*, June, 1958.

[19] Mark Sullivan, *Our Times . . .*, p. 72.

The Model T ushered in a revolution in American rural social life for it was the Model T which made the automobile a common article of consumption for the American rural family. The farm family began to experience the freedom of a startling increase in mobility. The cross-roads store and the country church received death blows in the decades in which the Model T was the dominant farm vehicle. Increasingly, the farm folk could get to town for their shopping and worship. The whole family could be whisked to an evening movie in the nearest town, or to larger centers than the nearest village for a Saturday afternoon of shopping or to worship in a more colorful church than the rural edifice. The relative isolation of rural society in the open-country neighborhood was on its way to replacement and rural sociologists soon noted its breakdown.[20]

The Polk records of motor vehicle registrations in the United States show that for 1924, 1925 and 1926, more than fifty per cent of all registrations were Model T cars and Model TT Ford trucks.[21] The more prevalently agricultural the state and the lower the per capita income, the greater the percentage of Model T's to all other cars. In 1926, for example, Mississippi, with the lowest per capita income in the nation, showed three Model T registrations to every other car registered.

One reason the Model T was so popular with farmers was its low first cost—but a more important basis of its popularity was its flexibility. It was nicely adapted to appeal to the strong streak of practical ingenuity of the American or Canadian farmer, and the farmers took to Model T as to no other vehicle in history. Here was a car that, with a bit of imagination and energy, could be used to do a hundred tasks.[22]

Among the many uses of the Ford on the farm were transport of all sorts, and as a power plant to turn such machines as cream separators, wood saws, feed mills, ensilage cutter and cider presses. Many a Ford car could and did find use to tow a wagon, pull a stump, drag a log or lead livestock. By 1915, truck conversion kits and tractor attachments by the thousands actually converted Model T's to usher in the day of the small truck and the farm tractor which came in the form of the Model TT trucks and the full-fledged Fordson tractor in 1917.[23]

20 See H. E. Barnes, *Society in Transition* (New York: Prentice-Hall, 1939), chap. xii, "The Revolution in Rural Life"; J. H. Kolb and E. Brunner, *A Study of Rural Sociology* (Boston: Houghton Mifflin Co., 1935).

21 R. L. Polk, *Motor Vehicle Registrations in the United States,* 1924, 1925, 1926.

22 This statement is supported in dozens of reports culled from many sources. The three best sources are *Ford Owner* Magazine, Milwaukee, Wisconsin, 1914 through 1925; *Ford Facts,* weekly news organ of Ford Motor Company, 1916 through 1924; *Ford Times,* monthly organ of Ford Motor Company, 1908-17.

23 See *Ford Owner* Magazine from 1914 through 1917, especially.

Wheeler Coy, a rural bard, summarized the farmer's son's sentiments in verse in 1916.[24]

Things are changing over our way,
Better than they were by far,
No more longing; no more sighing;
Father's gone and bought a car.
Now as daylight comes serenely,
In the calm and dewy morn,
Father wakes me with the summons:
"Take the Ford and plow the corn."

Time was, when I spent an hour,
Watering, feeding, brushing mules,
Chasing up and down the pasture,
For the on'ry pesky fools;
But we've sold our mules and horses,
All those beasts have had their day,
Father merely smokes and mentions,
"Take the Ford and rake the hay."

In the eve I once walked weary,
Over where the cattle browse,
Now I hear my father calling:
"Take the Ford and get the cows."
Quick I start and quick I'm back there,
Hardly started, so it seems,
After milking, father tells me:
"Take the Ford and churn the cream."

So it changes ever better
Farmer's lives are full of play,
Father says we have it easy,
Different from the olden way,
But the best thing, Father told me
Best thing happened in my life,
Father said so nice and quiet:
"Take the Ford and find a wife."

That great American educational institution, "the little red schoolhouse" immortalized in American folklore, suffered a sharp decline as the number of consolidated rural schools rose by 275 per cent, from 1915 to 1927.[25] School consolidation has continued since but never again at

[24] Wheeler Coy, "Take the Ford," *Ford Owner* Magazine, November, 1916, p. 16.
[25] *Biennial Survey of Education, 1926-1928,* U. S. Dept. of Interior, Office of Education, Bulletin No. 16, 1930, p. 452.

the rate of growth in the heyday of the Model T—when the Model TT truck chassis, equipped with a bus body, was the outstanding vehicle in use for transport of children to the rapidly growing number of consolidated rural schools.

The influence of the Model T on town and city life was hardly less than on the farm. In the first decade of its production, the little car was the near universal vehicle of the village R.F.D. mail carrier, the doctor and the traveling salesman or "drummer." Fire and police departments soon used them in large numbers. During 1911, Police and Fire Departments of New York City put fleets of Model T roadsters in service as district headquarters cars.[26] Los Angeles replaced twenty downtown patrolmen with four officer-driven Model T roadsters per shift, in 1916.[27]

The use of Model T's as taxis in many cities ushered in motorized taxicabs across the nation from the very advent of the little car. In 1914, the Model T foreshadowed the failure of the electric trolley car when hundreds of privately operated "jitneys" began service in Los Angeles.[28] The movement mushroomed, and by 1915, it had spread to every corner of the country. The trolley car was doomed as the motor bus was soon developed to provide the more flexible and rapid service so forcibly demonstrated by the jitney.

Mass production of Model T's got underway with the world's first moving assembly lines in 1913, and touring cars sold for $490 the following season.[29] At this point the motorized vacation tour rapidly became a commonplace for urban families. "Tourist camps" became standard equipment of thousands of town and city parks across the nation. The widespread ownership of the popular little car by manual laborers as well as white collar workers, contributed much to bringing to the townsman the pleasures of the country. The significance of touring and tourist tent camps as forerunners of the later tourist cabins and the modern day motel requires little documentation.

Another role of Model T, almost unsung, was to reinforce capitalism by giving to millions of workers a stake in the system in the form of motor car ownership or the expectation of such ownership. Plentiful

26 *Ford Times,* IV (1911), 282-83.

27 *Ford Times,* X (1917), 326.

28 The "jitney" obtained its name from a slang expression for five cents or a nickel coin. It was an owner driven private car which cruised main streets bearing an announcement such as "five cents to City Center." Its driver picked up riders as it proceeded toward its announced destination until the car was crowded. It operated without benefit of public charter or franchise in direct competition with a public transport system. See: F. W. Doolittle, "The Economics of Jitney Bus Transportation," *Journal of Political Economy,* XXIII (1915), 663-86.

29 Allan Nevins, *Ford, The Times, The Man, The Company,* pp. 471-74, 511.

evidence of the shortcomings of American capitalism to the workingman was accumulating in the years from 1890 to 1915. Virtual civil war marked the relation of labor and capital in the mining camps of the Rocky Mountains. The "Bull pens" of the Coeur d'Alene and Colorado mining camps into which striking miners were herded bore a striking resemblance to the concentration camps of Hitler Germany a generation or so later.[30] The battles of Homestead, Pennsylvania, and Pullman, Illinois and the Ludlow, Colorado, "massacre" were widely interpreted as notice that workers could not expect to better their lot under capitalism. There were indications, too, that labor increasingly accepted the socialist-communist-syndicalist rallying cry that worker wage-slaves "had nothing to lose but their chains." After 1905, the Industrial Workers of the World were creating havoc in the empires of the "lumber barons" of the west. To add to their challenge to capitalism, the I.W.W. made sallies into the textile centers of Lawrence, Massachusetts, and Paterson, New Jersey. Incidents of warlike activities as widely spaced as Spokane and Everett, Washington and McKee's Rocks, Pennsylvania, followed I.W.W. organizing activities.[31] After years of struggle and strife, in 1915 needle trades workers of both men's and women's clothing were brought in to labor organizations committed to the destruction of capitalism.[32] John Wayland's weekly newspaper, the socialist *Appeal to Reason,* achieved the widest circulation of the American press, with weekly sales of from four to six millions per edition in the years from 1910 to 1915 or so. To make matters worse, workers' real full-time weekly earnings remained at the same level in 1914 as they had been in 1891, more than twenty years earlier.[33] In 1920 amidst the troubled days of postwar discontent, Eugene V. Debs, as Socialist party candidate for President, polled an all-time record vote for his party of nearly a million ballots.[34]

It was upon this scene that the Model T dramatically demonstrated to the workingman the possibility that he could acquire the status symbol of the middle and upper classes. Henry Ford's policies of continuous price reductions after 1909, and mass assembly line production coupled with the $5 daily wage after 1914, made him a workingman's hero. In consequence, the tide of worker opinion quietly and inconspicuously turned away from anti-capitalist ideologies as the "pie in the sky,

[30] Selig Perlman and Philip Taft, *History of Labor in the United States, 1896–1932* (New York: Macmillan Co., 1935), pp. 189-207.

[31] *Ibid.*, pp. 262-81, 386-402.

[32] *Ibid.*, pp. 289-317.

[33] H. A. Millis and R. E. Montgomery, *Labor's Progress and Problems* (New York: McGraw-Hill, 1938), p. 98.

[34] Perlman and Taft, *History of Labor in the United States,* p. 425.

bye and bye," taunt of the radicals promised to become a reality in the form of a cheap automobile in the "here and now."[35] This shift in worker opinion was almost completely missed by the social scientists of the time, but not so by men in the labor movement itself. Probably the most accurate and authoritative opinion on the matter which survives is that of an old-line union man of Muncie, Indiana, made in the early twenties: "The Ford car has done an awful lot of harm to the unions here and everywhere else. . . . As long as men have enough money to buy a second-hand Ford and tires and gasoline, they'll be out on the road and paying no attention to union meetings."[36]

Did American workers justify the complaints of the Muncie union leader by buying Fords? Apparently millions did, although no statistics by owner status were ever compiled. However, a quick look at facts is suggestive.

As the years of its production increased, rising money wages and Henry Ford's policy of price reduction made it increasingly easy to own the little car. (See following chart.) In 1909, the first full year of Model T production, the factory price of a Model T touring car was $950 and the earnings of American workers in manufacturing, mining and transport were $516 a year. The average worker's total money income for 22 months would be insufficient to buy a Model T Ford. By 1919, the average worker's income had risen to $1,167 and the Ford touring car had declined to $575, so that six months' earnings would buy Mr. Average Worker a Ford. A small but growing number of workers could own new Fords, and second-hand cars could be bought by many more. Now came the big change. By 1923, the basic Ford touring car's factory price was

[35] "Pie in the sky, bye and bye" are words of derision from an I.W.W. song, widely sung among casual and migratory workers of the West in the decades from 1906 to 1925 or so. On the meaning of the Ford innovation of a $5 wage for 8 hours of work, for a recent evaluation, see: *Life* Magazine XLVII, No. 2 (July 13, 1959), 94-106. R. L. Bruckberger, "A Second U. S. Revolution that Shook All Mankind." See also Raymond Leopold Bruckberger, *Image of America* (New York: Viking Press, 1959), for an extended elaboration of the thesis that the Ford wage policy and price policy initiated a change in American capitalism which has won labor's loyalty to a private enterprise economy.

[36] R. S. Lynd and H. M. Lynd, *Middletown* (New York: Harcourt, Brace & Co., 1929) p. 254. By the mid-twenties, large numbers of the migratory work force, perhaps a majority of the people who followed the harvests of fruit picking, wheat, hops and other crops had motorized themselves with rattletrap Model T's and the lives of the railroad traveling "bum," the "blanket stiff" and other varieties of part-time or short-term workers were transformed in revolutionary fashion. This change was duly noted and reported in American literature: R. L. Duffus, *The Innocents at Cedro* (New York: Macmillian Co., 1944), p. 119; John Steinbeck, *Cannery Row* (New York: Viking Press, 1945), see chaps. xi, xiii; also John Steinbeck, *Grapes of Wrath* (New York: Viking Press, 1939).

RATIO OF PRICES OF MODEL T TOURING CARS TO WAGES OF FACTORY, COAL MINING AND TRANSPORT WORKERS U. S. A. 1909–1925

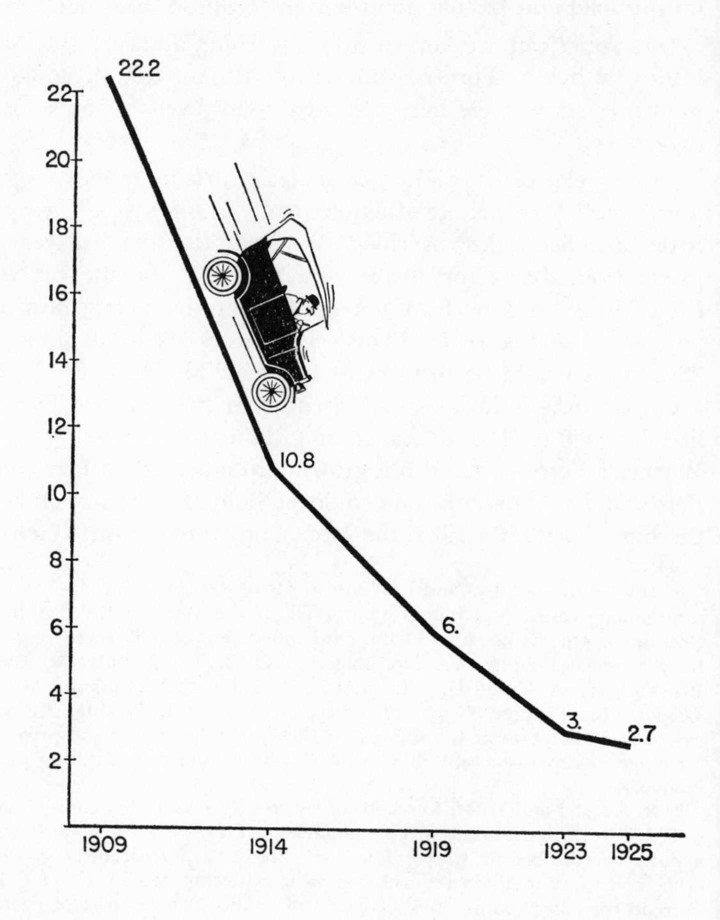

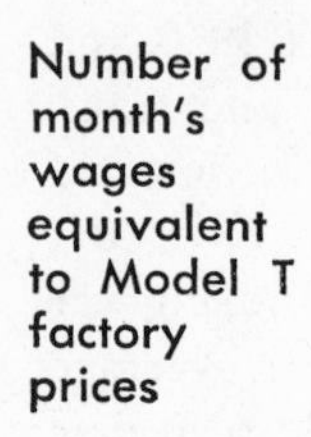

$295 and the average annual earnings had risen to $1,256. An average workingman could buy a new Ford with three months' earnings, and by 1925, he could do even better—he could have a $290 touring car with two months' and three weeks' wages.[37]

The relation of the automobile to religion and morals is no less significant. The impact of rapid transportation in reducing the importance of the rural houses of worship is clear and obvious. Thousands of rural worshippers found it easy to transfer their formal religious activities to more attractive and larger congregations and did.[38] But as often as not, the younger generation found the call of the open road too attractive and discontinued their formal church attendance completely except for weddings and funerals. The reports of sermons of the time are full of ministerial protestations against the loss of support of the younger people to the rival enticements of the automobile.[39]

Perhaps the cheap automobile had as great an impact on the religious thinking of the younger generation in those early years of its general use as it had on their church attendance. A recent recollection by an adolescent of the period serves to illustrate what Veblen termed "the impact of the machine process upon traditional religion." In this instance, however, the "machine process" in the form of the Model T Ford had its impact on the traditional religious beliefs of a user-consumer rather than on the fidelity of Veblen's factory worker to supernatural values. Our reporter recalls:

> "Our little Epworth League flock of five high school boys and girls was returning for a religious retreat shepherded by our minister. The road home led up Pine Canyon from the Columbia River to Waterville [Washington]. It was a long steep grade of four miles or so. The day was hot. We were not yet halfway up when the minister's Model T balked. The radiator boiled and the motor failed. Our good minister suggested that we call for God's help so all six of us knelt in the road on the shady side of the car and prayed. The radiator soon ceased to boil, and we got under way again. Our prayers were answered but momentarily. Stops became frequent, and prayers increased in length. Three or four prayers later, the Model T topped the hill, and we were profoundly impressed with our convincing demonstration of the power of prayer.
>
> "Imagine the shock to my newly demonstrated convictions at what

37 These prices are Ford Motor Company advertised retail prices for the touring car without accessories or extras, f.o.b. Michigan factories, in the respective years. Worker annual earnings are quoted from various publications of the U. S. Bureau of Labor Statistics, 1910-26.

38 H. E. Barnes, *Society in Transition* (New York: Prentice-Hall, 1939), pp. 597, 598; "Good Roads and Better Churches," *Literary Digest*, LXVII (November 6, 1920), 35.

39 Lynd and Lynd, *Middletown*, p. 259.

we learned from the owner of the service station in Waterville where we stopped to replace the radiator water which had boiled away and for gas. On hearing of our difficulties on the Pine Canyon Grade, he commented that all Model T's behaved similarly on that hill. The customary and necessary way to get a Model T up that hill or any other which overheated the motor, he declared, was to stop at the instant the radiator boiled and wait to let the heated motor cool off as the Ford thermo-syphon cooling system operated too slowly on hills to keep the motor at a safe operating temperature. When I learned that our prayers had merely provided the time for the thermo-syphon to overcome the motor heat, I was crushed. My faith in prayer suffered a mortal blow."[40]

This account suggests the possible influence of such everyday experiences with the Model T upon beliefs of the relationships of the spiritual and material orders.

The changes in morals, especially in sex behavior of unmarried young people in the years when the Model T was in greatest use, caused great concern on the part of the clergy and uneasy parents. They were quick to recognize the use of the Model T and other cars to carry young people quickly to secluded "lovers' lanes" or to the anonymity of distance in hotels or tourist cabins many miles from home. As Frederick Lewis Allen said, "One of the cornerstones of American morality had been the difficulty of finding a suitable place for misconduct; now the cornerstone was crumbling."[41] He characterized the automobile as a veritable "living room" on wheels.[42] The Lynds commented in 1928, "Buggy riding in 1890 allowed only a narrow range of mobility. . . . In an auto, however, a party may go to a city halfway across the state in an afternoon or evening."[43] In their review of the records of the juvenile court of "Middletown," the Lynds reported that over half the girls charged with "sex crimes" in 1924 had committed the offense in an automobile.[44] Although the Model T probably played a role no different than other makes as a participant in the changing behavior of the sexes, by sheer weight of numbers, the Model T must have been most important in the change of behavior from 1915 to 1925.

In 1927, when the Model T assembly lines ground to a final halt, more

[40] A personal experience of 1919 or 1920, reported to the writer by a woman who is now the wife of a well-known dean of a state university.

[41] Frederick Lewis Allen, *The Big Change* (New York: Harper & Bros., 1952), p. 123.

[42] *Ibid.*, see also Frederick Lewis Allen, *Only Yesterday* (New York: Harper & Bros., 1931), p. 101.

[43] Lynd and Lynd, *Middletown*, p. 137. See also A. C. Kinsey, W. B. Pomeroy, C. E. Martin and P. G. Bebhard, *Sexual Behavior in the Human Female* (Philadelphia: W. B. Saunders & Co., 1953), p. 336, Table 78, 5th section.

[44] Lynd and Lynd, *Middletown*, p. 258.

than fifteen million of the little cars had been produced in twenty calendar years. Never since has production of any single model of a motor car gone to a number even one-half as great. By 1927, the nation's population might all have been transported simultaneously, five to a car, and the car industry had grown up. No other country, except Canada, had reached an equivalent car-population ratio even by the year 1959.

The Model T had been so successful in making the motor car an article of common consumption that the country was well on its way toward its present-day organization of social life. By 1927, paved roads had been increased over one million times in the nineteen years since the Model T was born. The social forces were now all present—awaiting organization—to bring about the pattern of social life based on the automobile which we know in 1960. America had entered the "Age of Plenty," as *Business Week* observed in 1956, and "Model T" marked "a great divide in modern times. It can be used to date the transition from the Age of Production to the Age of Distribution." [45]

The automobile industry of this country has matured. It operates mainly on the basis of the replacement market demand. In the recession year of 1958, leaders of the industry were earnestly seeking market stimulants or harbingers of consumer demand changes. General Motors, Ford and Chrysler companies were reported to be grooming small cars for presentation to the market in 1959. One unnamed auto company official was quoted as declaring, with an air of disgust, when asked if his firm would offer a small, modestly priced car of 100 inches wheelbase or thereabouts: "I can't say that. It's just not a sure thing yet. If we build one, it won't be in response to public demand—it'll just be a case of panic." [46]

Meanwhile, as other nations of the world gear their economies to consumer demands in a world which shows promise of better standards of living for the common man, many candidates for the American role of the Model T in their respective countries have appeared. Among them

[45] "Selling to an Age of Plenty," *Business Week*, May 5, 1956, p. 121. The problems of adjustment to highly productive economic processes have been a repeated theme in American literature. Some social writers who have treated the subject are Stuart Chase in a number of books, particularly his *The Economy of Abundance* (New York: Macmillan Co., 1934). A more recent example is that of John Kenneth Galbraith in *The Affluent Society* (Boston: Houghton Mifflin Co., 1958). A different and more original approach is provided by David Morris Potter in *People of Plenty* (Chicago: University of Chicago Press, 1954), in pursuing the thesis of the relation between abundance in American cultural traditions and the American character.

[46] *Wall Street Journal*, July 9, 1958, col. 6, p. 1, "U. S. car makers shroud preparations to drive into small car market." By midsummer of 1959 plans of the "Big Three" to offer three new "compact" car models in the 1960 model year were public knowledge. See: *Business Week*, Aug. 8, 1959, pp. 60-78.

are the Volkswagens and Lloyds of Germany, the Austin A-30's, Morris Minors and Ford Anglias and Populars of Britain, the Renault Dauphines and the Citroen 2-cylinder 2 CV's of France, the Saabs of Sweden, the Moskvitz's of Russia, the Vespa and Lambretta Scooters and the Fiat 600's of Italy, the Datsuns of Japan and the Holdens of Australia. In this decade, tourist camp grounds are becoming as common in Western Europe as they were in America forty years ago and "camping" has become a word common to all languages on this side of the Iron Curtain. If general war can be avoided by the powers for another decade, we may well see other counterparts of America's transportation revolution which was so largely based on the Model T, in these and other nations of the world. But it is doubtful if any one car model will ever again be as socially influential and dominant in the market as was the Model T. As a cultural classic and symbol of the Age of Plenty for the common man, it has a unique place in history.

Perhaps the planners of the United States exhibit at the 1958 Brussels Fair were thinking of the role of the Model T in making America and our social life what it is today when they chose to place an early model of the car in the exhibit.[47] They may have been seeking to display symbols of the forces which made America's economic life the most bountiful in the world's history, rather than to exhibit, as sales bait, the chrome bedecked juggernauts of our current commercial offerings in a year when the American motor car industry was suffering the most severe slump in sales since the early years of the great depression of the thirties, and American imports of small foreign counterparts of the Model T are running at an all-time high after a rate of increase that had come close to doubling each year since 1953. The Model T had a revolutionary influence on America's social and economic life in ushering in an Age of Plenty and just possibly it may have carried that connotation to the millions of people who viewed it in the American Brussels exhibit.

The Model T exists now principally as memory. More than two hundred thousand Model T's were reported still running in June, 1953.[48] For certain, a few thousand are still in existence—mainly in the hands of the dilettantes, collectors, car dealers and service stations who preserve

[47] Apparently American planners of the United States Cultural Exhibit in Moscow in 1959 had learned a lesson from critics of the 1958 Brussels exhibit. Contemporary reports indicate that all American motor cars on display in Moscow were of the latest (1959) year model.

[48] Leslie R. Henry, "The Ubiquitous Model T" in the *Antique Automobile*, June, 1953; the R. L. Polk "Motor Vehicle Registrations in the United States for 1948," reported 73,111 Model T passenger cars and Model TT trucks registered as of July 1, 1948.

the cars as conversation or human interest pieces. Occasionally, one is seen still carrying on in the day's work. Last year, at the Oxford-Cambridge boat race, there was a perfectly maintained Model T doing duty in hauling produce on the streets in West London. Last week in a New England supermarket parking lot, an elderly couple drove up in a well-groomed 1918 Model T. It is an unusual Sunday if there are no Model T cars offered for sale in the classified "Automobiles for Sale" columns of *The New York Times.* Even today, a limited variety of Model T parts may be purchased through the catalogues of Sears, Roebuck and Montgomery Ward mail order houses.[49]

A strong case might be made for the proposition that the central material culture pattern of America at the end of the sixth decade of the twentieth century is the automobile complex. The present generation of Americans live in an environment of supermarkets, shopping centers, motels, service stations, used-car lots, wrecking yards and a series of "drive-ins"—movies, banks, restaurants, car washeries and so on. The American moves on rubber tires, over passageways characterized by traffic lights, complex road signs, highway numbers, toll booths, overpasses, underpasses, traffic separators, four, six, and eight lane separated turnpikes, trailer camps and parking meters. In terms of national consumption expenditures, the nation's motor transport accounts for more spending than does its food or its educational, health and library expenses combined, or its housing inclusive of depreciation and new construction outlays.

If American life of 1959 seems to be materially organized more around the motor car than around any other artifact, it is a safe generalization that the longest step in bringing about this material organization was that taken when the automobile first ceased to be a bauble of the rich and came within the reach of the common man. That step began just a half century ago with the advent of the Model T.

49 Sears, Roebuck's catalogue for Fall and Winter 1959 listed piston rings, intake and exhaust valves, cylinder heat gaskets, front wheel bearings and spark coils for the Model T. Montgomery Ward's catalogue for the same period listed king bolts for the front axle, piston rings and motor-overhaul gasket sets. In addition, Montgomery Ward offers in its catalogue for Fall and Winter 1959 (Catalog No. 61A5470F, p. 904) a complete engine and transmission "remanufacturing" service for Model T Fords with a "New car guarantee" on such rebuilt engines of "90 days or 4000 miles, whichever comes first." (p. 899)

Afternote

A subordinate thesis of my article is that the promise of property ownership and benefit for the common man in the form of potential or actual ownership of a Model T car was an important force in reducing the basic hostilities of the working classes to the capitalist employer corporations by giving great numbers of the workingmen a stake in the American capitalist system. I argued that such a force had a powerful influence in weaning large segments of the labor force from ideologies committed to the destruction and replacement of capitalism, especially after 1920 or so (ten years prior to the Great Depression of the 1930s). If I were to coin a term for this influence I should name it "the Model T effect" (with due apologies to Professor James S. Duesenberry of Harvard University who has given the economics profession the term "demonstration effect" to convey a somewhat different concept—of consumer behavior motivated by the desire for emulation).

Comparisons of the diffusion of the passenger automobile in some eight major nations during the years from 1900 to 1963 which are available at the time of this writing indicate that passenger car diffusion, as a rough measure of widening ownership of a form of property in durable goods, has advanced sharply among major European nations and Japan in recent years. On the assumption that these cars are privately owned, we may guess that their diffusion may have reached or passed the point where members of working classes are experiencing the "Model T effect."

An arbitrary method of estimating the "Model T effect" is to assume it can be related to the diffusion of passenger automobiles. As a measurement of this effect, I propose to adopt a speculative ratio of 50,000 passenger cars per million of population as the approximate point where expectations of passenger car ownership may begin to have the "Model T effect" on working class ideologies.

A tabular expression of such a diffusion of passenger automobiles follows:

Passenger Car Diffusion of 50,000 per million of population*
for some nations by year and number of cars and diffusion in 1963

Nation	Year	No. of passenger cars per million population	No. of passenger cars per million population — 1963
U. S. A.	1918	53,800	357,138
Canada	1922	51,800	264,000
Great Britain	1952	51,100	147,000
France	1954	62,100	148,000
West Germany	1958	56,300	136,000
Italy	1962	59,580	77,000

* Sources: Rostow, W. W., *The Stages of Economic Growth* (Cambridge, England: Cambridge University Press, 1960), p. 171 for figures through 1958.
Automobile Facts and Figures, Automobile Manufacturers Association, Detroit, 1961, 1962, 1963, 1964 and 1965 editions for figures after 1959.

Diffusion per million of population in Japan and Russia had reached 12,944 and 3,278 passenger cars per million of population, respectively, at the end of 1963.

Doubtless the strength of the appeal of anti-capitalist class struggle ideologies is not in simple inverse relationship to property ownership by the working class members. However, if property ownership is one significant force in workers' attitudes toward capitalist property holdings, as I am convinced it is, we say that it is reasonable to expect the waning of anti-capitalist attitudes in nations where automobile ownership is increasingly diffused.

This article was researched in the mid-fifties and was written in its published form in 1958–1959. One statement, factually accurate at that time, probably no longer holds. I asserted that when Model T production ceased in 1927, with more than fifteen million cars complete, the number was more than twice as great as any single car model ever produced. I believe the modern Volkswagen "bug" model has made that assertion obsolete. On the basis of the best information available now I believe the cumulative total output of that standard model was approximately 8,500,000 as of the close of the 1966 model production run about September 1, 1966.

I also nominated other cars as counterparts of the Model T, in the role of bringing individual motor transportation within reach of the "common man" and named the Russian Moskvitz as a candidate for the role in that country. On the basis of news reports of agreements between the Russian Government and the Fiat and Renault firms of Italy and France respectively, to build and operate automobile plants in the U.S.S.R. with combined capacities of upwards of one-half million units a year, it would appear that the popular models of the Fiat and Renault firms should be added to the Moskvitz as candidates for the Model T role in Russia.

F. Eugene Melder is a Professor of Economics at Clark University. [This article appeared in Vol. XII, No. 4 (Winter 1960).]

Marvin Fisher

The Iconology of Industrialism, 1830-1860

TO MANY EUROPEANS WHO VISITED THE UNITED STATES IN THE YEARS PRECEDING the Civil War, the sight of widespread technological development was usually unexpected, suddenly dramatic and largely admirable. Their response, however, is more varied than it first appears. For the most part, they saw in this new industrial pattern the most effective instrument of progress—a social force which paralleled and rivaled the frontier—but they could not consistently reconcile this obviously optimistic view of the new technology with their personal and, at times, unconscious reactions to it. These less obvious reactions tell us much about the mind of the European visitor as well as the social dimensions of the new technology in America. And although seldom based on purely aesthetic principles, their reactions also illuminate some of the reasons for the halting development of a functional approach to machine design.

The ambivalence in their response—common to Europeans and Americans alike, even to those most extravagant in their praise of industrialization—can be delineated best by analysis of imagery and metaphor, a sort of analysis which can often reveal unconscious or submerged associations and attitudes. To the psychologist analysis of such analogizing devices and the inconsistencies which they often involve is a projective technique; to the art historian it is the iconological method; to the sociologist it is a technique for observing covert culture; to the cultural historian it is a way of identifying the collective representations or the "myths" of a particular people at a particular time; and to the student of literature, it is the means of explicating his text and defining its structural integrity.[1]

[1] The method of iconological interpretation is presented in Erwin Panofsky, *Studies in Iconology* (New York, 1939) and has been reprinted as chapter I of *Meaning in the Visual Arts* (New York, 1955). In this chapter Panofsky explained why the values of medieval civilization prevented the union of classical forms and classical themes, even

The emotional reactions suggested by the various images of the machines were due only in part to some intrinsic feature of the machine. To a greater extent they stemmed from a conflict in value, a moral and aesthetic conflict, between the humane role of Nature in Western thought and its implicit denial by the machine. The American landscape, so vast and recently virgin, served in fact to heighten this conflict; for in one way it fulfilled the dream of the European romantic, but in the oft-repeated observation that "steam has annihilated space," that dream was dispelled. Nature could not simultaneously be revered by man and dominated by the machine which man had erected. It was this conflict in value which gave rise to the inconsistencies between the announced view of industrialization as a force for moral and material improvement and the image of the machine as a willful, malicious or destructive force. This conflict also confused the matter of a machine aesthetic and helps explain why so many nineteenth-century machines and products look so unlike what they were.

It hardly seems necessary to discuss the importance of Nature or landscape in the nineteenth century—its economic and moral antecedents in the minds of French physiocrats and Jeffersonian democrats, its aesthetic and moral eminence in the minds of European romantics and American transcendentalists, its sway over the popular mind and practical affairs of nineteenth-century Americans.[2] In slightly different ways, certainly, the

though these motifs and ideas were used separately throughout the Middle Ages. Since the reasons for this dichotomy lay in the inability of a commonly held set of values to accommodate a conflicting aesthetic and intellectual tradition, I feel the situation is not unlike the difficulties and inconsistencies involved in the mid-nineteenth-century response to industrialism.

In its scrutiny of symbolic elements in a work of art, the iconological method bears comparison with the new critical methods of recent literary circles. The most obvious difference, of course, is one of intention: iconological interpretation tries to integrate the work with broader cultural or historical phenomena, and part of the meaning of the work stems from our viewing it as a symptom of something in society. Panofsky termed the object of iconology "the discovery and interpretation of culturally or philosophically 'symbolical' values (which are often unknown to the artist himself and may even emphatically differ from what he consciously intended to express)." As a method, then, iconology employs detailed analysis, but its purpose is synthesis. *Meaning in the Visual Arts*, p. 31.

2 The degree to which Americans gave voice to and were influenced by conceptions of agrarian doctrine has been demonstrated by Henry Nash Smith, *Virgin Land, The American West as Symbol and Myth* (Cambridge, 1950). The considerable scholarship on the implications of the picturesque provides much pertinent background, especially works by Christopher Hussey, Samuel H. Monk, Marjorie H. Nicolson and Ernest L. Tuveson. Miss Nicolson's discussion of "the aesthetics of the infinite" in *Mountain Gloom and Mountain Glory* (Ithaca, 1959) is a particularly informative tracing of the worship of vastness and variety in nature and the veneration of space. This concept is basic to understanding the implications of a technology wherein virtue and progress are identified with the annihilation of space and taming of nature.

In an excellent essay "Nature and the National Ego," *Errand Into the Wilderness* (Cambridge, 1956), pp. 204-16, Perry Miller suggests the difference between American primacy of the land or the landscape was as important to Wordsworthians as to Jacksonians. And for Americans, their proximity to Nature seemed to confirm their superiority to European artificiality. For European visitors, however, the image of America was changing rapidly, far more rapidly than for most Americans: they saw the wilderness giving way. In America, where the Industrial Revolution was telescoped more suddenly and completely than elsewhere, it was not difficult for Europeans, surprised as they were, to recognize the importance of industrialization. But given their preconceptions, they could not easily shed the burden of inconsistencies which grew out of the seldom realized conflict in their beliefs. We find the range of this conflict revealed in the imagery they associated with the machine, and we find also the aesthetic confusion which it produced.

The image which reinforced the dominant response of optimistic acceptance and conveyed the idea of human supremacy over nature was the representation of the machine as a powerful servant, a beneficent slave to mankind. In an atmosphere of progress, the machine existed to do the bidding and improve the condition of its human masters. For example, Chevalier, whose task it was to study the fast-growing railroad system, voiced a seemingly unqualified faith in the machine as a means of extending man's creative abilities and his power to master the world:

> There is nothing in the physical order of things of which our race has a better right to boast, than of the mechanical inventions, by means of which man holds in check the irregular vigour, or brings forth the hidden energies, of nature. By the aid of mechanical contrivances, this poor weak creature, reaching out his hands over the immensity of nature, takes possession of the rivers, of the winds of heaven, of the tides of the ocean. By them, he drags forth from the secret bowels of the earth their hidden stores of fuel and of metals, and masters the subterranean waters, which there dispute his dominion. By them, he turns each drop of water into a reservoir of steam, that is, into a magazine of power, and thus he changes the globe, in comparison with which he seems an atom, into a labourious, untiring, submissive slave, performing the heaviest tasks under the eye of its master.[3]

---

and European conceptions of "Nature" and points out the often unrealized conflict between Christian belief and the widespread veneration of Nature's spontaneous goodness. And Miller tells us also that as civilization increasingly replaced the wilderness in the 1840s and 1850s, poets, painters and preachers tried desperately to identify the unique character of America with the special virtues of wild and unspoiled nature. As machines became more common, many Americans seemed driven to establish Nature as an element of national piety, as well as the physical representation of spiritual omnipresence.

[3] Michel Chevalier, *Society, Manners and Politics in the United States* (Boston, 1839), pp. 134-35.

In his words there seemed no hint that the machine could do anything but good. It was a servant to man, constructed to aid him in his mastery of nature. Although it served to subordinate nature there was no indication that the machine could in any way rival man, much less usurp his powers. This view of the machine is Promethean. It is aggressively man-centered, for the machine has supplied man the spark of power which had been reserved for the gods, and granted him a measure of importance out of proportion to his innate propensities. In this view, nature exists to be exploited rather than to be admired for its beauty or obeyed for its implied morality.

Somewhat paradoxically, Chevalier was, as we shall see, a devotee of the picturesque. And to the doctrine of the picturesque, which, with all its connotations of the sacred and the sublime in Nature, had permeated Western thought in the eighteenth and nineteenth centuries, this celebration of technology was fraught with troublesome conflict. If to the orthodox, the gospel of the sublime seems a species of sentimental heresy, this technological counterstatement, which posits man's triumph over Nature, must compound that heresy with increasingly secular concerns.

Transportation improvements made visible not only the sudden taming of raw nature, but also the degree to which man could overcome the vast distances of the new world, ostensibly bringing the benefits of civilization to all. Fredrika Bremer, the Swedish novelist, noted a steamboat "laboring and puffing, dragging along a large fleet of larger and smaller craft." [4] She saw this traffic in both directions, the exchange of the produce of fields for the product of factories. An even greater agency of man was the railroad, which unified the American nation by extending "its arms towards every city and every village," and which could "grasp with its iron hand, the most distant parts of the most extensive empire." [5] These images, whether they evoke a Promethean myth or an Arabian Nights jinni point to the apparent benefits of man's mastering a power greater than his own.

Miraculous communication was another way of annihilating space. One visiting clergyman, impressed by the low cost of sending messages to distant points, wondered why the businesslike operator appeared "utterly unconscious of the sublimity of the system in which he was acting a part." This operator, he thought, was unaware "that this almost magic system is consolidating the American continent . . . Little did he

[4] *The Homes of the New World,* trans. Mary Howitt (2 vols.; New York, 1854), I, 48-49.

[5] Guillaume Tell Poussin, *The United States; Its Power and Progress,* trans. E. L. DuBarry (Philadelphia, 1851), p. 375.

seem to anticipate the still more extensive results of this great discovery in the uniting of distant nations, the promotion of commerce and of peace, and incidentally, perhaps, the wide diffusion of the Gospel."[6] Thus the magic of the telegraph could make it an agency of morality as well as an instrument of progress. But because the miracle of the telegraph was embodied in no strange, bulky and unfamiliar form such as the charging locomotive, the puffing steamboat or some stationary power machinery, it elicited less of the apprehension which sometimes surrounded the latter machines, even though the imagery used to describe it stressed its role in overcoming the obstacles of nature.

In 1833, the author of a satire, supposedly the ex-barber to the King of England, devised a steam-operated shaving machine for his American clientele. He did not, however, realize the fortune which he expected, for his machine too neatly performed a job for which it was not intended: it sliced the noses of too many customers.[7] Though exaggerated for its humorous effect, Fibbleton's shaving machine would not have seemed funny had it not had some remote basis in reality. The fear that the machine could deviate accidentally or willfully from its assigned course of operation has recurred frequently in the human imagination; and the more complex the machine, the greater the fear. This fear was more than fear of accidental damage. It was rather the fear of subjecting oneself to the unfamiliar and often inexplicable machine, and of man's losing mastery over what he had created. The nineteenth-century traveler who was somewhat apprehensive about the immense power of a railroad locomotive was no less sophisticated than today's businessman who stands in awe of the retentive and the reasoning powers of an electronic computing device. Both have displayed the tendency to assign animistic or physiological characteristics to the machine—very likely an effort to bring the strange and fearsome thing into the circle of the familiar, to placate it and to calm their own fears by assigning to it the qualities of the living. Neither the "iron horse" nor the "mechanical brain" could be mistaken for an animate creature, but men have employed numerous metaphors and analogies to "domesticate" the locomotive and to "humanize" the mechanical computer. In many such instances the attempt to imbue the machine with the recognizable characteristics of living

[6] Henry Caswall, *The Western World Revisited* (Oxford, 1854), p. 276. Alexander Mackay, at about the same time, felt that the day was near "when the sensitive wires will extend in all directions, acting . . . like the nerves in the human system; when the framework of nature will, as it were, become sentient," so that important information could be transmitted simultaneously to all parts of the nation. *The Western World* (3 vols.; London, 1850), II, 258.

[7] George Fibbleton [Asa Greene], *Travels in America* (New York, 1833), pp. 99-101. Greene was an American satirizing British accounts of America.

creatures betrays the individual's unconscious apprehensions and his eagerness to fit the intruding machine into a familiar and comfortable system of thought.

For example, Chevalier, whose overwhelming praise of the machine is evident in the following passage, concluded with some disturbing implications. While he intended to exalt the power of man as an inventor, he suggested something different:

> Is there anything which gives a higher idea of the power of man, than the steam-engine under the form in which it is applied to produce motion on railroads? It is more than a machine, it is almost a living being; it moves, it runs like a courser at the top of his speed; more than this, it breathes: the steam which issues at regular periods from the pipes, and is condensed into a white cloud, resembles the quick breathing of a racehorse. A steam-engine has a complete respiratory apparatus, which acts like our own by expansion and compression; it wants only a system of circulation to live.[8]

Here, certainly, is a strong suggestion of the Frankenstein myth in this description of a creation so like a living creature but lacking a single characteristic. And in a succeeding passage that reached for images even deeper into the unconscious reserve of fear, Chevalier constructed a more terrifying portrait of the railroad engine. This locomotive he saw emerging from the depths of the forest, "formerly the domain of the great king Powhatan and his copper-coloured warriors, its chimney throwing sparks, its pipes breathing quickly." There in the very heart of primitive nature he had to call upon all his wits and his literal knowledge of mechanics as well as upon "the incredulity of the age, not to believe this flying, panting, flaming machine, a winged dragon vomiting forth fire."[9] Of course, railroads existed in Europe; and Chevalier, an expert in technological matters, was not in the least unfamiliar with railroad locomotives. Why then, should he be so struck by this American technological scene? His own words supply a very satisfactory answer: he saw the locomotive, the symbol of man's dominance over space, over time, over the very forces of nature, but this locomotive was emerging from the wilderness, the shrine of nature's supremacy. The locomotive was not itself unique, but the locomotive in the actual presence of the wilderness—the romantic wilderness of "great king Powhatan and his

[8] *Society . . . in the United States,* pp. 134-35. Employing the same kind of imagery and accidentally supplementing Chevalier's description, Fredrika Bremer wrote, "Locomotives are here like pulses, which impel the blood through the veins and arteries of the body to every part of the system." I, 540, *Homes of the New World.*

[9] *Society . . . in the United States,* p. 135.

copper-coloured warriors"—was entirely unique and obviously contradictory to the European's romanticized view of America.

Chevalier was not alone in his rather covert or submerged fear of the railroad locomotive. Alfred Pairpoint, while ostensibly praising American progress in locomotive production, endowed with life two engines being prepared for shipment to Egypt: "These locomotives, as they puffed and snorted—impatient, as it were, to get beyond the limits by which they were confined—appeared huge, powerful-looking monsters." [10] In his mind, these machines were not only living, feeling creatures; they were powerful *monsters*, more to be feared than admired. Alexander Mackay, a reputable journalist and barrister, resorted to the same sort of animism to explain why American cities prohibited locomotives within the city limits. Certainly, the incendiary locomotives were a danger to the inflammable wooden buildings, but Mackay suggested that the danger stemmed from the locomotive's too-stimulating diet and consciously mischievous spirit:

> With us, locomotives are fed on nothing but coke; in America they devour nothing but wood; and, like a horse kept exclusively upon oats, the latter are difficult to manage, from the nature of their diet. They are constantly attended by a formidable train of obdurate sparks, and sometimes amuse themselves on the way by setting fire to a barn, a hayrick, and the like, and, when they have nothing else to do, burning down a fence.[11]

There was clearly an element of playfulness in Mackay's mood, but it seems probable that his choice of imagery also indicated some covert fears. His analogy, which at first seems nothing more than clever, was selected after all from an almost infinite range of possibilities; still it returns us by metaphor to that willful, destructive creature, horselike but unnatural.

Charles Dickens, however, made no attempt to mask his fear and dislike of American railroads. Recalling a typical journey, he wrote, "On, on, on tears the mad dragon of an engine with its train of cars; scattering in all directions a shower of burning sparks from its wood fire; screeching, hissing, yelling, panting; until at last the thirsty monster stops beneath a covered way to drink, the people cluster round, and you have time to breathe again." [12] As a novelist, he was aware of the function of meta-

[10] *Uncle Sam and His Country* (London, 1857), pp. 310-11.

[11] *The Western World* (3 vols.; London, 1850), I, 148.

[12] *American Notes for General Circulation* (2 vols.; London, 1842), I. 151. Dickens' attitudes are of course most explicit in the moral allegory of *Hard Times*, which indicts industrial society not simply for economic exploitation but for depersonalizing the individual human being and mechanizing all human relations.

phor, and he was not so much concerned with reporting his reaction to American industrialization as he was with expressing its meaning within the broader context of human experience. This meaning is expressed in the cluster of terms suggesting not only the unhuman but the inhumane quality of an industrial civilization. There can be no mistaking this monstrous dragon with its beastlike noises for some benign bearer of burdens. It clearly did not harmonize with the sort of life Dickens valued. Fredrika Bremer passed a similar judgment, though her use of figurative language was more restrained than Dickens'. She recalled that she had left her hosts after a pleasant evening of conversation and entertainment and "hastened to the railway, which, as with an iron hand, had stopped the music of life." [13] Again, the railroad, with its inflexible and impersonal "iron hand," seemed in opposition to the amenities of civilized life. Of course, the railroad itself was not responsible for her leaving the scene of her enjoyment, but her response, as well as that of Dickens, was irrational. What gave rise to the emotion was not the machine itself, but rather its inharmonious presence against a background of human and humane interests.

The accident statistics spelled out in such gory detail in Captain Marryat's *Diary in America* offer a partial reason for travelers' fearing the railroad, but Marryat's three volumes are so loaded with anti-American bias that his laboriously gathered figures and descriptions must be suspect. His diary is more a product of artfulness than of experience. However, the element of danger in railroad travel cannot be lightly dismissed. T. C. Grattan, for many years the British consul in America, related an experience which suggested that the danger of American railroads was not only that they killed and maimed people but that they fostered a strong feeling of impersonality and unconcern about human life. He wrote that on one journey he felt "a violent jolt, accompanied by a loud crash" which alarmed the passengers. The train continued, nevertheless, with undiminished speed, and the passengers reassured themselves that all was well. At the next scheduled stop, Grattan approached the conductor and the engineer to inquire about the incident, and subsequently recorded the following dialogue.

In answer to his first question about the jolt, the engineer answered, "Well, it was in going over a chaise and horse." Grattan asked whether there was anyone in the chaise.

[13] *Homes of the New World,* I, 61. In his study of industrial imagery in nineteenth-century English poetry—"Poetry and Industrialism . . . ," *Modern Language Review,* LIII (April 1958), 160-70, Jeremy Warburg suggests that the difference between mere mention of a technological fact and the use of that fact as a basis of metaphor is a good index to the depth of a writer's response to what is new.

"Oh, yes, there were two ladies."

"Were they thrown out?"

"I guess they were, and pretty well smashed, too."

"Good God! and why didn't you stop the train? Can't you send back to know what state they're in?"

"Well, mister, I reckon they're in the State of Delaware; but you'd better jump into the steamer there, or you're like to lose your passage." [14]

Significantly, Grattan slighted the humor in this exchange to make a point about Americans. In their pursuit of progress, in their refusal to slow down or to go back, these "go-ahead" Americans seemed to sacrifice their humanity and their compassion, and satisfied the demands of the machine or of the system built around the machine.

Reactions to the steamboat closely parallel what we have noted in regard to the railroad. Here, too, the dangers were especially real when two or more steamboats raced each other, their fires growing hotter and pressure on the boilers increasing. There was one necessary difference in this vein of imagery. Whereas the point of familiar reference in many descriptions of the unfamiliar locomotive was the horse (and the locomotive became some grotesque transformation of the horse), the point of familiar reference for the steamboat was the sailing ship and the steamboat became some mad, restless mutation of the more "natural" sailing ship. A look at two such examples again reveals the writer's imagery conveying meaning beyond his explicit statement.

To Dickens the steam ferryboats around New York were restless insects, but the nearby sailing vessels were "creatures of a prouder kind." [15] On a trip across Long Island Sound, he described how his steamship

> shot in quick succession, past a lighthouse; a madhouse (how the lunatics flung up their caps, and roared in sympathy with the headlong engine and the driving tide!); a jail; and other buildings; and so emerged into a noble bay, whose waters sparkled in the new cloudless sunshine like Nature's eyes turned up to Heaven.[16]

The objects he noted strongly suggested danger, insanity and confinement until suddenly superseded by the pure and natural and even sacred beauty of bright sunlight and sparkling water. But the representation of lunacy, not of Nature, was in harmony with the rushing ship. Elsewhere on his American tour he admired the sentiment and apparently the sym-

[14] Thomas Colley Grattan, *Civilized America* (2 vols.; London, 1859), I, 161-62.
[15] *American Notes for General Circulation*, I, 187-88.
[16] *Ibid.*, p. 187.

bolism of a temperance poster showing the steamboat *Alcohol* exploding while the good ship *Temperance* sailed safely before a good wind.[17] And in another instance, he expressed his pleasure in lying on the deck of a canalboat at night—although he found the situation in the sleeping compartment below deck intolerable. The ship glided slowly past shadowy hills and dark trees, punctuated by an occasional campfire in the distance. He experienced "pure delights" in "the shining out of the bright stars, undisturbed by noise of wheels or steam, or any other sound than the liquid rippling of water as the boat went on." [18] Here, then, was a conveyance which, unlike the frantic steamboat, did not interfere with the sanctity of the natural order.

In a similar reaction to the machine, Miss Bremer insisted that sailing vessels were "infinitely more beautiful and more poetical than steam-vessels." The advantages of the former were not matters of safety nor, initially, of aesthetics, but of a moral commitment to the natural order; on board the steamboat one missed "the song of the wind or the billows, because of the noise caused by the machinery" and could "enjoy no sea-air . . . free from the fumes of the chimney." Steamboats, she continued, might have some virtue in the rivers, "but on the sea—the sailing-ship forever!" [19] The presence of the machine, after all, was the intrusion of the future on the present; the appreciation of art and natural beauty was the continuation in the present of the values of the past. And this moral preference for the system of Nature (and its implications) over the system of the machine (and its implications) provided a basis for aesthetic judgment.

The inevitable loss of the picturesque in regions newly turned to manufacturing was an obvious disadvantage of the new technology and emphasized the incompatibility of the systems represented by Nature and by the machine. The essentially rural features of New England formed a unique setting for industrial activity, and many Europeans thought it exceedingly fine for American workers "to have their dwellings and their occupation fixed in spots where the hills are heaped together, and the waters leap and whirl among the rocks." [20] Others, however, looked with considerably less favor on the factory-building habits of the enterprising Americans. Frances Trollope, who constantly lamented the lack of ruined

[17] *Ibid.*, II, 88.

[18] *Ibid.*, p. 62. Leo Marx has shown how Hawthorne's reactions to industrialism follow this same pattern and in fact supply the symbolism and color the meaning of "Ethan Brand." See "The Machine in the Garden," *The New England Quarterly*, XXIX (March 1956), 27-42.

[19] *Homes of the New World*, I, 531.

[20] Harriet Martineau, *Society in America* (2 vols.; New York, 1837), II, 38.

abbeys, feudal castles, domes, towers and steeples in America, made only one direct reference to industrialization—and that reference to reveal a boorish peculiarity of the American character. Traveling in upstate New York, she admired a romantic scene of untouched wilderness. A Yankee companion felt compelled to apologize for the phenomenon. Explaining that the wilderness property had until recently belonged to an Englishman, he added, "If you was to see it five years hence, you would not know it again; I'll engage there will be by that, half a score elegant factories—'tis a true shame to let such a privilege of water lie idle." [21] Chevalier, who, we must remember, was an ardent admirer of American technological accomplishment, was also a devotee of the picturesque. His musing over the American's demonstrated mastery of nature in the following passage strikes the same note as his shock at seeing the locomotive emerging from the wilderness; and it suggests again the systems of thought which center on Nature and on the machine:

> Those waterfalls which we admired as lovers of the picturesque, and the height of which our officers measured at the risk of their lives, he [the American] has shut up for the risk of his mills and factories, regardless of the scenery. If these countries had continued to belong to the French, the population would certainly have been more gay than the present American race; . . . but it would have had less of comfort and wealth, and ages would have passed away, before man had become master of those regions, which have been reclaimed in less than fifty years by the Americans.[22]

Though Chevalier seems to indicate that Americans were not troubled by their progressive domination of nature, current studies of our national literature—especially such figures as Hawthorne, Melville, Mark Twain, Henry Adams, William Dean Howells, Frank Norris, even Hemingway and Faulkner—and studies of political and economic thought from about 1830 demonstrate that Americans, consciously or unconsciously, confronted the same conflict.[23] But Chevalier, in his own day pulled by his split allegiances, would be the first to admit that the Americans had gained by their sacrifice of nature—while he stilled his questions and quieted his reservations.

[21] Frances Trollope, *Domestic Manners of the Americans,* ed. Donald Smalley (New York, 1949), pp. 372-73.

[22] *Society . . . in the United States,* p. 281.

[23] I am thinking particularly of an address by Leo Marx at the American Historical Association meeting in December, 1958, "'Two Kingdoms of Force': Technology and the Literary Imagination," which appeared subsequently in *The Massachusetts Review,* I (Oct. 1959), 62-95; and of Marvin Meyers' recent re-examination of a segment of nineteenth-century thought in *The Jacksonian Persuasion* (Stanford, 1957).

The imagery which many Europeans used to describe the growing industrial cities of America—such places as Pittsburgh, Cincinnati and Wheeling—again suggests the desecration of natural beauty and the perversion of health and morality, even though the majority of observers meant to emphasize the manifold benefits of industrialism in America. The stock comparisons, of course, were the English cities of Manchester, Birmingham and Sheffield; but for many Europeans the contrast between their preconceptions of America and the evidence of the new technology, the lack of transition between splendid nature and active factories, intensified their uneasiness.

James Stuart, so full of praise for most things and places American, found it necessary to warn emigrants of the clouds of smoke which hung over Pittsburgh and gave "a gloomy cast to the beautiful hills which surround it." [24] Buckingham, among the fairest and the most encyclopedic of all commentators, reported that neither houses nor streets, garments nor persons could escape sooty contamination: clean faces were "objects of rare occurrence and clean hands still more so." In fact, the sight reminded him of "the description given in the Scriptures of the appearance of the plain of Sodom and Gomorrah, on the day after the destruction of those cities by fire, when 'the smoke of the country went up as the smoke of a furnace.' " [25] Pairpoint, using a similar analogy, described the furnace room of a glass factory as a secular counterpart of Hell.[26] And when we discover in the words of another visitor that in some American cities "chimneys continued to vomit forth soot even on the day of rest, " [27] we realize the depth of the loss. This nineteenth-century smog, which impregnated the atmosphere, countered divine intention and continued simultaneously to despoil nature and defile the Sabbath.

Using the qualities of nature in a traditionally poetic way to suggest certain human qualities, another friendly visitor extended the charges against industrialism. Alexander Mackay found Pittsburgh distinguished by "the dingy and sickly character of the vegetation in its immediate vicinity," and in the same passage suggested that youth, purity and innocence were sullied by contact with the atmosphere of industrialism: "The fresh green leaf and the delicate flower being begrimed, ere they have fully unfolded themselves, by the smoke and soot with which the whole atmosphere is impregnated." [28] Indeed, Mackay's image is a metaphorical

24 *Three Years in North America* (3 vols.; London, 1833), II, 475.

25 James Silk Buckingham, *The Eastern and Western States* (3 vols.; London, 1842), II, 185.

26 *Uncle Sam and His Country*, p. 155.

27 Charles Mackay, *Life and Liberty in America* (New York, 1859), p. 122.

28 *The Western World*, III, 86.

introduction to the reactions of other observers to the girls tending their machines at Lowell.

Although most observers found Lowell a "philanthropic manufacturing college" and supported the rigid moral formula by which the workers' lives were ordered, the language of some again reveals a strong undercurrent of doubt and uncertainty. For Chevalier the characteristic sound of Lowell was the noise of hammers and spindles and of bells calling the hands back to their machines: "It is the peaceful hum of an industrious population, whose movements are regulated like clockwork." [29] And he termed the hundreds of girls there "the nuns of Lowell," who, "instead of working *sacred hearts,* spin and weave cotton" [30]—certainly a very revealing remark. First of all, he was emphasizing the excessive prudery and code of virtue imposed on the girls, but he also suggested that in this industrial situation no girl could realize her feminine potentialities. Somewhat ironically, then, he implied that they had taken their vows to serve their machines, "ere they had fully unfolded themselves." Another visitor, admiring the clean, neat factory and the girls' efficiency, noted "a certain pallor and anxious sadness on their countenances" as they worked at "the most beautiful specimens of machinery." [31] Like Melville or Henry Adams, these Europeans seem to be suggesting an inherent antagonism between machine production and human reproduction. Significantly enough, it was a woman who responded most directly to what was happening at Lowell. Very hopefully, Fredrika Bremer

> visited the manufactories, and saw 'the young ladies' at their work . . . . Only I noticed that some of 'the young ladies' were about fifty . . . . I was most struck by the relationship between the human being and the machinery. Thus, for example, I saw the young girls standing —each one between four busily-working spinning jennies: . . . and guarding them much as a mother would watch over and tend her children. The machinery was like an obedient child under the eye of an intelligent mother.[32]

These New England girls seem more like the victims than the beneficiaries of their industrial labor. The machines which they tend have usurped the most basic of human functions, and enforce a far more subtle and no more humane enslavement than the "peculiar institution" of the Southern States. Neither form of servitude could do much to advance the democratic principles of a nation proudest of its freedoms.

29 *Society . . . in the United States,* p. 129.
30 *Ibid.,* p. 143.
31 Pairpoint, *Uncle Sam and His Country,* pp. 164, 165.
32 *Homes of the New World,* p. 210.

Thus, beneath the generally favorable response of most Europeans, lay these covert fears about the dehumanization of the industrial worker —fears which grew most distinct at the sight of female operatives performing their mechanical duties,[33] fears which trouble us even today.

What holds this network of fears and objections together is the feeling that various features of the new technology violated certain commonly held attitudes toward Nature, whether it be natural beauty, natural health or purity, the natural observance of divine ordination, or the natural behavior, emotions and functions of human beings. That these fears were more often submerged in imagery than stated explicitly is symptomatic of the difficulty—common to both Europeans and Americans in the nineteenth century—of believing simultaneously in the benefits of inevitable progress (with the machine as chief instrument) and in the goodness of a quasi-religious conception of nature. The presence of this conflict, seldom fully realized, in the minds of men has affected the course of events, the shape of literature and the fine arts, and standards of machine design and machine production.

In this last regard I mean simply that the divided allegiances of many in the nineteenth century greatly hindered the diffusion of functionalism as a principle in architecture or industrial design. Thus, this conflict of commitments helps account for the fifty-year gap between the seeds planted by Horatio Greenough in America, Viollet-le-Duc in Europe, and the harvest of their heirs. And even these early theorists of functionalism worked from the moral hypothesis that Nature is structurally honest and exhibits in its organisms forms which express their function—an aesthetic counterpart of Darwin's biological hypothesis. This seems to me a subject worth more speculation and investigation than it has received.[34]

33 To an amazing degree, Herman Melville's sketch "The Tartarus of Maids" follows this same vein of imagery; see W. R. Thompson, " 'The Paradise of Bachelors and the Tartarus of Maids': A Reinterpretation," *American Quarterly,* IX (Spring, 1957), 34-45. And in *The Education of Henry Adams,* the polarities represented by the Virgin and the Dynamo express not only the conflict between past and present or the power of love and the power of machinery, but also the conflict between beauty and utility or religion and science.

34 Although John A. Kouwenhoven, in *Made in America* (New York, 1948), has argued persuasively and instructively that American artifacts characteristically developed simple, functional patterns which he termed "vernacular" forms, he has told only part of the story. He recognized the continuance, though never the dominance, of a more elaborate and ornamental "cultivated" tradition, but noted it only to stress the virtue of the "vernacular." And although he fits realistic landscape painting and literary realism into the vernacular along with functional machine forms and objects of daily use, my study cannot follow his distinctions. The problem is more than a semantic quibble over the meaning of a "realistic" response. It seems to me that the "realism" of functional design in machine forms and in architecture is quite different in both

To insist that all the imagery I encountered stresses the tension between a rising industrialism and cherished belief would be an oversimplification though not a misleading one, I think. A few observers, whose notions of beauty were less influenced by the idealizations and refinements of art and literature, found that the machine could express a beauty of its own. Though novel and unfamiliar, it need not be irreconcilable with the natural environment and human sensibilities; it could be evaluated simply as a machine designed to perform certain limited tasks. A few others, however, less able to deal with the machine in its own terms tried, perhaps too hard, to render it a harmonious addition to nature, even representing some of the traditional values of art and nature. Their attempt harbors some important confusions.

Those few who seemed to approach some concept of functionalism in their response to American machinery perceived "beauty" in machine construction and clearly associated "beauty" not only with workmanship but also with performance. In Philadelphia in 1831, the Englishman Godfrey T. Vigne wrote that "the waterworks on the Schuylkill are probably the finest in the world: they can scarcely be praised too highly for beauty of design, simplicity of construction, and real usefulness."[35] His words strongly suggest a functionalist creed, similar to that formulated by Greenough and well ahead of the time.

Both James Lumsden, a businessman, and J. F. W. Johnston, a chemist, made statements suggesting the beginnings of similar aesthetic standards. Also in Philadelphia, but in the early 1840s, Lumsden was impressed by the machinery at the United States Mint: "The steam engine that supplies mechanical power for the whole operations of the Mint is of the most ingenious construction, and it is scarcely possible to conceive anything of the kind more beautiful."[36] He clearly valued the design and construction and further supported his conclusion by citing the quiet, efficient operation of the machinery and the "exquisite" and "accurate" workmanship. Johnston, at Lowell, termed the functioning of "the self-acting machinery," which turned out carpeting as easily as calico, "a pleasing sight to see."[37] Numerous others stressed the superior

origin and implication from the "realism" of landscape and genre painting; and to equate them can overlook as much as it reveals. The iconography of most mid-nineteenth-century landscapes often countered "realistic" responses to the machine—not only in the genteel romanticism of the Hudson River painters or the unabashed grandiloquence of Bierstadt or Moran, but even in such a landscape as Inness' *Lackawanna Valley,* which clearly subordinates the railroad to the order of nature.

35 *Six Months in America* (2 vols.; London, 1832), I, 29.

36 *American Memoranda, by a Mercantile Man* (Glasgow, 1844), p. 17.

37 *Notes on North America, Agricultural, Economical, and Social* (2 vols.; London, 1851), II, 426.

efficiency of American machines and manufacturing processes without reference to the appearance of the machine. Even though none of these machines which appeared beautiful to a few might be termed "functional" today, the fact that beauty was linked with notions of utility, simplicity and efficiency indicates a rational response to the machine as something consistent with the purpose for which it had been constructed. The scarcity of this kind of comment, I think, indicates the strength of the cultivated tradition and of an emotional and intellectual commitment to "Nature."

Many of the previously mentioned instances of animal-like imagery applied to mechanical devices indicated attempts to reconcile the unfamiliar intruder with the more familiar setting. Although widespread, they represent, as I have said, attitudes that were neither deliberate nor rational but rather covert and unacknowledged. These responses are frequently the ingenuous expression of the preconscious, or to employ more of the psychologist's language, the result of free association which permits preconscious analogic processes. Less frank but no less revealing were the attempts to make the machine an element in complete harmony with nature, for frequently they constitute a kind of illusion—an instance of seeing what one wanted to see or not seeing what one was unwilling to see—what psychologists might call the operation of conscious or unconscious mentation to distort or repress the complex signals of the preconscious.[38]

To take such a striking and totally mechanized object as a railroad locomotive and to say that it fits right in with the scheme of field and forest may be a sort of transcendental self-deception. Yet, in several instances, precisely this was done. Emerson in his essay "The Poet" suggested that factory and railway were part of the vast order of Nature but indicated that it took the poetic imagination to overcome "dislocation and detachment" and restore the technological to the great Order. Harriet Martineau apparently had an easier time integrating the mechanical and the natural setting; but she is not entirely convincing as she explained that she "never saw an economical work of art harmonize so well with the vastness of a natural scene as here. From the piazza of the house at Branchville, the forest fills the whole scene, with the railroad stretching through it in a straight line, to the vanishing point."[39] In insisting that the line of track and the locomotive which traverses it are a harmonious part of the natural scene, she could be blocking out an

[38] I am using the terminology of L. S. Kubie in *Neurotic Distortion of the Creative Process* (Lawrence, 1958).

[39] *Society in America,* II, 8.

element from her experience. Psychologists, as we all know, use (or misuse) a variety of projective techniques to get at what has been forced out of conscious awareness. Admittedly conjectural, such a technique applied to these personal and historical materials can still be useful; and it is more than fancy to suggest that the writer who described the railroad's harmonizing with nature or the painter who fitted the railroad into a romantic landscape might have been ignoring or repressing what was least natural. He was at least expressing the desire to find sanction for the machine by emphasizing the natural environment. It is significant that on the page following the above passage Miss Martineau mentioned the train running down men on the track.

Another example might make my point more clearly. Chevalier, whose observations have already been so useful in outlining the conflict between Nature and the machine, tried very consciously to associate aspects of railroad construction with traditional ideas of natural and artificial beauty. He compared railroad tunnels with beautiful caverns, and said of a locomotive chimney that it was "not, perhaps, less perfect in its proportions than Pompey's Pillar." The trail of burning cinders, he proposed, made the railroad "the most poetical of all vehicles."[40] Certainly, he was suggesting that there was beauty in the machine, but it was the beauty borrowed from a concept of nature, of picturesque classic ruins and of romantic poetry—not the beauty of the machine itself, doing what it was constructed to do and reflecting its purpose in its appearance. His over-insistence on irrelevant standards of beauty suggests his great uneasiness about the machine—despite his intended praise—and also the lengths to which he went to reconcile the machine with the human imagination and the natural scene. He was no exception; like so many others, European and American, he was ready to accept the machine, but not simply as a machine. It had to reflect, enhance or harmonize with objects and ideas which its presence and its meaning contradicted. When the form of the machine reflected its purpose, it did not harmonize with "Nature." When, through embellishment and disguise, it fitted traditional notions of beauty, it could not be functional; but for many it could be "beautiful." The aesthetic principles derived from an intellectual, even a religious, commitment to Nature not only hindered a direct expression of function in form but also prompted a set of conventions (flowery scrolls, claw feet, classical imitations and even a somewhat specious arts and crafts program) which helped make the machine or its product acceptable at a time when the meaning of the machine was far from acceptable.

[40] *Society . . . in the United States*, p. 30.

The fact that early proponents of functionalism began with some of the same assumptions about "Nature" rather strengthens than weakens my argument. One need only recall the early differences between Frank Lloyd Wright and Le Corbusier to realize the differences between a functionalism based even sentimentally on Nature and a functionalism based on the logic of the machine. The mind of the nineteenth-century European responding to the dramatic emergence of industrialism in America helps locate the origin of contemporary conflict; helps place an aesthetic problem in a social context; helps us, as it were, to connect social fact with art and artifact.

Afternote

A revised version of this essay appears as Chapter 7 in *Workshops in the Wilderness: The European Response to American Industrialism, 1830–60* (New York: Oxford University Press, 1967).

Marvin Fisher is Professor of English at Arizona State University. [This article appeared in Vol. XIII, No. 3 (Fall, 1961).]

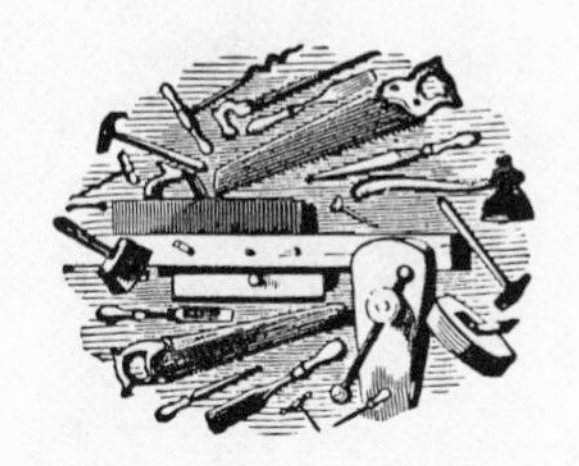

Mass Society

William E. Bridges

Family Patterns and Social Values in America, 1825-1875

THE HISTORY OF THE AMERICAN FAMILY IS PRESENTLY IN QUITE AS DISORganized a state as the family itself is often said to be. The conceptual sophistication of both sociology and social history since 1920 has left the only existing survey of this crucial social institution quite obsolete, for that survey was published during World War I.[1] In no major area of American social history will the investigator find so little work available and so much misconception passing for established fact. The situation is like that which would prevail if study had stopped forty-five years ago in the fields of religious or educational history. In a sense the situation is actually worse than that, for in disregarding the family, historians are disregarding what Margaret Mead has called "the basic institution of society."[2]

Before much sense can be made out of the family patterns in nineteenth-century America, the basic social function of the family must be clear.[3] As the context into which a child is born and within which he spends his most impressionable years, the family plays a double social role: first, it transforms an asocial biological entity into a human being, and by instilling in him the values endorsed by his culture it prepares him to meet the demands that his society will make upon him; second, it serves thereby to convey the culture's values across a critical gap in the social continuum—that separating one generation from its successor—and thus perpetuates the culture itself. This basic double function is performed in ways that are most appropriate to the values of the culture

1 Arthur W. Calhoun, *A Social History of the American Family* (3 vols.; Cleveland, 1915-18). Barnes and Noble reprinted this work in one volume in 1960.

2 Margaret Mead, *And Keep Your Powder Dry* (New York, 1942), p. 3.

3 For an extended discussion of this subject, see Paul Schrecker, "The Family: Conveyance of Tradition," *The Family: Its Function And Destiny*, ed. Ruth Nanda Anshen (New York, 1949), pp. 406-25.

in question. The way in which a child is acculturated is the product of the very values to which he is being acculturated. If, for example, his society is organized hierarchically, the child will be instructed in social subordination by domestic subordination; if his society expects sons to follow fathers in type of work and social station, the family patterns will aim at reproducing the father in the son; if his society emphasizes the importance of getting along with and fitting into "the group," the child will be encouraged to act in such a way that he will be popular with his juvenile peers. From a society's methods of acculturation, therefore, it is possible to predict the general outlines of its value patterns; conversely, a knowledge of cultural values will help one to make an educated guess as to the domestic methods by which they could be conveyed from generation to generation.

If all this is familiar to the student of American Civilization, it can only be said that the widely held conception of what nineteenth-century American family life was like suggests otherwise. For before the historian can make much headway in the task of describing that family life and its relationship to the society of which it was a part, he must deal with a surprisingly tenacious stereotype. *Snow-Bound,* "The Old Folks at Home," Currier and Ives prints, "The Children's Hour," Rogers Groups, "Home, Sweet Home"—from hundreds of such sources comes the image of a closely-knit, stable, patriarchal, self-sustaining, well-disciplined family group. As Carl Degler has recently suggested in these pages, this kind of family forms the basis for Riesman's study of "inner-directedness" in *The Lonely Crowd.*[4] The socialization of the child in such a family would presumably involve training in such qualities as self-control and self-denial; naturally the methods appropriate to such an end would call for considerable parental control and rigid discipline.

The person who brings such assumptions to the study of the nineteenth-century American family will find himself in a state of confusion very quickly. Surely the date of the following passage cannot be 1861; but for the diction it sounds more like 1961.

> In the genuine New England home of today, still that good old-fashioned thing called *obedience* lingers. In too many homes, judging by what we see and hear, it is deemed intrusive and turned out. . . . One may gather from his own observation and experience the most atrocious instances of disrespect and misrule, such as would disgrace an age of barbarism.[5]

[4] "The Sociologist as Historian: Riesman's *The Lonely Crowd,*" *American Quarterly,* XV (Winter 1963), 493-94.

[5] *Monthly Religious Magazine* (1861), quoted in Calhoun, III, 144-45.

Nor was a mid-century writer being affected in calling obedience "old-fashioned," for Americans and Europeans had been noting its absence for more than half a century. In the 1850s the Pulskys wrote that American children "have their own way" and described them as "tumbling and dragging about books and cushions and chairs and climbing up and down just as they please."[6] In the same decade Adam Gurowski complained of "the prodigality, the assumption, self-assertion, and conceit" of the American child.[7] When James Fenimore Cooper listed the "defects in American deportment" twenty years earlier, he began with "insubordination in children, and a general want of respect for age."[8] The children encountered in 1817 by De Montlezun "are absolute masters of their fates. The authority of the parents is no restraint at all."[9] And so it goes—the endless record of those who had been jostled, bellowed at and spilled upon by the pre-Civil War American child.

It may be objected, of course, that these were mostly observers who were generally disapproving in their views of American society, so let us turn to one less suspect on this score. Tocqueville devoted a chapter of his second volume to the American family, and it is well worth reading.[10] Obviously he saw the very things of which the other observers complained, but he did not confuse a lack of subordination and new patterns of training with insubordination and a lack of training. Instead he argued that the same forces that undermined the principle and practice of civil subordination also removed the need for most of the domestic subordination that was familiar to the European. He reasoned that the same principles on which the Americans had rejected the past politically and socially led them also to care less for the arbiters of and spokesmen for that past and, thus, to "the general want of respect for age" of which Cooper had complained. In keeping with his own domestic experience, he analyzed the situation in terms of the role of the father rather than that of the parents, but nonetheless many of his observations are astute. What he described was not a family in an advanced state of disintegration (as contemporary Europeans tended to) but rather a family that was being reconstructed so that it might more successfully acculturate the American child and prepare him thereby for life in his society. The kind of correlation he found between the values of American society and the patterns of its domestic life is evident when he writes,

6 Ferenc and Theresa Pulsky, *White, Red, Black* (1853) in *This Was America*, ed. Oscar Handlin (Cambridge, 1949), p. 239.

7 Quoted in Calhoun, II, 56.

8 *The American Democrat* (New York, 1950), p. 150.

9 *Voyage fait . . . de New-York a la Nouvelle-Orleans . . .*, in Handlin, p. 134.

10 "Influence of Democracy on the Family," *Democracy in America* (2 vols.; New York, 1948), II, 192-97.

> When the condition of society becomes democratic and men adopt as their general principle that it is good and lawful to judge of all things for oneself, using former points of belief not as a rule of faith, but simply as a means of information, the power which the opinions of a father exercise over those of his sons diminishes as well as his legal power.[11]

In this statement one can see the way in which Tocqueville's analysis differs from that of Riesman.[12] Whereas Riesman associates individualism with a process of close parental supervision under which the child "internalizes" parental restraints, Tocqueville associates individualism more logically with minimal parental supervision and early instruction in the importance of learning things for oneself. The complaints of most contemporary observers could be summed up in the words of an Englishwoman who wrote in 1848 that the American child "is too early his own master." [13] Her opposition to the system was almost as much one of principle as of results. If one could forget the principle and attend to the results, he might see the sort of thing observed by another Englishwoman who reported in amazement,

> Little creatures feed themselves very neatly, and are trusted with cups of glass and china, which they grasp firmly, carry about the room carefully, and deposit unbroken, at an age when, in our country mamma or nurse would be rushing after them to save the vessels from destruction.[14]

The only thing to add to such an account is that it seems very likely that the same child that carried the cup with such care also infuriated other visitors who tried to be helpful by taking it away from him. One suspects that much of the "willfulness" noted in the American child was triggered by the behavior toward him of the visitor who observed it.

It is significant, of course, that many of the criticisms of the American child's independence were voiced by those who found American men presumptuous, materialistic and restless. For the children were being fitted for life in a society whose main outlines were dangerous by European standards. It is interesting to compare the kind of child that we have been describing with the conclusions that several historians have reached about the demands made on the individual by society in this

[11] *Ibid.*, p. 194.

[12] *Cf.* Degler's statement that "Calhoun's chapter on 'The Career of the Child' has almost no point of contact with the view of the inner-directed child presented by Riesman." Degler, p. 493.

[13] Quoted in Calhoun, II, 67.

[14] Calhoun, II, 55.

period and the kind of man who was best suited to meet them. In his study of the effects of economic abundance on the American character, David Potter wrote,

> Historically, as new lands, new forms of wealth, new opportunities, came into play, clamoring to be seized upon, America developed something of a compulsion to make use of them. The man best qualified for this role was the completely mobile man, moving freely from one locality to the next, from one economic position to another, or from one social level to levels above. . . . In a country where the entire environment was to be transformed with the least possible delay . . . mobility became not merely an optional privilege but almost a mandatory obligation, and the man who failed to meet this obligation had, to a certain extent, defaulted in his duty to society.[15]

Potter's conclusion is supported by that of another historian whose approach and purposes are very different; in his study of Jacksonian democracy Marvin Meyers wrote,

> The central economic figure is . . . the speculative enterpriser who scents distant opportunities and borrows or invents the means for grasping them. A preference for high-risk, high-gain transactions is found at all economic levels. . . . Thus the American, in his urgent quest for gain and advancement, becomes to many witnesses the very opposite of the sturdy, stable citizen-producer; becomes an adventurer steered only by a bold imagination.[16]

To Potter's "completely mobile man" and Meyers' "adventurer" we may add the Adamic figure of self-containment described by R. W. B. Lewis as "an individual emancipated from history, happily bereft of ancestry, untroubled and undefiled by the usual inheritances of family and race." [17]

The composite image that can be formed from these three figures is very close, I would submit, to the image of man that the nineteenth-century acculturation practices were designed to produce. This impression is supported, moreover, by the findings of Daniel Miller and Guy Swanson, who summed up their survey of nineteenth-century child-guidance literature by identifying the following as one of the central and unifying themes in it:

> the notion that a youngster must be able independently to go out into the urban world, to capitalize on such opportunities as it may present, to carve out a life for himself which, in a rapidly changing society,

15 *People of Plenty* (Chicago, 1954), pp. 96-97.
16 *The Jacksonian Persuasion* (New York, 1960), p. 137.
17 *The American Adam* (Chicago, 1955), p. 5.

> may well require different tasks to be performed than were required of his parents. His is to be the active, manipulative approach to people and things.[18]

This statement may remind the reader of Riesman's figure, the inner-directed man; and assuredly the self-reliance and self-direction that Riesman emphasizes are present. What is also present and what has not been hitherto sufficiently remarked is a cluster of values that can be described as impersonality and emotional nondependence. The enemy of mobility is not only a static social structure but also the personal attachments that the individual develops in such a structure. Individualism, in these terms, is not so much an intellectual freedom as it is an emotional disengagement from others. This disengagement was an important element in Emersonian individualism.[19] What appeared to many observers to be domestic disintegration and lack of strong emotional ties within the family is better understood as training in detachment.[20]

The relationship between domestic practices and their social context in this matter of emotional independence was reciprocal. That is, the patterns of acculturation can be studied as both results and causes of an increasingly atomistic, impersonal, competitive socio-economic order. One area in which this two-way relationship is evident is that of paternal participation in family life. Contemporary reports make it clear that fathers were playing less and less of a part in domestic activities as their work took them out of the home for the major part of the day. In this matter as in so many like it, modern historians have underestimated the similarities between past and present—similarities that are clear in such a passage as this, written in 1860:

> The pressure upon a multitude of business and professional men is really frightful; combined with the necessity in many cases of going long distances to their places of duty, it produces little short of an absolute separation from their families.[21]

Not only is this the product of socialization along patterns of emotional independence; it also encourages such patterns in the next generation by fragmenting the family and by placing the father's central social concerns outside the domestic context.

18 *The Changing American Parent* (New York, 1958), p. 40.

19 "Let us feel if we will the absolute insulation of man . . . . Let us even bid our dearest friends farewell, and defy them, saying 'Who are you? Unhand me: I will be dependent no more.'" *Emerson: A Modern Anthology*, eds. Alfred Kazin and Daniel Aaron (New York, 1958), p. 168.

20 For reports of such "coolness," see Calhoun, II, 131-33.

21 *Monthly Religious Magazine* (1860), in Calhoun, III, 187.

It would be a mistake to assume, however, that this training in detachment was wholly successful, for one of the striking features of nineteenth-century family life resulted from its partial failure. There is plentiful evidence that striving to be the "completely mobile man" was a lonely and frustrating task. What Miller and Swanson called "the active, manipulative approach to people and things" dehumanizes not only others but oneself as well. The economic roles filled by these men were often narrow and not conducive to broad self-fulfillment. The problem and its bearing on family life have been described thus by Margaret Mead:

> In much of his ordinary adult activity, the individual expresses his personality in a segmented fashion. One aspect finds expression in his work or profession; another may be elicited from his social and recreational interests; still another may be called forth in his religious life. In the intimacies of family association, on the other hand, the entire personality is capable of integrated expression and receives response in terms of the whole rather than its parts.[22]

Here is another area in which the differences between the last century and this have been emphasized at the expense of the similarities. For although the social scientist's vocabulary would have been foreign to the nineteenth-century American, the notion behind the words would not. In the best-selling *Reveries of a Bachelor* (1850) the narrator decides that among the many attractions of home life to a man, the greatest is "the ecstasy of the conviction, that *there* at least you are beloved; that there you are understood; that there your errors will meet ever with the gentlest forgiveness . . .; and that there you may be entirely and joyfully— yourself."[23]

According to this view the home became a retreat from the world, a shelter from the impersonality and competitiveness of the society that surrounded it. This is, of course, the domestic image that fills the poetry and visual art of the period and is, thus, the source of the stereotype of nineteenth-century home life. In practice, however, the notion of home-as-retreat could only confuse domestic life, for it burdened the institution that was preparing children to face their society's demands with the task of rehabilitating adults that found those demands too great.

This confusion was compounded by another that stemmed from the father's absorption in extradomestic activity. In his absence the task of child raising, the acculturation process, fell largely to the mother. This

[22] Mead, p. 17.

[23] [Donald Grant Mitchell], *Reveries of a Bachelor* (New York, 1852), p. 90. See also the quotation from a *McGuffey Reader* in Richard D. Mosier, *Making the American Mind* (New York, 1947), p. 28.

shift of responsibility might have had less impact on our culture if, at the same time, the vigorous reform movements active in the society had not turned to the American mother and the acculturation process over which she presided as their best avenue of advancement. Mothers were barraged with a many-sided campaign to save the world by means of the family.[24] While the specific goals of the campaign were as various as the groups engaged in it, one of them deserves our notice. Its central figure was the editor of *Godey's Lady's Book,* the influential Sarah Josepha Hale, and its purpose is evident in the following passage from one of Mrs. Hale's editorials:

> In this country, there being no established rank and privileged class, wealth has been found to be the surest letter of introduction into the highest and most polished circles. . . . There is a cramping and debasing influence exerted by this systematic, absorbing pursuit after wealth. . . . And here it is that our country needs the power of female talent to be exerted, the efficiency of moral training to be tested. Let this besetting sin of our times be studiously watched by the Christian mother. Let us guard against this insidious influence of Mammon.[25]

Mothers were being urged, in short, to undermine the very pattern of values that the emerging economic order demanded.

The resulting tension between the values of the success ethic and those of Mrs. Hale's crusade did little to further domestic solidarity. But in the period between 1825 and 1875 it did achieve a precarious balance that was important. The home and the market place became the foci of opposite sets of values, one stultifyingly static and the other recklessly dynamic. Each was the more extreme for the presence of the other, while each acted as a brake on the other. The result was a tense amalgam of advance-with-safety, progress-with-restraint, exploit-with-control. It is the pattern of checks and balances that one finds in Howells' *The Rise of Silas Lapham* in which the male principle of material advancement is restrained by the female principle of moral advancement.

The hold of this polarity between home and market place upon the American imagination is considerable, even today. But just as the last quarter of the nineteenth century brought public criticism of the market as a threat to the individual, so the same period saw a disenchantment with the home on the same score. Huck Finn's flight from social control at both the beginning and the end of the novel is an escape from

24 See Anne L. Kuhn, *The Mother's Role in Childhood Education: New England Concepts, 1830-1860* (New Haven, 1947).

25 Quoted in Meade Minnigerode, *The Fabulous Forties: 1840-1850* (New York, 1924), p. 131.

the domestic context. "Aunt Sally she's going to adopt me and sivilize me, and I can't stand it" [26]—this is the complaint lodged against an institution and a set of values that it seeks to convey.

Yet even these attitudes are not new. The same narrator of *Reveries of a Bachelor* who depicted the home as a happy retreat decided finally to remain a bachelor because of the freedom he enjoyed in that state. Describing his house, he writes

> I take a vast deal of comfort in treating it just as I choose. I manage to break some article of furniture, almost every time I pay it a visit; and if I cannot open the window readily of a morning . . . I knock out a pane or two of glass with my boot.

He concludes that his behavior would "make a prim housewife fret herself into a raging fever." [27] His attitudes, though much more self-conscious, are like those of Huck, who announced, "there warn't no home like a raft, after all. Other places do seem so cramped up and smothery, but a raft don't." [28]

In comparing Huck's sentiments with those of the mid-century "bachelor," I am again suggesting that attitudes that we often consider modern do, in fact, run back well into the nineteenth century. Throughout the period the American family was equipping new generations to fit the social patterns described by Potter, Meyers and Lewis—an activity on which we have far too little information. At the same time the family, under maternal guidance, was serving as a counterweight to the effects of those values and as a retreat from the confusion they often produced. Most of our misconceptions about the nineteenth-century family come from assuming that its second, compensatory role was its only role. But the family's primary role, as we began by noting, is the acculturation of children. And until we know far more than we do now about the way in which the nineteenth-century American family functioned, vitally important pages will be missing from the historical record.

William E. Bridges is an Assistant Professor of English at Mills College, San Francisco. [This article appeared in Vol. XVII, No. 1 (Spring, 1965).]

[26] Mark Twain, *The Adventures of Huckleberry Finn* (New York, 1948), p. 293.
[27] Mitchell, p. 16.
[28] Mark Twain, p. 116.

Gregory P. Stone

Halloween and the Mass Child*

I SET THESE NOTES DOWN WITH A SENSE OF *déjà vu*. CERTAINLY IT HAS ALL been said before, and I may have read it all somewhere, but I cannot locate the sources. I have often thought about these things in the past. Then, too, as a sociologist, I like to think I am providing observations as well as impressions for my audience. I cannot recall any other counts and tabulations of the very few facts and happenings that I counted and tabulated this year in a small "near southern" town on the traditional hallowed evening.

In brief, I found that Riesman's "other-directed man" may have exported his peculiar life style—tolerance and conformity organized by the prime activity of consumption—from his suburban northeastern habitat to areas westward and southward perilously close to the Mason-Dixon line.[1] The town I speak of is a university town. As such, it has undoubtedly recruited "other-directed's" from the universities of the northeast. For example, I have been there. Moreover, the part of town in which I carried on my quantitative survey (properly speaking, a "pilot study") is a kind of suburb—a sub-village, perhaps an "inner-urb"—the housing section maintained by most large universities where younger faculty are segregated from the rest of the community in World War II officers' quarters. "Other-directed's" are younger and better educated than "inner-directed's."

* This paper has had the benefit of criticism provided by Dr. Stuart Cuthbertson, retired Chairman of the Department of Romance Languages at the University of Colorado, and Dr. David Bakan, Professor of Psychology at the University of Missouri.

[1] It may well be argued that "other-direction" is, like Babbitry, a midwestern phenomenon. Riesman has probably been unduly and misleadingly cautious in circumscribing his observations as he did. Thus, the notion of "other-direction" as an incipient character type originating in the northeast is probably more a consequence of the locale in which his early investigations were conducted than a reflection of the actual spread of "other-direction" in the United States. I am grateful to David Bakan for the presentation of this point of view.

You will recall the main theme of *The Lonely Crowd:* the very *character* of American life has been revolutionized as the fundamental organizing activity of our waking hours has shifted from production to consumption. We used to work—at least ideally and Protestantly—because work was our life. By our works we were known. Max Weber, among others less careful and profound, has attempted to explain this in his *Protestant Ethic and the Spirit of Capitalism,* showing how a vocabulary of motive was required to consolidate the spread of capitalism in society and arguing that the sheer dialectic of class antagonism was not always sufficient to account for the institution of pervasive economic change. *Every social change requires a convincing rationale.* Protestantism supplied this in part, and its persistence may still be seen in the contrasting attitudes toward gambling *(gaming),* for example, held by Protestant and Catholic churches. Only in the 1920's did the American Protestant churches relax their bans on such games, and then it was with the stipulation that they be played for amusement only. Risk and gain were cemented in the context of work; never in the context of play. The place of consumption in the "old" society—the industrial society—may be caricatured by referring to Marx's view that the cost of labor was the money and goods required for laborers to exist and reproduce themselves. Abbreviated: we consumed so that we might work. Today, for the most part, we work to live and live to consume. Abbreviated: we work to consume.

"Trick or Treat" is the contemporary quasi-ritual play and celebration of Halloween. Characteristically, the "trick-or-treater" is rewarded not for his work, but for his play. The practice is ostensibly a vast bribe exacted by the younger generation upon the older generation (by the "other-directed's" upon the "inner-directed's"?). The doorbell rings and is answered. The householder is greeted by a masked and costumed urchin with a bag—significantly, a *shopping* bag—and confronted with dire alternatives: the unknown peril of a devilishly conceived prank that will strike at the very core of his social self—his property; or the "payoff" in candy, cookies or coin for another year's respite from the antisocial incursions of the children. The householder pays.

In his *Psychology of Clothes,* J. C. Flügel has noted that the mask and costume free the individual from social obligation by concealing his identity and cloaking him in the absurd protective anonymity of a mythical or legendary creature—a clown, a ghost, a pirate or a witch. The householder must pay. For, by "dressing out," the urchin is symbolically immunized against those punishments that might ordinarily inhibit the promised violations of property and propriety. Punishment presupposes the identity of the offender.

Nonsense! This conception of "trick or treat" is clearly and grossly in error. In the mass society, the "protection racket" seems as archaic as the concepts of psychoanalysis. To revive either in the analysis of contemporary life betrays the nostalgia of the analyst. Both are but the dusty wreckage of long dead romances. Moreover, as we shall see, the mask invites the ready disclosure of the wearer's identity. Instead of protecting the urchin, the costume is more akin to the Easter bonnet, designed to provoke the uncritical appreciations of the audience.

Even so, we can apprehend the "trick" as a production; the "treat" as a consumption. Just twenty-five years ago, when I was an urchin, Halloween was a time set aside for young tricksters—a time for creative productions. Creativity, I might remind the reader, is inevitably destructive, as it pushes the present into the past. Of course, it is never merely nor exclusively the destruction of established forms. Our destructive productions were immense (I wonder at my adolescence, as Marx wondered at the *bourgeoisie*!). I don't know now how we managed silently to detach the eave troughs from the house of the neighborhood "crab," remove his porch steps, then encourage him to give chase by hurling those eave troughs, with a terrifying clatter, upon his front porch. I do know it was long, hard and careful *work*. The devices of Halloween were also artfully and craftily produced, like the serrated spool used to rattle the windows of more congenial adults in the neighborhood. We had no conception of being treated by our victims, incidentally, to anything except silence which we hoped was studied, irate words, a chase (if we were lucky), or, most exciting of all, an investigation of the scene by the police whom we always managed to elude. Our masks, we believed, did confound our victims' attempts to identify us.

In sharp contrast to these nostalgic memories are the quantitative findings of my "pilot study." Being a sociologist, I must apologize for my sample first of all. An editorial in a local newspaper warned me that between seventy-five and one hundred children would visit my home on Halloween. Only eighteen urchins bedeviled me that evening, a fact that I attribute to two circumstances. First, I unwittingly left my dog at large early in the evening. A kind animal, a cross between a Weimeraner and some unknown, less nervous breed, she was upset by the curious costumes of the children, and, barking in fright, she frightened away some of the early celebrants. Second, I think that our segregated "inner-urb" was neglected in favor of more imposing, perhaps more lucrative, areas of town. My eighteen respondents ranged in age from about four years to about twelve. Half were girls and half were boys. Two of the six groups—one-third—were mixed. Twenty-five years ago the presence of girls in my own Halloween enterprises was unthinkable.

Was the choice proffered by these eighteen urchins, when they whined or muttered, "Trick or treat?" or stood mutely at my threshold, a choice between production and consumption? Was I being offered the opportunity to decide for these youngsters the ultimate direction they should take in later life by casting them in the role of producer or consumer? Was I located at some vortex of fate so that my very act could set the destiny of the future? Was there a choice at all? No. In each case, I asked, "Suppose I said, 'Trick.' What would you do?" Fifteen of the eighteen (83.3%) answered, "I don't know." The art of statistics, taken half-seriously, permits me to estimate with 95% confidence that the interval, .67–1.00, will include the proportion of children who don't know what a trick is in that "hypothetical universe" for which the eighteen constituted a random sample (this is a ruse employed by some sociologists who find out belatedly that the sample they have selected is inadequate). Yet, it seems that at least two-thirds of the children like those who visited my house on Halloween probably have no conception of producing a trick! They aren't bribing anybody. They grace your and my doorsteps as consumers, pure and simple.

What of the three—the 16.7%—who did not respond, "I don't know"? One said nothing at all. I assume he really didn't know, but, being a careful quantitative researcher, I cannot include him with the others. Another did, in fact, say, "I don't know," but qualified his reply. Let me transcribe the dialogue.

Interviewer: Hello there.
Respondent: (Silence)
Interviewer: What do you want?
Respondent: Trick or treat?
Interviewer: Supposing I said, "Trick"?
Respondent: (Silence)
Interviewer: What would you do, if I said, "Trick"?
Respondent: *I don't know.* (Long pause.) I'd *probably* go home and get some sand *or something* and throw it on your porch. (Emphasis mine.)
Field Notes: The porches of the old officers' quarters are constructed from one-by-three slats so that about an inch of free space intervenes between each slat. In short, the porch simply would not hold sand, and the "trick" of the urchin could never be carried off!
Interviewer: O. K. I'll have to treat, I guess.

The third answered, without prompting, that he'd go home, get a water pistol and squirt my windows (which could have used a little squirting). The "tricks" did not seem so dire, after all! Moreover, the "means of production"—the sand and the water pistol—were left at home, a fact that reminds me of one of Riesman's acute observations to the effect that the home has become a workshop (work is consumed) and the factory, a ranch house (consumption is work).

Did the masks and costumes provide anonymity? To the contrary! I asked each child who he or she was. Happily and trustfully each revealed his or her identity, lifting the mask and disclosing the name. Had they ripped off *my* eave troughs, I would have had the police on them in short order! "Trick or Treat" is a highly personalized affair so that even its ritual quality is lost (for their persistence, rituals depend upon impersonal enactments, and my earlier use of the term, "quasi-ritual," is explained.

On the possibility that the costume might have been a production or a creation, I noted the incidence of ready-to-wear costumes. Two-thirds had been purchased in their entirety. Four of the others were mixed, consisting of homemade costumes and commercial masks. Two were completely homemade: one a ghost outfit, consisting of an old tattle-tale gray sheet with two eye holes; the other, a genuine creation. It was comprised by a mesh wastebasket inverted over an opening in a large cardboard box with armholes. On the front of the box, printed in a firm adult "hand," were the words: Take Me to Your Leader. Occasionally, adults produced, but only to ratify or validate the child in his masquerade as a consumer.

To ascertain the part played by adults in "Trick or Treat," I must, unfortunately, rely on recollections. In preparing my interview schedule and observational data sheets, I had not anticipated the adult, thinking that the celebrants of Halloween would be children. This impression was confirmed by my local newspaper which published the rules of Halloween, stipulating its age-graded character. "Trick or Treat" was set aside for the preadolescents of the town, while teen-agers were obliged to celebrate the event at parties. The rules were apparently enforced, as this news item on the November 1 front page shows:

> Police yesterday afternoon arrested, then released, a youth they said was dressed in a Halloween costume and asking for tricks [*sic*] or treats at downtown stores.
>
> They said the youth was about 17. He started the rounds of the stores early, he said, because he had to work last night.
>
> Police said they lectured the youth and explained the traditional [*sic*] trick-or-treat routine is normally reserved for children.

What adults were to do was not clarified by the local press. What many did do was to ease and expedite consumption by clothing their preadolescent children for the role, providing them with shopping bags and, in many instances, accompanying them on the rounds. At least three of the six groups of urchins that called at my house on Halloween were accompanied by adults (the father was always there, one alone!) who lurked uneasily and self-consciously in the darkness where night was mixed with the shadowed shafts cast by my porch light. In one case, a peer group of adults lurked in the shadows and exceeded in number the peer group of children begging on my porch. There they were: agents of socialization, teaching their children how to consume in the tolerant atmosphere of the mass society. The "anticipatory socialization" of the children—accomplished by an enactment of roles not normally played at the time, but roles that would be assumed in the future—was going on before my eyes. I wondered whether the parental preoccupation with the child's adjustment in the larger society could not have been put aside just for Halloween. Perhaps the hiding in the dark allegorically complemented my wish in the tacit expression of shame.

They were teaching a lesson in tolerance, not only a lesson in consumption, encouraging their children to savor the gracious and benign acceptance of their beggary by an obliging adult world. My questions made them nervous. The lone father was silent. He turned his face skywards, studying the stars. One couple spoke rapidly in hushed whispers, punctuating their remarks with nervous laughter. In another couple, the mother said sheepishly, "I wonder what they'll say? They've never been asked that." All the parents were relieved when I tactfully rescued the situation from deterioration by offering to treat the children with (purchased) goodies. Consider a typical protocol.

Field Notes: The bell rings. I go to the door. On the porch are three children between five and nine years old, two boys—one in a clown suit, the other in a pirate suit—and a girl in a Japanese kimono, holding a fan. On the sidewalk are a mother and a father whose faces are hidden in darkness.

Interviewer: Hi!

Respondents: (Silence.)

Interviewer: What do you want?

Respondents: (Silence.)

The clown: Candy.

Interviewer: Why?

Field Notes: The married couple giggles. They shift their feet.

Japanese girl and clown: (Silence.)

Pirate: I don't know.

Field Notes: I look questioningly at the girl and the clown. Each is silent.

Interviewer: What are you supposed to say?

Japanese girl: I don't know.

Interviewer: Have you heard of "Trick or Treat"?

Clown: No.

Field Notes: The married couple is silent. They lean forward expectantly, almost placing their faces in the circle of light arching out and around my porch and open front door, almost telling me who they are.

Interviewer: Well, I guess I'll have to treat.

Field Notes: I get a handful of corn candy from the living room, and divide it among the three outstretched open shopping bags. All the respondents laugh in an appreciative, relieved manner. My study is passed off as a joke. The world has been tolerant after all.

I am reminded of Ortega's remonstrances against the Mass Man, for whom *privileges had become rights.* Standing there, existing, it was the clown's right to receive the treat, the candy. The treat or gift was at one time an act of deference in recognition of esteemed friendship. Herbert Spencer wrote of it in that way—the gift was a privilege. On Halloween, the gift has become the right of every child in the neighborhood, however he or his family is esteemed. Now, rights are not questioned. That such rights would be questioned was hardly anticipated by those who claimed them. It made them ill-at-ease and nervous, perhaps lest the questions betray an indignation—a state of mind more appropriate to an age when people were busy, or perhaps busier, more productive.

Yet, this is not a plea for a return to the "good old days"—ridiculous on the face of it. Certainly, the farther south the tolerance of the mass society creeps, the happier many of us will be. It seems to be unquestionably true that the younger people of the south are less opposed to segregated schools than the adults. There is nothing morally wrong with consumption, per se, as production was often the setting for ruthless destruction. The conformity of "other-direction" (no trick-or-treater came to my door by himself) need not disturb us. Each society must secure conformity from a substantial majority of its members if that society is to persist. Instead, I have tried to show only two things. First, Riesman's character type of "other-direction" may, indeed, be a *prototype* of American character and not some strange mutation in the northeast. Consumption, tolerance and conformity were recognizable in the Halloween masquerade of a near-southern town. Production, indignation and autonomy were not. Second, national holidays and observances may have been transformed into vast staging areas for the anticipatory socialization of mass men. By facilitating this change in life style, they can give impetus to the change in character conceived by Riesman (and many others). I am being very serious when I say that we need studies of what has happened to all these observances—the Fourth of July, Thanksgiving, Christmas and Easter—in all parts of America. After reading this report, you will agree that we need a study of Halloween.

It is not only as a sociologist, however, that I ask for these studies. Something does trouble me deeply about my observations—the "I don't know." Here is the source of our misgivings and dis-ease with respect to the mass man. It is not that he consumes, but, to the profit of the "hidden persuaders," that he consumes, not knowing why or just not knowing. It is not that he is tolerant, but that he is *unreasonably* tolerant. It is not that he conforms, but that he conforms for conformity's sake. *The mass society, like the industrial society, needs a vocabulary of motive—a rationale—to dignify the daily life.* That's what troubles me about my findings on Halloween. It was a rehearsal for consumership without a rationale. Beyond the stuffing of their pudgy stomachs, they didn't know why they were filling their shopping bags.

Afternote

It has been seven years since the appearance of this little study, and I can report only one negative instance for its conclusions — and that, a matter of chance. In 1960, my colleague, Howard S. Becker, with all the assurance that scientific wisdom provides, confidently replied, "Trick!" to the query of a Kansas urchin and was promptly squirted in the face with a water pistol. Yet, in the article, I reported only 95 percent confidence that from two-thirds to all Halloween beggars will not know what a trick is. Becker was undoubtedly a victim of confidence limits and not mass society. There will always be strange mutation in large populations, and we can never know with precision where, when or at whom it will strike.

More scientific replications of the study provide only strong support and signal an inexorable advance in the established trends. In 1965, a younger colleague, Richard Travisano, repeated my procedure in a working-class suburb of Minneapolis. Of 104 visiting beggars, nineteen (18.3 percent) responded to his question, "What would you do, if I said, 'Trick'?" Of these, two "didn't know" what they would do, two threatened to soap his windows and fifteen conceived the "Trick" to be one of a number of insipid performances, like inept somersaults, in *payment* for the treat. I had observed this earlier in St. Louis in 1960. More than 200 interviews conducted there with Halloween celebrants established that the query was most often "Trick *for* Treat." The transformation had gone full circle: production had literally become the cost of consumption! Travisano also reported that two children offering tricks *for* treats removed their masks, without bidding, before performing their clumsy somersaults.

In 1965, I received this flash from Brandeis University, courtesy of Everett C. Hughes: Item, Boston *Globe*, October 28, 1965:

HAVE A SAFE HALLOWEEN

Spooks and hobgoblins will be abroad this week-end. What better time of year for safety reminders to the youngsters in your family?

Flashlights are safer than candles out of doors. And for all family members, flashlights should be standard equipment when walking out doors at night.

Sweep away leaves and debris from walks and doorsteps and turn on the porch lights for the young ghosts, avoid dangerous falls.

Long skirts and masks can be hazardous on this jolly [sic] week-end, so the careful parent should check the Halloween costumes before the children depart. Eye holes in masks can be easily enlarged; long skirts can be shortened. Fluorescent cloth strips can be sewn to the backs of costumes for better visibility and for safety's sake too.

This article is included as a chapter in my book, *Sports, Play and The Implications of Leisure: Essays in Sociology* to be published by Bobbs-Merrill.

Gregory P. Stone is Professor of Sociology and American Studies in the University of Minnesota. [This article appeared in Vol. II, No. 4 (Winter, 1950).]

Eugene D. Balsley

The Hot Rod Culture

I

THE following statement by Thomas W. Ryan, director of the New York Division of Safety, presents the typical image of the hot rodder in the mediums of mass communication. He is shown as a deliberate and premeditated lawbreaker: "Possession of the 'hot rod' car is presumptive evidence of an intent to speed. Speed is Public Enemy No. 1 of the highways. It is obvious that a driver of a 'hot rod' car has an irresistible temptation to 'step on it' and accordingly operate the vehicle in a reckless manner endangering human life. It also shows a deliberate and premeditated idea to violate the law. These vehicles are largely improvised by home mechanics and are capable of high speed and dangerous maneuverability. They have therefore become a serious menace to the safe movement of traffic. The operators of these cars are confused into believing that driving is a competitive sport. They have a feeling of superiority in recklessly darting in and out of traffic in their attempt to outspeed other cars on the road . . ."[1]

This point of view is lavishly dramatized in the comic-strip character Hot Rod Happy, a lawless, spoiled, delinquent, disrespectful cad, who is the antithesis of good, clean-living American youth. Recently Hot Rod was near death as the result of an automobile accident for which he was apparently solely responsible. Presumably he has returned as a cautionary exemplar of the evils of the hot-rod culture.

The hot rodder's picture of himself is somewhat different, though

[1] *New York Times*, June 19, 1949.

obliquely cognizant of the mediums' image. Thus, in a letter to the creator of Hot Rod Happy protesting the cartoonist's picture of the hot rodder, a hot-rod organization wrote as follows: "A hot rod accident or incident is newsworthy, while an accident involving ordinary cars is so common that it is usually not newsworthy. We wonder whether you appreciate the very real contribution that the hot rod industry, for it is an industry, has made to automotive transportation. The automotive industry has the equivalent of a million dollar experimental laboratory in the hot rod industry from which they can get valuable technical information free of any expense or risk of reputation . . ."[2]

The publication of the hot rodder, *Hot Rod Magazine*, which claims a circulation of 200,000, devotes many of its editorials to presenting a true picture of the hot-rod car and driver. One of them said, "A real hot rod is a car that is lending itself to experimental development for the betterment of safety, operation, and performance, not merely a stripped-down or highly decorated car of any make, type or description, or one driven by a teen-ager. As to the menace or nuisance element, very few hot rod enthusiasts want to risk their specialized equipment for use as battering rams. The fact their cars are built so that they attract attention becomes an automatic psychological brake which governs their driving activities . . ."[3]

II

Most Americans are sure that American cars are the best and cheapest in the world. They will argue that we are the leaders and innovators in motor-car design. Judging from the Detroit car one sees on the street, it looks as if Americans believe that "chromium makes the car" and that only a big, heavy car will hold the road. The predispositions of American automobile designers shine through the enamel and chromium strips. This standard of taste appears to be as unshakable as the erroneous American belief that the cars and drivers at the Indianapolis Memorial Day Race are representative of the best in the professional racing world. In contrast to this complacency, the hot-rod culture is committed to the everlasting modification of what it casually calls "Detroit iron" — the American production car.

[2] *Hot Rod Magazine*, September 1949, p. 4.

[3] *Ibid.*, December 1949, p. 6.

The hot rodder and his circle are highly articulate in their objections to the Detroit product as an automobile, and the reason is that they have little respect for the Detroit solution of a problem in transportation, engineering, and esthetics. The hot rodder says that this production car is uneconomical, unsafe at modern road speeds, and uglier than it has any right to be. What is more, it is too costly, too heavy, and too complicated by class and status symbolism to be a good car. Designed in ignorance of the hot rodder's credo that driving should not be so effortless that one forgets one is driving until after the crash, this car appears to the hot rodder to be a sort of high-speed parlor sofa. In general, the hot rodder protests against the automobile production and merchandising which fail to give the public a sufficiently wide range of models to permit judgments of value. The huge scale of the hot rodder's protest is immediately suggested by the sales of its parts industry—a cool eight million per year gross income.

III

When the hot rodder rebuilds a Detroit car to his own design, he is aiming to create a car which is a magical and vibrant thing. Yet, back of his dream design we can see the workings of the practical engineering standards that dominate the hot-rod culture. There are sound reasons for the hot-rod builder's selection and rejection of the various components of the Detroit car.

Any given car, when rebuilt by the hot rodder, can be loosely assigned to one of four classes of design. Let us talk in terms of ascending ranks of merit or prestige, distinguishing two illegitimate and two legitimate categories of hot rods. Implicit in this description is the assumption that the hot rodder has the knowledge to be critical, that, in fact, he possesses a kind of critical responsibility.

Cars rebuilt by means of the simplest changes can be classed in the lowest, the fourth rank. The owner in this category changes only the exterior of the body. He is, unfortunately, aided by the countless manufacturers of doll-up accessories, who provide such mechanically useless items as cutout mufflers, "supercharger pipes," and the ubiquitous Buick-like ventilator ports that do not ventilate. The owner of this kind of car spends most of his time driving around, playing provocative tunes on his four-note horn while flying three foxtails from his car aerial.

Transformations in cars of the next higher rank are dictated by considerations of function, although ornamentation may still be used. While in cars of the lowest category the engine remains substantially unaltered, the engines of third-rank cars are changed in order to increase horsepower and acceleration. A number of manufacturers make accessories which can be attached to their cars by fans with a minimum of mechanical skill. The old part, in most cases, is removed, and the hot-rod accessory is merely bolted on. The higher horsepower obtained is often dangerous if other compensations are not also made.

Now who are the mediums talking about when they speak of the irresponsible hot rodders? They are talking about cars in the two lowest ranks. Actually such cars are hot rods only in the loosest sense of the word. This was recognized by an official of the California Highway Patrol, who said in a letter to the editors of *Hot Rod Magazine*, "Along with the true hot rodder will come the chaps with the shot rods." [4]

When we move up to the second rank we cross the line into the true mysteries. The hot rodder in the second rank strips his car of all chromium and ornaments. He lowers the body of the car, often as much as ten inches, to increase roadability and safety. He stresses clean lines, lightness, simplicity, and gasoline economy in his design. He may not change the chassis but he will surely add disc or hydraulic brakes if needed. He has failed in his avowed objective if the car is poorly constructed, or if it is not safer, better looking, and more efficient than ordinary cars. His car is a pleasure car, and all the changes he makes are practical for everyday road use. If he happens to be interested in competition he is likely to drive against time at the dry lakes outside Los Angeles, or at the various national meets. Generally, however, a great deal of his time is spent talking about performance figures with his cronies at the garage or at his hot-rod club; dry-lake racing tends to force him toward ownership of a top rank car.

What are the cars of the top rank? They are superstreamlined, often made of surplus aircraft wing-tanks, and will run only at top speed. They can be started only if they are pushed, one of the many reasons why they cannot be run on the highway. They are of interest

[4] *Hot Rod Magazine*, May 1950, p. 7.

in the hot-rod complex mainly because their owners are the designers and innovators in the hot-rod field. Many automotive manufacturers, knowing the excellence of the timing apparatus at the lakes, time their own test models there.

Between August 21 and 27 of this year at Bonneville Salt Flats, Utah, there were hundreds of sleepy hot rodders fuming around trying to gap spark plugs and adjust carburetors in the early morning dark; these were the dry-lake drivers of the fourth category. They made dust and noise, and broke AAA records as soon as it was light enough to run. The stark, white salt desert, the blue of the far-off mountains, the brilliantly colored cars, and the tight roar of the engines drew hot rodders from all over America. To those who savor the smell of gas fumes and hot oil as others savor mountain air, a week at the salt flats is a kind of oil-drunken ectasy. Driving against time, not against each other, mixes competition with teamwork in an unforgettable blend.

IV

While the hot-rod culture can be seen largely as an engineering protest against Detroit, some students of American culture have looked for other sociological and psychological meanings in the activities of the hot rodder. The hot-rod culture has been called an attack on the existing channels of expression — channels which grant success and acclaim only to those who fulfill certain occupational roles. It is said that the hot rod is especially suited to this search for spheres in which it is possible to obtain nonoccupational status because its prestige points are exhibited freely and personally in the very act of driving it. David Riesman and Reuel Denney have emphasized that the hot rod is more than an isolated phenomenon, that it is rather a single example of a process that may go on in the consumption of all mass-audience products. "As the hot rodder visibly breaks down the car as Detroit made it, and builds it up again with his own tools and energies, so the allegedly passive recipient of movies or radio, less visibly but just as surely, builds up his own amalgam of what he reads, sees, and hears; and in this, far from being manipulated, he is often the manipulator."[5] Thus, apparently, the consumer can attain a measure of autonomy despite the at-

[5] "A Research Program in American Leisure," mimeographed study, University of Chicago, page 4.

tempts of mass-producers to channel consumption in "respectable" directions. The hot rod has offered a real challenge to the automotive producers in the past — a challenge that threatens to grow. It is even thought that since the hot rodder is a good critic of the automobile, he might also be a good critic of many other industrial products; indeed, he may, in some instances, generalize his critical flair to include such subjects as politics and modern art.

Such hypotheses suggest that we need to learn more about the formation of a critical attitude among consumers of our mass-produced commodities. They also suggest that we might use small samples such as the hot-rod culture in order to obtain insight into the psychological processes, methods, and standards employed by the critical consumer. And, of course, if we assume that the hot rod is a key variant in the mass-consumption complex, the logical next step is to know more about the hot-rod culture itself. Perhaps the researcher will find this easier than many other comparable investigations, since the hot rodder is highly articulate about what he is doing and his car is as concrete a piece of data as one could wish.

Afternote

This paper was originally written for a course conducted by Professors Reuel Denney and David Riesman in the College of the University of Chicago. I am presently studying the middle class motorcyclist as perhaps a related expression of what I thought I saw in the hot-rodders of 1950.

Eugene D. Balsley writes fiction and verse and produces documentary films for D.B.A. Productions, Inc., of New York. [This article appeared in Vol. II, No. 4 (Winter, 1950).]

Albert Roland

Do-It-Yourself: A Walden for the Millions?

THE SHORTAGE of skilled workmen and climbing labor costs have been determining factors in the inception and phenomenal growth of the do-it-yourself trend. But they are not enough to explain its impact on American society. In a decade, do-it-yourself has revolutionized the patterns of domestic life in millions of American homes, and it now cuts across income brackets, educational levels, social distinctions. It almost seems as if, a hundred years later, millions have taken to heart Thoreau's example, withdrawing to their basement and garage workshops to find there a temporary Walden. Starting from nuts and bolts, from simple and concrete things, they may be trying to take hold of their lives at this immediate level. In specific, concrete jobs, carried through from beginning to end, they find the satisfying feeling of individual identity and measurable accomplishment they fail to get from their everyday routine in an office, at the assembly line or behind a counter. The temporary do-it-yourself withdrawal may help them get at that distance from society which is needed for a better perspective, making possible an intelligent return to it.

The stereotype of a romantic Thoreau communing with Nature and meditating by the pond does not square too easily with millions of people busily engaged building knick-knack shelves, painting the walls, re-shingling the roof or tinkering with the plumbing. Yet if they were to express their attitudes about it, some might say with Thoreau: "Drive a nail home and clinch it so faithfully that you can wake up in the night and think of your work with satisfaction."[1] Most of them would share his fascination for lists of materials and costs—the minute essentials of everyday life. The simple,

[1]Henry Thoreau, *Walden* (New York: Harper & Bros., 1950), p. 436.

the concrete may be one touchstone for evaluating life around them—and their own. In a less dramatic way than Thoreau's, these people too are perhaps rebelling against a society where meanings have lost their edge. The analogy holds in a number of ways, but of course we don't intend to press it too literally. And before suggesting it as the basis for a tentative evaluation we ought to take a closer look at do-it-yourself: what it is, who engages in it, how and why.

If you look at it in business terms, do-it-yourself is today an economic reality that runs into over $6 billion a year. According to industry estimates, this "shoulder trade" will boom into a $10 billion business by 1960.[2] Manufacturers have recognized its special demands both in their production and in their merchandising. Do-it-yourself installation is now an essential requisite for most building materials, and it is even becoming quite important for such major home equipment as water heaters and air conditioners.

Cartoons poke fun at inept amateurs painting themselves in corners. General magazines have stressed safety hazards and bungling. But according to a recent estimate by *This Week Magazine,* do-it-yourself is the No. 1 American hobby, with some sixty million people engaging in it.[3] The Department of Labor reported that in 1953 week-end carpenters and the new Sunday painters brushed on three-fourths of the country's paint, pasted up 60 per cent of all wallpaper, installed 50 per cent of all asphalt tile. They bought some 25 million power tools to saw and drill, among other materials, 500 million square feet of plywood in one year.[4] This is big business. And the figures make do-it-yourself sound like a massive, homogeneous trend. But is it? When you try to find out what people are looking for, in their do-it-yourself activities, what do you find?

If you ask, the two standard answers (depending on the group values and on the character of the person you talk to) are that such activities save money, or that they provide something to do—they're fun. However, when you try to understand the motivations behind do-it-yourself, it begins to appear as if it were many things to many people. The differences seem more than just individual variations within one fairly well defined category. They seem sufficient to justify a breakdown of do-it-yourself addicts into at least three main groups: the craftsmen-hobbyists, the handymen and the do-it-yourselfers proper. Each group is distinct both in the type of activity and in the kind of motivation we find prevalent. It would take considerably more information than is available to present more than a few tentative

[2]*Time,* August 2, 1954, pp. 62-68.

[3]*This Week Magazine,* June 3, 1956, p. 12. The article in which the editors of the magazine presented this and other estimates of the number of people involved in various recreational activities, was the first in a series on leisure living.

[4]*Time,* August 2, 1954, p. 62.

suggestions. But even from limited observation some patterns emerge, perhaps of sufficient validity to at least suggest possible relations between do-it-yourself styles on the one hand and character types and social groupings on the other.

Let's take Mr. T. first.[5] He has a responsible managerial position and a comfortable five-figure income. His basement workshop represents an investment of at least $1,400. Power tools for both wood and metalworking are efficiently arranged on separate stands, each with its own motor. His 10-foot-long workbench has well-planned cabinets above and below for storage of tools and supplies. The returns from his investment are quite craftsmanlike (mainly copies of Early American furniture, with homemade hardware), but certainly not justifiable from an economic standpoint. He is the real craftsman-hobbyist, the kind of man for whom a craft is a most absorbing and desirable leisure activity. There have always been such people, and it is quite understandable that the mastery of the necessary skills, the competence required to achieve craftsmanlike results should have had a strong appeal for men whose paramount preoccupation was mastering their physical environment and molding raw materials into finished products. Their avocational interest in a craft was merely another expression of their production-oriented personality. Often there was an even more direct relationship, when skills learned at play were used for work improvement—as still happens with some factory workers, whose hobby is parallel to their job, and whose off-hours tinkering may result in suggestion-box prizes. On the whole, however, our society has shifted the emphasis from production to consumption, and we are much more preoccupied with manipulating people than with manufacturing things. Why then the dramatic postwar boom in home workshops?

Twenty years ago, the pioneering *Leisure: A Suburban Study* mentioned crafts only briefly in a ten-page section on "Painting, sculpture, and crafts."[6] The grouping itself is indicative of the place of handicrafts in the society of the thirties. Though the authors say that, "a workbench and a small lathe in the basement of a home is by no means unknown" (today it would

[5]This example is based on the author's experiences as do-it-yourself editor of a "home service" magazine. Mr. T., as later on Mr. M. and the L.'s, were selected because they are representative of attitudes and of situations observed frequently, throughout the country, in contacts with people involved in do-it-yourself activities.

[6]George A. Lundberg, Mirra Komarovsky, Mary Alice McInerny, *Leisure: A Suburban Study* (New York: Columbia University Press, 1934), pp. 280-89. Crafts fared even worse in *Leisure and Recreation,* by Martin H. Neumeyer and Esther S. Neumeyer (New York: A. S. Barnes, 1936). While it is understandable that it should be so in earlier studies, one wonders how any discussion of do-it-yourself could be so conspicuously absent in contemporary literature on the subject of leisure—such as Florence Greenhoe Robbins, *The Sociology of Play, Recreation, and Leisure Time* (Dubuque, Iowa: Wm. C. Brown Co., 1955).

be a drill or a saw), one gets the impression that an easel was about as common. Throughout the chapter, the various crafts (woodworking, pottery, basketry, etc.) are discussed pretty much as if they were merely different in form, not in significance, from painting and sculpture and even poetry. "The practical utility of handicrafts has been almost entirely destroyed by the machine," the authors state; "but the avocational and recreational significance of these activities remains and is perhaps destined to increase."[7]

However incorrect the first statement has proved recently, the last prediction has turned out to be quite accurate. Handicrafts as a hobby—not only woodworking but gardening and hot-rodding and boat-building—have become a favorite leisure pursuit of millions of people. Mr. T. is in very good company. Workshop enthusiasts include business, government and military leaders such as U. S. Steel Vice President David Austin, Dean Acheson, General Curtis LeMay; entertainment figures such as Desi Arnaz, Dick Powell, Edgar Bergen, Fibber McGee, Jane Russell, Perry Como. Watching Ed Murrow's "Person to Person" one is struck by how often his hosts turn out to be, to a greater or lesser extent, do-it-yourself addicts. And workshop hobbies are certainly not a pastime for the very well-off alone. A 1955 study by the Research Department of the Capper Publications found that nearly 60 per cent of *Household* magazine's 2½ million readers have a workshop.[8] Ownership of tools—including some specialized tools such as cement finishing, linoleum and plastering tools was even higher, over 80 per cent. It seems that we could safely assume that a large majority of the readers reporting a home workshop are not just fix-it men, but spend part of their leisure time working on hobby projects in the workshop.

A prerequisite of this widespread interest in craftsmanlike hobbies is of course the increased possibility for leisure, both in terms of more free time and of generally less tiring work. Still, our surplus energy and our short workdays and long week ends could have resulted in different leisure patterns; they allow, but do not account for, the popularity of handicrafts.

In Mr. T's case, the strongest motivation seems to be that of the old-time craftsman—the satisfaction of mastering difficult techniques and shaping hard materials into craftsmanlike objects.[9] Also, woodworking or

[7]Lundberg *et al., Leisure: A Suburban Study,* p. 280.

[8]*Household Magazine Subscribers' Report*: *Building and Improvements,* published in 1956 by the Research Department of Capper Publications, Inc., in Topeka, Kansas.

[9]A noted sociologist, who has contributed much to the study of contemporary man and of his work and play patterns, is himself a perfect example of this striving after perfection in do-it-yourself. In his case, it was car painting. It started as a disgusted answer to body-shop sloppiness. It progressed, week end after week end, through many trials and not a few errors. The result? In a letter to the author, he described it thus: "I can now honestly say my car has one of the finest paint jobs in the country. It happens to be a 1949 Buick which is probably worth all of $300 in the used-car

gardening provides a readily accessible physical release after a day spent at one's desk, behind a counter, at the assembly line. And for people like Mr. T., the basically inner-directed persons who carry on the tradition of craftsmanlike hobbies, another consideration may be relevant. Such activities offer a "purposeful" way to employ leisure time, freeing people of guilt feelings about their abundant leisure. Like frantically "broadening" vacation trips and compulsive cultural appreciation, craftsmanlike hobbies resemble work closely enough to avoid the stigma attached by the Puritan conscience to leisurely laziness and sheer enjoyment of one's own living.

In some cases, the withdrawal to a workshop indicates, as David Riesman points out, "an unconscious or barely conscious desire to run away from the problems set up in the play worlds of taste exchanging and criticism."[10] This kind of escape may be dictated by an incapacity to deal with such problems, and provide a plausible excuse for not facing them and attempting to work out a satisfactory adjustment. If so, it is probably an obstacle to a well-integrated personality development. But we feel that for many people it is good to find respite from constant "interpersonalizing" and get a chance to deal, more or less creatively, with things—rather than to spend every hour of their time, at work and at play, practicing psychic ping-pong with people.

This business of dealing with things, of creating something, is obviously a very important aspect of craftsmanship, and of the do-it-yourself trend as a whole. A 1954 *Time* cover story found in it one of the main motivations for do-it-yourself. For people involved in today's huge, anonymous processes of production and distribution, the article said, "it is hard to see what they are really accomplishing. But in his home workshop, anyone from president down to file clerk can take satisfaction from the fine table, chair or cabinet taking shape under his own hands . . . and bulge with pride again as he shows it off to friends."[11]

We should perhaps pause, at this point, and take a closer look at what these people are making in their workshops—president or file clerk—and just how that fine table or cabinet is "taking shape" under their hands. It's easy to get carried away and think of millions of people creating like craftsmen of old, getting a pile of fine lumber and through their ingenuity and skill producing beautiful objects. But let's not forget the kits, the

market, and in materials and time I spent the equivalent of $800 to $1000. From any rational viewpoint, in short, it was a silly thing to do. Yet I got a tremendous charge out of it, as I felt I was coming closer and closer to some sort of perfection—the kind impossible in the more normal pursuits of life."

[10]David Riesman, *The Lonely Crowd* (New Haven: Yale University Press, 1950), p. 354.

[11]*Time,* August 2, 1954, p. 63.

iron-on woodworking patterns, the detailed how-to instructions in books and magazines and newspaper columns, the ever-easier products and tools that commercial initiative turns out at an increasing rate, and that eliminate the need for long practice and the learning of complicated skills. Mr. T. would not dream of assembling a piece of furniture from a kit, but the great majority of today's craftsmen-hobbyists rely heavily on all kinds of do-it-yourself aids in their workshop projects.

This evolution of craft-hobbyism has brought about a significant change in the attitudes of its practitioners. For the oldtime craftsman, as for Mr. T., the greatest source of satisfaction is in doing. In *Time's* words, it stems "from the fine table, chair or cabinet taking shape under his own hands." But for today's average craftsman-hobbyist, the main object seems to be to have done. Kit assembly is the extreme example of this. And certainly putting bolt A through hole B and fastening with nut C, as per instructions, leaves little room for pride in the process. What counts most here, we feel, is the satisfaction of having built something, and being able to show it off to friends. This doesn't mean that the craftsman-hobbyist does not enjoy working with things—he does—but it suggests a different motivation for his activities than the mastery of the techniques of woodworking or boat-building. He engages in his craft partly as a pleasurable pursuit in its own right but perhaps even more as a means to taste competence as an asset to exploit in his relationship with other members of his group. A pretty good indication of this can be found in the innumerable groups organized to bring together fellow craftsmen, such as the Men's Garden Clubs. Trading information and practical know-how is an important function of these groups. But even more important, even if not often acknowledged, is the trading of connoisseurship that the meetings make possible.

In *The Lonely Crowd,* Riesman contrasted "the taste-exchanging use of leisure with craftsmanlike use of leisure," describing the contrast as "one between two worlds and two character types."[12] This holds true for Mr. T., and there may be quite a few like him, as strongly inner-directed people turn to craftsmanship to find a welcome relief from an increasingly personalizing environment. But on the basis of our experience in the how-to field, and the booming sales of anything that promises easy do-it-yourself results in a hurry, we think they are exceptions. For most Garden Club members, and members of do-it-yourself groups, and for all the people who assemble authentic Colonial furniture from kits and order iron-on patterns to make a cutting board—craftsmanship has a different meaning. The attention has shifted from materials and techniques to the finished

[12]David Riesman, *The Lonely Crowd,* p. 357.

product. And concentrating on getting bigger and better roses than one's neighbor grows is not so very different from competitive sun-tanning at the beach, or comparing notes on how one dines and wines.

Mr. M. is a very different case. He is an older man, with a routine office job, and a house that looks as if it had been furnished right after his marriage 20 or 30 years ago, and never a change since. Apparently, he has not built a piece of furniture or grown roses in his whole life. He doesn't have a workshop, and keeps his few tools helter-skelter in a corner of his garage. But he has fixed leaks in the roof, poured a concrete walk from house to driveway, puttered with the plumbing when something went wrong, patched this or that as the need arose. He is the typical handyman, the fix-it man. There have always been people like him who took care of most repairs around the house, without any inclination to build furniture or to tackle ambitious and, to them, marginal projects such as a pool or a patio. With the postwar housing boom and shortage of skilled workmen, coupled with rising labor rates, millions have joined the ranks of part-time handymen.

Fairly reliable evidence of this widespread interest can be found (aside from just spending an hour or two in a hardware store and watching the customers) in the large percentage and consistently high readership of straight home maintenance articles in such magazines as *Better Homes and Gardens* and *Household,* the two most down-to-earth home service magazines, with over 4½ and 2½ million reader families respectively. Through these growing numbers of handymen our country seems to be finding an answer to the problem of mass-producing services in the field of home maintenance. Modern appliances have pretty much done away with the maid. Repair kits, easy-to-use and readily available supplies and tools may well make the plumber, the painter and the carpenter nearly obsolete except as part of the building industry.

This radical change in the economy of the home is bound to affect the patterns of life at home. It will channel part of the handyman's leisure time into home maintenance activities and thus influence the family's recreation patterns. It may sometimes tend to draw man and wife and children into a closer partnership through work done together. But the most significant development takes place when handymen stop drawing the line at "essential" repairs, as Mr. M. does, and gradually widen their spheres of activities. Handymen such as Mr. M. can still be found at the lower end of the socio-economic scale and among people for whom the inner-directed virtues of thrift and economic self-reliance remain strong, vital motivations. The great majority of the new, postwar handymen, however, seem of a different breed. After finding that they can use hammer and saw to fix a screen, they will put up some shelves for storing assorted junk in the basement, then build a table for the kids—and perhaps tackle next a major kitchen remodeling job or add a family room. More likely than not, their wives play an active part in giving their activities this less strictly utilitarian bent, urged on by those most enthusiastic avocational counselors of do-it-yourself, the home service magazines. What we find then is not the now atypical Mr. M., the fix-it man who has always been with us. We have instead a do-it-yourself man (oftener, a do-it-yourself couple), ready to tackle almost any project thought to enhance living comfort and the looks of the home. In this process, purely economic considerations lose their paramount importance, and cultural values come to exert a significant influence on the direction of do-it-yourself activities.

Let's look now at the third group, the do-it-yourselfers. They have no immediately apparent ancestor—such as the old-time craftsman and the fix-it man were to the other two groups. They are usually fairly young, with an income from average to slightly better than average. And though the husband's and wife's contributions will vary, they usually work as a couple. The L.'s are a good example. They are in the late twenties, college graduates, with two children. Their income barely reaches the $5,000 to $7,500 bracket, and it is geared to what William H. Whyte called budgetism, the "smooth, almost hypnotic rhythm" of regular, unvarying monthly payments.[13] After the "fixed" expenses—house and car payments, food, nursery school, payments on their new automatic washer and TV set (next it will probably be a dryer)—and the usual incidental expenses such as doctor bills, recreation, etc., there is not quite enough left over for expensive furnishings and home improvements. So the L.'s have built a dining table and benches from some oak planks they found in their parents' attic, they have refinished a few pieces of second-hand furniture and they are now spending part of his vacation painting their house. Do-it-yourself is a way to get around budget limitations and to furnish and decorate their house as the home service magazines say it should be. They are the audience *Living for Young Homemakers* is edited for—and as a matter of fact, the L's do subscribe to *Living.*

On the surface, the motive is purely economic. The L's do some of it themselves because they can't afford to add more payments for all the expensive furniture their taste requires, and because their monthly budget won't easily stretch to include a contractor's paint job. Yet, these are the kind of people who are "so unconcerned with total cost or interest rates that they provide a veritable syllabus of ways to make two dollars do the

[13]William H. Whyte, *The Organization Man* (New York: Simon & Schuster, 1956), p. 323.

work of one."[14] It is not old-time thrift nor pioneer, necessity-born enterprise that impels them to do it themselves. "They are acquisitive, yes, but" as Whyte puts it, "for the good life."[15] Do-it-yourself is not a means to save money, but to upgrade their living standards, to afford more of the luxuries their peer group sets up as necessities of life.

An interesting recent development along this line was discussed in the advertising and marketing magazine *Tide*. The article noted that "some appliance makers are pushing a . . . controversial technique for breaking through the distribution and price barrier to the sale of packaged kitchen, air conditioning and heating: capitalizing on the burgeoning do-it-yourself trend." After listing a number of specific industry promotions by some of the major companies, *Tide's* comment was that, "appliances you can install yourself may help unlock the distribution blocks in major appliance marketing."[16] Here again, as we noted earlier in the field of home repairs, do-it-yourself provides a means to mass-produce services in the home and to help American industry distribute more efficiently and reach more people. Our economy is gearing itself to it in so many and so permanent ways that it doesn't seem justified to expect that an economic downturn and the resulting labor surplus would mean the end of the do-it-yourself boom, as some have predicted.

From all we have been saying, do-it-yourself appears as the domestic answer to some important needs of our economy of plenty. It is not, though at first glance it may seem so, a return to artisan production. It has developed rather, in a spontaneous, haphazard way, as a mechanism of distribution of goods and of "canned" services in the home. As such, it is another result of the shift from a production-oriented to a consumption-oriented culture. Some people might stress its utilitarian aspect of keeping the house in good working order, others its hobby aspect. But a close look at today's craftsmen-hobbyists and handymen show that even for the great majority of them do-it-yourself is essentially a means of taste-exchanging consumership.

We have come a long way from our opening suggestion that do-it-yourself might be a sort of contemporary Walden. In fact, stressing the importance of the group in giving it direction, we have seen it predominantly as a social phenomenon focusing on relationships among people, not between the craftsman and his materials. It would thus be in opposition to Thoreau's withdrawal from society and emphasis on the individual. And yet, there are

[14]William H. Whyte, "Budgetism: Opiate of the Middle Class," *Fortune*, May, 1956, pp. 133 ff. This article gives an excellent portrayal of the economics of today's young middle-class couple.

[15]William H. Whyte, *The Organization Man*, p. 324.

[16]*Tide*, July 22, 1956, pp. 34-35.

important points of contact, if we keep in mind that Thoreau was a nineteenth-century New England thinker and the millions engaged in do-it-yourself are contemporary, average Americans.

For one thing, do-it-yourself is an obvious symptom of a widespread craving for individuality, for the "custom," even if it does usually rely on mass-produced components and seldom goes beyond seeking a variation within the accepted group standards. This is not the individualism of "Civil Disobedience," but it is perhaps a healthy sign that we too often overlook. There is certainly much that is spurious and fake about do-it-yourself creativeness—the paint-yourself-a-picture-by-numbers kits are but one horrible example. Yet, aren't we rather snobbish if we spurn the pie baked from a mix (if it's good, and it can be), simply because the lady didn't start from scratch as her grandmother used to do? Actually, mass-produced tools and products that are easier to use do not increase conformity, but put diversification within reach of more people. And because they make it easier to produce craftsmanlike results than it is to play good tennis or to speak authoritatively of vintages, they afford people a better chance for that taste competence which lets them stand on their own feet and strengthens their feeling of individual identity within their group.

There is another way in which do-it-yourself helps individual realization, and that is through the confrontation with things—specific and concrete things. In an essay on "Freud and the Crisis of our Culture," Lionel Trilling remarked "how open and available to the general culture the individual has become," and how, in this light, "we may think of Freud's emphasis on biology as being a liberating idea. It is a resistance to and a modification of the cultural omnipotence."[17] We may be stretching his meaning here, but we feel that something of the same sort happens when one is confronted with wood and nuts and bolts. "Getting close to the soil" is a romantic ideal, yet it perhaps makes some sense. In our abstract, too verbal society we may not be materialistic enough. The hard touch of the things we do ourselves may be a needed corrective; they help us define our selves at least at a simple, biological level. Thoreau's fascination with sounds and sights and smells and things he touched had some of this quality, was in a way a search for an elementary touchstone as to what was real to men.

One final consideration, which is closely connected to what we just said, has to do with the relation of do-it-yourself to society as a whole. Eric Larrabee commented a few years back in *Harper's* that, "while the thoughtful commentators of the world of better letters were exercising themselves about the apathy of their audience, the audience was out in

[17]Lionel Trilling, *Freud and the Crisis of Our Culture* (Boston: Beacon Press, 1955), p. 53.

the garage building bookcases . . . . In apathy was their defense, in non-participation was their independence."[18] These people pay their taxes, and they are certainly far from articulate about their philosophy of government. Yet they may share the outlook of the author of "Civil Disobedience" to a much greater extent than they are given credit for. They are busy in their gardens, in their workshops, painting their houses. Their refusal to get involved—however frustrating to political activists and impatient liberals—may be a healthy protest against society's ever increasing demands for participation. Their do-it-yourself activities, as we have suggested, are largely in function of a group. But this is participation of a different kind. It is active, it is specific, it equips each of them to feel individually more competent, and thus helps them assert personal identity. And it is at the same time a healthy withdrawal from that other world which keeps making inordinate—and vague—emotional demands on them. In workshops or gardens, do-it-yourself may be just as close as millions of Americans can get today to a personal Walden.

Afternote

In the course of travel and residence abroad, the author has repeatedly been struck by how typically American the do-it-yourself attitude discussed here is, although some of the "Americanized" younger couples in Western Europe may tend to emulate the L.'s we chose as an example. Throughout much of Asia, certainly, a deep-rooted contempt for manual labor makes it unlikely that do-it-yourself will find many converts. The man who can work with both his brains and his hands — taking pride in the products of either and without any need to apologize for dirty hands — seems still to be peculiarly the American.

The author has explored further the role of do-it-yourself in the contemporary American's search for the good life in "Notes on the Family Room," (*Discourse*, I (October, 1958), 217–25 and in "Home Service: Counselors of the Good Life," *The Antioch Review*, XXI (Fall, 1961), 347–59.

Albert Roland, of the United States Information Agency, is currently in charge of editorial operations for the USIA publishing center for Southeast Asia and the Far East at Manila. [This article appeared in Vol. X, No. 2, Pt. 1 (Summer, 1958).]

Parker Tyler

Hollywood as a Universal Church

IF it were stated as a thesis that Hollywood is indifferent to everything but the personal-professional triumph, and that therefore it constitutes (since its influence is virtually limitless) a Universal Church of professionalism, with Money as the presiding deity, that thesis might be called "obvious." On the other hand, it might be flatly contradicted by those who admire, or at least take seriously, the recent films of social purpose, the "problem pictures." For aren't these films "about something"—something contemporary, close, and verifiable in terms of facts existing beyond Hollywood's doors?

My answer is "Yes!" But what determines their true content is neither the statistics which inhere in them nor the ostensible message of social toleration which they carry like a picket sign, but rather the precise inflections of their plots and the form inevitably given them by various Hollywood prejudices and conventions. I intend to marshal first a number of general facts which are well enough known by some, but which, when taken in relation to the perspective of the problem films, assume a new edge and importance, and reveal thereby the tacit presence of what may be dubbed Hollywood's "Higher Creed." The reader is asked therefore to be patient while, preliminarily, certain basic ground is surveyed.

A single fact permeates the background of commercial film in the United States. Professional society in Hollywood is a cohesive group in which the *unit* does not emerge as an "individual" until his name appears in letters of a certain height and thickness and placement—and stays that way. The resulting internal snobbery means that social gatherings and the standards observed therein are dominated precisely by size of salary, and "culture" is thus unequivocally equated with money. Not that purely social cliques are nonexistent. They exist, assuredly, but are dominated exclusively by top professionals.

A prime theme of Hollywood for many years, we may note, has been the success story, and especially the internal success story — that of theatrical talent on stage and screen. The dramatic resources of such film stories have been limited, naturally, both by standard taboos and by the narrow material usually chosen. One thing has been easy and frequent: to show that the road to success is hard, and that even when fame and fortune are achieved by the individual, his bed may be expensive but not all of roses. This formula has been applied at large, of course, to all professional groups; to the Vernon Castles and Pasteur, John L. Sullivan and assorted aviation pioneers, George M. Cohan and the Curies, Bell and Gershwin, Zola and Al Jolson. Moreover, there has been the garden variety of success epic, usually about fictitious composers or showgirls (for example, the mythologically conscious *Ziegfeld Girl*).

The current inflections of this archetype have actual precedents not altogether without implications of social prejudice. While anti-Semitism as such did not hamper John Garfield in his roles as the violinist in *Humoresque* or the prize fighter in *Body and Soul,* no secret was made of his national origin; indeed, what may be called his "race" served well to accent, however implicitly, his rise if not also his fall. Such tacitness in the studios operates the more forcefully in those biographic romances where, as with Al Jolson (two installments) and Gershwin, the Jewish hero is a resounding celebrity of real life. Wherever professional snobbery might have operated against singer or composer on the rise, prejudice as a factor was excluded simply because of the secure truth that the theater, especially Hollywood and the musical-comedy stage, has long been democratically open to whoever could make the grade — "regardless of race, creed, or color."

For us in the United States, the world of professional entertainment is an economic democracy where the artistic product ("entertainment") is without true ethical responsibility, and the human objective is profit and nothing more. Society at large is less particular about those who *entertain* it than about those it *receives at home*. This is mostly because stage and screen are realms of make-believe, of masquerade, where — to begin with — the rule for general purposes is for the Jewish entertainer, on every but the highest artistic level, to forget or disguise his Jewishness. In passing, two monumental facts should be explicitly recorded: First, nose operations may be *de rigueur* where topflight success is concerned, and are commonly desirable in lay life; and, second, religion is taboo in Hollywood stars' publicity.

The argument for Hollywood standards as a strong democratic force might be thought, offhand, well based, because of the very conditions I have been describing. But what is the formal mode of this "democratic force" which creates universal criteria for noses, manners, and acting talent? It is monolithic and hierarchic with only a slight modification of uniformity. This modification is a dualism derived from comic values, symbolic evil, and old age; this means that screen stories require, no less than "heroes" and "heroines," character actors, deep-dyed villains, and comedians, the last of whom may have outrageous noses and be geniuses of clumsiness. At the same time, even comedians appear in the mufti of private life, and to a certain extent, if famous enough, they even have "glamour"; thus, we must assume that comedians also may develop the drawing-room manners of a Fredric March (who, after all, can in turn impersonate Mr. Hyde); and if physically a comedian is too much unsuited to the role of romantic lover in real life, he may — like Jimmy (Snozzola) Durante — bob his nose a little.

If we are to conclude, as seems inevitable, that Hollywood's standards set up an internal convention perpetually refining itself toward universality, the instance of Danny Kaye offers a very particular import. Here is a comedian "resembling life" as much as did Harold Lloyd, who was the most normal-looking of the outstanding silent-screen comics. Both are Jewish and both achieved the big-time; both have exploited a semipathological awkwardness, primarily of sexual origin. But in Kaye's case one will note that he has an especially flashy personality and is a whiz (as seen in *Up in Arms*) at impersonation. A nightclub "emcee" rather than a clown, Kaye began his career in the Borscht Belt and, without getting permanently into costume or devising a genre manner, climbed to a command performance before English royalty and a visit with Bernard Shaw.

Kaye seems to illustrate the very pith of social-professional success in a handicapped person who has overcome his liability (perhaps stuttering or girl-shyness, or both, as elements of his routine indicate) by inverting it into an asset. Does anyone stop to consider that Kaye is Jewish? I hazard that many Jews do, and that his triumphant caterwauls echo intimately in many a breast in his audiences, especially in that of someone as young and personable as he, who hopes it is as short a step to Broadway as Kaye's film, *The Kid from Brooklyn,* demonstrates.

We have in Hollywood, then, in or out of mufti, nothing less than a Universal Church absorbing both Jewry and Christianity by means of a rigid social-professional creed. Yet, as we have seen recently, social reality has brought about an external modification of the monolithism: an explicit recognition of the "race prejudice" which, with respect to Jews, is so irrelevant in the social strongholds of professionalism. Recently, there have been five important commercial films on this theme: *Crossfire, Gentleman's Agreement, Home of the Brave, Lost Boundaries,* and *Pinky*. The idea that Hollywood should even *seem* to take sides in such large issues as social prejudices against Negroes and Jews was so shocking that the desire to exploit the commercial opportunity has not prevented big-time movie producers from begging off indirectly by insistence on the internal creed. In fact, except for a fresh opportunity to spread the professional doctrine, the producers would not have considered doing films on these public moral issues. Let us see what light may be thrown on this point by an analysis of these films.

It was a "natural" for John Garfield to take the part of the race victim in *Gentleman's Agreement*. Having been typed as rugged and sympathetic, rather than refined or handsome, his face was just right for that of the deserving underdog. And who is the gentile hero who finally takes up Garfield's cause? No one but Gregory Peck, correspondingly typed as handsome and noble, thus overwhelmingly ideal as the "Aryan" movie hero. What happens? Peck starts out by impersonating Jewishness (in name only) in order to write a series of feature articles for an important magazine. Thus we do not see humiliated, eventually and somewhat ludicrously, a *real* Jew but a *charade* Jew. Through this odd initiation rite, Hollywood spares the real Jew until, as Garfield, he has gentile Peck in there punching for him. We hardly need Peck's masquerading girl secretary in this movie to inform us that, in Hollywood and every other business, Jews, male and female, disguise their national origin "for professional reasons." Yet the point receives more than adequate emphasis when Peck's conspicuously gentile fiancée cannot persuade him at first that she would marry him even if he were *really* Jewish. The plain issue is that of "successful masquerade"—for which the best, and certainly the most lucrative, formula (it sticks out like Peck's manicured thumb) is that of being a Hollywood actor. Significantly, the fate of Garfield, Peck, and wives in their anti-Semitic suburb is never seen; Hollywood knows very well when to draw the curtain.

Crossfire provided a perfectly complemental example of the professional ethic; here a candid-camera Jew is dealt death by an equally candid-camera Gentile. Moral: Those who passively and naively accept their Jewishness (that is, do nothing to "improve" accent or physiognomy or mannerism) are open to victimization. Once again, the nominal Gentile is physically superior to the Jew with whom he is juxtaposed; by this "superiority" is indicated that social eligibility residing in a limited brand of personal attractiveness. For the gentile fascist, the casting department wittily employed an ideal "G.I." physical type if ever there was one, Robert Ryan, who found it as possible to look villainous as Sam Levene, who played the Jew, has found it possible in many a villain's role *he* has played in the past. The social eligibility ratio, according to the Hollywood telescoped standard of sex appeal, manners, and looks, is the same in both the movies under discussion; the higher ratio lies, whether he be hero or villain, *with the Gentile*.

In these "problem films," we are viewing a "realism" self-consciously equating itself with life, so that our cue is not to think of lack of personability or physical irregularity as a "talent possibility," having an internal side exploitable by comedian or character actor, but only as something to be *compensated for* in society and the extratheatrical business world. Thus, Hollywood, by indirectly elevating Gentile above Jew, is "anti-Semitic" only in that its absolutist creed is *pro-assimilative*.

Now, how may this simon-pure creed be stated in broader terms? It is precisely the kind of snobbery operating in "beauty" and "talent" contests everywhere, based on the truly *mass* ideal of good looks and good manners encompassing every element important for any job except the specific technical competence. In other words, Hollywood pre-eminently stands for the showcase aspect of all business—if, above all, of its own. Its pleas for social tolerance can be only a side dish simply because it is never serious about anybody's business but its own.

Amazingly enough, the Negro films follow suit in being fables of mere illusion despite the indelible sign of black skin which, in two cases, "haunts" the protagonists. Here, too, the human personality is presented as a showcase, reinforcing the implication that, legally white or colored, the human being is to be regarded, as far as possible, as a flexible and a surface phenomenon. The legend of *Gentleman's Agreement* is archetypal because it possesses an automatically reversible logic as though it were two sides of a magician's cloak: A Jew may successfully masquerade as a Gentile just as a Gentile may successfully masquerade as a Jew. Isn't this the *easiest way* to deal with prejudice? Of course, when it comes to the Negro situation and its known statistics, the shoe must be subjected to a certain compensation mechanism to prevent its pinching too hard (in Hollywood) the other foot of the social problem. The Negro G.I. in *Home of the Brave,* being a pure African type, can never conceivably pass himself off as white. This man's absorption with the color of his skin is so pathological that his dearest wish might be that, some night, the Lord would change his color and modify his features so that, even as Scott Carter of *Lost Boundaries* and Pinky herself (both bred "white" through intermarriage), he too might "pass."

The producers of *Home of the Brave* went to a great deal of trouble to prove that a Negro may have all the characteristics of one of filmdom's leading juveniles except a white skin and the corresponding type of feature. The young Negro here has dignity, natural gentility, and most personable African-ness, suitably exploited by close-ups in which a trembling lip (signifying suppressed emotion) puts him in a histrionic class with Jennifer Jones. Hence, while showing the character thus impersonated as a victim of race prejudice, largely due to his own neurosis, Hollywood sneaks in a good dose of its own cult of personability. Where, however, does "Hollywood talent" land this black hero, Peter Moss? Paradoxically, it doesn't save him from the trauma doubly occasioned by the persecution of a white G.I. and by the gruesome death of his own white G.I. chum. A psychological fault of the film is that this persecution by a G.I. (malcontent with the war because it has displaced him from a well-paying desk job) is shown as a routine, subcultural prejudice against black skin. The truth, according to Moss' personality, is that the white G.I. is irritated specifically by Moss' modest, tacit assumption of social equality as a well-spoken, educated being, a "Hollywood talent" supposedly out of place with a black skin.

However, the Negro's downfall (shown physically by his inability to walk) is duly staged under excruciating circumstances on a Japanese island, and has to be unstaged by the rather melodramatic maneuvers of an omniscient army psychiatrist. Presumably, Moss is enabled to walk again through the destruction of his delusion that a black skin is a fatal curse; thus he is restored to normal life and locomotion by yet another delusion: that some sort of neutral skin color exists in the abstract, indeed, the very "color" that is meant by "equality" on the democratic politico-economic "palette." Since the Hollywood "glamour act" is unachievable in the case of an indelibly black skin,[1] recourse must be taken to the larger and more hazardous "act" of the equality myth. Just how hazardous this is, is cruelly indicated at the end, when a white G.I. amputee offers to become Moss' partner in the restaurant business the Negro wants to start. The moral is made overt through the film's articulate testimony: A white man must lose an arm to equate himself in worldly eligibility with a black man having both arms.

Yet soon after *Home of the Brave* appeared, *Lost Boundaries* arrived to show, in no minced terms, that racial intermarriage is one sure-fire way for the black race, eventually, to stage its "equality act." This is the story of a Negro doctor and his bride, light enough to pass easily for white, whom circumstance effectually tempts into betraying their original decision to live "as Negroes." Unlike *Gentleman's Agreement,* it is an *explicit* tale of successful masquerade by members of an underdog group. Certainly, with its conventionally attractive hero and heroine typifying the millions of technical "Negroes" passing as white in the United States, *Lost Boundaries* is quietly aimed at sensationalism and quietly hits its mark.

We have already seen a roster of films in which persons extraordinary and ordinary have been restored to normalcy and/or their regular professions by psychiatric treatment (*The Seventh Veil,*

[1] Of course, black Negroes succeed in Hollywood only as comedians or character actors.

Spellbound, The Snake Pit, and the like). In *Lost Boundaries*, orthodox religion performs a very similar restorative role as a public act; here, a minister's sermon persuades the small-town community which has discovered, with appropriate alarm, that its well-loved doctor and his family are "Negroes" that, since God made us all and this doctor is an incarnate symbol of good deeds, the town should continue to keep him and to behave as if no Negro blood flowed in his veins. The townspeople decide in Dr. Carter's favor.

But what, the question instantly supervenes, has made possible such a ceremony of purification? Not merely the factor that the Carters are absolute models of the conservative middle class (though this too is essential) but most necessarily the a priori factor that they were made eligible for such a socio-economic success *through racial intermarriage*. Thus, what the white minister fundamentally puts forward in the Carters' behalf *as Negroes* is that their progenitors showed the good intention of *assimilation*, a good intention which Scott Carter and his bride personally have carried out to the last dot. Assimilation is thus placed before the Negro and white public by this movie as a sensational transformation act that has an excellent chance of success without as much trouble as the Carters ran into when their secret leaked out. Hollywood's internal angle is simple—only through the supplementary asset of "good breeding" (speech, deportment, and so on) could the Carters have put across their "act" as whites! To have a white skin is only the beginning; one must learn to live up to it in every way.

In her film, Pinky too is equipped in no mean sense to put across her act in the South as she has done up North, but she is harassed by a "race conscience" into sacrificing the prospective social career of being a white doctor's wife in the North in order to establish and head a nursing clinic for Negro children in her home town. An eccentric old lady whom Pinky tended on her deathbed has left her the means by willing her a fine house and grounds. Worthy of note is that the letter of the law (including especially the "human law" involved in the Hippocratic oath) receives a great deal of tacit respect in these problem pictures about Negroes. In *Pinky*, the process of legal justice, somewhat to one's surprise, triumphs below the Mason-Dixon line as the process of divine justice in *Lost Boundaries* triumphs above it. The southern court decides against the claim of the rascally relatives who contest the old lady's will. The issue of both movies is that of national institutionalism: religious and civil law as nondiscriminating toward race. The hint to Negroes is plain enough: Keep within the law at all costs because it intends to save you as the army psychiatrist saved the black victim of "race trauma" in *Home of the Brave*. As for Pinky, she is certainly no "Red." Her film vehicle backs up democratic institutionalism 100 percent by means of racist intention and racist result; before the last fade-out, we witness Pinky's clinic in full bloom.

In transcending orthodox religion, while offering no opposition to it, Hollywood is the one "church" whose shibboleths cannot even be remotely construed to interfere with any economic or political law in the United States, or democratic amendment thereto.[2] When the studios have portrayed the Negro as worthy of the smiles of divine and civic justice as well as of the fickle goddess, Fate, the ostensible inference is that Hollywood has contributed its tithe to racial tolerance as one tin cup and to patriotism as another. Does it matter that the racial thesis of *Pinky* in terms of general ethics contradicts that of *Lost Boundaries*? For one thesis does contradict the other. Substantially, *Lost Boundaries* says to the white-skinned Negro: "Pass if you will—and God be with you!" *Pinky* says to him: "Don't pass even if you can—adopt racism: It needs you." This quite unintentional propagandistic *double-entendre* is made possible only by one thing, which is underlined by another visible phenomenon that is coincidental only in the temporal sense.

On the same bill with *Pinky* at its original Broadway run, a newsreel carried the face and Charles Laughtonish voice of an American Federation of Labor official who, just returned from Europe and reporting in behalf of the theatrical professions, said that American movies are having an "impact" on European audiences grown tired of the "propaganda" handed out by Russia and reacting in favor of the American films' "entertainment." The apparent contradiction between this opinion and the social message of *Pinky* and the others, is more complex than the sort to be solved merely by a semantics of rhetoric. It is not that the function of propaganda is also to be enter-

[2] One may technically remain a Negro, of course, while not looking or behaving like, or pretending to be, one. The law does not require white "Negroes" to declare themselves except for the possible purpose of legal documents.

tainment, but that the function of entertainment is also to be propaganda—not only for American democracy, of course, but likewise for that Universal Church of monolithic socio-economic eligibility which is a tangible element of this democracy, and of which Hollywood (with its AFL locals as well as its stars) is, as I am arguing, the self-conscious shrine.

Does the ideology of one Hollywood product contradict another's? What do you know! The wiseacres of show business—naturally including everyone involved and certain others—are not disturbed; only a "nut" would bring up the point in the first place. If, in *Pinky*, the Hollywood cult casually sacrifices, to the ethical ideal of racism, the rewards automatically open to white-skinned beauty (for example, the chance to win the title of Miss America), there is a bromidic cachet right in the plot to justify it in cardinal terms of "the faith." The film guilds of the AFL can hardly be wrong on a question of this type: In motion pictures, "entertainment" precedes and ultimately defines "propaganda." Our heroine experiences one of those "private failures" combined with a "public success" which is a sentimental cliché of the biographic romances; if she deliberately flops in putting across her private act, she stages her public one with a vengeance, converting a southern ancestral mansion into a black social institution right in the faces of her white tormentors.

All over again, we have the perennial Hollywood underdog's smashing, publicity-getting triumph. One can imagine the solemn "radical" minds of the West Coast congratulating themselves that Pinky voluntarily gives up the kind of glamour that the "pinkies" of real life presumably would choose without hesitation: marriage to a white man and a white future! The "sacrifice," however, is obviously predicated on a richly furnished *power of choice* which, on the whole, should be received as welcome flattery by numerous individuals of the Negro race. With box-office receipts on the downgrade, the sensationalism from the white viewpoint is ideally wedded to a sensationalism from the black viewpoint. It is, as it might be phrased, "the sort of publicity which Negroes couldn't pay to get." Even the Universal Church of Hollywood cannot get along without journalism, and it is elementary journalistic wisdom that, on such a scale, the problem film accomplishes, beyond all speculative "social good," one unquestionable and massive public mission: It super-glamourizes the commonplace act of "passing."

From the serious ethical standpoint, the pith of the matter has not even been touched by Hollywood's innocents, though it is right under their noses. It is nothing but the problem of "identity" of whose "mistaken-ness" they have made such straight-faced sport with Jew and Negro. Long before existentialism, the drama of Oedipus helped to teach us, through art, the importance of personal identity. What is the true problem of identity in *Pinky* and *Lost Boundaries*? Aunt Dicey, Pinky's black grandmother, who can neither read nor write, is a more instinctive metaphysician, one would hazard, than any of the movie's creators. However blindly, she puts her finger on the essence of the matter when she says reproachfully to Pinky: "People shouldn't deny *what they is*." Aunt Dicey's point is that *being* a Negro, Pinky should behave as though she were.

But Aunt Dicey, and Hollywood too, should be told that Pinky, as her white skin informs all and sundry, "is" a "Negro" *only because of a legal technicality*, only because white society arbitrarily ordained that she be "black" rather than "white." On the contrary, biology plainly states that she is both, and probably more "white" than "black." Strictly speaking, although the color line is a legal and in some regions a social absolute, the mulatto is a *borderline identity*. But Pinky finds the borderline problem insoluble and must cheat 50 percent of her rights as a human individual by deciding only for the black side. How literal the classic "black or white" choice of moviedom's fiction has become! It was overlooked, dramatically, that Pinky's "white" blood symbolizes just as much a *group* duty, biologically speaking, as her "black" blood, and in choosing a black social identity, she is convicting her progenitors of the social "crime" of assimilationism—she is, in effect, denying the very moral will of fused black and white that brought her into being.

In giving up "personal glamour" for "race glamour," Pinky is the heroine of a curiously paradoxical exploitation of the Hollywood professional myth, whose conditions I have already explained. Objectively, one might quarrel over Pinky's logic as conceivably reactionary in that Negroism perforce militates against tolerance in putting up sexual barriers that hold the races apart. But patently, Hollywood's angle leaps clear of the argument. Behind all the means which white-passing Negroes and potentially gentile-passing Jews have in common for attaining and consolidating their "masquerade" is a simple motto for garden-variety (or Hollywood-conscious) democrats: Every De-Racializing Move is a *Sure* Move in the Direction of Glamour. This axiom, indeed, is uncontradictable on the level of personal charms and personal success so ascendant in an era of individual competitiveness and in a society where the dominant moral ideas derive their ideal nature from the ideal aspect of the economy.

Hollywood, I dare say flatly in conclusion, fulfills the place of a Universal Church in propagating the sacred image of a basically snobbish democracy: an anti-intellectual, "nonsectarian," and socially crass *personability*. Essentially, it is but a hardened vaporization of the old melting pot doctrine on which the economy of the New World is explicitly built. It has been gradually converted to the Hollywood perspective, I should say, because the existing economy structures have been found inadequate to totally unite a democracy retaining (all sentimental optimism to the contrary notwithstanding) serious racial and religious differences.

In placing a quasi-celestial ideal of human appearance and behavior before a democratic public, the melting pot doctrine via Goldwyn and Zanuck veers from its original economic status to a socio-biological status, by whose regulation orthodox religion as a serious force goes underground, and is allowed to speak up for all to hear (as in *Lost Boundaries*) *only* in behalf of the melting pot doctrine. In this Hollywood ideology, assimilation is a higher stage of tolerance, as $5000 weekly is a higher stage than $1000 weekly and as going out with Jeanne Crain is a higher stage than going out with her stand-in. It might be nominally identified as the Cult of the Divine Robot, in which mixing all the racial colors is supposed to produce, not a depressing grey, but a glowing pink, and in which an undesirable religion may be overcome by changing one's nose or taking a course in diction.

Afternote

After almost two decades, in accord with the stepped-up licence regarding sexual relations in international film, love affairs between blacks and whites are being graced with more candid treatment than that given them in the Hollywood films covered by the above article. The social issue of "integration," which lately has torn up various parts of the United States, is simply an official version of the pro-assimilative tendency I have discussed here. With true social equality, the term "mixed marriage" would become a misnomer. *Shadows* (1959), an independent film, portrayed with a remarkably imaginative documentary touch the deeply subjective issue of "passing" for a girl with Negro blood who has an illicit affair with a white man. However unhappy an incidental outcome, the tensions of the drive toward a universal ideal of race and color remain and are put in dramatic relief, today, by the slogan of Black Power raised by Negro racists. No better evidence exists for the viability of Hollywood's Universal Church than the emergence of a very personable Negro actor, Sidney Poitier, who has graduated from "race" roles to the part he played in *The Bedford Incident* (1965), a reporter who (for all the evidence in the story) might be white instead of black: his voice and manner are as cultivated and "white" as those of any stage or film juvenile one might name. Poitier, having "made it" in every sense, is the triumphant existential heir of the hopelessly handicapped, fictitious Peter Moss in *Home of the Brave*.

This essay was reprinted in my book, *Three Faces of the Film* (New York: Thomas Yoseloff, 1960).

Parker Tyler is an art critic who specializes in the film. He lives in New York. [This article appeared in Vol. II, No. 2 (Summer, 1950).]

Stuart Levine

Some Observations on the Concert Audience

BECAUSE THE PURPOSE OF THIS PAPER IS RATHER COMPLEX, AND BECAUSE limitations of space have made it perhaps too concise—gnarled, I fear—I thought it best to begin with a group of attitudes, assumptions, theses which might help to explain what I am about.

First, I am struck (and a little troubled) by a confusion in the meaning of the word "mass." In a good and recent article, Roy Harvey Pearce [1] argues for a healthy relationship between popular art and both folk and elite art. He would have us leave the way open for gifted people to move from one to another: "*My Fair Lady* to *Pygmalion;* advertising layout to Mondrian; Paddy Chayefsky to Chekov; Ted Williams to Nick Adams." [2] But the limitation of this article for the student attempting to define the place of the arts in American culture is that, at least to some extent, Mr. Pearce confuses mass *culture* with *a* culture under the influence of the mass media. He says that ours is the society in which mass culture "has taken deepest root." [3] What we have here is a case of unintentional equivocation. Ortega y Gasset's mass man is defined as "unthinking" man; in the work of semi-pro sociologists like Mr. Pearce (and myself, or any of us who take a fling at drawing large-scale social conclusions on the basis of our competence in our own fields and our subjective understanding of others), this mass man has become confused with "man in a room with a TV set"—that is, "man under the influence of the mass media." The two are not in every way identical. Indeed, as we shall see, the two different uses of the word "mass" are derived from two sharply contrasted models of social structure.

Confusion of a related sort appears even in the works of those who

[1] "Mass Culture/Popular Culture: Notes for a Humanist's Primer," *College English,* XXIII (March 1962), 417-32. [2] *Ibid.,* p. 429. [3] *Ibid.,* p. 424.

should know better. Daniel Bell, in his splendid critique, "The Theory of Mass Society,"[4] says that he doubts that western civilization can properly be understood as "mass." To make his point, he turns to an examination of American society, citing that tendency, noted by Alexis de Tocqueville, to be a nation of "joiners," and such phenomena as the surprising growth and proliferation of small newspapers. Evidence of this sort suggests that he is dealing with the word "mass" in its implications of sameness; the vigor of voluntary associations of various sorts is taken to indicate that in a world situation in which other peoples have felt themselves "lost," Americans have been able to "find" themselves by achieving status within the limits of smaller groups of their own invention. It also offers documentary evidence for the contention of liberals recently that ours is a pluralistic society, and indeed that it is this pluralism that we are fighting to maintain in the Cold War.[5]

Mr. Bell goes on to argue that since change is our norm, ". . . those consequences of change predicted by theorists basing themselves on European precedent find small confirmation." This is an extremely important point. Historians of immigration like Oscar Handlin have long argued that if there is a determining characteristic in the American personality, it is probably less the result of those frontier influences which Frederick Jackson Turner limned out than it is of that one basic trait which every immigrant almost by definition shared: something was drastically wrong with his position in the society which he left. Otherwise he would not have left. From these premises, it is possible to develop a theory of American personality based on a national capability to live with insecurity, change and social mobility. We often say of politically unstable countries that they are "not ready for a democracy"; it may be that it would be more accurate for us to say that since every new freedom brings a new insecurity, they are not yet accustomed to living with insecurity. At our best, on the other hand, we, in e. e. cummings's words, "wear the dangerous looseness of doom and find it becoming."

Curiously, having argued that American society is not "mass," and that this may be best seen by comparing it with European society, Bell ends his article by repeating that he doubts that western civilization is a mass civilization. As nearly as I can make out, what he has demonstrated, and rather convincingly, is that American society and the American social structure are radically different from what exists in Europe. Ortega y Gasset saw society as composed of a small elite with elite values and a large mass with "mass" values; the threat was that as "mass" man broke down the barrier between the two groups, he destroyed an elaborate

[4] *Commentary,* XXII (July 1956), 75-83.

[5] See, for example, Arthur Schlesinger Jr.'s contribution to "The Cold War and the West: A Symposium," *Partisan Review,* XXIX (Winter 1962), 77-81.

traditional framework in many ways admirable. I doubt whether this analysis of the situation fits the American experience.

A second controlling assumption in the discussion of the concert audience which follows is this: it is a truism (or it should be) in American Studies that each field must be treated in its own terms, and that each field is in some ways peculiar. For example, if one treats an art *only* in cultural terms, one does violence to the art. As Kenneth J. LaBudde pointed out in a recent article, the naïve notion of interdisciplinary study which seemed to be a guiding force in the early days of American Studies seems pathetic in retrospect.

> The correlation seemed so evident. One could perhaps show on a screen a slide of a painting such as Alexandre Houge's "Drought-Stricken Area." . . . At the same time one could play a recording of Woody Guthrie's "Dust Bowl Ballads." Now if one were really a frustrated producer, one could, I suppose, play the record softly as background music to one's reading aloud from *The Grapes of Wrath*.[6]

Proceed in this manner and all three works of art suffer. This is not to say that interdisciplinary discussion is impossible; certainly the cultural milieu out of which a work of art grows is important to an understanding of it, and if two or more arts seem to be reacting to the same cultural forces, the interdisciplinarian is probably onto something. But if he ever loses sight of the fact that changes in the different fields are not merely a reaction to historical and cultural tendencies, but also to the historical and purely artistic development of the individual field, he is clearly oversimplifying and cheating. I would be the first to agree that abstract expressionism in painting and atonalism in music bear some common relation to social conditions in our century, but I would also insist that they can be accounted for in terms of the development of each art: it is a cliché of music history that Schoenberg represents a logical step beyond Wagner; similarly, one could trace the artistic ancestry of Franz Kline back to tendencies in late-nineteenth-century French painting.

A third assumption: I will take the position that it would be a Good Thing if composers had a large and lively audience for their music. My work in this area began as an attack on music critics' ideas about how to enlarge the concert audience. It therefore seems reasonable to retain their concern; after all, it *would* be nice to have a big audience.

Social critics earlier than de Tocqueville and more recent than Ortega y Gasset have concerned themselves with the place of the arts in a democ-

[6] "Regionalist Art and American Studies," *Journal of the Central Mississippi Valley American Studies Association,* II (Fall 1961), 49-65, 57.

racy and, being a notoriously self-conscious people, Americans have taken them seriously. In the field of concert music in particular those who would like to help the cause of the art have been far too willing to take the warnings of such experts at face value, without careful examination of the peculiarities of the situation. It is, to select an obvious analogy, as though economists attempted to account for the American economy in purely Marxist terms, without considering the limitations of Marx' formulation, the surprising flexibility of American governmental institutions or America's apparent social fluidity.

If we look at the matter closely, we can see that the problem which most worried Ortega y Gasset—that is, that newcomers to the arts would pollute tastes because they do not bring with them the proper values—is not really relevant in the concert hall. While it is true that in the nineteenth century popular taste in the United States to a considerable extent did corrupt concert music (and examination of any of the volumes of memoirs written by barnstorming virtuosi will bear this out), it is also true that we did not have at the time a concert audience large enough to be worthy of the name. Whether they knew it or not, the barnstormers were functioning as popular entertainers. And what is more, the situation in the twentieth century is totally different. If anything, composers have been hampered not by too much audience influence, but by too little.

The special problem of music (and this is an over-simplification) is that for the first time in the modern world the composer in the early part of this century got too far ahead of his audience. Composers have been shocking audiences for centuries, but the gap between audience and composer certainly was never so great as it was then. A sign of its magnitude is that in this century we have had the unusual phenomenon of major composers writing music with no specific performance, commission, prize competition or artist in mind. The composer, deprived of that immediate audience reaction which, whatever its disadvantages, is an essential part of any healthy art, retreated to his garret, from which generations of philanthropists, propagandists and musical reformers have attempted to rescue him. They still concern themselves with vigorous windmill-tilting and assaults on dead horses. They are worried, for instance, about listener comprehension of the new music; this is no longer a serious problem: decades of movie and television sound-tracks have conditioned us to accept, even to "understand," almost anythng which the composer is likely to do.

It is revealing to compare what happened to the concert audience in the fifty years from 1900 to 1950 to what happened in jazz in the ten years beginning, let us say, with 1943. The situations are surprisingly similar. Some time during the Second World War, for reasons which are partially social and partially a matter of a logical development of their art, the front line of jazz performers lost touch with the audience. In a very brief time, these men reached a position so far ahead of what their listeners could comprehend that the music which they were producing seemed as mad to its listeners as did the music at those famous concerts early in the century which produced riots and flying vegetables. It took roughly ten years for an audience to catch up with what the bopsters had done, and, just as the various directions in which the concert musical rebellion at the turn of the century were woven together in a synthesis usually called the International Style, the developments in bop were assimilated into the fabric of what came to be known as Modern Jazz. Jazz reached a workable solution to its audience problem in ten years as compared to the fifty it took concert music. It has as yet been unable to solve the problem of patronage.

Concert composers are a little better off: the universities have taken over the job which the eighteenth-century patron and the nineteenth-century concert audience used to perform, so that by now the garret has been transformed, by and large, into a poor man's split-level in a faculty slum. Critic and crusader, however, go on undaunted, believing that all it takes to restore the composer to his rightful position (whatever that is supposed to be—no composer in the last two centuries, to my knowledge, has ever been able to support himself solely on the proceeds earned from music written for the concert hall, though a few have managed if they wrote music for the stage) is propaganda for the new music aimed at some hypothetical established body of listeners.

The facts are that the special reasons for the failure of the new music to hold a large audience are unrelated to this line of thinking. They are simple, almost physical, and they are peculiar—to this one art. I will list them briefly.

1) The new music, of whatever variety or quality, is music of great tension and demands careful listening. It will not work (as much of the good music of the past will) as fashionable background to a cocktail party. You can't even read to it. And since few people, even serious music-lovers, really spend more than a few minutes a week listening intently, it does not get listened to in the home.

2) If it is any good, it works very well in the concert hall, even when performed for musically unsophisticated audiences. But concert managers are afraid of it. They believe that it frightens away audiences, and, what is worse, they know that it is terribly expensive to perform. The cost shows up less in royalties than in rehearsal time; if you study the programs of the major orchestras, you discover that the appearance of a new work on a program usually means the appearance of a thundering herd of war-horses in the programs surrounding its performance.

New works take extra rehearsal time; rehearsal time is frightfully expensive; all orchestras are broke. So the new piece must be padded about with works from what orchestra librarians call "the first repertoire," works which can be played with little or no rehearsal.

Moreover, any work, new or old, takes repeated listening to establish itself; very few new works, even most of those which the critics take to on first hearing, are ever re-performed. The late Serge Koussevitsky had a deserved reputation as a "pioneer." [7] Under him the Boston Symphony premiered an impressive number of new works. But if one reads back through the program books of the Symphony, one quickly discovers that most of the new works performed were played once or twice, then forgotten.

FIGURE ONE: WORKS BY CONTEMPORARY AMERICAN COMPOSERS PERFORMED BY THE BOSTON SYMPHONY UNDER KOUSSEVITSKY UP TO 1949

Composer	*Number of works*	*Repeats*	*Composer*	*Number of works*	*Repeats*
Barber	6	2	Gershwin	3	0
Bernstein	2	0	Griffes	3	2*
Bloch	11	9*	Hanson	6	2
Copland	13	5	Harris	7	5**
Cowell	2	1	Loeffler	12	32*
Diamond	2	0	Piston	11	1***
Fine	1	0	Schuman	5	3
Foss	3	0	Sessions	1	0
Foote	2	0*	Thomson	3	1

* Perhaps these should not be on the list. They belong to an older generation, and Bloch is an immigrant.

** The Third Symphony, played thrice in 1939, repeated the same year in a special concert, and then in 1941 and 1949. This work is always spoken of as a sensationally successful exception to the rule that new pieces are not popular.

*** Up to 1949, not one symphony repeated in a subsequent season.

---

[7] John H. Mueller in *The American Symphony Orchestra* (Bloomington, Ind., 1951) points out a possible reason for the surprising courage shown by conductors in America. He says that in this country there was a wider gap in sophistication between audience and conductor than in Europe. The first major American conductors were Europeans who brought with them nineteenth-century German romantic ideals; orchestral management and orchestral audiences were more likely to hold the conductor in awe and to accept as standard opinions of those "in the know" ideas which were, in fact, avant-garde. The result, according to Mueller, is that if one compares American symphony orchestra programs of the period to those in Europe, one discovers that American concertgoers were listening to "heavier" and more experimental programs than were their European counterparts. It would seem, then, that Koussevitsky was working in an established tradition. Americans expected the conductor to blaze the trail. It is also worth observing that Ortega y Gasset's fear seems once again unjustified; if anything, these early concert audiences seem to have been too timid about imposing their own tastes.

3) And this is our main point today: it is my thesis that if we examine the listening career of the individual music lover, we find that a taste for the new music is usually the last taste he acquires, if he acquires it at all. I believe that the concert audience is pyramidical in structure, and that tastes are dynamic, not static. As one moves upwards from the base of the pyramid, where tastes are limited to the familiar chestnuts and the best-known music of the best-known composers, the ranks of the audience thin out. The new music, alas, occupies a position near the apex.

If these assertions are true—and I hope to demonstrate that they are—the way to get more listeners at the apex would be to enlarge the pyramid: before there can be more customers for the product which the avant-garde is selling, we must get more traffic in the store. How do people come to like concert music? How large is the audience?

Much of what little reliable data we have on this latter topic comes from a series of studies financed by the American Federation of Musicians in the years following the Second World War. While these data are limited in many ways and certainly out of date, they at least indicate unambiguously that the concert audience, however defined, is growing.

FIGURE TWO: CASH OUTLAY FOR ADMISSIONS TO MOTION PICTURES COMPARED TO THAT FOR CONCERTS, OPERAS AND LEGITIMATE THEATER (in millions of dollars)

Year	*Movies*	*Index*	*Concerts, etc.*	*Index*
1939	659	100	32	100
1940	709	107.6	36	112.5
1941	756	114.7	40	125.0
1942	924	140.2	48	150.0
1943	987	149.8	68	212.5
1944	1175	178.3	82	256.2
1945	1359	191.0	80	250.0
1946	1427	216.5	91	284.4
1947	1380	209.4	103	321.9

Limitations: 1) Since the figures are based on admissions receipts, records and radio are specifically excluded. 2) The "concert" figures include receipts for admissions to plays. 3) The figures stop at the beginning of a great boom in concert music triggered by the long-playing record and the high-fidelity craze. 4) The movies in 1947 provide a poor basis for comparison; they were just entering a brief period of declining receipts. Source: *International Musician,* December 1948.

How fast it is growing I do not know. It is discouraging to note that its size until about the period of the A. F. of M. study was a steady 1 per cent of the total population: it kept pace with population growth but seemed unable to engage a proportionally larger group. I am prone to trust those rather subjective indices, the mass media, which, in the years since the study, give one the distinct feeling that the rate of growth has finally increased; I think that something which one wants to label "common sense" tells us that increased leisure means increased audience, but of course one should be wary of common sense when dealing with social and cultural issues. For our purposes, it hardly matters anyway, since even were the audience merely keeping pace proportionally, it would still be growing. If it is growing, new listeners must be coming from somewhere. Where?

Here is another list: six hypothetical "paths" to the concert hall. First: undoubtedly many people inspire a taste for good music simply because it is present in the atmosphere of the homes in which they are brought up. If one reads the music critics, particularly the big ones in the eastern papers, and especially Virgil Thomson, one soon learns that most of them tacitly assume that all sophisticated listeners come from this source. That most people agree with them can be inferred from the aura of snobbism which surrounds the concert hall; the assumption is that "our kind of people" like good music; these critics are distinctly writing for "our kind of people." If you are not "in," you are "out," and your snickers only demonstrate how real you think the difference is.[8] But the idea that this process, which we can call "the traditional path," is the only way to the concert hall is absurd, first, because it presupposes a more rigid class structure than we have; second, because, as we have seen, the concert audience is growing, and the hypothetical social class to which this group of critics thinks it is addressing itself is precisely that class which students of population and fertility tell us is unable to keep pace with rapid population growth. This explanation would make sense were our society clearly split between "mass" man and "elite" man. But, as we have seen Daniel Bell argue, it is not.

If we return to the *International Musician* and the A. F. of M., we can discern the outlines of a second path to the concert hall (and we should make clear from the outset that these paths overlap and intertwine). According to that magazine, as of 1948, one out of every eight Americans played a musical instrument, and the author of the article in which this figure was reported goes on to say that it is "axiomatic that the audiences for professional performances of all types, popular and serious, are recruited at least fifty per cent from amateurs who have taken a fling at playing an instrument." One would like to know where on earth the author came up with his figure, but his point is certainly well taken.

[8] John H. Mueller's *The American Symphony Orchestra* contains a good discussion of such non-musical attractions—social prestige and civic pride, for example.

Certainly amateurs pick up an interest in music from playing. But if we examine the type of music which they play, we discover some interesting facts: most amateurs who participate in instrumental playing belong to bands; almost all band music is what we will later define as standard music. Those who do not for the most part also play standard music—popular songs which have become "standards," light classics, old favorites, popularized versions of the more familiar classics. This is easy enough to document; one has merely to examine the selections included in elementary and intermediate music instruction books for the various instruments.[9]

Then I suppose that one should map a third path, that taken by those attracted to music by the hi-fi craze. The totally naïve listener who buys a rig has to buy some records. Presumably he starts with pops—the hit parade—but if he wants to show off his device, he has to buy LPs. Since most LPs are not really pops—the hit parade comes out on 78s and 45s—and since he will soon tire of recordings of sonic boom and cannon, the chances are good that he too will turn to standard music. Perhaps this is as far as he will ever get: 101 Strings and no content. But he may get farther.

Yet a fourth path is that of the music appreciation industry (or "racket," as one hostile critic calls it) and music education; I group them together not to imply anything about their relative merits but for convenience and brevity. I have no idea of the ultimate effectiveness of compulsory music education—the so-called "appreciation" courses required in many school systems—beyond the subjective reports of friends and students who have gone through them. They say that generally such courses are ineffective except in the cases of students already highly motivated to learn about concert music.

Motivation, which would seem to be the critical element in the grade and high schools, certainly is the critical element on the college level. What is going on is perhaps best understood in terms of reference-group theory.[10] If we pick the brain of a hypothetical serious minded student

9 The reasons are easy to understand. Concert selections are too difficult for the beginner (unless they are simplified, in which case they are best understood as standard music); popular songs are carefully protected by law and extremely expensive to quote. What is worse, their popularity disappears so quickly that one would have to bring out a new edition of one's book every three weeks.

10 This is a useful sociological concept designed to enable one to pin down the sources of ideas, ideals, attitudes, value-judgments, etc., by discovering from which groups the subject has acquired them, against which groups, in other words, he is measuring himself. If one were studying a group of students, for example, one might expect to find among their important reference groups their peers, their parents, their teachers, members of professional or fraternal groups, and so forth—any group to which the subjects might "refer" themselves.

and attempt to discover what he wants to get out of college, I think that we will find that, besides specific or specialized training, it is something which can be defined, albeit vaguely, as an understanding of matters which people he admires or would like to imitate care about. A recent exploratory study of reference groups on a large campus, besides demonstrating that it is almost impossible to pin down a subject's reference groups without the sort of prompting which gives the gag away and invalidates the study, did suggest something of the sort. If the people to whom the student in one manner or another "refers" himself are interested in good books, art and music, he feels that he should know enough about such matters to enjoy them himself and/or to be able to talk about them. Most of us are, I believe, aware of how common this attitude is, especially among our better students.

Presumably, if the student does not pick up the requisite information socially or through required courses, he will go out of his way to acquire it. He is thus *using* whatever course he takes to equip himself for what is probably best understood as a change in social class, although he himself, perhaps through double-think, does not refer to class. "Educated," "intelligent," "sensitive," "knowledgeable," "people who count": these are the ways the students describe those they wish to emulate; they do not use the term "upper class," probably because this would imply a lack of democratic feeling and an acknowledgement of their own inferior class position at the present. If classes in our society should be understood not merely in terms of cash income but also in terms of style of life (which includes tastes and interests) and if, as also seems obvious, the college is for a great many students a place in which to cast oneself in the mold of a desired level of society, it would not be surprising to find students using introductory art and music courses for social purposes. (I should make clear that I am neither applauding nor criticizing the process; I do not want to imply anything about the sincerity of the student's commitment to the arts.) [11]

Moreover, motivation of this type would seem also to account for the prosperity of the do-it-yourself culture industry. The magazines are full of invitations to join clubs which offer a quick introduction to the better things in life; all such advertisements stress the "informative booklets by well-known authorities" which accompany each selection. The entire

11 It is, indeed, possible to argue that their commitment to the arts is of the best possible sort. Russell Lynes, for example, praises the enlightened dilettante, whose enthusiasm is genuine, and who encourages "a high degree of performance in whatever field of interest happens to be his." He can "determine the quality of our culture." "Time on our Hands," *Harper's Magazine,* CCXVII (July 1958), 34-39.

come-on is quite consciously designed to suggest that the club offers answers to the question which the novitiate wants answered: How can I learn about those things which people I want to be like talk about?

But I am convinced that by far the most worn path to the concert hall runs through that music most despised—and perhaps deservedly so—by critic and connoisseur, so-called "standard music." By this I mean such things as "all-time favorites," popularized versions of the classics, "popular classics," the sound of Muzak and other sonic wallpaper, Kostelanetz, Waring and even Liberace: in short, all that "middle-brow slush and slop" which music historians have found aesthetically less interesting than pops, rock and roll, hillbilly and even rock-a-billy, and compared to which the Twist is an artistic movement of great significance.

I have some sketchy evidence to support my assertion, and hope soon to obtain more. First, we may examine more of the data gathered by the A. F. of M., this time printed in the *International Musician* for June 1948.

FIGURE THREE: AMERICAN HOMES IN WHICH AT LEAST ONE PERSON SAYS THAT HE ENJOYS A GIVEN TYPE OF MUSIC, BY SECTIONS

Section / *Type of Music*	*EAST*	*MID-WEST*	*SOUTH*	*WEST*	*OVER-ALL*
Church Music	44.0%	63.4%	74.3%	57.6%	60.8%
Old Favorites	53.3	58.0	51.4	54.4	54.4
Semi-Classical	49.8	44.9	28.2	52.5	42.3
Classical	40.2	32.9	22.1	45.8	33.3

Limitations: 1) These figures do not give a clear indication of number of listeners. 2) The categories selected seem badly designed for our purposes. What we have called "standard music" includes both what the chart calls "Old Favorites" and "Semi-Classical." 3) A good many people unfamiliar with concert music call Johann Strauss "classical." Indeed, they would also include Mantovani. If the tune in question is twenty years old, there are "strings" in the orchestra, and the thing has been played in Carnegie Hall (even once), or has some snob appeal (some of their friends call it "longhair"), they think of it as "classical." Curiously, on this level of understanding, no music is called classical if it has lyrics. It is because of such misunderstanding of these terms that in my own work I use the term "concert music" instead of "classical music," and concern myself with the listening history of people who are already initiates.

Whatever their limitations, these figures suggest that there exists a connection between interest in standard music and interest in the classics. Where the figures for "Old Favorites" and "Semi-Classical" are high, so are those for "Classical"; the low figures also coincide. If we lump together the two standard categories (in which cases the figures can no longer be called percentages, but have rather to be termed "indices"), this becomes even more apparent. The index for the eastern U.S. would be 103.1; for the Mid-West, 102.9; the West, 106.9; but in the South, only 79.6.

In all fairness we should point out that these figures could be accounted for in terms of the "traditional" notion about the sources of the concert audience. If musical tastes follow solidified class lines, there may simply be more members of the "properly established classes" in those areas which score high. But I find this implausible: it is based on an hereditary conception of class inapplicable to this country. Our class lines are far too fluid, especially if we consider class as partially a matter of tastes.

Some years ago I conducted a very limited and statistically unsound study of my own, designed to determine something about the listening careers of people from near the top of the audience pyramid. I hope, in 1964, to try it again, still on a limited scale, but this time with a well-designed universe and adequate controls. My respondents the first time were subscribers to the program guide of a concert music station who were also, first, regular listeners to my radio program, and second, interested in the new music. The questionnaire, which I plan to use in the second study as well, reads as follows:

> Many people come to like concert music because it was important in the homes in which they were brought up; others come to like it through a long, slow process of taste development. Undoubtedly there are many other routes to the concert hall. This questionnaire is designed to determine what path you followed.

I. Background

A. Would you say that you were brought up in a "musical" home? That is, was there an active interest in music, something more than a feeling that it would be nice if the children studied a little piano?

B. Did you ever play a musical instrument? If so,

1. What instrument?
2. How seriously?
3. Ever play in an orchestra, band or recital?
4. Do you play now?

(Please elaborate where necessary; the more detail the better.)

II. Present activity

A. How many concerts a year, on the average, do you attend?
B. Where do you go to hear concerts?[12]
C. In order of preference, would you rather hear orchestral, operatic or chamber music? If you can't make so simple a choice, please elaborate.
D. Do you prefer programs which include contemporary music?
E. Do you have a record collection? What sort of music predominates?

III. Development of tastes

A. Do you now, or did you once like

	NOW LIKE	ONCE LIKED	NEVER LIKED
1. Jazz (of any sort)			
2. Popular music—that is, the "hit" songs			
3. Standard music [a description of what was meant by "standard music" was given]			

B. What was the first piece of "classical" or concert music which you can remember liking? If you can't bring back a specific work, say something about the kind of music it was.

C. In the order in which you developed a taste for them, list the kinds of concert music which you have liked since that type described in the previous question. If you can, name a work or two in each type to give us a clear idea of the sort of music you mean.

IV. Comments

If our questions in any way do not fit your case, or if you can further clarify anything you have said above, please use this space to explain.

The decidedly long-haired respondents to my first small survey had, in every case, at one time preferred standard music. According to their age, they named such favorites as Freddy Martin (he of the popularized arrangements of tunes borrowed from Tschaikovsky), Fred Waring or Montovani; according to their experience in performance, they named simplified arrangements of familiar classics for their instruments, or band music. And the first piece of concert music they could remember liking

[12] This question was included for reasons unrelated to our main point in the present paper. A study done at Brown University a few years ago revealed the surprising fact that listeners apparently go to favorite halls more because there is a concert at the hall than because of a favorite type of music which is being played.

was invariably a work like the Rachmaninoff Second Piano Concerto (which we may call "mama"), Gershwin's Rhapsody in Blue (which we may call "papa"), the Warsaw Concerto (which one waggish critic called the bouncing baby offspring of the first two works), a Tschaikovsky symphony or the 1812 Overture, Scheherazade: in short, those serious works in the most immediately accessible romantic tradition, and exactly those works most copied in standard music arrangements and rifled through for themes for pop songs.

It would seem, then, that the best plan for the crusaders for the new music to follow would be to "lay off" their favorite targets, standard music and the warhorses, and to concentrate instead on helping nature take its course. It is easy enough to see practical ways in which this can be done. For example, when the Mantovani orchestra (perhaps "organization" would be a better word) made its American tour a year or so ago, it would have been helpful had a few serious music critics in different cities attended and reported. They would not have had to lower their standards in any way. An honest description of what went on would have sufficed to make clear to those who attended the concert just what the music they were listening to represented, and even to suggest to them that the "real thing" might be preferable. Similarly, an understanding of the manner in which listeners get to the concert hall might give the programers of educational concerts clearer principles on which to select works. I have played hundreds of educational concerts, and can report that school children are bored by most of the stuff performed at them. But they respond well to what musicians call "real rousers"—melodic and emotional late romantic music, noisy overtures, contemporary works with strong rhythmic vitality, even if, as was sometimes the case, of questionable worth. Most of the audience for the new music is recruited from the existing concert audience. One should encourage anything which will enlarge its ranks.

As to the larger problem of the arts in a mass society, I would say that the development of the American musical scene has been so totally different from anything which an earlier student of democratic culture could have predicted that we had best base our generalizations on empirical grounds. Alexis de Tocqueville's fear of a prevailing mediocrity in the arts makes no sense for concert music precisely because it *does* make sense for popular music, and popular music simply did not exist in his time: undoubtedly popular tastes corrupt the quality of our popular music (although even that has its defenders, notably Henry Pleasants), but the entire process serves to protect the concert music from corruption of any sort. It may be that popular and standard music serve as an artistic chastity belt to preserve the purity of our elite arts from the advances of tastes which would despoil them. But I think it more accurate to say that the popular audience is quite separate from the "elite" audience, and that when a listener makes the slow transition, he accepts fully what goes on in the concert hall. He in no sense corrupts concert music by his presence. If anything, he is liable at first to be too willing to conform to accepted canons of behavior. We do know that people new to a class are the most concerned with propriety and the rules. Silas Lapham spends a whole chapter worrying about whether or not to wear those white gloves. Silas may be in the concert hall because he is a culture-vulture; he may be impressed by radio announcers whose tones suggest that they are introducing music pressed on records of burnished gold; he may, in short, be coming to music for class reasons, and perhaps the chances are even good that he will never develop beyond his present state. But, to mix a few metaphors, he has ears, and may very well enlarge his tastes. Many of his fellows are at the base of our pyramid. We know at least this much about Cheops' pyramid: it was not built from the top down.

Afternote

The more systematic survey mentioned has now been conducted. Our universe was composed of the audiences for three chamber music concerts, two in the Los Angeles County Museum and one at the University of Kansas. The process which I postulated seems to apply to an overwhelming majority of these concertgoers; they do come into concert music through standard music, and the first works of "real" concert music which they heard are almost always the familiar warhorses "in the most immediately accessible romantic tradition." Indeed, the first work named in the answers to question III C was so frequently one of the same works that the key-punch operator was able to assign a code not merely to *types* of music, but to individual pieces, for example, The Nutcracker Suite, William Tell Overture.

Contemporary music, despite the fears of critics and concert-managers, seems to hold no terror for these listeners: 46.6% said that they had no strong feeling one way or another; 34.9% actively preferred concerts which included contemporary works; only 18.3% said "No" to question II D. A surprise to me was that a great many of these concertgoers *still* like popular and standard music or both. Elite critics lead us to believe that no self-respecting chamber music lover would be caught dead listening to "middlebrow slop," but 74.9% of our audiences said that they do. I had assumed that they once liked such music, but had rather expected them to voice distaste for it now. This suggests that categories are less important than our critical pundits believe. It may also suggest that some standard music has genuine value. They say that if you want to pinpoint the art which the future will consider worthy and culturally meaningful, look to the art which critics despise most, but which the public supports. And so, of late, I have been forcing myself to listen seriously to standard music. Muzak and its ilk still seem drivel, but I am beginning to feel that there is a kind of aesthetic which will apply to a good deal of slick "arranged" music. The "arranger" is, at his best, an original artist. We are dealing with concert music, a serious critic once wrote, whenever the material is less important than what is done with it. This probably applies to arranged music, and our shades would be deservedly embarrassed if good critics of a century hence chided us for being blind and deaf to the most meaningful music around us.

Stuart Levine is an Associate Professor of American Studies and Chairman of the American Studies Program at the University of Kansas. He is also editor of the Midcontinent American Studies Journal. [This article appeared in Vol. XV, No. 2, Pt. 1 (Summer, 1963).]

Joseph L. Blau

A Philosophic View of the City

THE MOST significant question that philosophers have raised concerning the urban trend that has developed in modern America and has been studied in many perspectives is whether there can be any real community in the modern city. That this is a philosopher's question is evidenced by the fact that it asks about "real" community. Baker Brownell in his recent and extremely able book, *The Human Community,* has argued the negative very strongly. For community—real community—to develop, Brownell maintains, there must be an integral relationship with natural processes, such as one finds in rural areas, and there must be repeated opportunities for face-to-face, person-to-person, human relationships that are between "whole" persons, rather than fragments. Those with whom we may chance to share our working hours in the city get to know a fragmentary part of us extremely well. But our human relations are specialized just as our work is specialized. There is a division of our humanity that corresponds to our specialized division of labor. You may know everything about me as a salesman and nothing about me as a man. By extension, Brownell holds, although we may physically relate ourselves to a multitude of people in a city day, these superficially personal relations are *really* impersonal. Is the elevator operator a person to us? Are our fellow passengers in the subway or bus persons? The waitress at our favorite table in our favorite restaurant? In terms of their personal relevance to our lives, we must answer that they are less personal than our mattress or our pillow. Lumpiness in our mattress at least guarantees that our attention will be wholeheartedly focused on it; an equivalent disorder in the mind or heart of the waitress (I dare not speak of her external aspect) would not be noticed, or if noticed would not lead us to any concern for her problem.

In urban living, Brownell says, all men are instrumentalities in the lives of each other; whatever else of Kant's thought may today be disregarded, ethical and social philosophers constantly reassert his insistence that ethical living is subverted unless each man is regarded as an end in himself. I take Brownell as illustrative here of a general tendency among social philosophers to deny that the big city can produce community. In our very use of words in common discourse there is frozen a similar if unformulated tendency of popular thought. "Urbanity" and "civility" are both, if not pejoratives, at the very least references to the external rather than the internal life of man. They are descriptive of ways of avoiding friction at the surface in contact, not "external and visible signs of an inward and spiritual" engagement.

Now Brownell and Arthur Morgan and others who argue along the same lines may be sentimentally nostalgic in their memories of the rural places in which their boyhood years were spent, and I don't blame them for that. If one can't be sentimental about boyhood, then there's nothing left to be sentimental about. Furthermore, Morgan, in working with Antioch College Community Service and the T.V.A., and Brownell, in working with the Montana Study, have both had the opportunity to see some artificially stimulated but nevertheless highly successful rehabilitation programs on the level of rural community. These they admit into evidence; indeed most of their evidence is derived from the successful cases, although Brownell mentions some of the failures of the Montana program. Their views on what cities are like, however, take no account of comparable programs in city neighborhoods, or of the possibility that comparable results might be reached in whole cities if the same techniques and an investment in proportion were undertaken. One of Brownell's examples concerns a rehabilitation of one rural church, for 50 families, at a cost to the general body of that denomination of $34,500. If that much money were put into the rehabilitation of city churches for each 50 families, there might be a real boom in religion; God-power might really become more important in our society than horsepower. But no! the city churches must provide funds for the rehabilitation of rural churches so that city folk may be told that only a rural group can develop true community.

I should like to suggest that these philosophers are presenting an argument that is not only specious in the way I have already brought out, but also and more fundamentally in their insistence on a structural (and therefore static) definition of "community." For them, "community" is always "*the* community," and "*the* community" is defined in terms of face-to-face relationships between "whole" men. Having defined "*the* community" in a way that only rural areas can fulfill, and equated "*the* community," a social entity, with "community," a spiritual fact, they proceed to rest their case. It would be easy to construct to order a similar circularity to prove that real community can only occur in a metropolis; the view would be less popular because less sentimental, less effective because less nostalgic, and none the less fallacious.

The hint toward a better view is contained in a single sentence by Martin Buber. "Community is," he said, "where community happens." This deceptively simple and remarkably astute aphorism implies, in the first place, that "community" cannot be defined as a fixity. It is an event, a crossroads of many processes. It may be extremely transitory; or it may last a bit longer. But it does not remain; community is, essentially, a moment of communion with our fellow men at their (and our) best. And we are at our best but rarely and but fleetingly. Have you not been in a subway car, a mere agglomeration of men and women, cut off from each other by the film we draw over our eyes in public places, when a garrulous cherub has danced up and down the aisle and for a moment transformed that grimy car into a church in which each man and woman reveals his soul to the others in a blinding flash and all are joined together in ultimate humanity? This is community happening; it cannot be planned. Or the unity of men—whole men and not fragments—at the climax of a concert or a great theatrical performance? Here again community happens and then is gone.

Surely it would be wonderful if we could force it to stay. But it is quicksilver, and the more we press to hold it, the faster it glides away. The question to be asked is whether these moments will come to the city dweller as well as to the resident of the small town, the urbanite as well as the ruralite. And I for one am prepared to say that community will happen more often in the city than in rural areas simply because it is easier and less shaming to bare one's soul before strangers. It is easier to be one's self where one is not known, except as oneself. Indeed, I would venture to suggest that the very continuities of rural groups, lauded so loudly by the Brownells and Morgans, act to prevent true community because they lead each man to play a part, that of the descendant of his ancestors, rather than to reveal himself. Let this be as it may be; it is not my intention here to decry rurality, but merely to rescue urbanity from unmerited dispraise.

Let me move from social considerations to matters of ethics, also the concern of philosophers, until recently, at least, pausing in the twilight zone between to note that one of the obligations of society to the individual is that of providing occasions for solitude. These occasions, as Whitehead realized, are the essence of religion; "Religion," he said, "is what the individual does with his own solitariness." Now it is obvious that Whitehead here does not mean merely alone-ness or loneliness. Solitude or "solitariness" may occur in a crowd; it is a man's coming face-to-face with himself. For this, not alone-ness but privacy is prerequisite. And by what seems a paradox in the perspective of physical existence but is none in the spiritual perspective, occasions of privacy occur more often in the urban press than they do in rural dispersion. For it is of the essence of urbanity that one's soul is his own. One's "station and its duties" consume but a portion of one's time and spiritual energies; the remainder, wherever it be spent, is time and energy uncoerced. Rural time is not so; it is all coerced, all public, because it is never secure from observation. Even in the family, traditionally the locus of possessiveness, urbanity is learning to allow the individual his solitariness, his privacy, not of body but of spirit.

It seems to me, perhaps perversely, that one of the reasons for the increased spiritual privacy in urban living is precisely the closeness of our physical living. As a consequence of apartment house construction, I have a considerable body of information about the ultimate physical patterns of my neighbors' lives, and I know they must have similar information about mine. Some of this information, achieved without the wish to achieve it, is of the intimate kind that rural neighbors will snoop and pry for years to gain. The very ease with which this knowledge comes to us puts us on our guard against spiritual snooping, against invading the true privacy not only of our neighbors, but even of our family. Urbanites are respecters of privacy; even in suburban living, but a short step from urban living, this respect for privacy has already begun to decline.

Similarly, I conceive that the crowded physical conditions under which urbanites live have led to an increased moral sensitivity. I mean precisely what I have said: city dwellers have higher ethical standards than the inhabitants of rural areas. If, as someone or other wisely said, my freedom to swing my fist ends where your nose begins, then clearly the closer your nose is, the more limited is my freedom, and the sooner I must learn control —self-control, if possible, and if not, control by the law's majesty. In many respects, in the course of any day, a city dweller exercises, as a routine matter, moral restraints that would tax the strength of even the most moral of country folk. On a single subway ride, the male urbanite may be in physical contact with more women than a ruralite has to resist in a lifetime, and considering the fantastic number of these contacts, the number of aggressions is very small. We readily learn to assume an impersonal attitude toward stimuli that the ruralite would regard as deliberately provocative and would therefore feel justified in taking personally. We may be exposed to more temptations to covet or to steal in an hour than he in many years. The proportion of those who fall, considering the magnitude of the temptation, is exceedingly small. Urbanity is not a mask drawn over corruption, but a genuine expression of an ethical attempt to reduce aggression against others, to minimize the violations of human personality and property.

There are two considerations that are often raised that should be mentioned here. First, divorce is more prevalent in urban than in rural areas.

This is often held up as evidence that moral standards are higher in rural areas. I say to you that it is precisely the reverse; that the lower incidence of divorce in rural areas is evidence of a lower moral standard there, a standard that permits all manner of aggressive acts by mate against mate, provided the aggression and violation takes place within the holy bonds of matrimony. It is immoral narrowness and bigotry that compels people who hate each other and hurt each other to continue in "holy deadlock" in order to satisfy the obsolete ethical standards of their rural neighbors.

And, second, what about delinquency? Robert Frost, on his 80th birthday was asked what he thought about juvenile delinquency, and he said that we seemed today to brand as delinquency what in his youth was called boyish high spirits. Juvenile delinquency is not new, nor, I suspect, proportionately on the increase. More of it gets in the newspapers these days, partly because many changes in the canons of good taste permit the publication of what was once regarded as unfit to print. Absolutely, there may be more delinquency, because our population has increased. What is, I suspect, the real issue is that our ethical standards have improved more than our ethical performances. It is not that our young people act worse than we did, but that we demand more of them than was demanded of us, and we do so, in part at least, because of the more crowded conditions under which we live. For all the sensationalism of our "Blackboard Jungles," as Ernest Melby has pointed out, school discipline is better, not worse than it was, and we are holding many more youths in school for a far longer time. We must remember too, not to compare the youth of today in an American city with the youth of fifty years ago in the same American city; we must add, for 1907, comparative studies of the places from which these youths' parents came. If the knife is a more frequent weapon in New York streets now than it was then, I should hazard the guess that the knife was a far more frequent weapon in 1907 in the streets of San Juan; it takes time for acculturation to be completed.

Whether we talk in terms of social philosophy or of ethics, then, I maintain that urbanity is a source of improvement, not of degeneration. And, in conclusion, I echo the words of St. Augustine, "The life of the city is a social life"—for it seems to me that these words are true whether we are talking of the city of God or of the city of man. Indeed, in the broadest perspective, these two are one.

Afternote

This *jeu d'esprit* was prepared for a conference at which most of the other papers were to be read by sociologists. The conclusions of this paper would, however, not be different if I were to rewrite it today for a less special situation. I remain firmly convinced that the cities of the world are its chief civilizing agencies, that, to use Lewis Mumford's telling reminder, civilization *is* "the culture of cities."

In some respects I could put the case for urbanity even more strongly than I do here. American sentiment has begun to catch up with American reality. Jeffersonian sentimental agrarianism has lost some of its hold on American intellectuals, a generation after the center of gravity in American life has shifted from the farms and small towns to the cities. The wide interest in Harvey Cox's *The Secular City* (New York: The Macmillan Company, 1965) is evidence of a newer concern. So, too, is the creation of a Federal department of urban affairs and the channeling of some of the cities' tax payments back to the cities for urban renewal. Finally, I should call the reader's attention to the "urban renewal" of the churches, the development in both theory and practice of the "inner city churches," a development that has led not only to the revivication of urban parishes, but also to the revitalization of their ministry.

Joseph L. Blau is Professor and Chairman of the Department of Religion at Columbia University. [This article appeared in Vol. IX, No. 4 (Winter, 1957).]

Varieties of Cultural Evidence

J. Merton England

The Democratic Faith in American Schoolbooks, 1783-1860

FROM NOAH WEBSTER IN THE 1780s TO EMMA WILLARD IN 1860, THE AUTHORS of American school textbooks emphatically believed that there was such a thing as national character and that they had a duty to help form and preserve it. They set out to create a usable past for republican America—an agreed-upon national myth, we might say now. Fundamental elements in the canon they constructed were the enduring shibboleths of the American democratic faith—liberty, equality, morality. Taken together, their schoolbooks present a composite picture of a chosen people and a unique nation, especially favored by Providence and endowed with a world mission to spread democratic government and pure religion.

In the rhetoric of schoolbook patriotism, the words liberty and freedom appear more often perhaps than any others, unless it be their antonyms, tyranny and oppression. (Indeed, one of the most striking characteristics of schoolbook authors is the habit of polarization, the tendency to see things in terms of their opposites.) Nowhere are the dimensions of "liberty" defined. It does not seem to have meant simply the absence of restraints upon the individual, since the authors themselves wove a tight net of moral constrictions around individual conduct. Essentially, liberty seems to have meant release from foreign monarchic rule and a dictated religion. Once "crown and crosier rul'd a coward world," a Fourth of July poem said, but then the Pilgrim Fathers, "by faith impell'd, by freedom fir'd,/By hope supported, and by God inspir'd," helped to break the "vile chains" which had bound "earth's torpid children." [1] "The principles of civil and religious liberty," Benson J. Lossing wrote, were asserted before Columbus made his first voyage, and "had shaken thrones and overturned dynasties before Charles the First was brought to the block." In Europe the "love of liberty . . . germinated beneath the heat of persecution." In

[1] Montgomery Robert Bartlett, *The Juvenile Orator* . . . (Philadelphia, 1839), p. 139.

America it "budded and blossomed. . . . Here king-craft and priest-craft never had an abiding place, and their ministers were always weak in the majestic presence of the popular will." [2]

Although schoolbook "liberty" was primarily political or religious, occasionally it also meant economic free enterprise. In 1800 Mathew Carey linked "liberty and the security of property." [3] To a politician whose Fourth of July speech in 1837 was anthologized in a school reader, freedom was a creative power. He called the "magic changes" since 1776—growth "in population, in wealth, and in all that constitutes individual prosperity and national power"—"the natural results of that perfect freedom of enterprise, and security of person and property" guaranteed by our political institutions. He asked: "Will any one tell me that these, instead of being the legitimate fruits of free government and free institutions, are the result of the native energies of the country?" [4] This idea was exceptional. The texts usually did attribute the growth of the United States to the "native energies" of the people as well as to their freedom; and freedom was a boon they deserved because they had won it by their determination and valor. Yet it was essentially a negative boon, an escape from the injustice of "a tyrant king" [5] and from "the curse of moral and political despotism" like that which still prevailed in Hispanic America.[6]

Equality, not liberty, Tocqueville considered the great passion of democratic America. A prolific author and editor of school texts, Samuel Griswold Goodrich ("Peter Parley"), agreed: "The tendency to exclusiveness [in America] is checked and repressed by public opinion, which is exercised more to secure equality than even liberty." [7] Nevertheless, equality received much less emphasis than freedom in school texts; and much more than liberty, it was a negative value, a safeguard against relapse into monarchy. William Grimshaw, the author of an early school history of the United States, commented:

> . . . although . . . aristocratic customs are so generally denounced by the laws, they are eagerly followed by the people. . . . There are in the United States more nominal nobility, than any country in the world exhibits, of legitimate creation. Every governor is Excellent; every

[2] Benson J. Lossing, *A Pictorial History of the United States for Schools and Families* (New York, 1854), pp. 158-59.

[3] *The School of Wisdom: or American Monitor . . .*, ed. Mathew Carey (Philadelphia, 1800), p. iii.

[4] Lyman Cobb, *Cobb's New North American Reader; or, Fifth Reading Book . . .* (New York, 1852), p. 340.

[5] William S. Cardell, *The Middle Class Reader . . .* (new ed.; Philadelphia, 1853), p. 57.

[6] Lossing, *Pictorial History of the United States*, p. 33.

[7] Samuel G. Goodrich, *Manners and Customs of the Principal Nations of the Globe* (Boston, 1845), p. 21.

> judge, senator, and representative, is Honourable; and every justice of the peace, distinguished by the chivalric title of Esquire. These frivolities should be carefully discouraged, and the dangerous assumptions, by every real friend of liberty, opposed. They are the first robes in which a republic advances to aristocracy; thence, to monarchy; and, from monarchy, to oppression and extravagance.[8]

In the texts equality is a lackluster hero to whom the authors pay canting tribute. The villains of the piece, kings and nobles, are lusty and colorful. There is, perhaps, unacknowledged envy in the words of latter-day Puritans as they denounce "proud and haughty" English aristocrats who "live in great castles and palace-like halls" and revel in sensual pleasures. As rulers, Jacob Abbott wrote, "instead of being the wise and the good, they are only cunning and wicked. It is not possible for the imagination to conceive of characters more selfish, profligate, and vile, than the line of English kings, with two or three doubtful exceptions, have uniformly exhibited from the earliest periods to the present day." [9]

One of the foreign aristocrat's worst vices, Abbott thought, was "to look with scorn on every species of peaceful industry." [10] Similarly, other Yankee authors disparaged Southern slaveowners as aristocratic scorners of the secular Puritan ethic—industry, thrift and sobriety—which the textbooks sought to make universal. Southerners were "haughty and imperious," Nathaniel Dwight wrote, and "attached strongly to pleasure and dissipation." [11] They were indolent, the author of a geography said, and self-indulgent devotees of "dancing, horse-racing, cock-fighting, and chiefly hunting." [12]

Rarely does one find in the schoolbooks of pre-Civil War America an ardent plea for equality as a moving force for democratic development. William H. Seward, in a Fourth of July speech in 1839 that soon found its way into a school reader, struck this rare positive note:

> Our institutions, excellent as they are, have hitherto produced but a small portion of the beneficent results they are calculated to bestow

[8] William Grimshaw, *History of the United States* . . . (rev. ed.; Philadelphia, 1826), p. 193.

[9] Jacob Abbott, *Narrative of the General Course of History from the Earliest Periods to the Establishment of the American Constitution* (New York, 1856), pp. 300, 388-89.

[10] *Ibid.*, p. 315.

[11] Nathaniel Dwight, *A Short but Comprehensive System of the Geography of the World* . . . (2nd Conn. ed.; Hartford [1797?]), pp. 183, 186. The American Antiquarian Society copy of this book gives the publication date [1795?]. But it tells of the admission of Tennessee to the Union.

[12] Daniel Adams, *Geography; or, a Description of the World in Three Parts . . . for the Use of Schools and Academies* (5th ed.; Boston, 1820) pp. 136-37, 140-41, 145, 150.

> upon the People. The chief of these benefits is EQUALITY. We do indeed enjoy equality of civil rights. But we have not yet attained, we have only approximated toward, EQUALITY OF SOCIAL CONDITION. . . . [Aristocracy unfortunately exists even in America.] We should be degenerate descendants of our heroic forefathers, did we not assail this aristocracy, remove the barriers between the rich and the poor, break the control of the few over the many, extend the largest liberty to the greatest number, and strengthen in every way the democratic principles of our constitution.

In this great work, he told his audience at a Sunday School celebration on Staten Island, "Sunday Schools and Common Schools are the great levelling institutions of the age." [13]

"Levelling institutions"! On the "levelling" role of the schools, most textbook authors of Jacksonian America agreed with Seward. Their opposition to aristocracy extended even to an aristocracy of brains. They valued creativity less than uniformity, trained intelligence less than the spreading of useful knowledge and the cultivation of virtue.[14] After quoting Benjamin F. Butler on "The Necessities and Advantages of the General Diffusion of Knowledge," the compiler of a reader asked: "Will all remember, however, that it would be better for the community to have all the children and youth of our country grow up in UTTER IGNORANCE, if they are not *morally* educated at the same time that they are *intellectually* educated, so as to become GOOD, MORAL, and VIRTUOUS citizens as well as WISE and LEARNED men, as a *learned* wicked man can do *ten* times as much mischief in society as an *ignorant* wicked man?" [15] "We have, indeed, been desirous to cultivate the memory, the intellect, and the taste," Emma Willard wrote. "But much more anxious have we been to sow the seeds of virtue." [16]

Education meant indoctrination—indoctrination in the familiar catalogue of moral virtues of Protestant, agrarian-commercial America: industry, thrift, practicality, temperance, honesty, plain living, patriotism and piety. These moral values were the props of the state. Without them the flourishing republic of the New World could not endure.

The incarnation of all these virtues was George Washington, the gigantic hero-figure of pre-Civil War America. American schoolbooks often

[13] *Cobb's New North American Reader,* p. 286.

[14] "The primary intellectual value embodied in these books is that the only important knowledge is that which is 'useful.'" Ruth Miller Elson, "American Schoolbooks and 'Culture' in the Nineteenth Century," *Mississippi Valley Historical Review,* XLVI (December 1959), 413.

[15] *Cobb's New North American Reader,* p. 253.

[16] Emma Willard, *Abridged History of the United States, or Republic of America* (new ed.; New York, 1860), p. 5.

called the Revolution the supreme event in human history, and Washington dwarfed all its other heroes. In writing of him, bombastic authors drew upon their lushest prose. The compiler of *The Juvenile Orator* wrote:

> The history of the Old World records the names of those whose deeds and daring cast a passing glare upon the age in which they lived, and whose memory yet survive[s] the waste of time; but to the New World was reserved the glory of giving existence to one, the lustre of whose virtues lighted the habitable globe with a noon-tide splendor, that can subside only with subsiding nature. Upon the broad page of the history of man, GEORGE WASHINGTON stands in unclouded sublimity, an unmatched model of self-created greatness.[17]

Washington stood alone in the American pantheon, but much can be inferred about the nation's culture merely from a listing of other schoolbook heroes: Christopher Columbus, intrepid discoverer; John Smith, successful colonizer; Benjamin Franklin, practical philosopher; Israel Putnam, patriotic Cincinnatus; Patrick Henry, eloquent agitator; Robert Fulton, useful inventor. Sometimes their virtues may now sound strange. In Noah Webster's *Little Reader's Assistant* we read: "What a *hero* was Capt. Smith! How many Turks and Indians did he slay! How often was he upon the brink of death, and how bravely did he encounter every danger! Such a man affords a noble example for all to follow, when they resolve to be *good* and *brave*." [18]

Even fictitious heroes were mustered to illustrate the schoolbook virtues of industry, patriotism and piety. Jack Halyard, the "Sailor Boy" of William Cardell's *Middle Class Reader,* was a rural American prototype of the popular version of the Gilded Age Alger hero. Jack's father, a sailor turned farmer, died when the boy was young, leaving a destitute, invalid widow and four children. The family soon lost its New Jersey farm and moved to New York. Jack, the elder son, went to sea, and in his letters home told his family of the strange places and people he saw on his travels. On one of his voyages Jack was shipwrecked just off the American coast. Although most of the passengers and crew lost their lives, Jack saved a young English girl, Harriet Temple, and her mother was also rescued. Mrs. Halyard and Mrs. Temple became fast friends, and Jack and Harriet were married. By the end of the book, Jack has retired from seafaring, bought back the old family farm and settled there with his bride. His prospects are bright. In summing up Jack's career, the author tells us

17 Bartlett, *Juvenile Orator,* pp. 149-50.

18 Noah Webster Jr., *The Little Reader's Assistant . . .* (2nd ed.; Hartford, 1791), p. 12.

that the young man had made his way in the world "by persevering industry and upright conduct." He had always been honest and trustworthy, always "the dutiful son, the kind brother, the sincere friend, the lover of his country, and of his fellow-men." Jack, "the Christian hero," had at all times kept "two prime objects in view: to gain useful knowledge and to practise right." His life served as an example "that there is no real greatness on earth, but the will and power of being greatly good." The Halyards were among "the virtuous poor" who possess "that inward peace which the sons of vice, with all their power and state, can never find." The author assured his schoolchildren readers: "Bad men cannot be happy. If the wicked appear sometimes to prosper, their deceitful success must soon come to an end; and the good, though their day may be clouded with misfortune for a while, will surely have their reward; for truth and virtue are from the beginning, and, unchanging, shall last as long as the throne of GOD endures."[19]

Other textbook writers agreed with the chronicler of the Halyards in emphasizing "the throne of GOD." Morality depended upon religion—more specifically, Protestant Christianity. The zealous spirit of anti-Catholic evangelical religion permeated the schoolbooks of nineteenth-century America.[20]

Pious textbook authors, many of them ministers, had no doubt that God was on the side of the United States, indeed had a special mission for His "American Israel." "God hath not dealt so with *any* other people," said Hall and Baker's *School History of the United States*.[21] The Puritan idea of a chosen people's "city on a hill" and the idea of inevitable progress gained new vigor and momentum with the rise of millennialism in the religious revivals of the nineteenth century. "God did not design this continent to remain a wilderness," Lossing wrote.[22] Here was a new Eden: "The great garden of the western world needed tillers, and white men came."[23] Before the occupation of New England, a plague annihilated local Indian tribes. "Thus," Emma Willard wrote, "Divine Providence prepared the way for another and more civilized race."[24] The

19 Cardell, *Middle Class Reader*, pp. 205-6, and *passim*.

20 Anti-Catholic bias shows especially in comments in geographies on Spain, Portugal, Italy and Ireland. For example: "The Roman Catholic religion, to the exclusion of all others, is the religion of the Spanish monarchy; and it is, in these countries, of the most bigotted [*sic*], superstitious, and tyrannical character." Jedidiah Morse, *The American Geography* . . . (2nd ed.; London, 1792), p. 496.

21 Samuel Read Hall and A. R. Baker, *School History of the United States* . . . (new ed.; Andover, Mass., 1839), p. 4.

22 Benson J. Lossing, *A Common-School History of the United States* . . . (New York, 1864), p. 9.

23 Lossing, *Pictorial History of the United States*, p. 12.

24 Willard, *Abridged History of the United States*, p. 19.

coming of the settlers "opened a new era in the history of man— . . . the dawn of a *new civilization,* higher and more perfect than had yet been born," wrote Jesse Olney on New Year's Day 1851, in the preface to his school history of the United States. He continued:

> In these United States, the great Republic of the World, lies the grand and imposing theatre of the *future* progress of the race. We are to work out, not alone our destiny, but that of the whole world. . . . Here, for the first time in human history, man will be *truly* man. . . . Here shall be realized the long-prophesied, long-expected *Golden Age.* . . . From this Free and Happy Land shall go forth the power to perfect the Civilization of the World. . . . The arts of Freedom and of Peace shall be brought home to the ancient cradle of the race, and the deserts of Asia made to rejoice and blossom with the fruits of the highest culture. . . . The inferior races shall be educated . . . and made fellow-laborers in the great work of human progress. To the portal of this Golden Future, the consummation of man's earthly destiny, *America* holds the key. *She* only can accomplish the work to which she is pledged, and thus make the sublimest prophecies and aspirations of the Past the bright *realities* of the Present, and the foundation for a yet nobler Future.[25]

Yet under such brave words of millennial vision lay anxieties and fears. If one reads beneath the surface of the schoolbooks, he can feel insecurity and tension, which were no doubt personal with the authors but also part of the culture. There was the habit of polarization referred to before—for example, the contrasts between England and America: age and youth, smallness and bigness, past and future, oppression and liberty, aristocracy and equality, a state church and religious freedom, decay and vigor, depravity and innocence. This simple black-and-white way of seeing things did not, one feels, reflect the assurance of certitude. It reveals tautness, not relaxation—a kind of whistling in the dark to keep up one's courage. Textbook emphasis upon self-control through the exercise of will power resulted in part from the abundant evidence of rampaging, often violent individualism in romantic mid-century America, a society of hectic growth and change. But perhaps it also sprang from the authors' personal, unconscious straining against the built-in bonds of the culture.

What is called "millennial hope" can just as easily be felt as a hovering apocalyptic despair. Throughout the texts recur such phrases as "to the end of time,"[26] "when time is no more,"[27] "the last shock of time."[28]

[25] Jesse Olney, *A History of the United States, for the Use of Schools and Academies* (rev. ed.; New Haven, 1851), pp. v-vii.

[26] *The American Speaker* . . . (3rd ed.; Philadelphia, 1816), p. 354.

[27] Caleb Bingham, *The Young American's Speaker* . . . (Philadelphia, 1857), p. 44.

[28] Noah Webster Jr., *An American Selection of Lessons in Reading and Speaking* . . . (Boston, 1790), p. 140.

Over and over the schoolbooks recount the decay and death of glorious empires of the past and point the cautionary moral. The New World empire would last only so long as it kept its youthful innocence and virtue. Caleb Bingham's *Columbian Orator* brought to the attention of schoolboys the words of a Harvard commencement speaker: "Warned by the fate of her predecessors, may she [the United States] escape those quicksands of vice, which have ever proved the bane of empire. May her glory and her felicity increase with each revolving year, till the last trump shall announce the catastrophe of nature, and time shall immerge in the ocean of eternity."[29] "Protect us from evil!" the texts cry out. The subject was America, but the feelings, one suspects, were often personal and morbid.

European travelers in Jacksonian America marveled at the way New World citizens lived in the future. By some incredible alchemy, the swaggering backwoods booster transformed a sleepy village into a bustling city—and he actually saw it! But progress created anxiety. If the divine event toward which creation moves is far off, one can contemplate its advent calmly. But what if it is at hand, may come at any moment in a blinding flash? If I read the schoolbooks right, boastful Americans were shouting down inner voices of doubt and fear. Vaunting optimism had an undertone of desperation. This was cultural, and it was personal. America was beautiful, and so was life. For Young America it was a dawning time, but perhaps, whispered *timor mortis*, a dying time too.

A favorite poem of the American schoolbook anthologist was Bishop Berkeley's "The Muse's Hopes for America." It prophesied that

> In happy climes, the seat of innocence,
>
> . . . .
>
> There shall be sung another golden age,
>
> . . . .
>
> Westward the course of empire takes its way;
> The first four acts already past,
> A fifth shall close the drama with the day:
> Time's noblest offspring is the last.[30]

Of similar theme was Timothy Dwight's poem "Columbia." The first stanza has the line: "Thy reign is the last and the noblest of time."[31]

Planet Earth's great drama began, the textbooks said, in 4004 B.C. America was the fifth and final act. It was an exciting but an awesome thought.

29 Caleb Bingham, *The Columbian Orator* . . . (Boston, 1797), p. 34.
30 *Cobb's New North American Reader,* pp. 419-20.
31 Bingham, *Young American's Speaker,* p. 44.

One must hesitate before equating the democratic faith of Young America with the schoolbook interpretations of liberty, equality and morality. Nor can we assume that the texts performed a dominant role in shaping the minds of their readers. Although reflecting opinions widely held in American society, the texts did not faithfully mirror republican sentiments, if we may trust other sources that indicate more positive democratic beliefs and a happier, more carefree spirit.

Few of the textbook authors were representative men of their age or of their sprawling country. Most of them spoke with the twang of the New England town, not the drawl of the Southern plantation or the careless slurring of the Western farm. Heirs of the Puritans, whose memory they perpetuated, they had accepted a modified Calvinism, in that they believed that man could by his own efforts curb his inherent sinfulness and follow the narrow path of virtue, but they could not stomach Methodist Arminianism or a Jeffersonian confidence in the essential goodness of human nature. Diehard Federalists, many of them, they wrung their hands over the passing of antique values—and of their own former status—in the pushy society of Jacksonian America. Soft breezes from the South, murmuring of aristocratic ease in the land of slavery, and hurly-burly gales from Western clearings, carrying the raucous shouts of coonskin democracy, did not moderate but made more bitter the winter of their discontent.

In such persons of the "Mugwump" type an anxious temper would prevail.[32] They would incline toward a negative view of the trinity of democratic values: Liberty was release from slavery, not opportunity to develop one's talents to the full; equality was a barrier against aristocratic privilege, not a force to promote universal respect for human dignity; morality was a checkrein upon vice, not a spirit to motivate the development of free, responsible individuals living in harmony in an open society.

In what ways, then, did the schoolbooks reflect, transmit and shape popular culture? Most important, perhaps, they imposed restraints upon a people who lacked them. They helped to establish and maintain a tradition in a society that tended to forget or scorn the past. They perpetuated the secular ethic of Puritanism, emphasizing work, thrift and earnestness, and made it seem as fresh and valid for urban-industrial America as for the simpler agrarian republic. They intensified the concern of the age with individual morality, under the guidance of religion, and the belief in man's capacity and responsibility to do good. And they reaffirmed the general belief in the superiority of American institutions and in America's unique mission in the world.

[32] See Richard Hofstadter, *The Age of Reform: From Bryan to F.D.R.* (Vintage ed.; New York, 1960), pp. 137-43; William R. Taylor, *Cavalier and Yankee: The Old South and American National Character* (New York, 1961), pp. 55-65.

Afternote

Since this article appeared, a fine full-length study, based upon more than a thousand elementary textbooks, has been published — Ruth Miller Elson's *Guardians of Tradition: American Schoolbooks of the Nineteenth Century* (Lincoln: University of Nebraska Press, 1964). Mrs. Elson's comprehensive "study of attitudes which make up the lowest common denominator of American intellectual history" convinces me that at least one of the impressions I have set down here is misleading, and in part wrong. "It would be a serious mistake . . . ," she writes, "to conclude that nineteenth-century American schoolbooks were not class conscious, or that they opposed the idea of distinctions of rank" (p. 268). Jacksonian ideas of equality did not appear prominently in schoolbooks until after the Civil War.

In this article I referred to the textbook contrasts of England and the United States. I have discussed these contrasts and their contribution to an American myth in "England and America in the Schoolbooks of the Republic, 1783–1861," *University of Birmingham Historical Journal*, IX (1963), 92–111. A valuable study of the harmful influence of more recent school histories (American and British) is Ray A. Billington and others, *The Historian's Contribution to Anglo-American Misunderstanding* (New York: Hobbs, Dorman & Co., 1966).

Formerly Professor of History at the University of Kentucky, J. Merton England since 1961 has been Director of the Institutional Grants Program, National Science Foundation. [This article appeared in Vol. XV, No. 2, Pt. 1 (Summer, 1963).]

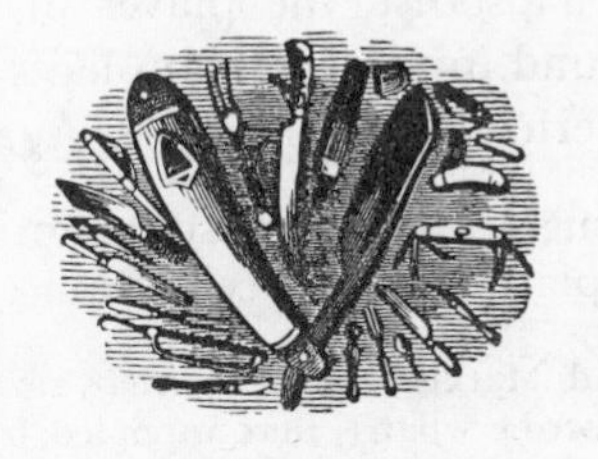

Clarence Mondale

Daniel Webster and Technology

A MAN'S PRIVATE LIFE IS NOW THOUGHT OF AS REAL, AND HIS PUBLIC LIFE as a mere projection of that private life, as second-hand and conventional.[1] As one consequence, "oratory" for us signifies a somewhat shady business of manipulating commonplaces or a defunct kind of hyperdramatics, and "rhetoric" connotes empty talk. The greatest of our orators, Daniel Webster, is about to be consigned to oblivion. The few scholars who make oratory their study still rank Webster with Demosthenes and Cicero,[2] but the rest of us can't see much importance to such ranking, even if deserved. Webster's most recent biographer, Richard Current, baffled by a platform manner which extended all the way to a grandly dramatic deathbed scene, concludes that his subject was, basically and at heart, a player of roles.[3] Richard Hofstadter, deciding that Webster had no important part in *The American Political Tradition,* suggests that he should be remembered only as the "quasi-official rhapsodist of American nationalism," [4] i.e., as a mere orator.

Surely Webster, the rhapsodist, the player of roles, is, as alleged, an orator. His speeches abound in the commonplaces of his time: civilization is progressing, and America leads the way. Again and again he says,

> No schemes can be suggested to us so magnificent as the prospects which a sober contemplation of our condition . . . fairly spreads before

[1] Romantics, Freudians and Marxists have in their several ways debased the very words one wants to use to describe what is here intended by the word "public." I have in mind our intentionally conventional civil life, what Webster lauded as "respectability," what we have for the past half-century condemned for being "genteel." "Public" life has to do with the quality of social manners and morals, and with generally agreed upon convictions as to the nature of the good, the true and the beautiful.

[2] For a recent estimate of Webster by rhetorical critics see the article by Wilbur Samuel Howell and Hoyt H. Hudson, in *A History and Criticism of American Public Address,* ed. William N. Brigance (New York, 1943), II, 666-733.

[3] *Daniel Webster and the Rise of National Conservatism* (Boston, 1955), pp. 180-83.

[4] (New York: Vintage Books, 1955), p. 68.

> us. A country of such vast extent, with so much public spirit and private enterprise, with a population increasing so much beyond former example, with capacities of improvement not only unapplied or unexhausted, but even, in a great measure, as yet unexplored,—so free in its institutions, so mild in its laws, so secure in the title it confers on every man to his own acquisitions,—needs nothing but time and peace to carry it forward to almost any point of advancement. [5, 64][5]

Here is rhapsody, and we can guess that on the platform Webster was wonderfully dramatic. And no one can mistake this passage for "original" thought or expression, for the whole message is a commonplace. But it had to be if it was to reach its audience. As Richard M. Weaver argues, repetition of these commonplaces did not necessarily make them hackneyed, as we have been taught to suppose; from the right man in the right place they constituted a vital, meaningful expression of communal tradition.[6] Webster's published orations sketch for us the postures of contemporary public belief.

In this essay we will limit our discussion to what Webster said about technology and its public consequences. We already know how he began opposed to, and later took the side of, governmental support to manufactures. This development of his politics is only incidentally our concern. We are interested, rather, in the development of his rhetoric. The coming of steam and of factory production was a novelty, and of almost imponderable consequence. Because of their public effect, steam and the factory had to be dealt with. Because of their novelty, they demanded a novel rhetoric. This rhetoric, to be effective, had to be congenial to Webster's auditors and subservient to his own objectives, his own reasons for appearing before them. As literature, Webster's remarks about technology lack coherence. We will try to show how as oratory they fall into place.

In his earliest political speeches, Webster represented commerce and agriculture as companion interests. "Indissoluble bonds connect him who ploughs the land with him who ploughs the sea" [15, 541]. But it is wrong, the young orator declared, to take the side of an exclusive agrarianism against the rights of commerce: the United States is not "a great land animal, whose walks are confined to his native forests, and who has nothing to do with the ocean but to drink at its shores, or sooth its slumbers by the noise of its waves" [15, 541]. As spokesman for New Hampshire commerce, we would expect Webster to make some such

[5] References in brackets are to volume and page numbers of the National Edition of *The Writings and Speeches of Daniel Webster* (Boston, 1903).

[6] See Weaver's *The Ethics of Rhetoric* (Chicago, 1953), pp. 164-85.

remarks. Confronted with the possibility of a growth in manufactures, however, he drops any distinctions he may have made between commerce and agriculture, and identifies himself with agrarian values.[7]

In 1814, Webster secured the repeal of federal prohibitions on commerce. Manufacturing had thrived on those prohibitions.[8] The true policy of government, Webster had then argued, was "to suffer the different pursuits of society to take their own course, and not to give excessive bounties or encouragements to one over another" [14, 15]. So far as manufactures themselves are concerned, Webster affects to be disinterested. "I am not, generally speaking, their enemy. I am their friend, but I am not for rearing them, or any other interest, in hot-beds." America is not yet ready for heavy industry, and anyway, "I am not in haste to see Sheffields and Birminghams in America" [14, 43].

This last remark is transitional and marks a shift of ground. The issue thereafter becomes moral rather than political and economic. The populous manufacturing city, says Webster, brings with it vast capital investment, minute subdivision of labor and the employment of masses of children. Immorality, dependence and despotism follow in their train. Much better that America stay a country of farms (and farm homes):

> I am not anxious to accelerate the approach of the period when the great mass of American labor shall not find its employment in the field; when the young men of the country shall be obliged to shut their eyes upon external nature, upon the heavens and the earth, and immerse themselves in close and unwholesome workshops; when they shall be obliged to shut their ears to the bleatings of their own flocks, upon their own hills, and to the voice of the lark that cheers them at the plough, that they may open them in dust, and smoke, and steam, to the perpetual whirl of spools and spindles, and the grating of rasps and saws. [14, 43-45]

Webster argues against protection (and at some remove, for commerce) by appeal to radically agrarian values.

In 1816, Webster moved from New Hampshire to Massachusetts. It seemed likely, in 1820, that Congress was going to boost tariff rates. Boston shippers and importers called a protest meeting in Faneuil Hall. Webster gave the main speech.[9] The thesis of the speech is that the proposed tariffs would ultimately prove fatal to the small merchants,

[7] I derive my notion of ante-bellum agrarian value and myth from Henry Nash Smith, *Virgin Land* (New York: Vintage Books, 1957), chaps. xi and xii.

[8] Current, p. 20, describes the legislative battle between Webster and Calhoun, the South Carolinian taking the side of protection.

[9] For a description of the occasion see Claude Moore Fuess, *Daniel Webster* (Boston, 1930). I, 272.

and seem so intended. As in 1814, Webster, to defend commerce, upholds agrarian ideals, but in this later speech (as a protest meeting would demand) the contrast between farming and factory work is lurid. *Any* family man, proclaims our orator, would move beyond the Rockies—in 1820!—to maintain the "respectability and the independence of a freehold," rather than go into a factory, "taking the chance of the ignorance and the vice, the profligacy and the poverty, of that condition, although it were the best manufactory in the world." The tariff issue is therefore critical. Two generations of the protective tariff "would change the face of New England society." "Of all public measures it was among the last," Webster said, "to which he should give his approbation" [13, 16-19].

This climactic agrarian statement is followed by an anticlimactic and conciliatory conclusion, which argues that the manufacturers have adequate protection under existing laws. This conclusion is appropriate. As in 1814, Webster is not attempting any reform. He is not trying to exclude manufacturing, but to prevent its undue encouragement and to protect commerce. His radical agrarian arguments serve just such modest ends. Four years later Webster leaves the way open for his subsequent endorsement of manufactures.

At the outset of his speech on the 1824 tariff, Webster identifies himself to the House as a representative of a district "highly commercial, and deeply interested in manufactures also" [5, 95]. The proposed tariff on cotton gives many of his constituents advantages, Webster concedes, but "they are greatly counterbalanced by other advantages enjoyed by other portions of the country. I cannot but regard the situation of the West as highly favorable to human happiness . . ." Webster then describes the happy state of "him . . . who cultivates his own fee-simple inheritance" [5, 136]. Notice that he is balancing interests between manufacturing and farming, and that agriculture is now depicted as a Western and so, like manufacturing, a sectional interest. He argues from expediency rather than from morality and nature: the earlier radical agrarianism is abandoned. Webster votes against the 1824 tariff because he supposes commerce the dominant interest among his constituency, but his argument leaves him free to vote for protection once manufactures take first rank.

When Webster addressed the Boston Mechanics' Institution in 1828 (the year he first votes for a protective tariff), he found the conventions of formal discourse awkward means of eulogizing the technology he was on the platform to promote. His address begins in a tone redolent of profound and liberal scholarship: "The visible and tangible creation into which we are introduced at birth, is not, in all its parts, fixed and stationary. Motion, or change of place, regular or occasional, belongs to all or most of the things around us . . ." Step by rational step Webster arrives at his subject. Motion is the result of force; force and its practical application is the province of mechanical philosophy; mechanical philosophy thus takes its place among the sciences—it is suited to "the elevated rank and dignity of reasoning beings." Mention of dignity supplies adequate occasion for praise of the most dignified of reason's accomplishments, higher mathematics, which Webster praises for "penetrating into the secret principles which hold the universe of God together" [2, 30].

But the penetration of God's secret principles makes Webster uncomfortable. He changes tone as argument flounders. He immediately reassures his audience that man can never unmask all the secrets of nature. Even if the reach of reason is "indefinite, though not . . : infinite," the number of secrets is "indefinite also, if not infinite." "The field, then [!!], is vast and unbounded" [2, 31]. The quibbling between indefinite and infinite, and the very tenuous logic which attends it, is symptomatic. Webster wants the infinite. The "vast and unbounded" excites wonder; it puts off to one side, if it does not quite banish, the specter of God to earthly eyes unveiled.

What the quibbling suggests, Webster's handling of the history of technology confirms. Our orator traces machinery back beyond knowledge to wonder. The Greeks are praised for their known contributions, but the burst of eloquence comes in the praise of the vast and wondrous pyramids of Egypt. We don't know, we can only wonder, what marvelous machines may have constructed those pyramids, and so to our moral:

> God seems to have proposed his material universe as a standing, perpetual study to his intelligent creatures; where, ever learning, they can yet never learn all; and if that material universe shall last till man shall have discovered all that is now unknown, but which by the progressive improvement of his faculties he is capable of knowing, it will remain through a duration beyond human measurement and beyond human comprehension. [2, 32]

The moral is curious but consistent with what had preceded it. Webster reaffirms the values of science and of progressive knowledge, but on behalf of enduring mystery.

His history of technology concludes with a depiction of the myriad activity of America's spindles and wheels and saws, involving a eulogy of steam as the tremendous new power behind it. In earlier years this power and activity was invidiously contrasted with life on the farm; now Webster makes the new steam power complement a sentimental emphasis upon human frailty. He has steam, personified, say to man, "Leave off your manual labor, give over your bodily toil; bestow but your skill and reason to the directing, and I will bear the toil,—with no muscle to grow weary, no nerve to relax, no breast to feel faintness" [2, 35-36].

The unfaint breast reasserts the presiding sentimental tone, and the rest of the discourse aims at regaining the polite altitude at which it commenced. In a properly dignified conclusion, architecture is praised as an art involving both technology and politely classical taste. Webster suggests that America might give peculiar emphasis to *domestic* architecture, as a final grace note to the performance.

Clearly the formal conventions appropriate to the occasion were incongenial to the subject matter. Perhaps because of this, very little of Webster's discourse on mechanical philosophy ever gets to its subject. But in spite of the conventions Webster does make out a case for the industrial arts—a rhetorical or platform case, as the occasion required. So far as his speech succeeded, we can imagine Webster's auditors going away feeling that the new technology was more dignified, and even a more fit subject for wonder and tenderness, than they had up to then supposed.[10]

From the Hayne debate (1830) to his death, Webster became for many Americans the champion of the Union as over and against the section and state. His ambitions were national; he hoped, from 1836 to 1852, for the Presidency. In geographical fact, however, the industrial and commercial interests to which he was committed were markedly sectional. If he were to attain national prominence and still publicly support those interests, he had somehow to sell them to an audience that was better than eighty per cent agricultural. This selling job was to require every bit of his rhetorical ingenuity.

Webster would sometimes argue that even if his interests were sectional, they complemented rather than competed with the interests of other sections: "Why the chief consumption of wheat flour in this country is in the East, where the great manufacturing interests are carried on . . ." [3, 288]. But more typically he tells his audiences that the non-agrarian interests he represents are really the interests of the nation as a whole. To make his argument he has to circumvent the very agrarianism he had appealed to in earlier years, an agrarianism still dear to the populace he addresses. Webster effects this circumvention by identifying farmers and factory workers, all the "laborious, industrious, and productive classes," with what he calls "labor." This makes labor, in effect, the national

10 Webster delivered a somewhat similar address before the Society for Diffusion of Useful Knowledge in 1836, but apparently his audience was more miscellaneous, and he made less effort after polite elegance.

interest. "Strike out the laborers of the United States . . . and you reduce the population of the United States from sixteen millions to one million" [3, 24-25].[11] Webster, as spokesman for "labor," speaks for the nation, and so at least qualifies for the Presidency.

In 1824 Webster's praise of American labor (as against European serfdom) derives from an agrarian bias, the dignity of the native workingman depending upon a safety valve of arable land, and that dignity compromised, already and in America, in our "large cities" [2, 141-42]. Before a convention of Whigs at Andover, Massachusetts, in 1843, the agrarian bias is gone, or, rather, transformed. Here is Webster's "rhetoric of labor" as finally perfected:

> There is, indeed, no subject which so much requires an essay to set forth all its prominence, importance, and peculiarity, as American labor; there is nothing like it on the globe; and there never was any thing like it. . . . Gentlemen, the labor of the United States is respectable. We are emphatically a country of labor; and labor with us is not reluctant drudgery. It is cheerful, contented, spirited, because it is certain of its reward. Labor everywhere mixes itself with capital. The fields around us, how many are occupied by their owners! The shops in our towns, how many are occupied by their proprietors, for the convenient pursuit of their callings! Hence, in the United States, we see labor and capital mixed together in a degree unequalled in the world. What is the value of a hundred acres of land at the feet of the Rocky Mountains . . .? Nothing at all. There is no value till man has mixed his labor with it. But the moment an American laborer drives his plough through these acres, or fells a tree upon them, that moment he creates a capital, which every step he takes, and every stroke he gives, constantly augments. He thus not only lives by labor, but every day's work, while it gives him subsistence, adds to his means, his property, his capital. Where else in this world shall we find the same state of things to such a degree? [3, 175-76].

This passage defends labor in general, but gains its imaginative charge from agrarian rhetoric. The American laborer (like the yeoman) is *uniquely* happy, a concrete realization of the age-old American dream. The American laborer and yeoman are, in contrast to their European counterparts, eminently respectable. American shops, like American farms, are owned in fee simple. Our laborer is not servile, works for his own gain: as Webster had said in an earlier speech, our laborers have

[11] Webster affects to be indifferent to capital, so far as government policy is concerned, expressing his concern instead for the workingman. Typically he argues (against Jackson-Van Buren money policy) that the laborer is the one victimized by economic dislocation—capital can take care of itself [2, 256].

an interest in "the soil they cultivate, . . . the fabrics they produce" [3, 25]. Webster's illustration of how American labor "mixes" itself with capital is the yeoman, and I suspect that the phrase itself borrows resonance from an agrarian rhetoric where the yeoman's mixing his labor with the soil suggested a mystical communion with nature.[12] The very virtues of Webster's laborer—he is "cheerful, contented, spirited"—are the virtues which Jefferson and Crèvecoeur had identified with American yeomanry. For a nation of independent farmers Webster asks his audiences to substitute a nation of independent labor-capitalists. The American laborer is rhetorically construed as the yeoman (on and) off the farm.

Throughout his public life, Webster had to argue the cause of non-agricultural interests to audiences with strong agrarian prejudices. In Portsmouth, New Hampshire, Webster had simply to ally his commerce with the popular agrarianism to make his argument against manufactures. Once committed to manufactures, however, Webster's rhetorical task is much more difficult. The agrarian rhetoric, invented to express antipathy to the Birminghams and Sheffields of the old world, was made by indirection to argue for the Walthams and Lowells of the new.

Modern readers, who have been taught to look to the semantics of words and to slight their rhetoric, may see in the appropriation of an agrarian bias to a non-agrarian cause a kind of disingenuousness. But as we have been suggesting, Webster had to appeal to the agrarian prejudices of his audiences to even begin to carry his case. Further, the "rhetoric of labor" was consistent with Webster's mature political convictions, which took the side of a wide distribution of property (as had the agrarian myth), of the interdependence of the nation's several interests (all of whom "labor" represented) and of government aid to business and industry, which Webster supposed the best way to further the interests of the nation as a whole. Finally, it seems likely that Webster

[12] I am enquiring after the rhetorical source of the phrase, why Webster chose to use it on the platform, and not after its literary origin. It happens, however, that in this case the relationship between literature and rhetoric is unusually direct. Locke defines property as that part of nature with which human labor has been "mixed" (*Second Treatise of Government,* chap. v, par. 27). A. Whitney Griswold demonstrates that Jefferson's theory of property was exactly coincident with Locke's, and in all probability derived from it. But, as Professor Griswold expresses it, Jefferson found "confirmation . . . not inspiration" in Locke (*Farming and Democracy* [New York, 1948], pp. 37-43). The inspiration—and the rhetoric—were American, Locke's abstract state of nature in the new world transformed into an agrarian ideal of individual independence and social democracy. Henry Nash Smith's *Virgin Land* (pp. 195-96) traces the further influence of Locke's theory of property to George Henry Evans' National Reform movement and to the Homestead Act.

had his own agrarian prejudices;[13] and, in any event, his "rhetoric of labor" extends, it does not subvert, agrarian ideals. It is characteristic of the conservatism informing Webster's whole career that he should keep sympathy with the old, that he should attempt consolidation of the new with the old, rather than allow—much less promote—a rupture between the two. If we conceive of his early agrarian rhetoric as a defense against such rupture with what had been a commercial-agricultural past; and if we give due weight to his conciliatory statement of that rhetoric and to its progressive amendment and transformation; then, at least when technology is his subject, the whole course of Webster's rhetoric, like that of his politics, follows the same conservatively progressive pattern. What we have been studying is not "mere" rhetoric, then, mere manipulation and talk, but rather a potent public expression of private conviction.

This argument can be further buttressed by a closer examination of the polite discourse before the Mechanics' Institution. That discourse is different from the other speeches which we have examined in that it is only indirectly political in its objective. It is what classical rhetoric calls demonstrative oratory, having as its object the persuasion of the audience to the honor (or blame) of the orator's subject. As we have seen, Webster found the discourse no easy assignment. Apparently his audience was unsure as to where honor in general (let alone in the particular of technology) belonged. Webster presumes polite science, higher mathematics, cosmic pride; at the very moment of presumption a transmutation occurs, and Greece loses itself in Egypt, higher mathematics in mystery, pride in humility. The pattern here is not unique to Webster. Emerson's

[13] Webster gloried in his country estate at Marshfield, and his many and minutely detailed letters home to his farm overseers testify that his interest in agriculture (of the manorial variety, anyway) was genuine and spirited. In addition to this manifest sympathy with agriculture, Webster very occasionally gives inadvertent expression to an agrarian aversion to the new technology. In a speech commemorating the opening of a railroad, he makes mention of the "thunder" and "screams" made by the train, and of the "awkward and ugly embankment" defacing what had been a "finely rounded field"; but it's all passed off as a joke [4, 107-11]. There is a pastoral mood to Webster's description of his childhood home, part of a letter to President Fillmore written the year Webster died: "The place is a spot of absolute quiet. It is a valley, lying in the bend of the river. Railroad cars run across it three or four times a day, and that is all the motion which is seen or heard. There is no manufacturing; no coach, wagon, or cart, going along the highway, except very infrequently. The fields are quite green . . ." [18, 535]. To another correspondent Webster confides that he wants a grave where "the clatter of railroads and the bustle of business are not likely to break the silence" [13, 581-82]. Webster's misgivings about the new industrial order are of the kind described by Leo Marx in "Two Kingdoms of Force," *Massachusetts Review*, I (October, 1959), 62-95. My point is that any generalization about Webster's loyalties to commerce and industry *as against* agriculture must be made with great circumspection.

thought aspires to demonstrate that the admitted progress of the sciences is transmuted evidence of the genius of poetry. Emerson, like Webster, attempts to reconcile the apparently incommensurate claims of head and of heart. I am arguing that Webster's transcendence of polite intention and scheme by appeal to sentiment is a public (crude and expedient) equivalent to the method of Emerson's transcendental philosophy.[14] Both men address themselves to what was fast becoming a radical bifurcation in American values. Here again, then, we do not have "mere" rhetoric—the issues are live as can be.

We don't need to be reminded that Webster differs grossly from Emerson in the attitude he takes toward, in the use he makes of, the issues he confronts. His performances are only accidentally contributions to literature or philosophy: he is concerned to exploit issues for immediate and practical public effect. This essay began with the declaration that we today have lost our respect for such dignifying of public effect, such attention to public expediency. So far as that is the case, we must remind ourselves that American respectability in Webster's time revered oratory as queen of the arts,[15] by direct implication making its kind of guidance of public deportment the highest duty of the educated man. If we are able to study Webster's orations (and those of his more able fellow orators) in the spirit in which they were delivered, we make ourselves familiar with what was, for at least several decades of our national experience,[16] a practical and powerful kind of popular education.

Such has been the assumption behind this discussion of Webster. The gradualness with which he perfects his "rhetoric of labor," the tentativeness in his effort to make technology a suitable subject for formal discourse, have been described as natural consequences of the orator's need to stay with his audience. And I trust it has been made evident that his need is our good fortune. First and incidentally because that nearness to audiences gives the speech document a peculiar immediacy. Since the recorded speech is a function of the rhetorical situation in which it occurred, it makes the whole situation come alive—the excitement of the Faneuil Hall protest meeting, the pretentious formality before the

14 Bronson Alcott's orphic pronouncements, in *Nature*, are perhaps the Emersonian equivalent to Webster's eulogy of the pyramid-building. With Alcott, Emerson would like us to believe, we leave behind the admittedly valid but "digested systems" of positive sciences and soar into the "undiscovered regions" of the soul.

15 For an appraisal of the status of oratory in the early years of Emerson's life, see F. O. Matthiessen, *American Renaissance* (New York, 1941), pp. 14-24.

16 Just which decades will have to be determined. In New England culture the long transition from theological to literary interests had a late middle phase of neoclassical influences, during which oratory flourishes wonderfully and the orator—Webster, or Everett—is supposed the type of high culture.

Mechanics' Institution. Specialists in rhetorical criticism have always insisted upon, and treasured, the wonderful immediacy of the speech document. They have not, however, shown enough awareness of the larger cultural context of the speech.[17] Because the orator has to stay with his audience, his oration reveals that audience; the *continuing* efforts of the orator, audience after audience, reveal the American public. Our discussion of the persistent agrarian ardor of Webster's audiences, and of the polite sentimentality of one such audience, has at least opened up larger questions of cultural context, of public belief. We have discussed only Webster and technology. For those years when oratory was a vital cultural institution, the investigation of other orators and other subjects should provide an illuminating record of the changing dispositions of public (as distinct from private) belief, at a time when public belief was supposed to have its own import and dignity.

[17] I take the three-volume *History and Criticism of American Public Address* to be typical of contemporary rhetorical criticism, in its emphasis upon criticism of individual performances and in its indifference to oratory as a cultural institution. Marie Hochmuth describes the principles of rhetorical criticism in the introductory chapter to the third volume, and the bulk of the volumes is devoted to criticism of sundry American orators, pretty much according to those principles. But the attempt to give historical continuity to public address during antebellum years ("The Early National Period, 1788-1860," I, 55-110) dissolves into a disconnected miscellany of generalization and anecdote.

Afternote

I am now convinced that public tradition, at least in New England, passes through several distinct phases: a first and Federalist phase (c. 1800–1815) employing a florid, copious style; a second and Whig phase (c. 1815–1830) employing what might be termed a style of homely elegance; a third phase (c. 1830–1860) involving a radical split within the polite community, between traditionalists and reformists. There probably is a fourth phase, involving a retreat from politics: Robert C. Winthrop spends most of the late nineteenth century out of politics, elegantly dignifying public occasions.

Principals of the New England polite tradition deserve fresh evaluations, of the kind found in Winfred E. A. Bernhard, *Fisher Ames* (Chapel Hill, N. C.: University of North Carolina Press, 1965). Leo Marx puts Daniel Webster and technology to his own shrewd and sensitive use in *The Machine in the Garden* (New York: Oxford University Press, 1964), pp. 209–14.

Clarence Mondale is an Associate Professor of American Civilization at George Washington University and is Project Director of the Rose Computer-Stored Bibliography in American Studies. [This article appeared in Vol. XIV, No. 1 (Spring, 1962).]

Howard Mumford Jones

Literature and Orthodoxy in Boston after the Civil War

ON December 1, 1868, the *American Literary Gazette and Publishers' Circular*, predecessor of the *Publishers' Weekly*, in a list of books recently brought out in the United States, announced the appearance of *Gates Ajar* by Elizabeth Stuart Phelps, a volume of 248 pages selling for $1.50. The publishers were Fields, Osgood and Company, heirs since October of Ticknor and Fields and ancestors of Houghton Mifflin. The book did not seem important enough to appear in the page advertisement by this firm in the "winter issue" and was not advertised until September 1, 1869, when another edition, illustrated, is presented as selling for $3.50 cloth and $6.00 Turkey morocco. Meanwhile controversy was carried on in the magazine as to whether or not S. C. Griggs and Company of Chicago had disposed of more than 2300 copies of *Gates Ajar,* a number which pales into insignificance when one learns that by the end of the century the book had sold 100,000 copies in America, a larger number in Great Britain, and an unknown number when translated into French, German, Dutch, Italian, and other languages.

Before its vogue was over, there were Gates Ajar tippets, Gates Ajar collars, Gates Ajar cigars, Gates Ajar hymns, a Gates Ajar funeral march, and a Gates Ajar floral offering at funerals. As late as 1893 the book was still so well known that the author, nearing fifty, was asked to contribute to a symposium in the *North American Review* on immortality. She wrote:

After the lapse of nearly thirty years I cannot recall without emotion the letters which fell like drops of a storm upon the author of the little book. . . . They were the letters of the bereaved;—from all countries, all ages, all sorts and conditions of men. They came with the deep, black margins that told their story before the seal was broken. They came with pages half illegible from the stains of tears.

Obviously *Gates Ajar* satisfied a need for spiritual comfort parallel to that satisfied by Rabbi Liebmann's *Peace of Mind* in our time.

Although Miss Phelps was only twenty when she began writing *Gates Ajar,* she had already produced a considerable body of fiction, some of it Sunday-school juveniles marked by humor and realism. The daughter of a Congregational minister who had once had the cure of a church on Harrison Avenue in Boston but who had been called to Andover Theological Seminary, and of a mother, the descendant of ministers and a writer of religious fiction, Miss Phelps grew up in an atmosphere of theology, spiritualism, and death.

Her grandfather, the Reverend Eliakim Phelps, was persecuted by spirits, tales of which sent the frightened little girl to bed, gasping under the bedclothes. Dishes leaped from the table, forks were bent by unseen fingers, turnips dropped from the ceiling, and spirit rappings told of the torments of hell or demanded the satisfactions of squash pie. Her mother was obsessed with the idea of death; and, dying soon after the birth of a third child, left directions for burial worthy of the genius of Hawthorne, for at the funeral the baby boy was baptized beside his mother's coffin just as the sun broke through the December clouds to illumine the dead woman's portrait at the end of the room. A tubercular stepmother deceased within three years of marrying the widower, albeit a third wife was of more lasting mettle.

Miss Phelps' first story for adults narrates the sorrow of a sewing woman for a sweetheart killed at Antietam, and her first impressive narrative, "The Tenth of January," published by the *Atlantic* in March 1868, is a play-by-play account of the deaths of several hundred millhands, mostly women, trapped in the Pemberton Mill at Lawrence in 1860 and there crushed or burned. As the flames rose female voices sang the hymn, "We're going home, to die no more." Finally, the young man Miss Phelps was in love with, Samuel Hopkins Thompson of the class of 1862, Phillips Academy, enlisting upon graduation to become a lieutenant, was killed in battle that same year while rallying his men.

It is out of these experiences that *Gates Ajar* was born. As in the case of *Uncle Tom's Cabin* and "John Brown's Body," however, its authoress disclaimed all personal responsibility for its inspired pages. "I had no more to do with the writing of it," she says in her autobiography, "than the bough through which the wind cries. . . . The angel said unto me 'Write!' and I wrote." The angel, however, had had considerable experience in libraries, inasmuch as during the course of the work he quotes Archbishop Whately, the Reverend Thomas Chalmers, the Reverend Isaac Taylor, Eugénie de Guérin, Mrs. Browning, Gottfried August Bürger, Thomas Gray, Adelaide Proctor, Charles Lamb, Goethe, John Greenleaf Whittier, and many other mundane geniuses.

Gates Ajar is the story, told in the first person, of Mary Cabot, whose brother Roy is killed in battle. Between brother and sister there had been a relation so close that a modern novelist would have treated the problem as one of abnormal psychology; Miss Phelps' generation preferred to see it in terms of religious consolation. Mary passionately revolts against the injustice of God in taking her brother from her; her icy sorrow is untouched until an Aunt Winifred, who has lost a ministerial consort of un-Calvinistic views and who has done a good deal of cheerful meditating on the afterlife, comes to visit her. The book then becomes a record of comforting conversations between the two about a cheerful deity and the pleasures of heaven, where, Mary is assured, brother Roy is presently talking to Abraham Lincoln. Personality somehow survives, and heaven is going to be mainly a purified earth. Because Roy silently communicates to the soul of his living sister, death becomes merely a beautiful gate into paradise. Here is a characteristic utterance by Aunt Winifred toward the end of the volume:

> You [that is, Mary Cabot] had all your life been directed to an indefinite heaven, where the glory of God was to crowd out all individuality and all human joy from His most individual and human creatures, till the "Glory of God" had become nothing but a name and a dread to you. . . . [But], my child; clinging human loves, stifled longings, cries for rest, forgotten hopes, shall have their answer.

Mary thereupon represents herself as thinking: "I *knew* that I loved Roy more than I loved such a Being as God [had] seemed to me then to be. Now . . . the more I love Roy, the more I love Him." In other words, the humanity of Christ as interpreted by Aunt Winifred is reassurance that these dead have not died in vain. Thus Miss Phelps comforted the stricken.

Gates Ajar marked a gentling, a softening, a feminization of Protestant Christianity, which was to have its greatest Boston triumph in the rise of the Christian Science church, the founder of which is known as Mother Eddy, and one of the tenets of which is that God is simultaneously Mother-Father. "Few manuscripts," remarks the impersonal *Dictionary of American Biography*, "have had a more remarkable influence upon American religious history than that which finally found its way into print in 1875 under the title *Science and Health.*" This humanization of Protestant creeds, this blurring of intellectual issues, this eschatological optimism is a salient fact in postwar Boston.

The struggle, however, was long and sometimes unpleasant. From the point of view of orthodoxy *Gates Ajar* was heretical, as a library of attacks insisted, but its continuing success makes it something more than a tear-drenched story. One must remember the rigidity characteristic of Protestant doctrine, even after Transcendentalism and the Civil War. Frank H. Foster's *Genetic History of the New England Theology* (1907) is a survey of this religious history. The "old theology" as there outlined was dogmatic, intricate, and rigid. It reduced the personality of Christ to a cog in a complicated machine. Its God was a god of justice rather than of love; it laid far more stress upon analysis of the probabilities of salvation than it did upon individual growth in Christian nurture; it asserted the punishment of sinners in hell; it tended to interpret the Bible as a charter like the American Constitution rather than as a mode of life like the British constitution; and its method of demonstrating religious truth had the unhuman objectivity and intellectual refinement of mathematical proof. Even after the catastrophe of war, it was more interested in sin than in salvation. It was against the spirit and manner of this approach to Christianity that revolt in Boston church life and in literature developed.

Three episodes in church history show the importance of the controversy. In 1884 the Reverend George A. Gordon was called from

Greenwich, Connecticut, to the Old South Church in Boston. He was to become one of the great preachers in the city and one of the principal proponents of the "new theology" in a succession of volumes intended for both ministers and laymen, *Humanism in New England Theology* (1920) being a late characteristic affirmation of a point of view which opposed the inhumanity of that school. But even as a young man Dr. Gordon frightened the orthodox, and the account of his installation both reveals the conflict and has its humors.

"Completely and honorably sincere," he tells us in his *Autobiography*, "as the orthodox body was in Massachusetts, a more provincial or unenlightened mind, upon the nature of religion in general, and of Christianity in particular, probably never existed than in my denominational environment in those painful early years of my ministry in Boston." Interviewed by the council of the church, he felt they were "panic-stricken, half-wild." A church supper to welcome the new minister had been set for six-thirty, and the council had gone into secret session at five-thirty. At six-thirty they were still in session. "The committee in charge delayed till they could delay no longer. The invited guests, representing all religious denominations, were escorted to the diningroom and partook of the supper. Speeches of welcome to the new minister were made, and greetings extended by Phillips Brooks and others. Still no council appeared. At a few minutes before nine o'clock the result was given out, forty-eight in favor, eighteen against installation. I fancied," the account concludes, that those who had battled for me "wondered whether I was really worth it all," when they saw only the cold fragments of the meal.

The second case is that of the Reverend Phillips Brooks, the most influential pulpit personality that Boston nourished in the post-bellum period, a preacher and writer whose immediate influence was far greater than that of Jonathan Edwards. His very first sermon, preached in Philadelphia, lamented the absence of free inquiry in New England theological circles. By 1867 he had rejected a call to be the head of the Episcopal Theological School in Cambridge, and in 1868 he had refused a call to Trinity Church in Boston, to which nevertheless he came in 1869. The power of his preaching was legendary, and the wide audience for his published sermons was international.

Nevertheless, Boston distrusted the Episcopal church; and the more orthodox Episcopalians distrusted Brooks, who was supposed to be tainted with Unitarianism. His sympathetic biographer notes eight important points in which Brooks departed from the theology in which he had been reared. Brooks' indifference to fine points of creed, his hospitality to all manner of Christians, and his subordinating of other religious topics to his burning belief in the personality of Christ—his Bohlen lectures of 1879 on the "Influence of Jesus" are his chief contribution to theology—shocked the orthodox (including his mother) so deeply that when on April 29, 1891, he was elected to the bishopric of Massachusetts, confirmation of the election, which is usually immediate, was postponed for ten weeks, to the scandal of his parishioners. Defenders of the old order spent the interval trying to find heresy in his sermons.

A famous passage in his *Essays and Addresses* of 1892 shows Brooks' impatience with theological niceties and indirectly indicates the nature of his battle with orthodoxy. He wrote:

> It seems to me as if, were I a layman in the days when some doctrine had got loose as it were into the wind and was being blown across the Common and up and down the streets, I should go to church on Sunday, not wanting my minister to give me an oracular answer to all the questions that had been started about it which I should not believe if he did give it, but hoping that out of his sermon I might refresh my knowledge of Christ, get Him, His nature, His work, His desire for me once clear before me, and go out more ready to see this disputed truth of the moment in His light and as an utterance of Him.

Humanly speaking, this is an admirable utterance; but the dismissal of the minister as an intellectual incompetent, the by-passing of a philosophical issue with an appeal to Christ seemed to more conservative Christians to reduce belief to mere personalism.

The third illuminating episode is the Andover heresy trials, which, beginning in 1886–87, were not settled until 1890–91 when the supreme court of Massachusetts ruled against orthodoxy. The founders of Andover Theological Seminary had, after anxious thought, produced in 1808 a statement of theological truth to which all professors in the seminary swore to adhere and which was intended to be the core of Christian orthodoxy for time and eternity. In the eighties, however, many alumni of the seminary were disturbed by the fact that the Reverend Egbert C. Smyth, professor of ecclesiastical history, had departed widely from this creed; and they accordingly demanded and received a formal hearing before its board of visitors. This hearing, famous in American intellectual history, had all the dignity and intricacy of a court trial. Professor Smyth, said his accusers, did not teach the inerrancy of Scripture; he had taught that Christ was a finite being; he had taught that no man has the power to repent without the knowledge of God in Christ; and he had heretical views of the nature of the atonement. Professor Smyth's reply was that theology, like any other science, was capable of development and could not be frozen into shape even in 1808; that his alleged heresies were legitimate developments from the creed or adaptations to modern scholarship of primary truths; and that therefore he had not violated his oath. Other teachers and writers became involved, and the state supreme court finally ruled for Professor Smyth.

In this third instance, only ten years before the end of the century, dogmatic theology again clashed with the point of view of intuitive or developmental theology, and again lost. Once more one notes the minimizing of definition of belief, the whittling down of the old Protestant theology to a few broad themes, the exaltation of the Christian life at the expense of the Christian intelligence. The sharp intellectual distinctions which for three centuries had seemed to Boston supremely important were being erased; and churches which had once inquired anxiously into a communicant's belief concerning salvation or sin or the nature of Christ, grew more and more content with demanding only that their communicants lead a Christian life if they were able to do so.

Against this philosophic history let me now project some writers whose importance in this regard historians do not always appreciate. I begin with Henry Wadsworth Longfellow, to whom the war years had brought tragedy, for Mrs. Longfellow was burned to death on July 9, 1861, while sealing packages of her daughters' curls. "How can I live any longer?" he wrote in his diary; and in a letter to George William Curtis he said, "I am inwardly bleeding to death." Many years later he wrote:

> In the long, sleepless watches of the night,
>   A gentle face — the face of one long dead —

Looks at me from the wall, where round its head
The night-lamp casts a halo of pale light.
Here in this room she died; and soul more white
Never through martyrdom of fire was led
To its repose . . .

In February 1862 his close friend Cornelius C. Felton died, a man of whom he said in "Three Friends of Mine":

Oh, what hadst thou to do with cruel Death,
Who wast so full of life, or Death with thee,
That thou shouldst die before thou hadst grown old!

And on May 23, 1864, Longfellow attended the funeral of Hawthorne. By then death had struck so often round him that he walked like a man in a trance:

The faces of familiar friends seemed strange;
Their voices I could hear,
And yet the words they uttered seemed to change
Their meaning to my ear.

For the one face I looked for was not there,
The one low voice was mute;
Only an unseen presence filled the air,
And baffled my pursuit.

It seemed to him, not only of Hawthorne's demise but of most human endeavor, that

The unfinished window in Aladdin's tower
Unfinished must remain!

If the poet raised his eyes above these domestic and personal griefs, there was around him only the vast sordid tragedy of the Civil War, the sacrifice of the young:

He is dead, the beautiful youth,
The heart of honor, the tongue of truth,

who rode whistling along the picket line only to be shot. Small wonder that the wind in the chimney at Craigie House whispered to Longfellow:

Hollow
Are the visions that you follow,
Into darkness sinks your fire!

How, then, did Longfellow find consolation? As in the case of Miss Phelps, intricate debates over the merits of sublapsarianism and supralapsarianism were meaningless to him; like her he turned to reconsider the whole vast problem of Christianity. He wanted, not the cold reasoning of Andover theologians, but some warmhearted cathedral, where, as he tells us in his magnificent sonnets on the *Divine Comedy,*

> [I could] leave my burden at this minster gate,
> Kneeling in prayer, and not ashamed to pray,
> The tumult of the time disconsolate
> To inarticulate murmurs dies away,
> While the eternal ages watch and wait.

The translation of Dante was an anodyne for his grief-struck spirit, and he produced out of his pain and desolation one of the great renderings of that poem in English. But this was, after all, scholar's work; it was not his own utterance; and though the last line of each of the three parts of the *Divine Comedy* contains the word "Love," the poem, however magnificent, was not his.

Could he not as a Protestant show that love is the central doctrine of the Christian religion? He returned upon an old project of his — a poetic version of Christian history on which he had long been laboring, the third part of which he published in 1868, the whole of which he completed by 1872. This was the lengthy dramatic trilogy, *Christus: A Mystery,* begun as early as 1849, but not finished until the lapse of almost a quarter century of thought, work, and sorrow. It includes "The Golden Legend," a varied and beautiful poem despite its indebtedness to *Faust,* and it includes some of the finest blank verse that Longfellow, a master craftsman, ever wrote.

We do not read the trilogy nowadays because fashions in poetry change and also because we do not understand its historical significance. Like the Catholic *Divine Comedy,* the Protestant *Christus: A Mystery* is an assertion that the heart of Christian faith is love. The "Introit" pictures an angel bearing the prophet Habakkuk high in the air; and when the prophet inquires why he has been chosen for this honor, the angel answers:

> In the harvest-field I beheld thee,
> When no man compelled thee,
> Bearing with thine own hands
> This food to the famishing reapers. . . .

In the "Finale" Saint John speaks and insists like Phillips Brooks upon the personality of Christ and upon the central significance of love in the Christian scheme.

> The Ages come and go,
> The Centuries pass as Years;
> My hair is white as the snow,
> My feet are weary and slow,
> The earth is wet with my tears!
> . . . .
> The world itself is old;
> The portals of Time unfold
> On hinges of iron, that grate
> And groan with the rust and the weight,
> Like the hinges of a gate
> That hath fallen to decay;
> But the evil doth not cease;
> There is war instead of peace,
> Instead of Love there is hate;
> . . . .
> From all the narrow rules
> And subtleties of Schools,
> And the craft of tongue and pen;
> Bewildered in its search,
> Bewildered with the cry:
> Lo, here! lo, there, the Church!
> Poor, sad Humanity
> Through all the dust and heat
> Turns back with bleeding feet,
> By the weary road it came,
> Unto the simple thought
> By the great Master taught,
> And that remaineth still:
> Not he that repeateth the name,
> But he that doeth the will!

Thus Longfellow, in the central work of his life, turned away from the old New England theology and against the alumni of Andover to the central doctrine of a creedless Christian.

The first drama, "The Divine Tragedy," a rendering of the Gospels into transparent and dignified blank verse, has its significance pointed out in an interlude spoken by the Abbot Joachim, whose speech concludes:

> . . . I am in love with Love,
> And the sole thing I hate is Hate;
> For Hate is death; and Love is life,
> A peace, a splendor from above;
> And Hate, a never-ending strife,
> A smoke, a blackness from the abyss
> Where unclean serpents coil and hiss!
> Love is the Holy Ghost within;
> Hate the unpardonable sin!

The second, poetically the richest of the three, is "The Golden Legend," a tale of the selfless love of a Christian girl for Prince Henry of Hoheneck. Of Lucifer, who struggles to thwart both her affection and the redemption of the prince, a Recording Angel says in an epilogue:

> . . . since God suffers him to be,
> He, too, is God's minister,
> And labors for some good
> By us not understood!

The third portion of the poem is made up of two historical plays about New England (perhaps a naive anticlimax)—one in which Longfellow unsparingly condemns the persecution of the Quakers in seventeenth-century Boston, and a second in which with equal severity he condemns the witchcraft persecutions. These he traces to a theology unillumined by love. Thus, in a final speech by Cotton Mather, that divine is unhistorically made to say:

> O sight most horrible! In a land like this,
> Spangled with Churches Evangelical,
> Inwrapped in our salvations, must we seek
> In mouldering statute-books of English Courts
> Some old forgotten Law, to do such deeds?
> Those who lie buried in the Potter's Field
> Will rise again, as surely as ourselves
> That sleep in honored graves with epitaphs;
> And this poor man [Giles Corey], whom we have made a victim,
> Hereafter will be counted as a martyr!

Because the last third of this enormous work is not satisfactory either as poetry or as drama, Longfellow seems at first sight to be beating a dead horse. But when one studies the "Finale" by Saint John, which I have quoted, when one projects Longfellow's trilogy against the clash of creeds in Boston and New England, both within Protestantism and between Protestantism and other faiths, *Christus: A Mystery* takes on a startling significance. One begins to realize that this vast poem is directed not merely against past wrongs recorded in history but also against the stony walls of Andover. It is a plea to rise above anti-Catholicism and anti-Protestantism into a universe where the soul of man can live in *l'amor che muove il sole e l'altre stelle*.

Equally revealing is it to pass from Longfellow to Whittier. Albeit the Quaker clung desperately to the belief that

> The riddle of the world is understood
> Only by him who feels that God is good,

the Civil War had been for him a long nightmare which led him to the brink of disbelief in God. In one of his poems in 1861 the firmament breaks up, light after light goes out in black eclipse, and the evil star of the Apocalypse drags the lights of heaven into the abyss. In "Amy Wentworth" of 1862 he wrote poignantly of the dilemma of noncombatants,

> Doomed to watch a strife we may not share
> With other weapons than the patriot's prayer,
> Yet owning, with full hearts and moistened eyes,
> The awful beauty of self-sacrifice.

To Whittier it sometimes seemed that

> through a weary day and night
> I watch a vague and aimless fight;

and another poem notes that

> pain
> Is bitter, and tears are salt: our voices take
> A sober tone; our very household songs
> Are heavy with a nation's grief and wrongs;
> And innocent mirth is chastened for the sake
> Of the brave hearts that nevermore shall beat,
> The eyes that smile no more, the unreturning feet!

In Whittier's situation the conditions of sanity required that he cling with almost pathological strength to the doctrine of the goodness of God, so that in the sixties and the seventies we find him returning again and again to the iteration of what was for the Quaker a cardinal religious truth. He stated the theological issue fairly in a poem of 1863.

> What if thine eye refuse to see,
>   Thine ear of Heaven's free welcome fail,
> And thou a willing captive be,
>   Thyself thy own dark jail?
>
> Oh, doom beyond the saddest guess,
>   As the long years of God unroll,
> To make thy dreary selfishness
>   The prison of a soul.

In 1865, in his well-known "The Eternal Goodness," he reiterated the Quaker faith. The poem explicitly repudiates theology of the Andover school.

> I trace your lines of argument;
>   Your logic linked and strong
> I weigh as one who dreads dissent,
>   And fears a doubt as wrong.
>
> But still my human hands are weak
>   To hold your iron creeds:
>
> . . . .
>
> Who fathoms the Eternal Thought?
>   Who talks of scheme and plan?
> The Lord is God! He needeth not
>   The poor device of man.

Holding this peculiar faith in the Inner Light, Whittier was not disturbed by the problems of biblical criticism, for the Scriptures, he wrote, "are *a* rule, not *the* rule of faith." Believing that God was actively at work in and through Nature—"The harp at Nature's advent strung," he sang, "Has never ceased to play"—he was undisturbed by the conflict between science and religion. Clinging to the personality of Christ, he was also unshaken by skepticism and doubt.

> Man judges from a partial view
> Man never yet his brother knew;
> The Eternal Eye that sees the whole
> May better read the darkened soul,
> And find, to outward sense denied,
> The flower upon its inmost side.

His democratic charity was boundless; it embraced all creeds, all persons, and clung persistently to cosmic optimism.

Yet howsoever changed or tost,
Not even a wreath of mist is lost,
No atom can itself exhaust.

So shall the soul's superior force
Live on and run its endless course
In God's unlimited universe.

But—for there is always a *but* in human affairs—though it was comforting to hear the Quaker poet sing

That life is ever lord of Death,
And Love can never lose its own!

the historian is compelled to point out that this fine spirit also exalted Christian love at the expense of Christian intelligence, to the impoverishment of philosophical Protestantism.

Oliver Wendell Holmes approached the same problem from two separate positions. As a poet he joined Longfellow and Whittier in celebrating the central place of love in the Christian scheme and in ignoring distinctions of creed.

O Love Divine, that stooped to share
Our sharpest pang, our bitterest tear,
On Thee we cast each earth-born care,
We smile at pain while Thou art near!

. . . .

On Thee we fling our burdening woe,
O Love Divine, forever dear,
Content to suffer, while we know,
Living and dying, Thou art near!

Unlike his two contemporaries, however, Holmes did not seek to conquer the old theology by indirection only; he charged against it, combining his knowledge of science and of evolution into an effective attack upon the orthodox theory of sin. Three direct assaults are the essays, "Mechanism in Thought and Morals" (1870), "Crime and Automatism," and "Jonathan Edwards" (1880), but equally cogent are the three "medicated novels," *Elsie Venner* (1860–61), *The Guardian Angel* (1867), and *A Mortal Antipathy* (1885), in which the chief characters, though they sin, or at least are tempted to, act as they do from causes outside themselves. Holmes is explicit in a preface to *Elsie Venner*:

> The real aim of the story was to test the doctrine of "original sin" and human responsibility for the disordered volition coming under that technical denomination. Was Elsie Venner, poisoned by the venom of a crotalus before she was born, morally responsible for the "volitional" aberrations, which translated into acts become what is known as sin, and, it may be, what is punished as crime? If . . . she becomes by the verdict of the human conscience a proper object of divine pity and not of divine wrath, as a subject of moral poisoning, wherein lies the difference between her position at the bar of judgment, human or divine, and that of the unfortunate victim who received a moral poison from a remote ancestor before he drew his first breath?

The theme of *Elsie Venner* is fantastic and the management of the story (as is true of its companion novels) unskillful, but these truths should not conceal the fact that Holmes is assaulting Augustinian Christianity. In the words of Dr. S. I. Hayakawa, a close student of this writer: "Professionally trained as he was to empiricism, the theological apriorisms that underlay Calvinistic dogmas about sin and moral responsibility seemed to [Holmes] relics of barbarism unbecoming the unenlightened Americans, so that he set about with great vigor to destroy, by mockery, logic, sentiment, and science, the notions prevailing among the general public about crime and sin."

In "Mechanism in Thought and Morals" Holmes neatly turns the argument from materialism against the theologians. After demonstrating that human thought depends in surprising degree upon the physiological makeup of the individual and upon his inheritance, he points out that orthodox theology is, however, more materialistic than science, inasmuch as the doctrine

> In Adam's fall
> We sinned all,

implies the mechanical transmission from one generation to another of a condition of sinfulness the individual can have no responsibility for. "I reject," he writes indignantly, "the mechanical doctrine which makes me the slave of outside influences . . . I claim the right to eliminate all mechanical ideas which have crowded into the sphere of intelligent choice between right and wrong."

The crucial difference between orthodox theology and the scientific view of man, in Holmes' judgment, was that the doctrine of inherited guilt removed all moral responsibility from man, whereas the findings of science, though they illumine the dependence of thought — and therefore of choice — upon matter, do not eliminate the possibility of morally independent volition. As he indignantly remarks in his essay on Jonathan Edwards, "What can be more utterly materialistic than to attach the idea of sinfulness and responsibility, and liability to eternal suffering in consequence, to a little organic bundle, with no more knowledge of its relations to the moral world than a marsupial embryo in the maternal pouch has of its geographical position?" The doctrine of innate depravity he dismissed as so much "Asiatic legend." Holmes differed from Longfellow and Whittier by carrying out an intellectual attack, not merely an emotional one, on the old theology; but like them he did not perceive that iconoclasm was not enough, so that, when he had finished, a hazy Christian emotionalism was all that the reader had left to lay hold on.

In Miss Phelps, Longfellow, Whittier, and others one reads from time to time that the unseen spirits of the dead are close to the living world. A characteristic passage is in Longfellow's "Palingenesis," printed in the *Atlantic* in 1864:

> . . . round about me all . . .
> Seemed peopled with the shapes
> Of those whom I had known in days departed,
> Apparelled in the loveliness which gleams
> On faces seen in dreams.

By way of coda to this inadequate discussion of a complex phase of cultural history, one notes an extraordinary revival of spiritualism in Boston during the seventies and eighties. The works of Andrew Jackson Davis, chief of the cult, were then garnered and republished by a Boston publisher. Epes Sargent in 1869 wrote a book to prove that the planchette was the despair of science and another in 1875 to show that spiritualism was the palpable proof of immortality. In 1886 Allen Putnam, having already explained the witchcraft delusion as a misapprehension of spiritualism, brought out *Post-Mortem Confessions*, which relates the mortification of the spirits of half a dozen Harvard professors, including President James Walker and Professor Benjamin Peirce, at having scoffed at spiritualism in their lifetime and so prevented the college from teaching its truths. By the eighties, in fact, Boston was one of the capitals of this belief, its mediums were celebrated, and many of its citizens, finding nothing in the old creeds, were turning to seances for ghostly comfort. The cult became fashionable; and in *The Undiscovered Country* (1880) by William Dean Howells and *The Bostonians* (1886) by Henry James one finds lengthy, if unsympathetic, fictional histories of this phase of belief, the novel of Howells being more directly concerned with spiritualism than is the book by James. Obviously, since in spiritualism any departed spirit in eternity may communicate with any living human being, systems of theology become, as it were, irrelevant; so that, as the climax in this outline of Bostonian revolt against an intellectualized Protestant theology, it is fair to regard spiritualism as the utmost limit reached by the deliquescence of Christian rationalism in the period. During the postwar battle between dogmatic theology and religious intuition the literature one associates with Boston enlisted heavily against theology.

Howard Mumford Jones is Professor Emeritus of English at Harvard University. [This article appeared in Vol. I, No. 2 (Summer, 1949).]

Everett Carter

Cultural History Written with Lightning: The Significance of *The Birth of a Nation*

ON FEBRUARY 20, 1915, DAVID WARK GRIFFITH'S LONG FILM, *The Clansman,* was shown in New York City. One of the spectators was Thomas Dixon, the author of the novel from which it was taken, who was moved by the power of the motion picture to shout to the wildly applauding spectators that its title would have to be changed. To match the picture's greatness, he suggested, its name should be *The Birth of a Nation.*[1] Only by a singular distortion of meaning could the film be interpreted as the story of a country's genesis; the birth it did herald was of an American industry and an American art; any attempt to define the cinema and its impact upon American life must take into account this classic movie. For with the release of *The Birth of a Nation* "significant motion picture history begins." [2] Its prestige became enormous. It was the first picture to be played at the White House, where Woodrow Wilson was reported to have said: "it is like writing history with lightning." [3] By January 1916 it had given 6,266 performances in the area of greater New York alone.[4] If we conservatively estimate that five hundred patrons saw each performance, we arrive at the astounding total of over three million residents of and visitors to New York who saw the picture, and forever viewed themselves and their country's history through its colorations.

[1] Lewis Jacobs, *The Rise of the American Film* (New York: Harcourt, Brace & Co., 1939), p. 175.

[2] Seymour Stern, "The Birth of a Nation in Retrospect," *International Photographer* VII (April, 1935), 4.

[3] Jacobs, p. 175.

[4] Stern, *International Photographer,* VII, 4.

And not only does significant motion picture history begin, but most of the problems of the art's place in our culture begin too. The picture projects one of the most persistent cultural illusions; it presents vividly and dramatically the ways in which a whole people have reacted to their history; its techniques in the narrowest sense are the fully realized techniques of the pictorial aspects of the motion picture; in the widest sense, its techniques are a blend of the epical and the symbolically realistic, and each part of this mixture has developed into a significant genre of cinematic art.

Griffith was a Kentuckian, a devout believer in Southern values, and these values, he was certain, were embodied in *The Clansman,* a sentimental novel of the Reconstruction which had appeared in 1905, had been widely read, had been seen in dramatic form throughout the South, and whose author had dedicated it "To the memory of a Scotch-Irish leader of the South, my Uncle, Colonel Leroy McAfee, Grand Titan of the Invisible Empire Ku Klux Klan."[5] In his introduction, Dixon went on to describe his theme: "How the young South, led by the reincarnated souls of the Clansmen of Old Scotland, went forth under this cover and against overwhelming odds, daring exile, imprisonment, and a felon's death, and saved the life of a people, forms one of the most dramatic chapters in the history of the Aryan race." [6] This strong suggestion that the South's struggle is a racial epic, involving all the people of one blood in their defense against a common ancestral enemy, became, as we shall see, a major influence upon Griffith's conception of his cinematic theme. And, in addition, the novel in so many ways served as what would later be called a "treatment" from which the story would be filmed, that we must examine the book closely before we can understand the significance of the film.

The Clansman told the story of "Thaddeus Stevens' bold attempt to Africanize the ten great states of the American Union . . ." It interpreted the history of the Reconstruction as the great Commoner's vengeance motivated partly by economics: the destruction of his Pennsylvania iron mills by Lee's army; [7] partly by religion: in his parlor there was "a picture of a nun . . . he had always given liberally to an orphanage conducted by a Roman Catholic sisterhood;" [8] but mainly by lust: his housekeeper was "a mulatto, a woman of extraordinary animal beauty . . ." who became, through her power over Austin Stoneman (the fictional name for

[5] Thomas Dixon, *The Clansman* (New York: Grosset & Dunlap, 1905), Dedication, without page number.

[6] *The Clansman,* Introduction, without page number.

[7] *The Clansman,* p. 95.

[8] *The Clansman,* p. 90.

Stevens) "the presiding genius of National legislation." [9] Stoneman was shown in private conference with Lincoln, whose words in his Charleston debate with Douglas were directly quoted: "I believe there is a physical difference between the white and black races which will forever forbid their living together on terms of political and social equality." [10] Stoneman's instruments in the South were all described as animals, demonstrating that the Civil War was fought to defend civilization against the barbaric and bestial. Silas Lynch, the carpet-bagger, "had evidently inherited the full physical characteristics of the Aryan race, while his dark yellowish eyes beneath his heavy brows glowed with the brightness of the African jungle." [11] The Negro leader, Aleck, had a nose "broad and crushed flat against his face," and jaws "strong and angular, mouth wide, and lips thick, curling back from rows of solid teeth set obliquely . . ." [12] The Cameron family of the Old South were the principal victims; Gus, a renegade Negro ravished Marion Cameron, the sixteen-year-old ". . . universal favourite . . ." who embodied "the grace, charm, and tender beauty of the Southern girl . . .;" [13] Silas Lynch attempted to violate Elsie Stoneman, the betrothed of Ben Cameron. The actual rape was a climax of a series of figurative violations of the South by the North, one of which was the entry of Stoneman into the black legislature, carried by two Negroes who made "a curious symbolic frame for the chalk-white passion of the old Commoner's face. No sculptor ever dreamed a more sinister emblem of the corruption of a race of empire-builders than this group. Its black figures, wrapped in the night of four thousand years of barbarism, squatted there the 'equal' of their master, grinning at his forms of Justice, the evolution of forty centuries of Aryan genius." [14] These figurative and literal ravishments provoked the formation of the Ku Klux Klan, whose like ". . . the world had not seen since the Knights of the Middle Ages rode on their Holy Crusades." [15] The Klan saved Elsie, revenged Marion, brought dismay to the Negro, the carpet-bagger and the scallawag and, in the final words of the book, ". . . Civilisation has been saved, and the South redeemed from shame."[16]

The picture followed the book faithfully in plot, character, motivation and theme, and became a visualization of the whole set of irrational

[9] *The Clansman*, p. 57.

[10] Paul M. Angle, *Created Equal?* (Chicago: University of Chicago Press, 1958), p. 235. *The Clansman*, p. 46 ff.

[11] *The Clansman*, p. 93.

[12] *The Clansman*, pp. 248-49.

[13] *The Clansman*, p. 254.

[14] *The Clansman*, p. 171.

[15] *The Clansman*, p. 316.

[16] *The Clansman*, p. 374.

cultural assumptions which may be termed the "Plantation Illusion." The Illusion has many elements, but it is based primarily upon a belief in a golden age of the antebellum South, an age in which feudal agrarianism provided the good life for wealthy, leisured, kindly, aristocratic owner and loyal, happy, obedient slave. The enormous disparity between this conception and the reality has been the subject of Gaines's *The Southern Plantation*[17] and Stampp's *The Peculiar Institution.*[18] But our concern is not with the reality but with what people have thought and felt about that reality; this thinking and feeling is the Illusion, and the stuff of the history of sensibility. The Illusion was embodied in Kennedy's *Swallow Barn* (1832), developed through Caruther's *The Cavaliers of Virginia* (1834) and firmly fixed in the national consciousness by Stephen Foster's "Old Folks at Home" (1851), "My Old Kentucky Home" and "Massa's in the Cold, Cold Ground" (1852), and "Old Black Joe," songs which nostalgically describe a "longing for that old plantation . . ." In 1905 Dixon summarized it in the assertion that the South before the Civil War was ruled by an "aristocracy founded on brains, culture, and blood," the "old fashioned dream of the South" which "but for the Black curse . . . could be today the garden of the world."

This was the image realized almost immediately at the beginning of *The Birth of a Nation.* A scene of Southern life before the Civil War is preceded by the title: "In the Southland, life runs in a quaintly way that is no more." A primitive cart is shown trundling up a village street, filled with laughing Negroes; there is further merriment as a few children fall from the cart and are pulled up into it; then appears a scene of a young aristocrat helping his sister into a carriage; she is in white crinoline and carries a parasol; the young Southerner helps her gallantly from the carriage, and the title reads: "Margaret Cameron, daughter of the old South, trained in manners of the old school." With the two levels of feudal society established, the scene is then of the porch of the plantation house. Dr. and Mrs. Cameron are rocking; he has a kitten in his arms, and puppies are shown playing at his feet. A pickaninny runs happily in and out among the classic columns while the Camerons look indulgently on; a very fat and very black servant claps her hands with glee.

A corollary of this aspect of the Southern Illusion, one might even say a necessary part of it, is the corresponding vision of the North as the land

17 F. P. Gaines, *The Southern Plantation* (New York: Columbia University Press, 1924), pp. 143-236.

18 Kenneth Stampp, *The Peculiar Institution* (New York: Alfred A. Knopf, 1956).

of coldness, harshness, mechanical inhumanity; expressed most generously, it is the description of the North as "Head" and the South as the warm human "Heart" which was Sidney Lanier's major metaphor in his Reconstruction poems. Although Lanier had called for the reunion of the heart and head, a modern Southerner, John Crowe Ransom, has scolded Lanier for preaching reconciliation when, Ransom said, what should have been preached was the "contumacious resistance" of the warm, agrarian South against the harsh industrialism and rationalism of the North.[19] *The Clansman* had emphasized the contrast between warm South and cold North by rechristening Thaddeus Stevens, "Austin *Stoneman*"—the man of stone; the radical republican who is the obdurate villain of the picture. He has a clubfoot and moves angularly and mechanically; his house, his dress, are gloomy, dark, cold, as opposed to the warmth and lightness of the Southern planation garments and scene. In the novel, Dixon had identified him as the owner of Pennsylvania iron mills, and Griffith took the hint, giving him clothes to wear and expressions to assume which, in their harshness and implacability, suggest the unyielding metal. The sense of commercialism, combined with rigidity and pious hypocrisy is identified with the North, too, by showing the presumed beginnings of slavery in America. We see a Puritan preacher sanctimoniously praying while two of the elect arrange the sale of a cringing slave; the following scene is of Abolitionists demanding the end of slavery; the grouping of the two scenes, the dress and features of the characters in both, make the point strongly that these are the same people; the montage is a dramatization of Ben Cameron's assertion in the novel, that "our slaves were stolen from Africa by Yankee skippers . . . It was not until 1836 that Massachusetts led in Abolition—not until all her own slaves had been sold to us at a profit . . .[20]

In these opening scenes, too, we have the complete cast of characters of the Plantation Ideal. The Camerons are shown as they go down to the fields to mingle with the happy and trusting slaves. A title tells us that "in the two hour interval for dinner given in their working day from six to six the slaves enjoy themselves;" then appears a view of slaves clapping hands and dancing. Ben Cameron places his hand paternally upon the shoulders of one, and shakes hands with another who bobs in a perfect frenzy of grateful loyalty: in several seconds a wonderful summary of a hundred years of romantic tradition in which "a beautiful felicity of racial contact has been presented, not as occasional but as constant; an

[19] John Crowe Ransom, "Hearts and Heads," *American Review,* II (March 1934), 559

[20] *The Clansman,* pp. 124-25.

imperious kindness on the part of the whites, matched by obsequious devotion on the part of the blacks." [21]

The Plantation Ideal had to explain the obvious fact that during the war and Reconstruction, many Negroes fought with the Union and greeted Emancipation with joy. The Illusion protected itself by explaining that the true, southern, fullblooded Negro remained loyal throughout and after the war. It expanded the truth of individual instances of this kind into a general rule. In the Civil War sequences of *The Birth of a Nation,* the Camerons' slaves are shown cheering the parade of the Confederate soldiers as they march off to defend them against their freedom. The fat Negro cook and the others of the household staff are described as "The Faithful Souls"; they weep at Southern defeat and Northern triumph; they rescue Dr. Cameron from his arrest by Reconstruction militia.

While the Illusion persistently maintained the loyalty of the true slave, it premised the disaffection of other Negroes upon several causes, all of them explicable within the framework of the Plantation Ideal. The major explanation was the corruption of the Negro by the North. The freed Negro, the Union soldier, is a monster of ingratitude, a renegade from the feudal code, and only evil can be expected of him. The picture shows The Faithful Soul deriding one such abomination; the title reads, "You northern black trash, don't you try any of your airs on me." And a little later, we see her lips saying, and then read on the screen, "Those free niggers from the north sho' am crazy." The second explanation was that the mulatto, the person of mixed blood, was the arch-villain in the tragedy of the South. Stoneman, the radical republican leader, is shown, as he was in the novel, under the spell of his mulatto housekeeper. A scene of Stoneman lasciviously fondling his mistress is preceded by the title: "The great leader's weakness that is to blight a nation." The mistress, in turn, has as a lover another mulatto, Silas Lynch, who is described as the principal agent in Stoneman's plans to "Africanise" the South. This dark part of the Plantation Illusion is further represented in the twin climaxes of the picture, both of which are attempted sexual assaults on blonde white girls, one by a Northern Negro, and the other by the mulatto, Silas Lynch.

The sexual terms into which this picture translated the violation of the Southern Illusion by the North underscores the way in which the film incorporates one of the most vital of the forces underlying the Illusion—the obscure, bewildering complex of sexual guilt and fear which the Ideal never overtly admits, but which are, as Stampp and Cash and

21 Gaines, p. 210.

Myrdal [22] have pointed out, deeply interwoven into the Southern sensibility. The mulatto, while he occasionally would be the offspring of the lowest class of white woman with Negroes, much more commonly was the result of the debasement of the Negro woman by the white man, and, not infrequently, by the most aristocratic of the characters in the plantation conception.[23] At the very least, then, the deep convictions of the Protestant South about the nature of sin would cause the Southern Illusion to regard a living, visible evidence of a parent's lust as evil in itself, and at the most, and worst, and most debilitating, as a reminder of the burden of guilt the white must bear in the record of sexual aggression against the Negro. *The Birth of a Nation* gives all aspects of these sexual fears and guilts full expression. Typically, the burden of guilt is discharged by making the mulatto the evil force in the picture, evincing both the bestial, animal sensuality of the unrestrained Negro, and the perverted intellectual powers of the white. And the full-blooded, but renegade, black justifies any excess of the Klan, by accomplishing that final most dreaded act of the sexual drama, the violation of the blonde "little sister." The book had made the rape actual: "A single tiger-spring," it narrated, "and the black claws of the beast sank into the soft white throat." [24] The picture shows us the little sister as she jumps off a cliff to escape dishonor; but a scene of Gus, kneeling blackly over the white-clad, broken body, makes the sexual point without the overt act. And this point is further reinforced by a description of Lynch's attempts to possess Elsie Stoneman, by a portrayal of the passage of the first law of the black Reconstruction legislature legalizing miscegenation, and by a scene of Negroes who carry signs reading "Equal rights, equal marriage."

The descriptions of Gus as "tiger-like" and of Stoneman's mistress as a leopard, brings us to the last element of the Plantation Illusion—the defense of the system on the basis of the essential non-humanity of the Negro. The book had been blatant in its statement of this position; the picture projects this attitude by its shots of the eyes of mulatto and Negro displaying animal lust and ferocity, and by its view of Gus as a slinking animal, waiting, crouching, springing.

As the record of a cultural illusion, then, *The Birth of a Nation* is without equal. Furthermore, it is the film to which, as the historian of the art declares, "much of subsequent filmic progress owes its inspira-

[22] Stampp, pp. 350 ff., W. J. Cash, *The Mind of the South* (New York: Alfred A. Knopf, 1941), pp. 114-17. Gunnar Myrdal, *An American Dilemma* (New York: Harper & Bros., 1944), p. 562.

[23] Stampp, p. 355.

[24] *The Clansman,* p. 304.

tion." In order to understand its significance, one has to remind oneself of the nature of the motion picture art. It is not an art of external events and the people who perform them; it is an art of the camera and the film. Before Griffith, the camera was treated as a fixed position, much like the spectator of the drama. The interpretation was by the actors, by their bodies, by their faces, by physical objects and by the settings before which these performed. Griffith made the ordering and interpretation—the art, in brief—one of the location, the angle, the movement of the camera and of the juxtaposition of the images the camera records by means of cutting and arranging these images to bring out their significance. An example of the first technique—camera position—was the famous scene of Sherman's march to the sea. The camera shows the serpentine line of Union troops in the distance, winding over the landscape. War is distant; it is simply a move of masses over territory; the camera turns slowly until it includes, in the left foreground the figures of a weeping mother and child. Immediately a perspective is achieved; what was remote and inhuman becomes close and humanized; the human implications of such mass movements are illustrated clearly, sharply, poignantly simply by the perspective of the camera.

An example of the second aspect of the purely filmic technique was Griffith's juxtaposition of the two parallel scenes in the introduction to the Plantation Ideal: Negro cart and white carriage. Alone the first shot would be at worst meaningless, at best a bit of atmosphere; the second would serve merely to introduce two characters who might have been presented in an infinite variety of ways. Placed together, both scenes become significant forms because of the two elements they have in common: means of transportation, and the perfect fitness of each group of characters to that means; the juxtaposition thus serves to summarize the feudal theory—the rightness of each part of society in its place.

A second aspect of this editorial technique—the cutting and arranging of images—was also brought to its fullness of possibility in *The Birth of a Nation* after Griffith had experimented with it in earlier films. This was the intercutting of parallel scenes occurring at different locations in space, but at the same location in time, each of which has a bearing upon the other, with the meanings of both carefully interwoven, and with the tensions of either relieved only when the two are finally brought together. The famous example of this, an example which has been followed faithfully from then on, was the intercutting of shots of Lynch's attempted forced marriage to Elsie Stoneman with shots of the gathering of the Klan which will effect her rescue. A series of six shots of Lynch and Elsie is superseded by seven shots of the gathering of the Klan; then two single shots of the Klan and two of the attempted ravishment are quickly alternated; fourteen shots of Lynch and Elsie are followed by one of the Klan; a shot of long duration during which the Elsie-Lynch struggle becomes more intense is then followed by seven shots of the Klan's ride to the rescue; and so it goes until both sequences are joined in space when the Klan finally reaches Elsie. As an early critic described the meaning of this achievement: "Every little series of pictures . . . symbolizes a sentiment, a passion, or an emotion. Each successive series, similar yet different, carries the emotion to the next higher power, till at last, when both of the parallel emotions have attained the *nth* power, so to speak, they meet in the final swift shock of victory and defeat."[25] To these epoch-making achievements of camera placement, significant juxtaposition and intercutting, Griffith added the first uses of night photography, of soft-focus photography and moving camera shots, and the possibilities of film art were born.

And with it were born most of the problems of those of us who wish to take the art seriously. For what can we make of so awkward a combination of sentimental content and superb technique? We must admit, first of all, that the effect of the film's detachable content was pernicious. It served the ugliest purposes of pseudo-art—giving people a reflection of their own prejudices, sentimental at best, vicious at worst, and a restatement of their easy explanations of the terrible complexities of their history as Americans. It demonstrated how easily and how successfully the art could pander to the sentimentality of the public, how effectively and profitably it could transfer melodrama from the stage and false values from the novel. The enormous commercial success of the film at a time when men like Louis B. Mayer, later to become the head of the greatest studio, were starting their careers as exhibitors, cannot have but fixed the melodramatic, the cheap and obviously emotional, as the index to the potential economic success of a film.

But it showed, as well, two directions in which the film would move: one is in the direction of the epic, and the other in what may be termed "symbolic realism." Its move in the first direction, of course, was an immense and shocking perversion. Griffith apparently sensed the truth that great epics are involved with the destiny of whole races and nations, and had seized upon Dixon's hint that the South's struggle was part of an "Aryan" saga. The Klan was described in the book, and on the screen, as part of an "Aryan" tradition. The term is used again at a crucial point in the screen narrative, when a mob of Negro soldiers attack the em-

[25] Henry MacMahon, "The Art of the Movies," New York *Times*, June 6, 1915; section 6, p. 8.

battled whites. The battle of the Caucasians, the title on the screen tells us, is "in defense of their Aryan birthright." Griffith improved upon Dixon in emphasizing the "epical" quality of the story: before they ride, the Klansmen are shown partaking of a primitive barbaric rite; they dip a flag in the blood of the blonde white virgin before they go out to destroy.

The picture is no epic, but rather an epic *manqué*: partial, fragmentary and therefore necessarily inartistic; in attempting to be the saga of a shattered fragment of a nation, in attempting to erect upon false premises a series of racial responses reputedly instinctive, it was immediately self-defeating. An epic is justified in its radical simplifications, its stereotypes, its primitive terms, by its appeal to a real national unity of belief, and by its power to reinforce that unity. The oversimplifications of *The Birth of a Nation,* however, are not the controlled and ordering images of an art based upon a set of beliefs to which an entire people subscribe, images which emotionally order and control the world of that people's experience; instead it is the projection of images of disorder, an attack upon cultural and moral unity; the images of the film are the debilitating images of a false myth, a pseudo-epic.

The picture did, however, provide another cinematic genre with many of its basic situations. In 1908, with the "Bronco Billie" series, the Western setting had begun to be realized as particularly suitable to the enactment of the drama of simple primitive faiths and national aspirations. After *The Birth of a Nation,* its images of elemental struggle and black and white moral values, and its techniques for making these exciting and significant, were transferred to the "Western." The epic qualities of *The Birth of a Nation* were false and vicious because they impinge upon contemporary reality, and oversimplify both actual history and contemporary social circumstance; transferred to a realm of pure mythology—the Western scene of Richard Dix, *Stage Coach* and *High Noon,* and to the moral blackness of outlaw and moral whiteness of law, these simplifications, and the techniques for pictorializing them, have given us something much more artistically valid.

But more important, *The Birth of a Nation* pointed in the second, and the major direction of the motion picture art. This direction we can call "symbolic realism"—the apparent imitation of actuality which brings out the symbolic or representational meaning of that apparent reality. This "significant" or "symbolic" realism was demonstrated to be effective in the portrayal of either deep psychological or wide universal meanings. To take a rather titillating example in *The Birth of a Nation* of the first kind of surface realism arranged to illustrate unexpressed psychological truths: Lillian Gish plays an innocent love scene with the hero, returns to her room, and seats herself dreamily on the bed; the bed happens to be a four-poster each of whose posts is almost embarrassingly suggestive of masculinity; she dreamily embraces and caresses the bedpost. Some years later, Greta Garbo, as Queen Christina, after three days in bed with John Gilbert, used the bedpost in similar fashion. More significant, perhaps, is the way in which images were juxtaposed in this pioneering picture so as to bring out the universal significance of the concrete instance. The view of the army winding past the mother and child to symbolize the agony and displacements of war; the cart and the carriage as symbols of feudal levels of society; Stoneman's clubfoot representing the maimed wrathful impotence of the mechanical North; little sister adorning her coarse post-bellum dress with a bit of cotton rescued from the destroyed plantation fields—these were but a few of the large number of symbolic extensions of the surface, and they pointed the way toward the great documentary symbolic realism of Flaherty, and the imaginative symbolic realism of *The Informer, Sous les Toits de Paris, The River* and the whole run of wonderful Italian neo-realistic films: *Open City, Paisan, The Bicycle Thief* and *La Strada.*

A preliminary examination of a significant motion picture, then, has yielded some profit as well as some disappointment. The disappointment is largely in the failure of this pioneering picture to measure up to standards of artistic greatness: its failure to achieve that fusion of content and technique which together make up a great work of art. Its failure is doubly disappointing, because it involves an inversion and debasement of epic powers in which those powers pander to popular taste instead of attempting to reach a whole vision, sinewed with moral responsibility. But in this very failure lies some of its profit for us as students of American civilization; better than any other art work, it summarizes every aspect of the Plantation Illusion which is so vigorous a force in the history of American sensibility; for the student of the art form, it will demonstrate the beginnings of techniques which both rescue *The Birth of a Nation* from ugliness, and which, when used to embody more aesthetically malleable content, give us the possibilities of the art of the movie.

Afternote

Two afterthoughts, one small, one large. The fact that, for the scene of the ritual dipping of an emblem into the blood of the ravished white girl, Griffith substituted a flag for a cross does not now seem to me to justify my contention that Griffith emphasized the pseudo-epical more than did Dixon. The change now seems to me probably due to some religious hesitations. And my attempt to make a critical distinction between "epic" and "pseudo-epic" on the basis of the failure of the South's bid for full nationhood seems to me to raise, without sufficient argumentation, an extremely knotty problem of the difference between the tawdry mass art which consciously panders to the preconceptions of an audience, and an epic art which uses these same preconceptions for valid aesthetic ends.

Everett Carter is Professor of English at the University of California, Berkeley. [This article appeared in Vol. XII, No. 3 (Fall, 1960).]

Henry M. Littlefield

The Wizard of Oz: Parable on Populism

ON THE DESERTS OF NORTH AFRICA IN 1941 TWO TOUGH AUSTRALIAN BRIGADES went to battle singing,

> Have you heard of the wonderful wizard,
> The wonderful Wizard of Oz,
> And he is a wonderful wizard,
> If ever a wizard there was.

It was a song they had brought with them from Australia and would soon spread to England. Forever afterward it reminded Winston Churchill of those "buoyant days." [1] Churchill's nostalgia is only one symptom of the world-wide delight found in an American fairy-tale about a little girl and her odyssey in the strange land of Oz. The song he reflects upon came from a classic 1939 Hollywood production of the story, which introduced millions of people not only to the land of Oz, but to a talented young lady named Judy Garland as well.

Ever since its publication in 1900 Lyman Frank Baum's *The Wonderful Wizard of Oz* has been immensely popular, providing the basis for a profitable musical comedy, three movies and a number of plays. It is an indigenous creation, curiously warm and touching, although no one really knows why. For despite wholehearted acceptance by generations of readers, Baum's tale has been accorded neither critical acclaim, nor extended critical examination. Interested scholars, such as Russel B. Nye and Martin Gardiner, look upon *The Wizard of Oz* as the first in a long and delightful series of Oz stories, and understandably base their appreciation of Baum's talent on the totality of his works.[2]

The Wizard of Oz is an entity unto itself, however, and was not ori-

[1] Winston S. Churchill, *Their Finest Hour* (Cambridge, 1949), pp. 615-16.

[2] Martin Gardiner and Russel B. Nye, *The Wizard of Oz and Who He Was* (East Lansing, Mich., 1957), pp. 7 ff, 14-16, 19. Professor Nye's "Appreciation" and Martin Gardiner's "The Royal Historian of Oz," totaling some forty-five pages, present as definitive an analysis of Baum and his works as is available today.

ginally written with a sequel in mind. Baum informed his readers in 1904 that he had produced *The Marvelous Land of Oz* reluctantly and only in answer to well over a thousand letters demanding that he create another Oz tale.[3] His original effort remains unique and to some degree separate from the books which follow. But its uniqueness does not rest alone on its peculiar and transcendent popularity.

Professor Nye finds a "strain of moralism" in the Oz books, as well as "a well-developed sense of satire," and Baum stories often include searching parodies on the contradictions in human nature. The second book in the series, *The Marvelous Land of Oz,* is a blatant satire on feminism and the suffragette movement.[4] In it Baum attempted to duplicate the format used so successfully in *The Wizard,* yet no one has noted a similar play on contemporary movements in the latter work. Nevertheless, one does exist, and it reflects to an astonishing degree the world of political reality which surrounded Baum in 1900. In order to understand the relationship of *The Wizard* to turn-of-the-century America, it is necessary first to know something of Baum's background.

Born near Syracuse in 1856, Baum was brought up in a wealthy home and early became interested in the theater. He wrote some plays which enjoyed brief success and then, with his wife and two sons, journeyed to Aberdeen, South Dakota, in 1887. Aberdeen was a little prairie town and there Baum edited the local weekly until it failed in 1891.[5]

For many years Western farmers had been in a state of loud, though unsuccessful, revolt. While Baum was living in South Dakota not only was the frontier a thing of the past, but the Romantic view of benign nature had disappeared as well. The stark reality of the dry, open plains and the acceptance of man's Darwinian subservience to his environment served to crush Romantic idealism.[6]

Hamlin Garland's visit to Iowa and South Dakota coincided with Baum's arrival. Henry Nash Smith observes,

> Garland's success as a portrayer of hardship and suffering on Northwestern farms was due in part to the fact that his personal experience happened to parallel the shock which the entire West received in the later 1880's from the combined effects of low prices, . . . grasshoppers, drought, the terrible blizzards of the winter of 1886-1887, and the juggling of freight rates. . . .[7]

[3] L. Frank Baum, *The Marvelous Land of Oz* (Chicago, 1904), p. 3 (Author's Note).
[4] Gardiner and Nye, *Wizard,* pp. 5-7, 23.
[5] *Ibid.,* pp. 20-22.
[6] See Calton F. Culmsee, *Malign Nature and the Frontier* (Logan, Utah, 1959), VII, 5, 11, 14. The classic work in the field of symbolism in Western literature is Henry Nash Smith, *Virgin Land* (New York, 1961), pp. 225-26, 261, 284-90.
[7] *Ibid.,* p. 287.

As we shall see, Baum's prairie experience was no less deeply etched, although he did not employ naturalism to express it.

Baum's stay in South Dakota also covered the period of the formation of the Populist party, which Professor Nye likens to a fanatic "crusade." Western farmers had for a long time sought governmental aid in the form of economic panaceas, but to no avail. The Populist movement symbolized a desperate attempt to use the power of the ballot.[8] In 1891 Baum moved to Chicago where he was surrounded by those dynamic elements of reform which made the city so notable during the 1890s.[9]

In Chicago Baum certainly saw the results of the frightful depression which had closed down upon the nation in 1893. Moreover, he took part in the pivotal election of 1896, marching in "torch-light parades for William Jennings Bryan." Martin Gardiner notes besides, that he "consistently voted as a democrat . . . and his sympathies seem always to have been on the side of the laboring classes." [10] No one who marched in even a few such parades could have been unaffected by Bryan's campaign. Putting all the farmers' hopes in a basket labeled "free coinage of silver," Bryan's platform rested mainly on the issue of adding silver to the nation's gold standard. Though he lost, he did at least bring the plight of the little man into national focus.[11]

Between 1896 and 1900, while Baum worked and wrote in Chicago, the great depression faded away and the war with Spain thrust the United States into world prominence. Bryan maintained Midwestern control over the Democratic party, and often spoke out against American policies toward Cuba and the Philippines. By 1900 it was evident that Bryan would run again, although now imperialism and not silver seemed the issue of primary concern. In order to promote greater enthusiasm, however, Bryan felt compelled once more to sound the silver leitmotif in his campaign.[12] Bryan's second futile attempt at the presidency culminated in November 1900. The previous winter Baum had attempted unsuccessfully to sell a rather original volume of children's fantasy, but that April, George M. Hill, a small Chicago publisher, finally agreed to print *The Wonderful Wizard of Oz.*

8 Russel B. Nye, *Midwestern Progressive Politics* (East Lansing, Mich., 1959), pp. 63, 56-58, 75, 105. See also John D. Hicks, *The Populist Revolt* (Minneapolis, 1931), pp. 82, 93-95, 264-68.

9 See Ray Ginger, *Altgeld's America* (New York, 1958).

10 Gardiner and Nye, *Wizard,* p. 29.

11 See William Jennings Bryan, *The First Battle* (Lincoln, Neb., 1897), pp. 612-29. Two recent studies are notable: Harold U. Faulkner, *Politics, Reform and Expansion* (New York, 1959), pp. 187-211 and Nye, *Politics,* pp. 105-20.

12 See Richard Hofstadter's shattering essay on Bryan in *The American Political Tradition* (New York, 1960), pp. 186-205. Nye, *Politics,* pp. 121-22; Faulkner, *Reform,* pp. 272-75.

Baum's allegiance to the cause of Democratic Populism must be balanced against the fact that he was not a political activist. Martin Gardiner finds through all of his writings "a theme of tolerance, with many episodes that poke fun at narrow nationalism and ethnocentrism." Nevertheless, Professor Nye quotes Baum as having a desire to write stories that would "bear the stamp of our times and depict the progressive fairies of today." [13]

The Wizard of Oz has neither the mature religious appeal of a *Pilgrim's Progress,* nor the philosophic depth of a *Candide.* Baum's most thoughtful devotees see in it only a warm, cleverly written fairy tale. Yet the original Oz book conceals an unsuspected depth, and it is the purpose of this study to demonstrate that Baum's immortal American fantasy encompasses more than heretofore believed. For Baum created a children's story with a symbolic allegory implicit within its story line and characterizations. The allegory always remains in a minor key, subordinated to the major theme and readily abandoned whenever it threatens to distort the appeal of the fantasy. But through it, in the form of a subtle parable, Baum delineated a Midwesterner's vibrant and ironic portrait of this country as it entered the twentieth century.

We are introduced to both Dorothy and Kansas at the same time:

> Dorothy lived in the midst of the great Kansas prairies, with Uncle Henry, who was a farmer, and Aunt Em, who was the farmer's wife. Their house was small, for the lumber to build it had to be carried by wagon many miles. There were four walls, a floor and a roof, which made one room; and this room contained a rusty-looking cooking stove, a cupboard for the dishes, a table, three or four chairs, and the beds.
>
> When Dorothy stood in the doorway and looked around, she could see nothing but the great gray prairie on every side. Not a tree nor a house broke the broad sweep of flat country that reached to the edge of the sky in all directions. The sun had baked the plowed land into a gray mass, with little cracks running through it. Even the grass was not green, for the sun had burned the tops of the long blades until they were the same gray color to be seen everywhere. Once the house had been painted, but the sun blistered the paint and the rains washed it away, and now the house was as dull and gray as everything else.
>
> When Aunt Em came there to live she was a young, pretty wife. The sun and wind had changed her, too. They had taken the sparkle from her eyes and left them a sober gray; they had taken the red from her cheeks and lips, and they were gray also. She was thin and gaunt, and never smiled now. When Dorothy, who was an orphan, first came to

[13] Gardiner and Nye, *Wizard,* pp. 1, 30.

her, Aunt Em had been so startled by the child's laughter that she would scream and press her hand upon her heart whenever Dorothy's merry voice reached her ears; and she still looked at the little girl with wonder that she could find anything to laugh at.

Uncle Henry never laughed. He worked hard from morning till night and did not know what joy was. He was gray also, from his long beard to his rough boots, and he looked stern and solemn, and rarely spoke.

It was Toto that made Dorothy laugh, and saved her from growing as gray as her other surroundings. Toto was not gray; he was a little black dog, with long silky hair and small black eyes that twinkled merrily on either side of his funny, wee nose. Toto played all day long, and Dorothy played with him, and loved him dearly.[14]

Hector St. John de Crèvecoeur would not have recognized Uncle Henry's farm; it is straight out of Hamlin Garland.[15] On it a deadly environment dominates everyone and everything except Dorothy and her pet. The setting is Old Testament and nature seems grayly impersonal and even angry. Yet it is a fearsome cyclone that lifts Dorothy and Toto in their house and deposits them "very gently—for a cyclone—in the midst of a country of marvelous beauty." We immediately sense the contrast between Oz and Kansas. Here there are "stately trees bearing rich and luscious fruits . . . gorgeous flowers . . . and birds with . . . brilliant plumage" sing in the trees. In Oz "a small brook rushing and sparkling along" murmurs "in a voice very grateful to a little girl who had lived so long on the dry, gray prairies" (p. 20).

Trouble intrudes. Dorothy's house has come down on the wicked Witch of the East, killing her. Nature, by sheer accident, can provide benefits, for indirectly the cyclone has disposed of one of the two truly bad influences in the Land of Oz. Notice that evil ruled in both the East and the West; after Dorothy's coming it rules only in the West.

The wicked Witch of the East had kept the little Munchkin people "in bondage for many years, making them slave for her night and day" (pp. 22-23). Just what this slavery entailed is not immediately clear, but Baum later gives us a specific example. The Tin Woodman, whom Dorothy meets on her way to the Emerald City, had been put under a spell by the Witch of the East. Once an independent and hard working

[14] L. Frank Baum, *The Wonderful Wizard of Oz,* pp. 11-13. All quotations cited in the text are from the inexpensive but accurate Dover paperback edition (New York, 1960).

[15] Henry Nash Smith says of Garland's works in the 1890s, "It had at last become possible to deal with the Western farmer in literature as a human being instead of seeing him through a veil of literary convention, class prejudice or social theory" *Virgin Land,* p. 290.

human being, the Woodman found that each time he swung his axe it chopped off a different part of his body. Knowing no other trade he "worked harder than ever," for luckily in Oz tinsmiths can repair such things. Soon the Woodman was all tin (p. 59). In this way Eastern witchcraft dehumanized a simple laborer so that the faster and better he worked the more quickly he became a kind of machine. Here is a Populist view of evil Eastern influences on honest labor which could hardly be more pointed.[16]

There is one thing seriously wrong with being made of tin; when it rains rust sets in. Tin Woodman had been standing in the same position for a year without moving before Dorothy came along and oiled his joints. The Tin Woodman's situation has an obvious parallel in the condition of many Eastern workers after the depression of 1893.[17] While Tin Woodman is standing still, rusted solid, he deludes himself into thinking he is no longer capable of that most human of sentiments, love. Hate does not fill the void, a constant lesson in the Oz books, and Tin Woodman feels that only a heart will make him sensitive again. So he accompanies Dorothy to see if the Wizard will give him one.

Oz itself is a magic oasis surrounded by impassable deserts, and the country is divided in a very orderly fashion. In the North and South the people are ruled by good witches, who are not quite as powerful as the wicked ones of the East and West. In the center of the land rises the magnificent Emerald City ruled by the Wizard of Oz, a successful humbug whom even the witches mistakenly feel "is more powerful than all the rest of us together" (p. 24). Despite these forces, the mark of goodness, placed on Dorothy's forehead by the Witch of the North, serves as protection for Dorothy throughout her travels. Goodness and innocence prevail even over the powers of evil and delusion in Oz. Perhaps it is this basic and beautiful optimism that makes Baum's tale so characteristically American—and Midwestern.

Dorothy is Baum's Miss Everyman. She is one of us, levelheaded and human, and she has a real problem. Young readers can understand her quandary as readily as can adults. She is good, not precious, and she thinks quite naturally about others. For all of the attractions of Oz Dorothy desires only to return to the gray plains and Aunt Em and Uncle Henry. She is directed toward the Emerald City by the good Witch of the North, since the Wizard will surely be able to solve the problem

16 Hicks declares that from the start "The Alliance and Populist platforms championed boldly the cause of labor. . . ." *Revolt,* p. 324. See also Bryan's Labor Day speech, *Battle,* pp. 375-83.

17 Faulkner, *Reform,* pp. 142-43.

of the impassable deserts. Dorothy sets out on the Yellow Brick Road wearing the Witch of the East's magic Silver Shoes. Silver shoes walking on a golden road; henceforth Dorothy becomes the innocent agent of Baum's ironic view of the Silver issue. Remember, neither Dorothy, nor the good Witch of the North, nor the Munchkins understand the power of these shoes. The allegory is abundantly clear. On the next to last page of the book Baum has Glinda, Witch of the South, tell Dorothy, "Your Silver Shoes will carry you over the desert. . . . If you had known their power you could have gone back to your Aunt Em the very first day you came to this country." Glinda explains, "All you have to do is to knock the heels together three times and command the shoes to carry you wherever you wish to go" (p. 257). William Jennings Bryan never outlined the advantages of the silver standard any more effectively.

Not understanding the magic of the Silver Shoes, Dorothy walks the mundane—and dangerous—Yellow Brick Road. The first person she meets is a Scarecrow. After escaping from his wooden perch, the Scarecrow displays a terrible sense of inferiority and self doubt, for he has determined that he needs real brains to replace the common straw in his head. William Allen White wrote an article in 1896 entitled "What's the Matter With Kansas?" In it he accused Kansas farmers of ignorance, irrationality and general muddle-headedness. What's wrong with Kansas are the people, said Mr. White.[18] Baum's character seems to have read White's angry characterization. But Baum never takes White seriously and so the Scarecrow soon emerges as innately a very shrewd and very capable individual.

The Scarecrow and the Tin Woodman accompany Dorothy along the Yellow Brick Road, one seeking brains, the other a heart. They meet next the Cowardly Lion. As King of Beasts he explains, "I learned that if I roared very loudly every living thing was frightened and got out of my way." Born a coward, he sobs, "Whenever there is danger my heart begins to beat fast." "Perhaps you have heart disease," suggests Tin Woodman, who always worries about hearts. But the Lion desires only courage and so he joins the party to ask help from the Wizard (pp. 65-72).

The Lion represents Bryan himself. In the election of 1896 Bryan lost the vote of Eastern labor, though he tried hard to gain their support. In Baum's story the Lion, on meeting the little group, "struck at the Tin Woodman with his sharp claws." But, to his surprise, "he could make no impression on the tin, although the Woodman fell over in the road and lay still." Baum here refers to the fact that in 1896 workers were often

[18] Richard Hofstadter (ed.), *Great Issues in American History* (New York, 1960), II, 147-53.

pressured into voting for McKinley and gold by their employers.[19] Amazed, the Lion says, "he nearly blunted my claws," and he adds even more appropriately, "When they scratched against the tin it made a cold shiver run down my back" (pp. 67-68). The King of Beasts is not after all very cowardly, and Bryan, although a pacifist and an anti-imperialist in a time of national expansion, is not either.[20] The magic Silver Shoes belong to Dorothy, however. Silver's potent charm, which had come to mean so much to so many in the Midwest, could not be entrusted to a political symbol. Baum delivers Dorothy from the world of adventure and fantasy to the real world of heartbreak and desolation through the power of Silver. It represents a real force in a land of illusion, and neither the Cowardly Lion nor Bryan truly needs or understands its use.

All together now the small party moves toward the Emerald City. Coxey's Army of tramps and indigents, marching to ask President Cleveland for work in 1894, appears no more naively innocent than this group of four characters going to see a humbug Wizard, to request favors that only the little girl among them deserves.

Those who enter the Emerald City must wear green glasses. Dorothy later discovers that the greenness of dresses and ribbons disappears on leaving, and everything becomes a bland white. Perhaps the magic of any city is thus self imposed. But the Wizard dwells here and so the Emerald City represents the national Capitol. The Wizard, a little bumbling old man, hiding behind a facade of papier mâché and noise, might be any President from Grant to McKinley. He comes straight from the fair grounds in Omaha, Nebraska, and he symbolizes the American criterion for leadership—he is able to be everything to everybody.

As each of our heroes enters the throne room to ask a favor the Wizard assumes different shapes, representing different views toward national leadership. To Dorothy, he appears as an enormous head, "bigger than the head of the biggest giant." An apt image for a naive and innocent little citizen. To the Scarecrow he appears to be a lovely, gossamer fairy, a most appropriate form for an idealistic Kansas farmer. The Woodman sees a horrible beast, as would any exploited Eastern laborer after the trouble of the 1890s. But the Cowardly Lion, like W. J. Bryan, sees a "Ball of Fire, so fierce and glowing he could scarcely bear to gaze upon it." Baum then provides an additional analogy, for when

[19] Bryan, *Battle,* pp. 617-18, "During the campaign I ran across various evidences of coercion, direct and indirect." See Hicks, *Revolt,* p. 325, who notes that "For some reason labor remained singularly unimpressed" by Bryan. Faulkner finds overt pressure as well, *Reform,* pp. 208-9.

[20] Faulkner, *Reform,* pp. 257-58.

the Lion "tried to go nearer he singed his whiskers and he crept back tremblingly to a spot nearer the door" (p. 134).

The Wizard has asked them all to kill the Witch of the West. The golden road does not go in that direction and so they must follow the sun, as have many pioneers in the past. The land they now pass through is "rougher and hillier, for there were no farms nor houses in the country of the West and the ground was untilled" (p. 140). The Witch of the West uses natural forces to achieve her ends; she is Baum's version of sentient and malign nature.

Finding Dorothy and her friends in the West, the Witch sends forty wolves against them, then forty vicious crows and finally a great swarm of black bees. But it is through the power of a magic golden cap that she summons the flying monkeys. They capture the little girl and dispose of her companions. Baum makes these Winged Monkeys into an Oz substitute for the plains Indians. Their leader says, "Once . . . we were a free people, living happily in the great forest, flying from tree to tree, eating nuts and fruit, and doing just as we pleased without calling anybody master." "This," he explains, "was many years ago, long before Oz came out of the clouds to rule over this land" (p. 172). But like many Indian tribes Baum's monkeys are not inherently bad; their actions depend wholly upon the bidding of others. Under the control of an evil influence, they do evil. Under the control of goodness and innocence, as personified by Dorothy, the monkeys are helpful and kind, although unable to take her to Kansas. Says the Monkey King, "We belong to this country alone, and cannot leave it" (p. 213). The same could be said with equal truth of the first Americans.

Dorothy presents a special problem to the Witch. Seeing the mark on Dorothy's forehead and the Silver Shoes on her feet, the Witch begins "to tremble with fear, for she knew what a powerful charm belonged to them." Then "she happened to look into the child's eyes and saw how simple the soul behind them was, and that the little girl did not know of the wonderful power the Silver Shoes gave her" (p. 150). Here Baum again uses the Silver allegory to state the blunt homily that while goodness affords a people ultimate protection against evil, ignorance of their capabilities allows evil to impose itself upon them. The Witch assumes the proportions of a kind of western Mark Hanna or Banker Boss, who, through natural malevolence, manipulates the people and holds them prisoner by cynically taking advantage of their innate innocence.

Enslaved in the West, "Dorothy went to work meekly, with her mind made up to work as hard as she could; for she was glad the Wicked Witch had decided not to kill her" (p. 150). Many Western farmers have held these same grim thoughts in less mystical terms. If the Witch of the West is a diabolical force of Darwinian or Spencerian nature, then another contravening force may be counted upon to dispose of her. Dorothy destroys the evil Witch by angrily dousing her with a bucket of water. Water, that precious commodity which the drought-ridden farmers on the great plains needed so badly, and which if correctly used could create an agricultural paradise, or at least dissolve a wicked witch. Plain water brings an end to malign nature in the West.

When Dorothy and her companions return to the Emerald City they soon discover that the Wizard is really nothing more than "a little man, with a bald head and a wrinkled face." Can this be the ruler of the land?

> Our friends looked at him in surprise and dismay.
>
> "I thought Oz was a great Head," said Dorothy. . . . "And I thought Oz was a terrible Beast," said the Tin Woodman. "And I thought Oz was a Ball of Fire," exclaimed the Lion. "No; you are all wrong," said the little man meekly. "I have been making believe."

Dorothy asks if he is truly a great Wizard. He confides, "Not a bit of it, my dear; I'm just a common man." Scarecrow adds, "You're more than that . . . you're a humbug" (p. 184).

The Wizard's deception is of long standing in Oz and even the Witches were taken in. How was it accomplished? "It was a great mistake my ever letting you into the Throne Room," the Wizard complains. "Usually I will not see even my subjects, and so they believe I am something terrible" (p. 185). What a wonderful lesson for youngsters of the decade when Benjamin Harrison, Grover Cleveland and William McKinley were hiding in the White House. Formerly the Wizard was a mimic, a ventriloquist and a circus balloonist. The latter trade involved going "up in a balloon on circus day, so as to draw a crowd of people together and get them to pay to see the circus" (p. 186-87). Such skills are as admirably adapted to success in late-nineteenth-century politics as they are to the humbug wizardry of Baum's story. A pointed comment on Midwestern political ideals is the fact that our little Wizard comes from Omaha, Nebraska, a center of Populist agitation.[21] "Why that isn't very far from Kansas," cries Dorothy. Nor, indeed, are any of the characters in the wonderful land of Oz.

The Wizard, of course, can provide the objects of self-delusion desired by Tin Woodman, Scarecrow and Lion. But Dorothy's hope of going

[21] Professor Nye observes that during 1890 (while Baum was editing his Aberdeen weekly) the Nebraska Farmer's Alliance "launched the wildest campaign in Nebraska history." *Politics*, p. 64-65. Bryan was a Senator from Nebraska and it was in Omaha that the Populist party ratified its platform on July 4, 1892. See Henry Steele Commager (ed.), *Documents of American History* (New York, 1958), II, 143-46.

home fades when the Wizard's balloon leaves too soon. Understand this: Dorothy wishes to leave a green and fabulous land, from which all evil has disappeared, to go back to the gray desolation of the Kansas prairies. Dorothy is an orphan, Aunt Em and Uncle Henry are her only family. Reality is never far from Dorothy's consciousness and in the most heart-rending terms she explains her reasoning to the good Witch Glinda,

> Aunt Em will surely think something dreadful has happened to me, and that will make her put on mourning; and unless the crops are better this year than they were last I am sure Uncle Henry cannot afford it. (p. 254)

The Silver Shoes furnish Dorothy with a magic means of travel. But when she arrives back in Kansas she finds, "The Silver Shoes had fallen off in her flight through the air, and were lost forever in the desert" (p. 259). Were the "her" to refer to America in 1900, Baum's statement could hardly be contradicted.

Current historiography tends to criticize the Populist movement for its "delusions, myths and foibles," Professor C. Vann Woodward observed recently.[22] Yet *The Wonderful Wizard of Oz* has provided unknowing generations with a gentle and friendly Midwestern critique of the Populist rationale on these very same grounds. Led by naive innocence and protected by good will, the farmer, the laborer and the politician approach the mystic holder of national power to ask for personal fulfillment. Their desires, as well as the Wizard's cleverness in answering them, are all self-delusion. Each of these characters carries within him the solution to his own problem, were he only to view himself objectively. The fearsome Wizard turns out to be nothing more than a common man, capable of shrewd but mundane answers to these self-induced needs. Like any good politician he gives the people what they want. Throughout the story Baum poses a central thought; the American desire for symbols of fulfillment is illusory. Real needs lie elsewhere.

Thus the Wizard cannot help Dorothy, for of all the characters only she has a wish that is selfless, and only she has a direct connection to honest, hopeless human beings. Dorothy supplies real fulfillment when she returns to her aunt and uncle, using the Silver Shoes, and cures some of their misery and heartache. In this way Baum tells us that the Silver crusade at least brought back Dorothy's lovely spirit to the disconsolate plains farmer. Her laughter, love and good will are no small addition to that gray land, although the magic of Silver has been lost forever as a result.

22 C. Vann Woodward, "Our Past Isn't What It Used To Be," *The New York Times Book Review* (July 28, 1963), p. 1; Hofstadter, *Tradition*, pp. 186-205.

Noteworthy too is Baum's prophetic placement of leadership in Oz after Dorothy's departure. The Scarecrow reigns over the Emerald City, the Tin Woodman rules in the West and the Lion protects smaller beasts in "a grand old forest." Thereby farm interests achieve national importance, industrialism moves West and Bryan commands only a forest full of lesser politicians.

Baum's fantasy succeeds in bridging the gap between what children want and what they should have. It is an admirable example of the way in which an imaginative writer can teach goodness and morality without producing the almost inevitable side effect of nausea. Today's children's books are either saccharine and empty, or boring and pedantic. Baum's first Oz tale—and those which succeed it—are immortal not so much because the "heart-aches and nightmares are left out" as that "the wonderment and joy" are retained (p. 1).

Baum declares, "The story of 'the Wonderful Wizard of Oz' was written solely to pleasure children of today" (p. 1). In 1963 there are very few children who have never heard of the Scarecrow, the Tin Woodman or the Cowardly Lion, and whether they know W. W. Denslow's original illustrations of Dorothy, or Judy Garland's whimsical characterization, is immaterial. *The Wizard* has become a genuine piece of American folklore because, knowing his audience, Baum never allowed the consistency of the allegory to take precedence over the theme of youthful entertainment. Yet once discovered, the author's allegorical intent seems clear, and it gives depth and lasting interest even to children who only sense something else beneath the surface of the story. Consider the fun in picturing turn-of-the-century America, a difficult era at best, using these ready-made symbols provided by Baum. The relationships and analogies outlined above are admittedly theoretical, but they are far too consistent to be coincidental, and they furnish a teaching mechanism which is guaranteed to reach any level of student.

The Wizard of Oz says so much about so many things that it is hard not to imagine a satisfied and mischievous gleam in Lyman Frank Baum's eye as he had Dorothy say, "And oh, Aunt Em! I'm so glad to be at home again!"

Afternote

Following the publication of this article a number of letters pointed out the interesting composition of southern Oz. The writers claim that brittle little people made of Dresden china, bogs, marshes, brooding monster-ridden forests, hammer-headed folk who prey on travelers in the hills, combined with the rich, red Quadling farm country, render that part of Oz a Tennessee Williams treasury of social and geographic stereotypes. Perhaps and perhaps not; I'm unconvinced. However, all correspondents agree that students thoroughly enjoy following and adding to this blueprint left us by L. Frank Baum.

Because so many of his children's stories contain strong social commentary, they remain interesting to a variety of readers. I look forward to the time when major libraries will accept Baum as the genuine and subtle craftsman he was.

A public school teacher, Henry M. Littlefield is Director of the Federal History Project, D. A. Sullivan School, Northampton, Mass. [This article appeared in Vol. XV, No. 4 (Winter, 1963).]

Chadwick Hansen

Social Influences on Jazz Style: Chicago, 1920-1930

BEFORE THE FIRST WORLD WAR JAZZ WAS PRIMARILY A MUSIC OF THE southern Negro, and especially of the Negro in and around New Orleans. It was, in the southerner's disdainful and distasteful phrase, "nigger music": one component of a subculture that was thoroughly segregated, detested and exploited by the dominant culture. But during and after the First World War, during the "Great Migration" of Negroes to the North, jazz moved north as well, and Chicago, which attracted more Negroes than any other northern city in the Mississippi Valley, soon replaced New Orleans as the center of the jazz world.

Migration to the North placed the Negro jazz musician in a social environment radically different from that in which his music had been formed. He was, to be sure, still a member of a minority group, a subculture, but the dominant culture in the North was open to him to an extent that would have been unthinkable in the South. Furthermore, it opened up to him the possibility of further change, the possibility of suppressing the traits of his own subculture and acquiring the traits of the dominant white middle class.

The result was a series of social pressures on the jazz musician, which, operating throughout the decade of the twenties, effected a marked change in jazz style. By 1930 jazz was a new music; many of its own traditions had been abandoned and were replaced by elements adapted from the popular music of the white middle class.

The most important of these social pressures was the Negro's own recognition that in moving north he had made one step toward escaping from a vicious and degrading social situation, and his desire to continue this escape, rejecting the hated past and replacing it with something better.

The old southern spirituals were full of escape images, after emancipation as well as during slavery: the gospel train, which would take you away from your present misery; the promised land, for which you were bound; the delivery of the Lord's anointed out of Egypt or out of the lions' den; the journey to "the city of refuge." Secular folksong and folklore as well were permeated by the theme of escape, as in the legend of Lost John: "hounds couldn't catch him . . . he's long gone, Lost John." This pervasive Negro folk motif found concrete realization in the Great Migration.

It must be admitted that many of the Negroes who came north during the First World War and the twenties found the city a lonesome and impersonal place, and many of them were occasionally homesick for old friends and old places, familiar cooking and familiar smells. The common term for the South among these people was "down home." Almost none of them went back down home, however, for with their nostalgia went too many bitter memories. Their South had not been the South of magnolia blossoms and the cool grace and proportion of Greek-revival plantation houses. Their South was a land of fear and hatred, dirt and disease, malnutrition, degradation and violence. In 1921 Chicago's Negro newspaper, the *Defender,* carried an article which began, "A letter came from Jelly Roll Morton, and in it he claims that the report of his death, which is raging throughout the civilized world and the South, is exaggerated." [1] Morton put lightly what he and others felt deeply. They had escaped from the South to civilization; they had found a city of refuge.

The black belt of Chicago's South Side, where jazz musicians of the twenties and their audience were located, would hardly seem like paradise to most Americans. But the words of an old blues say "I've been down so long that it seems like up to me." Even the Chicago Black Belt seemed like up, since compared to down home it *was* up. Furthermore, it brought the Negro to a place where he could see a world that was even further up: the world of the middle-class Chicago white man.

E. Franklin Frazier speaks of what the motion pictures represented to the southern Negro who saw them for the first time: "an undreamed

[1] The sources for my quotations from *The Chicago Defender,* in the order in which they appear in the text, are as follows: November 12, 1921, p. 7; January 21, 1928, part 1, p. 8; September 13, 1924, part 1, p. 6; April 30, 1921, p. 8; April 28, 1928, part 1, p. 8; April 7, 1928, part 1, p. 10; May 19, 1928, part 1, p. 11; February 25, 1928, part 1, p. 8; January 28, 1928, part 1, p. 8; February 28, 1928, part 1, p. 8; March 10, 1928, part 1, p. 8; May 12, 1928, part 1, p. 10; May 19, 1928, part 1, p. 10; April 24, 1920, p. 6; December 6, 1924, part 1, p. 1; June 4, 1921, p. 6. I wish to thank Mrs. Roi Ottley, librarian of the *Defender,* for her consistent courtesy and helpfulness.

world of romance and adventure." [2] The world of the motion pictures and the advertisements, the slick magazines and the sentimental song—the world of American popular culture—looks rather tawdry to some Americans. But to many of the inhabitants of Chicago's South Side in the twenties it had the glitter of the dimly apprehended golden streets of heaven. It lay beyond them, but since they had been able to make the step from a very real hell to the purgatory of the Black Belt they knew they might make this step, too, and many of them began to try.

The militant *Chicago Defender* had played an important part in the Great Migration in the entire Mississippi Valley area, by urging southern Negroes to move north.[3] And the *Defender,* which had given many southern Negroes their first picture of the advantages of the North, also gave its readers a picture of the world of white, standard, middle-class culture, the next step in race progress. Dave Peyton, who led one of Chicago's Negro bands and wrote a regular column called "The Musical Bunch" for the *Defender*, gave classic form to this picture when he wrote, in 1928, under the subheading "Opportunity,"

> In Chicago an opportunity is offered musicians [i.e., Negro musicians] in another field [i.e., another field than jazz] and we must make good if humanly possible. Friendship must be cast aside. It is the reckoning hour for our musicians. We have ballyhooed along for the past 10 or 12 years fooling ourselves. We have played music as we think it should be played without trying to find out if we are playing it correctly. So few of us have the time to visit the grand symphony orchestras, the deluxe picture houses and other places where things musically are done correctly. . . . With the coming of the new Regal theater in Chicago, operated by a corporation of theatrical magnates who know just what it's all about, a new era is dawning upon Race musicians. In the pits of the deluxe houses things are done machine like. . . . The orchestra leader must register with the picture operator and every department in the deluxe house, directly under the orders of the stage director, must function their part in the cogwheel [*sic*]. . . . The opportunity is here, the door has opened for us, we have entered . . . let's make good.

This is a fabulous picture in the true sense of the word: a picture of a world of fable in which music is played "correctly," rather than the

[2] E. Franklin Frazier, *The Negro Family in the United States,* revised and abridged edition (New York: Dryden Press, 1948), p. 92.

[3] For the *Defender's* role in the Great Migration see Emmett J. Scott, *Negro Migration During the War,* Preliminary Economic Studies of the War No. 16 (New York, 1920), pp. 29-33, or chap. x, "The Uneasy Exodus," of Roi Ottley's *The Lonely Warrior* (Chicago, 1955).

way in which Negroes think it should be played. It is a "grand" and "deluxe" world. Since a symphony orchestra was to Peyton nothing more than a large orchestra that played from a written score, the "grand symphony orchestra" and the pit orchestra of the "deluxe picture house" are musically one and the same. Peyton has chosen technology as the most logical source for the imagery that enables him to construct a world of mindless efficiency directed by a "corporation of theatrical magnates who know what it's all about." Having entered this world, it is the business of the Negro musician to make good.

The compulsion to conform to socially-approved standards is, of course, a characteristic of the Negro who is on his way up in American society. Frazier quotes an instance from an earlier time, of an ex-slave who had been almost completely unmanageable during slavery but took up the middle-class white man's virtues of sobriety and respect for property after emancipation:

> Since he has been freed, he has grown honest, quiet, and industrious; he educated his children and pays his debts. Mr. Barrow asked him, one day, what had changed him so. "Ah, master!" he replied, "I'm free now; I have to do right." [4]

There is an instructive parallel between the two cases. In the process of advancing in social status neither Peyton nor the ex-slave has gained any real freedom of choice: they have gained instead barely enough equality so that they are permitted the opportunity to fit themselves into a cultural pattern established by the white man. Both have accepted cultural masters: the ex-slave, the man who was formerly his literal master; Peyton, the "corporation of theatrical magnates." [5]

Since the traditional New Orleans jazz style was clearly identified in the Negro's mind with the southern past he had rejected, since it was clearly unlike the white man's popular music that was played in theaters run by "theatrical magnates," the *Defender's* staff had few kind words for jazz.[6] They were, however, always pleased by the success of individual

[4] Frazier, p. 130.

[5] "Advancing the race" is so common a concept among American Negroes that Drake and Clayton use it as the title of chap. xxii of *Black Metropolis*. The primary meaning of the phrase is, of course, simply advancing toward equal status, but it has been characteristic for Negroes to assume that any cultural differences between Negro and white are a hindrance to equal status.

[6] The *Defender* staff was not unique in this. Morroe Berger, in "Jazz: Resistance to the Diffusion of a Culture Pattern," *Journal of Negro History*, XXXII (1947), 465-66, writes: "Leaders of Negro communities have spoken out against the influence of jazz. This is to be expected of those 'race leaders' who believe that Negroes can improve their status mainly by acceptance of the standards of the white community,

jazz musicians. They were proud that A. J. Piron's orchestra was employed in the more expensive white restaurants in New Orleans: "the successful achievement of Piron and his orchestra in the South is another milestone covered by the Negro musician." They were proud that Tony Jackson, the New Orleans pianist, had written popular tunes which were known outside the Negro community (one of them is the perennial *Pretty Baby*), and added that "it is said that there are many of the better grade [vaudeville] acts using numbers which were sold to them outright by him." They were proud of the individual musician who could stand out as a star: "Louis [Armstrong] is the only musician I know of who stops the ball, just as an actor stops a show."

The Negro community was proud of an outstanding individual like Armstrong, since to most white men Negroes were nameless nonentities. Negroes' names were a matter of supreme indifference even to some of the recording companies which sold their music. Ferdinand "Jelly Roll" Morton's name was spelled "Fred Morton" on one of his early records, and "Jelly Roll Marton" on another.[7] Sometimes the names might be absent altogether from the record label, or a pseudonym invented by a record company executive might be used.

If a Negro musician could make himself a star the record companies would use his name, and learn to spell it correctly: Morton's name was never misspelled on his later recordings. The name of a star meant money to the record companies, and it meant status to the Negro community. A man who made a name for himself in music was a race hero to the Negro community for the same reason that Jackie Robinson and

---

which clearly disapproved of jazz as barbaric and sensual—characterizations which Negroes have tried to dissociate from themselves. . . . The treatment of jazz by Negro writers reveals that it is not considered the kind of cultural achievement of the race that ought to be mentioned or recommended. . . . The most prominent chroniclers of Negro achievement in America . . . scarcely mention jazz in their books." Mr. Berger is dealing with Negro leaders and writers in general. I have chosen to depend primarily on the *Defender* because it represented militant Negro leadership in Chicago in the twenties, and may therefore be expected to have exercised more immediate influence on jazz men than the similar national attitudes which are Mr. Berger's subject.

[7] Rialto 535 and Paramount 12050. Since Paramount's executives were Negroes, this misspelling may be attributed to the middle-class Negro's contempt for jazz musicians. Paramount's tastes are clearly indicated in the following paean to musical propriety, taken from their 1924 catalogue: "Paramount is proud to offer you records by the celebrated soprano—Florence Cole-Talbert. She is the premier concert star of the Race, and is known to millions from Coast to Coast because of her concert tours of the United States. These records are undoubtedly the highest type of Race music sold today." Mrs. Cole-Talbert's records are Paramount 12096: *Homing* and *Swiss Echo Song*, accompanied by Sammy Stewart's Symphonic Orchestra, and Paramount 12187: *The Kiss (Il Bacio)* and *The Last Rose of Summer*, accompanied by the Black Swan Symphony Orchestra. This portion of the catalogue is reprinted in *The Record Changer*, September 1950, p. 11.

Ralph Bunche are race heroes today: because names are generally reserved for white men.

Negro musicians on the way up wanted more than names, however. On April 7, 1928 Dave Peyton announced in his column that

> Fess Williams and his Jazz Joy Boys of the Regal theater made some fine recordings for the Vocalion records which will soon be released. Manager Jack Kapps[8] says this is the first "Sweet Record" our musicians have recorded and it was perfect. Heretofore, our orchestras have been making jazz and hokum numbers, but Fess insisted that if they wanted him to record he would have to be given the same breaks as the white bands were getting and that is making real sweet musical song and dance records. Good for Fess.[9]

Peyton praised Fess Williams' preference for sweet music over jazz again, a month later:

> Fess and his boys are doing sweet numbers and are the first of our orchestras to get into the legitimate line. Heretofore our orchestras have confined themselves to hot jazzy tunes.

He spoke of his own theater orchestra as playing "first class standard music" and as "highly trained symphony players [who] will characterize the screen classics with symphonic music and offer from time to time standard overtures, animated by interesting stage characterizations." It must have pained him to admit that among his "highly trained symphony players" was jazz drummer Jasper Taylor, whose chief contribution was a "washboard specialty." He advised Negro musicians: "if you are now in a jazz band, do not give up the proper study on your instrument. You may be called upon to render real service and to play good music."

Peyton's conception of good music is most clearly stated in the two following quotations:

> Jazz is on the wane, and the better class of music is coming back into favor with the critical public. . . . The country raves about Leroy

[8] This is, of course, the late Jack Kapp, later co-founder and president of Decca Records.

[9] This was not actually the first sweet record made by Negroes, but it was probably the first Peyton knew of. *My Oriental Rose,* recorded by Fletcher Henderson and his Orchestra in 1922, and issued on Black Swan 2022, is sweet enough for the most saccharine taste, and there may have been sweet records made by Negroes before this one. Peyton's ignorance of Henderson's early recordings may be explained by the fact that Henderson and Black Swan were in New York and Peyton in Chicago, and by the absence of national Negro communication media at this time.

> Smith's orchestra and Fletcher Henderson's orchestra, both of New York. [Henderson, at this time, was half way between sweet music and jazz. He had started his career with a band that sounded like a white popular band. In 1923 he began adding jazz musicians, and began the process of combining sweet and jazz that was to make him one of the famous men of the swing style in the thirties.] They have the goods, they have the same quality of Lopez, Whitman [*sic*], Paul Ash, Dornberger and other prominent [white, successful, sweet] orchestras. They play together, they play even, they sound like an orchestra and no individual stands out above the ensemble, unless in solo rendition. Practice and direction has made this efficiency and that is what the majority of our orchestras need.
>
> To know Paul Whiteman is to understand at last the phenomenon of American jazz. Whiteman did not invent jazz—he specifically disclaims this—but he was the first to write an orchestral score for jazz, and from its inception ten years ago right to the present he has been its acknowledged chief exponent all over the world.

Peyton was not the only *Defender* writer to prefer the correct social status of sweet music to jazz. Indeed, he is typical of the writers on music, whether their articles appear on the entertainment page, in the general news, or on that traditional home of genteel journalism, the Woman's Page. The *Defender's* writers were generally not interested in music as such. They were interested in status, and, as a result, the *Defender's* coverage of jazz in Chicago is inadequate throughout the twenties. A historian who wanted to trace the careers of jazz men would find more information in the advertisements of night clubs, theaters and phonograph record companies than in the news columns. The news columns would tell him that a particular blues singer had a large and expensive wardrobe. They would tell him that a theater built for Negroes was lavishly decorated. They would tell him that a vaudeville performer had entertained the "elite" of New York City. In the early twenties they would tell him when Negroes made recordings, since in the early twenties this was still an unusual event. But "race records" included popular music as well as jazz, and since the *Defender's* writers preferred the former, the historian would not find much material even here.

The music criticism he would find would not differ significantly from Peyton's. For example, under the heading "Soft and Slow" he would find the following, by an anonymous "admirer of C. W. [*sic*] Handy":

> There is a vast difference between 'Blues' and Jazz. The public is just beginning to learn the distinction. Many orchestra leaders who have assumed that the two forms of music were the same, and who have been

> prejudiced against Jazz, have recently taken up 'Blues' and are glad to get the genuine article. . . . The most effective way to play 'Blues' is the soft, slow, croony way, and . . . it is not necessary to be an acrobat to play this wonderful music.[10]

He would find a description of a pop concert under a New York date-line and the heading "Handiwork of Handy Lauded":

> At the Metropolitan Opera House here Sunday afternoon Vincent Lopez [the leader of a popular sweet band] and his augmented orchestra of 40 selected soloists rendered a symphonic 'jazz' concert, in which everything and every note known to music was featured.

The chief offering at this concert was a "tone poem" entitled *The Evolution of the Blues,* by W. C. Handy and Joseph Nussbaum, "with orchestral development by the latter and Vincent Lopez."

It is an ironic inconsistency that the *Defender's* staff preferred sweet music to jazz, for in its political and social policy the *Defender* was no friend of white middle-class gentility. The *Defender* followed the radical social position of W. E. B. DuBois, rather than the polite conservatism of the Booker T. Washington tradition. Yet one should not expect the music criticism of a Negro newspaper in the twenties to be consistent with its political and social criticism. The Negro who disliked the social assumptions of the white middle class still had good reason to dislike traditional jazz, since traditional jazz was part of the white stereotype of the Negro.

In Peyton's account of Fess Williams' sweet records, what pleased him most was that "Fess insisted that if they wanted him to record he would have to be given the same breaks as the white bands were getting and that is making real sweet musical song and dance records." It is quite true that the white world expected Negroes to stick to jazz and leave "respectable" music to the white man. Jazz, the blues and the spirituals were products of the Negro community, and the white world has put a racial tag on all of them. And this identification of the Negro with music of Negro origin has been a serious barrier to the Negro musician who wants to perform popular or classical music. The *Defender* gives the history of one such man, Carroll Clark, who had recorded for a company run by whites. The company's policy had been that this man's picture

> must not be identified with the finer ballads, but with the type of song which has come to be identified in the popular mind with the

[10] Handy's own recordings show that he played the blues in a sweet, popularized, "soft, slow, croony way." See, for example, *Aunt Hagar's Blues,* by Handy's Orchestra, Okeh 4789, recorded in the early twenties.

> smart, sophisticated "coon" who furnishes use [*sic*] with ragtime and jazz. Mr. Clark, a cultured Negro, with a fine and well trained voice, naturally rebelled against the imposition of this demand that he cheapen his art and belittle his race, and left the employ of the white concern.

This racial identification still persists today. For example, a Negro concert singer is expected to include a number of spirituals in his repertory. This is foolish, since the Negro uses the same concert arrangements of spiritual melodies as the white concert singer, and these arrangements are a far cry from the spirituals as they are sung by a shouting congregation. But the concert audience likes to get its spirituals from a Negro. The music carries a racial tag, and the Negro singer is expected to accept it.

Negro newspaper men were not, of course, the only Negroes who compared the rough, disturbing vitality of jazz unfavorably with the sugary "correctness" of popular music. The impact of popular standards may be seen very clearly in the tastes of jazz musicians as well. Louis Armstrong announced his fondness for Guy Lombardo on a number of occasions, and insisted that the men in his Savoy Ballroom band, in 1928, would never miss a Sunday night Lombardo broadcast.[11] These attitudes are not limited to the twenties nor to New Orleans jazz men. As late as 1943 Duke Ellington, one of the best of the swing musicians, wrote the following tribute to the producers of the insipid confections we call "semi-classical" music:

> Then, there is the school of Kostelanetz, Morton Gould and Dave Rose, who work with a different type of instrumentation [different from the instrumentation of the swing band]. I think they're wonderful, and the things they turn out are gorgeous. The music is beautiful to listen to and wonderful to write. It's the kind of thing everyone wishes he could write, and what we'd all like to be working on. It's such majestic music! Dave Rose is very modern, almost futuristic. Strayhorn [Ellington's staff arranger], too, has some ultra-modern ideas. His ideas are way ahead of those being used by most of the others, but he is reluctant to write them, as am I. Dave Rose has gone ahead and thus, in a sense, pioneered the modern field.[12]

To call the music of Kostelanetz, Gould and Rose "majestic," and to speak of their derivative popularizations of the late nineteenth-century European tradition as "very modern" seems fantastic. Only the worst of

[11] See "The Sweetest Music . . .," *The Record Changer,* July-August, 1950, p. 26.
[12] Duke Ellington, "Duke Ellington on Arrangers," *Metronome,* October 1943, p. 35.

Duke Ellington's music has approached the slick emptiness of these popular semi-classicists. It is fortunate that Armstrong and Ellington, no matter how hard they may have tried, have never been able to sound quite like Lombardo, Kostelanetz, Gould and Rose.

The impact of the standards of popular music on jazz musicians may also be seen in their curious contempt for the man among them who does not read music. Many of the best early jazz musicians could not read, or learned to read late and badly. This did not in any way diminish their excellence as performers of a music which has always been at its best when improvised or played in "head" (memorized) arrangements. Yet when *Down Beat* asked for comments on Kid Ory, the best that pianist Eddie Beal could produce as a compliment to one of the greatest of the New Orleans jazz musicians was this:

> The thing that comes to my mind first when thinking of Kid Ory is that he is one of the very few musicians of his era that could actually read music. In other words, he was one of the very few real musicians.[13]

Benny Goodman has said that some of the better jazz men he knew in Chicago "were terrifically talented guys, but most of them didn't read."[14] And a trombonist I talked with in Washington, D. C. told me he thought Sidney Bechet was wonderful—he could listen to Bechet all night long—but Bechet was "no musician," because he couldn't read.

It is said that some of the best of the older New Orleans cornetists used to hold one hand over the fingers that were manipulating the valves, if they thought a rival was watching them, so that the rival could not steal their fingering, and thus steal their phrases. But since the twenties the test for "real" musicianship has become reading, a technique that every hack in the Guy Lombardo band is sure to possess.

Big Bill Broonzy is rebelling against this definition of reality in music when he says:

> Some Negroes tell me that the old style of blues is carrying Negroes back to the horse-and-buggy days and back to slavery . . . and they say to me: "You should learn, go and take lessons and learn to play real music." Then I will ask them: "Ain't the blues real music?"

Yet Broonzy himself partially accepts the common phrase when he says, of a musician who had some experience with popular music, "He knew

13 *Down Beat,* August 10, 1951, p. 19.

14 Benny Goodman and Irving Kolodin, *The Kingdom of Swing* (New York: Stackpole Sons, 1939), p. 74.

more about real music than I did, but I knew more about the real blues."[15]

It *is* a definition of reality rather than a peculiar use of the word "real" that we are dealing with here, since the Negro jazz musician did feel that he was playing "music as we think it should be played" rather than "correctly," in Peyton's words. The Negro jazz man felt that he was living in a world of musical make-believe, playing "hokum," a term which was synonymous with jazz not only for Peyton but for Negro jazz men in general.[16]

Even when the question of "reality" is not involved, the jazz musician's sense of playing a stigmatized music may be summed up in his use of the word "legitimate." From the beginnings of jazz to the present, all jazz musicians have referred to the man who played the notes as he saw them in the score—either the popular or the classical musician—as a legitimate musician, and to the music he played as legitimate, and have referred to all jazz techniques as illegitimate. The white jazz man, as well as the Negro, has used this curious classification, since both have been aware that their music lacks the social approval and status granted to classical and popular music. Now that jazz is becoming respectable, this classification may die out, but the fact that it is still widely used is evidence of the extraordinary pressures the jazz musician has had to acknowledge, pressures to stop playing jazz and start playing "correctly."

I have outlined, in the attitudes of the *Defender's* staff and in the attitudes of jazz musicians themselves, one of the socially determined pressures toward change in jazz style during the decade of the twenties: the Negro's own compulsion to reject a music identified in his mind with a degraded past, and to replace it with the socially respectable popular music of the white middle-class majority. But the new social environment of Chicago exerted external as well as internal pressures on the jazz musician.

For one thing, the audience for jazz was changing. Much of it consisted of Negroes who were on their way up in American society and beginning to identify with the dominant popular culture. Many of the whites who were becoming an important part of the jazz audience could not understand a music too radically different from the popular music they were used to, and preferred sweetened jazz to the unadulterated variety. And when more members of the audience wanted popu-

[15] William Broonzy and Yannick Bruynoghe, *Big Bill Blues* (London: Cassell & Company, Ltd., 1955), pp. 4, 87-88.

[16] Johnny Dodds, the New Orleans clarinetist, used this word for his own music all his life (see Charles Edward Smith, with Frederic Ramsey, Jr., Charles Payne Rogers and William Russell, *The Jazz Record Book* [New York, 1942], p. 116).

larization, the musician, like any other professional entertainer, felt obliged to satisfy them. Richard M. Jones, a pianist and bandleader, announced at the beginning of one of his recordings, in a mock preacher's tone: "We are gathered here to give the public what it wants—and the public wants good first class music—and we gonna give 'em *Dusty Bottom Blues*." [17] Jones was recording in 1926, when his public was already beginning to want something quite different from *Dusty Bottom Blues.* Jones made almost thirty records during the twenties, but he made only five in the thirties, since by 1930 his taste differed too greatly from that of his public.

It was during the twenties that jazz really spread beyond the Negro community and became popular with America at large. Jazz men had, of course, been playing for some white audiences long before, but it was in the twenties that they acquired a truly national audience and found themselves a part of the national entertainment industry, subject to all its requirements. And it was in the twenties that entertainment first began to acquire the centralization and standardization that have made it an industry.[18]

There were always a few night club owners who liked their jazz unsweetened and managed to find enough local customers to stay in business. But many club owners, and most of the people who dealt with a national, undifferentiated mass audience—record company, radio and motion picture executives, and the agents of the national booking agencies—preferred the safety of a kind of jazz that was not too different from the standard product of the entertainment industry. The record companies will serve as an example. In the early twenties, when jazz records sold only to the Negro community and were listed only in special "Race" catalogues, the record company executives were content not to meddle musically with this profitable sideline. But when jazz began to be listed in the main catalogue they could not afford to let it alone. The company has a far larger economic stake in a nationally distributed record than in a record sold to a limited audience. And the nationally distributed record must strike an average of mass taste rather than the clearly defined taste of a special group, since the company must sell a large number of records simply to get its money back. In order

[17] Richard M. Jones Jazz Wizards, *Dusty Bottom Blues,* Okeh 8431.

[18] Some idea of the centralization within this industry may be gained from Irving Kolodin's statement in "The Dance Band Business: a Study in Black and White," *Harper's Magazine,* CLXXXIII (June 1941), 72: "These three booking offices [the Music Corporation of America, the William Morris Agency, and the General Amusements Corporation] *are* the band business, and every leader knows it." Mr. Kolodin remarks on the same page that booking "is a business that has flourished for only two decades."

to make money it must produce a certain proportion of "hits," and while a really original record may occasionally become a hit it is much more apt to lose money. Therefore the standard product is the safe product.

The musician who succeeds in the entertainment industry, then, is the musician who will produce the required standard product. Louis Armstrong, defending himself against the charge of wasting his talent on trivial popular tunes, said, "They put a piece of music up in front of you—you ain't supposed to tell the leader 'I don't want to do this.' And I was brought up that way." [19] Notice that "the leader" here is not the bandleader, since Armstrong leads his own band, but a metaphor for the entertainment industry.

Finally, it should not be forgotten that all of these pressures toward popularization were supplemented by the constant presence, in northern Negro communities, of popular music itself. The twenties, when Negroes had moved to the cities en masse, was also the period when the American entertainment industry first began to achieve mass distribution. Every radio, every phonograph, every sheet music counter was a channel for the standard variety of popular music.

It is hardly surprising, given the radical changes in the Negro jazz musician's social attitudes and environment, and the resulting social pressures upon him, that the first major change in jazz style was toward the socially sanctioned popular music of the white man, more than a change proceeding from innovations within jazz itself.

A convenient date for the ending of the first jazz style and the beginning of the second is 1930. Certainly it was about this time that this socially-determined impact of popular music on jazz had its most dramatic musical effects.

These effects may be seen very clearly by comparing two of Louis Armstrong's records. The first, *Yes! I'm in the Barrel,* by Louis Armstrong and his Hot Five, was recorded in 1925. [20] The composer credit is given to Armstrong: this is a jazz tune rather than a popular song made over into jazz. The instrumentation is cornet, clarinet, trombone, banjo and piano, a traditional New Orleans instrumentation except for the omission of bass and drums, which may have been left out because neither could be recorded well in 1925. All of the musicians but pianist Lil Armstrong are from New Orleans. The record opens with a three-note, stop-time riff against which Armstrong constructs the lead. (A riff

[19] From a broadcast of "The Dave Garroway Show," September 5, 1954.

[20] Okeh 8261, reissued on Columbia ML-4383. The "barrel" in the title is an abbreviation of "barrelhouse," a low-class bar.

is a short melodic or rhythmic pattern, repeated with minor variations. The equivalent term in European music is "ostinato." Stop-time leaves one or more accents of the meter unstated. The lead is the main melodic line.) At the end of this passage there is a marked sense of released tension as the band abandons the riff for the traditional New Orleans improvised ensemble style. The third section, a solo by clarinetist Johnny Dodds with rhythm accompaniment, is followed by a final ensemble passage, broken only by two short breaks by trombonist Kid Ory and Armstrong.

The second record, *Star Dust,* by Louis Armstrong and his Orchestra, was recorded in 1931.[21] The tune is, of course, a popular sentimental song, which must be made over into jazz. The instrumentation is two trumpets, trombone, three alto saxophones, tenor saxophone, piano, banjo, bass and drums, a band smaller than most of the white sweet bands of the period, but a step in that direction, especially in the saxophone section. Less than half the men are New Orleans musicians. The record consists of three parts: a trumpet solo by Armstrong, a vocal solo by Armstrong and a trumpet solo by Armstrong, with short bridge passages by the band. Armstrong is in magnificent form, better as a soloist than on *Yes! I'm in the Barrel,* since he has time to develop his ideas. His inventive trumpet and his gravelly voice break the sentimental melody into little pieces, and from those pieces build something new and exciting. But listen to the rest of the band! It plays in close harmony, with the mushy timbre of the saxophones dominating the orchestral sound. Behind the trumpet solos it plays a dispirited two-note riff, failing utterly to achieve the tension of the stop-time riff produced by the Hot Five. Behind the vocal solo and in the bridge passages it plays an arrangement of the melody so sickeningly sweet and sentimental that this band could not be distinguished from Guy Lombardo's except for Armstrong himself and for the fact that his rhythm section can keep interesting as well as accurate time.

Jazz has always borrowed from popular music, but this is something more than borrowing, something more than the adaptation of a melodic phrase or a harmonic device to a jazz framework. Here the very basis for Armstrong's jazz solos is a great, sticky, unassimilated glob of musical sweetness.

Armstrong's *Star Dust* is music with a split personality, jazz and sweet combined in a tissue of contradictions, the half-marvelous and half-monstrous issue of the socially-forced marriage of popular music to jazz. It is still clearly jazz because of Armstrong's dominating role as soloist:

21 Okeh 41530 (second master), reissued on Columbia ML-4386.

a role that satisfied both the Negro community's desire for a race hero and the entertainment industry's desire for an easily identifiable star. But the jazz solo is placed in a startlingly inappropriate setting, in the slushiest musical vulgarity of which popular music is capable.

Surely the southern Negro made a real social advance to the extent that he became acculturated to white middle-class society, for in spite of the faults of the latter it is clearly preferable to the social disorganization and degradation of the southern Negro's subculture. But since the Negro's jazz tradition was preferable to the popular music of the white middle class, the results of acculturation on the musical level were equally clearly unfortunate. Jazz at the end of the twenties was an unsuccessful mixture of two disparate musical traditions. Reconciling these traditions, synthesizing jazz and sweet, was the difficult business of the jazz musicians of the thirties, and the result of their synthesis was the music we call swing.

Afternote

My position regarding the central theme of this article has not changed. I still think that acceptance of the standards of the popular entertainment industry by jazz musicians has been musically unfortunate. If it had continued it would have meant the end of jazz as a separate music. But fortunately the acceptance of popular standards was never complete, and in the 1940's jazz musicians turned once more to standards of their own.

The chief qualification I would now make is that acculturation was by no means a one-way process. In the 1930's popular music was clearly the stronger of the two, but over the long run jazz has probably influenced popular music as much as popular music has influenced jazz. And for that we can all be grateful.

Chadwick Hansen is an Associate Professor of English at the Pennsylvania State University where he also serves as faculty adviser to the Major in American Studies. [This article appeared in Vol. XII, No. 4 (Winter, 1960).]

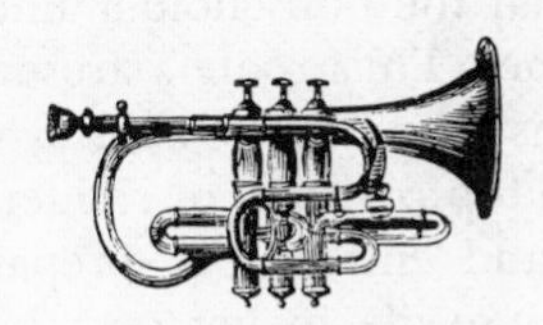

Arthur H. Cole

The Price System and the Rites of Passage

THE "RITES OF PASSAGE," THE ACTIVITIES OR CEREMONIES CONNECTED WITH birth, admission to adulthood, marriage and death, constitute a group of the most intimate family and social events in human history. In colonial times in America these events were regarded as distinctly family affairs: the new child welcomed in the main bedroom of the house; the marriage celebrated—in the presence of scarcely more than the two families—in the parlor of the bride's home; and the dead prepared for burial there in the quieted household, and his body interred in the family burying lot. To be sure, the ceremonies associated with these passages—baptism, wedding, burial—soon came to be solemnized by the offices of a clergyman; and the sociologist might see in the persistence in our society of religious sanctions to these ceremonies a link with the early past. Anthropologists in dealing with primitive peoples are disposed to look at the tone and character of the rites of passage for a reflection of the basic values of those social units; and typically we continue to exhibit our hold upon Christianity, Judaism or other domestic faith at such ceremonials.

Now the capacity of the price system to penetrate areas of human action and concern previously carried on by voluntary effort is a phenomenon long appreciated by historians. One facet of this development is the entrepreneurial action of providing a service or commodity at a price or in a condition that the householder finds attractive in terms of his available money income. Thus roofers arose in towns of appropriate size who, for considerations found reasonable by owners of houses, would repair the slate or shingle top covering of residences; or the "commercial bakery" was established and enlarged to prepare the bread and cakes erstwhile baked by the housewife in her own kitchen. Such productive and service institutions have now become so numerous, and their offerings so largely coterminous with household needs, that the function of the householder and housewife has greatly changed from earlier times. Aided also by mechanical devices now installed within the home, the woman of the family has been able, more definitely than ever before, to become a companion to her husband and a mother to her children, while, as the family matures, she is likely to re-enter the ranks of business herself. Except for a few chores such as the making of beds and the care of the lawns, the household has become institutionalized, its diverse functions being dispersed into the hands of numerous business units. This entrepreneurial aspect of the price system will be found to have achieved significance also in the area of the rites of passage.

The birth of children has, in the American culture, been the least publicized of the major passages to which human life here has been subject—perhaps because women felt a distaste for the unusual distention of their abdomens during the latter months of pregnancy, and perhaps because somehow their "delicate condition" advertised the pudendous aspect of sex life. Not many years ago, actual childbirth was almost universally referred to in polite circles as a woman's "confinement"; and I suspect that this euphemism derived from the withdrawal of the expectant mother from most social contacts, at least after the pregnancy had reached a stage of external obviousness. And one of the first loosenings of this traditional behavior came through the action of entrepreneurship. Lane Bryant of New York began in the years around 1910 to design and offer for sale "maternity" clothes; the products of this heroic action proved popular with women; the fashion spread; and — undoubtedly abetted by the rise in the capacity in America for a higher standard of living—the manufacture and sale of such clothing had by 1960 become an important element in the women's garment industry. The 1960 classified directory of the New York Telephone Company for Manhattan lists 34 enterprises engaged in the manufacture and wholesale trading in this form of apparel, and 14 retail stores that specialized in its sale. (It seems also true that Lane Bryant and her imitators succeeded in expanding the use of the words "maternity" and "pregnancy," beyond the unabridged dictionary, helped to give the coup to such phrases as "interesting condition" and "delicate condition," and converted "confinement" to "childbirth"!)

The actual delivery of the child was taken from the monopoly of the family at a very early period, perhaps first by other wives of the tribe or community, but then, as far back as ancient Egypt, by paid midwives. Women remained in control throughout the ancient and medieval periods, indeed down fairly close to our own times. Their hold on the business was strengthened by the vigorous sex-derived taboos, not only that no man should enter the room of delivery, but that no details of the physiology of childbirth should be printed. The beginning of a new trend in England seems to have occurred with the death at childbirth of Jane Seymour, wife of Henry VIII, in 1537. Doctors of that country began to take more interest in the problem; they became attendants at noble and royal births; and "male midwives" played a considerable role by the eighteenth century, especially when instruments had been introduced for use in difficult deliveries.

Midwives came to America in early shiploads of migrants, although none seems to have been present when Peregrine White was born on board the "Mayflower." Anne Hutchinson was a practitioner of the art or handicraft, even if she is remembered more widely for other activities. Indeed, such handmaidens of Lucina dominated childbirth in this country until the middle of the nineteenth century, except for limited urban areas as, for example, New York City and Philadelphia. As late as 1935, over 10 per cent of births in America were still attended solely by midwives, but the proportion had diminished to less than 3 per cent in the mid-1950s—and these remaining births almost exclusively in the nonwhite section of our population. The professional doctor had practically taken over.

While the midwife introduced a certain measure of commercialization into the procedure of childbearing, the latter process stayed on in the home, at least in most cases. The exponents of medicine, in England or in the United States, were not in a position vigorously to dispute the regime of midwifery or to attract their female patients into hospitals. The rising national income of the two countries, and especially of the United States, accompanied by a rising tide of benevolence at the hands of men of large fortunes, did permit the establishment of hospitals of various sorts in the middle decades of the nineteenth century, and, among them, hospitals with the euphemistic description of "lying-in." This term actually dates back centuries in England, and seems to have been synonymous with the later "confinement" or the action of childbearing; but it may have persisted to modern times in part because, in substance as well as in metaphor, the expectant mother came to "lie in" a hospital in the charge of an attendant physician. A minor proportion of such specializing hospitals, to be sure, were profit-oriented, commercial institutions; but the greater number were, at least in considerable part, supported out of charity or endowed by wealthy individuals.

The appearance of lying-in hospitals did not, of course, mean a complete, immediate transfer of all births to such institutions. Many an older person in such a settled region as New England can report his appearance into the world to have occurred at his parents' home. Families recently arrived from Europe were unaccustomed to births elsewhere than in the home, and anyway many could not afford the luxury of hospital attention. In addition to midwives and the local physicians, students in metropolitan medical schools, when they came to the study of obstetrics, used to gain experience in the homes of immigrants and the less well-to-do of the city's population. Their services were less costly than those of the local midwives.

A wider appreciation of the germ theory of disease, combined with the rising surplus of incomes above minimal living needs, moved childbirth almost wholly into hospitals, and these forces were supplemented in time by discoveries of procedures for saving the lives of "blue" or other abnormal children if hospital treatment were immediately available. An important impetus seems to have derived from the discovery of the origin and the means of preventing "childbed fever." At all events, a combination of factors had, before the middle of the twentieth century, moved the activities of childbearing outside the home.

Relative to activities subsequent to childbirth, other features of the price system have over a long time-period been evident. In early days, both abroad and here, the initial agent of this system was the wet nurse. In the days of frequent deaths at childbirth and of frequent illness of the mother after the ordeal, and when "baby-foods" were still largely a development of the future, there was a real social as well as economic service attached to the advertisements, so frequently inserted in early newssheets, of "a woman with a full breast of milk" who desired a child or children to suckle. Happily no one arose with a theory that a child took in more than nourishment with a stranger's milk, and the practice of wet-nursing continued down into the twentieth century, at least in certain areas. Added to this element of commercialization came something of a substitute arrangement. After certain advances in medical skills and after the introduction of refrigeration and aseptic conditions in institutions, all obstetrical hospitals in the larger metropolitan centers sponsored and maintained an affiliated enterprise—when the service was not actually made an integral part of the hospitals themselves—at which mother's milk could be purchased for the benefit of children who stood in need of that form of sustenance.

In the meantime, the proud father had achieved a modest place in the total performance: he was dispensing cigars to his friends, an action perhaps deriving from the hospitality offered at christenings. The manufacturers of cigars have given what encouragement they could to the continuance of this custom, even in a world where cigars are no longer the major form of tobacco consumption. One may secure boxes especially prepared for this joyous occasion, each appropriately provided with the designation "It's a boy" or "It's a girl."

Of recent years, commercialization has found new ways of attempting to improve the well-being of the happy parents. Even before she leaves the hospital, the mother may well be offered the chance to secure a photograph of her newborn. This is a result of a development—quasi-commercial and quasi-eleemosynary—which made its appearance in the mid-1950s. An entrepreneur of the Boston region conceived the notion of placing cameras in maternity hospitals—and maternity wards of general hospitals—and sharing with the local institution the profits secured from the operations of the picture-taking unit. The scheme seemed to satisfy a desire on the part of the new parents, hitherto unrecognized, or at least unsatisfied commercially; installations were rapidly extended to other regions of the United States; and by 1960 this added touch of business had become almost universal in the country anent the "rite" of birth.

Meanwhile, at the home, an interesting batch of mail is likely to be accumulating for the decisions of the new mother upon her return to her household position. The literature will contain advertisements ranging all the way from prepared foods to children's furniture, and from savings schemes to diaper service. Nor are the special needs of the parents left unnoticed. There may be an offering of abdominal belts to compress the mother back into shape, and the tendering of contraceptives to the household, lest such a tragedy strike the family again. (In states where the passage of such literature through the mails is forbidden, less specific pamphlets of the Planned Parenthood Association may well take its place.)

All in all, the activities in and around the typical American family, relative to the arrival of an "addition," have felt the impact of the price system, especially over the past fifty or sixty years. The advent of the child has for some period been an event in which at least one person outside the family was likely to have a share; but the enhancement of family incomes rather generally through the American society and the increase of pressures upon business institutions to stretch their markets to the maximum have conspired to make this advent almost a public affair. The assertion of a modest connection of the child with the Christian or other domestic faith may be broadcast at the immediate or ultimate christening or equivalent ceremony, but, in the meanwhile, the photographer at the hospital, the purveyor of prepared formulas, perhaps the forward-looking private school nearby, seem to have acquired operational beachheads on the family, even if a midwife should no longer be able to look upon the infant as one of "her children" or the lad in later years be duty-bound to look with special thanks to a strange woman who came to his rescue early with "a full breast of milk!"

Ceremonies connected with the attainment of physiological maturity have counted for little in Anglo-Saxon cultures. Given their relative niggardliness of free gifts from nature, these cultures were more concerned with the superfluity of population, even before England's Malthus, than with the joys of procreation. Social pressures and laws of property came early to tie procreation to marriage; marriage, at least in those days before the welfare state appeared, came to be associated with the capacity to support a family; and, in our northern climes, such capacity to secure so adequate an income delayed marriage until long after puberty had been passed. Even schooling, when it became common, tended to obliterate the physiological line; at first boys, and later girls, progressed from kindergarten or its equivalent to the university without definite break at any point correlated to physical change.

There has been a minor notion of "reaching maturity" in the admission of young people into full membership within religious bodies; the Jewish ceremony of "bar mitzvah," seems relevant; but the Catholic and Episcopal denominations have been disposed to give confirmation when the novitiates are still children; while the Evangelical denominations seem to prefer the act of joining the church to be the decision of persons who have really achieved the "age of discretion." Again, in voting laws, there is a differentiation drawn between men and boys; but here also the minimum voting age has always had some rough correlation with intellectual or moral faculties, not simply the capacity to reproduce one's kind.

Perhaps it is permissible, with only a modest stretch of imagination, to conceive the "coming-out parties" of young women as roughly analogous to the puberty ceremonies of primitive peoples. To be sure, for the most part, coming-out parties have been considered a phenomenon of the "upper strata" of communities and therefore perhaps not truly representative of society as a whole. However, it has been observed, at least in Boston, and seemingly elsewhere in the country, that as people acquire economic and social competence, they tend to follow practices previously established by their predecessors on the economic and social ladders. In recent years, for example, cotillions have been set up for the presentation to society of the debutantes of various minority groups—as Catholic, Jewish and Negro.

Historically such "presentations to society" have always been viewed as related to marriage. One reads of dinners and dances being given by English nobility in the eighteenth century at which daughters were "presented to society." If the families were of the Catholic faith, the daughters might be "coming out" of convent schools. More generally, the young ladies could be pictured as metaphorically "coming out" of the seclusion of their families; now they were on their own; now they could be courted by appropriate young men with an anticipation of ultimate marriage.

The practices of the nobility came to be imitated by the mere wealthy. Prior to 1860, festivities of corresponding character were offered by proprietors of southern plantations, and soon—in a group affair—at such a cotton-merchants' town as Charleston in annual "cotillions." Perhaps the greater stake in continuance of the plantations and therefore the greater desirability that the young women of families make "advantageous" marriages may have (unconsciously, to be sure) incited the fathers to such activities. "Dancing assemblies" had become a part of the social life of Philadelphia in the latter colonial years; and the practice was taken up by the St. Cecilia Society of Charleston about 1820, and in other mercantile communities of the Atlantic coast in these early decades of the new century—probably not discouraged by the proprietors of the City Tavern or equivalent hostelry at which the festivity might be held. Subsequently, when wealth came more markedly to the North, thus enhancing the importance of family strength, and when this importance was given wide-flung sanction with the publication of "social registers" in the larger cities—the result of entrepreneurial enterprise in the late 1880s—individualized "coming-out" parties began to be given in New York and other metropolitan centers. By this time, city hotels had arisen at which it was convenient to assemble the guests for the "presentation" of a lovely daughter to the established society. Caterers soon arose to serve families in the large residences which now the more affluent members of "the 400" had constructed for living—or display—purposes.

The characters of these performances may perhaps be correlated roughly with certain facets of the price system. The adoption of the form of group presentation, the cotillion, may have been originally a reflection of the modest financial resources of the merchants in the southern ports, or perhaps their greater pecuniary caution relative to the matrimonial ventures of their daughters. Cotillions were again embraced when a combination of inflation and a scarcity of servants struck the country in the years after the Second World War. In the period of ostentatious wealth, especially between the 1890s and the "great depression," individualized parties were the rule in the northern cities, each daughter being presented at her own cocktail party, dinner-dance or the like, and each party given with at least an avoidance of niggardly appearance, if not always with purposeful ostentation. That the latter type is not wholly forgotten was demonstrated in 1960, when Henry Ford gave his daughter Charlotte a lavish debut party at the Country Club of Detroit. Supposedly a year of planning was put into the affair; 1,200 guests were entertained; $60,000 went into flowers alone; and the total cost was reported to have reached or exceeded a quarter of a million dollars. However, such affairs are relatively rare these days.

On the other hand, entrepreneurial invasion of this "rite" has made comparatively little progress. Businessmen have found little opportunity to develop pressures upon parents to underwrite either individual parties for their offspring or participation in a group effort; nor have they been able to set up specifications relative to the apparel to be expected of participants in these performances so that much specialized activity is generated. Usually, for the cotillions, the girls being honored are expected to wear white evening gowns, white slippers and long white gloves. The last feature may make a contribution to the welfare of the somewhat sick glove-making industry, since long white gloves are otherwise hardly ever a requisite in the wardrobe of a young lady of the mid-twentieth century; but white evening gowns and white slippers are produced widely enough so that this debutante-party demand could make for no great jollity in the women's wholesale or retail trades. Perhaps the debutante season may have more specific effects on the male side. Many young men these days do not own full-dress paraphernalia; such garments would be *de rigueur* at dinner-dances or other evening parties; and shops for the rental of men's evening wear do a good business in consequence.

Business management does probably play a role in all sizable communities relative to the programming of the annual performances. Obviously the lack of some control might well result in the bunching of festivities on specific days or nights, so that none would be well attended, caterers would be pushed beyond practical limits, the supply of dance bands would prove insufficient and the like. In Boston, a quarter of a century ago, an office existed, operated by a woman who at least appeared to know the city's "society." In return for a fee, a reservation could be registered for a tea-dance, a supper or larger operation on a specific day or evening. The lady also supplied lists of other debutantes of that year, and a list of approved young men from the local secondary schools and the lower classes of the local colleges and universities. Now some part of these functions seems to have drifted into the hands of a leading stationer of the city, a man who sooner or later will be producing engraved invitations not only to the debutante parties but later to weddings and "at-homes," announcements of the arrival of children, and whatnot. All young women may register their desires at this gentleman's shop, paying a small fee.

At the close of the local school year, this list is published in the Boston newspapers, and turned over to a committee of selection which has meanwhile been assembled chiefly from mothers of girls who indubitably qualify as debutantes in that particular year. This group, burdened with the unpleasant task of selecting a hundred girls from the two or three hundred who have registered with the stationer, is assembled by the head of an enterprise which, since the close of World War II, has been active in the planning and directing of social events in the city. The choices are made as expeditiously as possible, and, when the office of this social manager has received the new list, it sends out invitations at once for participation in the annual cotillion to take place a fortnight later. The young ladies—or their parents—are free to decline such invitations, but those who do accept are required to pay approximately $75 to the enterprise, a sum which covers hospitality to the young lady's father, her escort and herself on the evening of the dance. Presumably the payments from the hundred selected debutantes provide an appropriate profit for the hotel at which the party takes place as well as a suitable honorarium to the management concern which engineers the whole operation.

In the meantime the debutantes sit for photographs at commercial photographers whose names will look well below the cuts appearing in the newspapers; glossy prints are supplied to the latter; and the pictures of all the season's debutantes are likely to be printed sooner or later in the society columns of the *Boston Herald* and *Boston Globe*. The young ladies have been appropriately launched on a social career.

It is recognized that the data presented here—and to some extent elsewhere in this essay—relate exclusively or predominantly to conditions in Boston. Investigation of phenomena such as the foregoing necessarily carries a limitation on the geography of coverage. Little has been written on such social practices as coming-out parties and wedding receptions, and one can obtain a view of representative habits only by living in the community, reading the local newspapers, talking to parents and the like; and such residence is particularly essential to perceive changes and current trends. Another and more practical reason for the concentration on affairs of greater Boston is that of space in an essay such as this. Perhaps Boston is atypical for the whole country; but once the observer has moved beyond a single community, where would he be able to stop? What would constitute a representative group or a full spectrum of American urban areas? Nevertheless, in regard to coming-out parties in other cities, it can be noted that in some centers larger than Boston, a body of professional family advisers has appeared, "social secretaries," women who "know the ropes," can advise the parents on where to hold a function, whom to invite and what refreshments to serve. For families who have newly risen into contact with the world of society, and for those who, already well adjusted to it, are too busy otherwise to attend to a special event, such guides with accumulated wisdom are highly useful. Here, as in other phases of the "coming-out" rite, the intervention of the price system contributes to the smooth performance of the social order.

By the time modern young folk arrive at the juncture of marriage, they are already pretty well educated to the services attainable in private entrepreneurship and, consequently, the relative unimportance of the family. No longer is the family hearth the center of courtship for the young lady, nor is it likely that she and her female relatives will labor days and nights to fill her wedding chest with dainty garments made by their own hands. Still more improbable is the production of a homemade wedding dress, even with the aid of an itinerant seamstress, unless it chances that the mother's wedding gown has been saved and can be altered to fit the daughter. The rise in the value of urban land with the further growth of cities, and the increase of urban congestion, have driven more and more families into apartment houses; and such living quarters lend themselves poorly to the enactment of marriage rites and the holding of wedding receptions. Similarly the growing scarcity of household servants and their increased wages have tended to diminish still further the flexibility of many families in the face of such an emergency as a social wedding. Now preparation for marriage and quite surely the ceremony itself involve agencies and institutions external to the household.

The publication of marriage intentions in the local newssheets is now enough to set enterprise in motion. The prospective bride will secure advertisements of stores offering silverware, china and glassware; stores offering linen and other items for her trousseau; shops expressing a willingness to design and produce wedding gowns with, if petitioned adequately, gowns for the whole bridal party; advertisements of caterers, of wedding directors and of limousines for hire. Meanwhile, the prospective groom will be informed, by advertisements, of opportunities to rent tuxedos or other formal wear, and of hotels particularly suited for honeymoons, and may be waited upon by insurance salesmen who would be glad to write new policies to protect his prospective wife.

The increased public character of weddings plus the enhanced financial resources of many families have conspired to promote the development of divers new institutions on both the local and the broader fronts. Of the former, the wedding directors may deserve special mention. Such persons are likely to pretend to competence in only individual facets of the marriage rite: dresses, food or music. Of course, the parents of the bride need consult only those whom they believe likely to be helpful. Then there are retail shops specializing in wedding apparel for the women in the proceedings and willing, with appropriate compensation, to supervise the costuming of the bride and her attendants on the day of the ceremony. In addition there are the local photographers, who have recently taken on increased importance. Now photographs of the chief participants, the two pairs of parents, the other members of the wedding party, the guests at the reception, even the table with the wedding cake, are all essential. When note is also taken of caterers, florists, musicians, society columnists on the local newspapers, etc., it will be evident that much business turns now upon the performance of the marriage rite in specific communities.

An interesting index of the acquiescence of the modern bride in the commercialization of her actions is provided in her registering a specific silverware pattern with a specific jewelry shop, nominating her selected pattern in china at another shop and the like. After such actions, the prospective bride can refer inquiring friends to the several shops, where these potential donors can learn what already has been purchased by other generous souls.

The actual fabrication of feminine apparel for appearance at weddings involves relationships with areas other than one's own. There may be specializing manufacturers of wedding dresses in such a city as Boston —where actually two manage to carry on operations — but orders are likely also to be transmitted to New York City, where no less than 25 or 30 are active. In fact, the volume of business in the whole country is large enough to encourage the maintenance of a Bridal and Bridesmaids Apparel [trade] Association. Then there is the *Bride's Magazine,* which has been published nationally for 25 years, and there are even local periodicals—supported by advertisers no doubt—such as New England's *Bride's Dutch Uncle* issued in Boston.

Not least important in the wider view has been the evolution of specializing honeymoon hotels. To be sure, the preference of honeymoon couples for specific locations—Niagara Falls, Old Point Comfort, Atlantic City, etc.—dates back well into the nineteenth century; but, by and large, the newly-weds had to take their place with all other visitors in the several hostelries at these places. There were "bridal suites" in a number of hotels, dating also from the nineteenth century. Now hotel establishments cater especially to such young folk. For example, the Reefs in Bermuda with its row of cabanas and its private beach, has, since the close of World War II, paid almost exclusive attention to the honeymoon trade; while the Farm on the Hill in Swiftwater, Pennsylvania, advertises its facilities as intended "for newlyweds only—your own exclusive cottage"; and in the *Bride's Magazine* there are advertisements of other such institutions extending over twenty pages, places suited to longer and shorter pocketbooks.

The matrimonial rite has indeed wandered far from the simple, intimate ceremony of the family's front parlor, with the bride largely content to have appareled herself in "something old and something new, something borrowed, something blue." Now, from the publication of an engagement until the return of the married couple from their honeymoon adventure, their activities induce attentions from entrepreneurs of various sorts and involve themselves, their parents and their friends in manifold commercial transactions so large in total volume as to produce specialization at both the local and national levels. In a sense, bridal business is big business.

The rites attendant upon death, no less than those provoked by other human "passages," have felt the impact of forces deriving from movement in the price system. Long gone is the simple course of actions upon the passing of a member of the household: the preparation of his body by loving relatives and friends, the procurement of a plain, deal box and the quiet interment of his earthly remains in the family plot of the local churchyard. Now funeral rites make manifest the series of changes which have converted this basically private ceremony into a quasi-public affair —forces stemming from both entrepreneurial forwardness and the movement of larger economic factors.

Some changes in these simple arrangements had supervened before the close of our colonial period. One such was the intervention of handicraftsmen, as had happened earlier in the case of childbirth. Here it was the appeal to carpenters and cabinetmakers to prepare the coffin; and, in the nineteenth century, the manufacture of such equipment—of ever increasing variety and quality—became a significant segment of American industry. In our colonial days also, the sexton became the usual grave-digger as older communities achieved church organizations and incidentally established graveyards as attachments to their places of worship. Finally, it may be noted that in the years shortly before the American Revolution, an individual called an "undertaker" put in an appearance, although it is uncertain just what he considered his appropriate functions. Individuals of the same designation had risen in England nearly a century earlier, individuals who seem fairly close both to funeral directors of the ancient world and to those of recent decades in America.

With the increase in the size of our population in the nineteenth century, and especially the growth of larger communities, both the number of undertakers grew and the nature of their functions expanded. For example, 16 such operators were listed in a Boston directory of 1830, and 63 in a Philadelphia directory of 1860. The Federal Census of 1870 reported 2,000 for the whole country, while an estimate for the mid-1950s placed the total figure at over 50,000. With such numbers, it is by no means surprising to discover that the business has promoted the organization of a half-dozen trade associations—of which the largest one of over 13,000 members was founded as long ago as 1882—and several trade periodicals.

The ranks of this "profession" had been expanded by accretions from several sources. Many of the earlier practitioners had been cabinetmakers and furniture dealers who took on the duties of undertaker as a corollary to the sale of their coffins, which apparently they had come to stock for prompt delivery. Another group was comprised of church sextons who, having effective control of the church burial plots, were in a position to "integrate backward," so to speak; they took on the preparation of the body for burial as well as the interment itself. Thirdly, there was a later accession of proprietors of livery stables, whose horses and carriages were required for funeral processions. They too extended backward their operations. Such additions to the total were all the more readily secured since, until the Civil War era, the process of embalming was practically unknown in this country. Subsequent to that period, specializing schools of embalming provided a flow of new talent—talent without necessary connections with carpentry or livery stables—for the enlargement of the "profession."

The expansion of the functions assumed by the undertaker is suggested by the foregoing account of sources of talent. The practitioners came gradually to bear more and more responsibility for the whole rite. They acted for the bereaved, bewildered and usually inexperienced family in making arrangements for the funeral service as well as the actual burial; they helped with the proper display of floral tributes at the church; and, as the communities grew in size and cemeteries sprang up at some distance from most residential districts, they provided, or arranged to secure vehicles — hearse and horse-drawn hacks — to convey the funeral party from church to the place of interment. Before the close of the nineteenth century, such "professional" men had come rather widely to be known—and had reached the point of wishing to be known—as "funeral directors." And, before the twentieth century was half gone, some of their numbers had grown so sure of their importance that the clergy was complaining at the domination of the funeral service by these directors—to the diminution of its religious values.

Perhaps equally significant with the foregoing matters, as far as the intrusion of business into the performance of the funeral rite in America is concerned, has been the development of central shops by these funeral directors, something much more elaborate—and appropriate—than the office of a livery stable. Both the spread of the practice of embalming—until it was almost universally employed—and the increase in the proportion of our population dwelling in apartment houses, contributed to the rise of mortuaries attached to the offices of the funeral directors. There bodies of the deceased could be cared for between death and the funeral service. Enlargement of the central premises was also encouraged when wakes became more extensive social events, perhaps as a consequence of our rising standard of living. Then, in the twentieth century, if not before, these central premises added on, or were converted mainly into a place where funeral services could be held. "Funeral homes" seem to have appeared in metropolitan areas as early as the 1880s, and had become rather common by the first decades of the new century. By 1960, the number of funeral homes, parlors, chapels, etc. had swollen to something like 20-25,000 in the United States. Death and its immediate consequences had now surely moved almost wholly out of the home.

Advance in the quantum of the economy's disposable income had, in the meantime, led to various developments in the business world more or less closely tied in with the rite of death. Probably changing social habits must also be given some credit in these connections. One such development was the appearance of houses in the women's clothing industry especially devoted to the manufacture of mourning garments—with perhaps some similar institutions in the production of hats, veils and gloves—and the advent of retail stores concerned particularly with the purveyance of such goods. "Widow's weeds" had been common enough at earlier times, but now they were prepared outside of the home and indeed kept on hand by retail establishments precisely for occasions of death. As early as 1861 J. B. Lewis of 441 Broadway in New York City advertised "crepe collars, veils, trimmings, ruches, buttons, and mourning goods in general." The men's wear industries were much less affected. Gentlemen limited themselves, in mourning, to dark outer clothing—which they might already possess for Sunday wear—and to black arm bands and black neckties, the latter pair disappearing after six months or a year of display.

Again, the cultivation and distribution of flowers on a commercial basis experienced a marked expansion, especially in the decades after the Civil War, in large measure because of demand arising in the provision of whole "blankets" and lesser "sprays" for use at funerals, and for the decorations of the graves of soldiers, particularly on Memorial Day. In the early years of the twentieth century, the business of retail florists was considerably enhanced by the demand for "set pieces," and ornamental wreaths, which might be ordered, for instance, by a Masonic lodge to honor a departed "brother." Some florists found 90 per cent of their business to be associated with funerals, and apparently a proportion of 50 per cent or more was not uncommon. (Another portion of the retail florist's activities was connected with the marriage ceremony, as has already been intimated. Another portion surely was connected with the maneuvers of courtship and with the more public debutante parties. If the demand deriving from funerals be added, it will become obvious that the whole commercial production and distribution of flowers has over past decades been primarily associated with the rites of passage. Recently the use of flowers in house decoration, in gifts to the sick and housebound and other purposes has diminished somewhat the dependence of this segment of American business upon such rites.)

One should perhaps also note the consequence in the business world of the desire for prompt action relative to the provision of funeral flowers; a new business institution made its appearance. The Florists' Telegraph Delivery Association was launched in 1909; it expanded rapidly; and a decade later, it was assisting in the transmission of the purchase of flowers all over the country. Orders are sent directly from one member of the Association to another, but the Association supervises the activities of the whole group and, as necessary, polices the members. Indeed, it maintains a sort of clearing house in Detroit equipped with IBM machines.

In a quite different field, the increase of disposable income had effect upon the activities associated with the rite of death. In the last decades of the nineteenth century, publishing houses sprang up which specialized in the production of county and local histories in which sketches of the careers of recently deceased citizens of such areas, together with steel engravings of their faces in latter life, would be inserted. The preparation and publication of these volumes—plus probably a profit to the publishing house—were derivations largely from subsidies provided by the descendants of the individuals honored in the specific volumes. Technically the payment was to cover the cost of the steel engraving, but the contribution from the surviving family might run as high as a thousand dollars. The production of such "mug books" has disappeared in recent decades. Perhaps other forms of memorial—from obituaries in trade journals to the erection of charitable foundations—have reduced the field in which such publishing enterprises could operate advantageously.

Finally, the increase in population and the somewhat corresponding increase in the number of deaths, gave encouragement to certain entrepreneurs to establish new and larger burial grounds. Municipalities took action in the establishment of public cemeteries, but privately incorporated enterprises also found profitable action in the purchase of sizable tracts of land not too far from cities, and the development of these areas as attractive resting places for deceased citizens. Some such enterprises as the Forest Lawn unit in California have quite surely proven profitable undertakings.

Practices reported by the historian and anthropologist relative to the disposal of dead human bodies—cremation among the Greeks, the catacombs at Rome and elsewhere, the funeral pyres of the devout Hindus, or the exposure of the remains to natural forces as among primitive people of South America—tend to raise the question whether there is not competition between the living and the dead for terrestrial space. Such competition may indeed have some general importance as far as burial laws in England or Germany are concerned. In England, for instance, local governments have in the twentieth century acquired the rights to close to further use crowded or ill-placed cemeteries, and, after a period of years, to level the mounds, remove the headstones and convert the area into open park, even into playing fields for children. In Germany, cemeteries have in recent decades become similarly subject to closure against further use, but here, after a relatively brief lapse of time, they may become subject to reuse as burial grounds.

In these latter cases as well as in that of the United States, the special situation of insufficient areas around urban centers and, not least in importance, the increased value of urban space, have been the crucial elements in the problem. It was urban burial—in France and England prior to 1850—which first brought state regulation of cemetery location and condition. Sanitary laws there and elsewhere, including cities of the United States, came to forbid burial within the city limits or close to residential sections of the metropolitan communities. Such matters have become rather generally subject to state regulation in modern industrial regions. But still the pressure of increased numbers of deaths within the areas continued.

The advent of cremation somewhat reduced the immediate demand for space. Actually this custom arose, it seems, without much, if any, relation to cost reduction; it was embraced merely as a matter of social preference. Court decisions as early as the 1880s cleared the way in both England and the United States for the erection and use of crematoria. The number of such institutions increased markedly in the twentieth century, until there were approximately 120 in England and 220 in the United States by the late 1950s, at which approximately 150,000 and 50,000 cremations per annum, respectively, were performed. The practice had gained considerably greater relative favor in England, where indeed cremations were a third of earth burials. In the United States, cremations were still less than 5 per cent of the older-style burial in the ground. Perhaps in the course of a few decades, this mode of bodily disposal may reach proportions in many countries, including the United States, whereby the pressure for space to be used for cemeteries will have become tolerable by the living members of the communities.

Another solution, however, has been gaining ground in the United States of recent decades—and the idea has found favor also in such countries as Japan. I have in mind huge mausoleums located on the outskirts of metropolitan centers. The number now operating in this country is uncertain, perhaps ten or a dozen in 1960. One in the neighborhood of New York City was described as encompassing several levels or stories, being equipped with elevators, electric lights and air conditioning, and capable of containing 30,000 bodies plus several thousand funeral urns. One recently erected in Los Angeles was advertised to possess fifty thousand crypts and several added thousands of niches for funeral urns. Each would seem destined ultimately to become a "city of the dead." Possibly this development—which the economist would label "capital-intensive"—may solve the conflict between the pressure of population upon urban land and the protection given by both public sentiment and court rulings, in Anglo-Saxon countries, that the dead are entitled to lie in peace through perpetuity.

In sum, then, the rites connected with the phenomenon of death have, it seems, changed most of all as compared with conditions that obtained in our earlier days. Far distant indeed seems the time when a citizen could die quietly in his own home, be prepared there for burial by his beloved relatives and friends, and be taken quietly to be placed beside his forebears in the nearby family burying plot or perhaps in the churchyard not so far away. Now the body of the deceased is entrusted promptly to the care of a strange funeral director, who spirits it at dead of night down the apartment-house stairs—so poorly constructed for the purpose—places it temporarily in his mortuary, and makes all the arrangements for a service in his own chapel or funeral home, and sees to it perhaps that these earthly remains are laid to rest in the seventh alcove of the fifth floor of some gigantic mausoleum! The price system here has surely made evident its penetrative power.

Mankind's pattern of living may be conceived in terms of concentric circles around the human ego. On the periphery there might in theory lie the ways in which his ships were constructed or his mines were exploited; somewhat closer to the central figure would perhaps be the manner in which his favorite newspaper was produced or his house kept in repair; in the circle close around him might be found the modes whereby his bread was cooked or his linen washed; and surely most intimate to him would be the procedures which accompanied and adorned those climactic events in his journey through life—his birth, his presentation to adult society, his marriage, the launching of *his* progeny, and his end when he has "shuffled off this mortal coil." Changes relative to the contents of all such circles are elements in the research of the historian, those of the outer areas perhaps more for historians with an economic orientation, and those of the inner regions more for historians drawing inspiration from the fountains of sociology.

It is of interest to the historian that in the end all the circles of man's requirements have been penetrated by entrepreneurial ingenuity or been altered by economic forces deriving their influence from the price system; and it is of interest to the historian also that the invasion of these circles has occurred more or less sequentially from the more remote to the most intimate areas of mankind's activities. There are exceptions such as the midwife or the somewhat differentiated funeral director, whose initial appearances date back to ancient times, but, by and large, the commercial construction of ships preceded that of dwelling houses, the business of shoe manufacture got upon its feet earlier than that of commercial fabrication of doughnuts or even plain white bread, and the placing of roof repairing in the hands of a handicraftsman took place earlier than the entrusting of one's daughter to the tender mercies of a wedding director. On the whole, indeed, the penetration of the innermost circle of human affairs has been a phenomenon of the twentieth century. Now, in a way of speaking, the social system and the economic or business system are coterminous. With the "rites of passage" now added to the domains of economic production, trade, communication and even entertainment and sports, there is little left for the energetic entrepreneur to conquer.

BIBLIOGRAPHICAL APPENDIX

In the collection of data for this essay, which for the most part involved personal inquiry, the author has been especially dependent upon the help of Mrs. Dorothy Lubin. He is also indebted to Miss Ruth Crandall for her assistance. The few books that were found pertinent to particular sections of the survey are the following:

LeRoy Bowman, *The American Funeral* (Washington, 1959).

Alfred Fellows, *The Law of Burial* (London, 1940).

Palmer Findley, *Priests of Lucina* (Boston, 1939).

Jürgen Gaedke, *Handbuch des Friedhofs und Bestattungsrechts* (Göttingen, 1954).

Robert W. Habenstein and William M. Lamers, *The History of American Funeral Directing* (Milwaukee, 1955).

Percival E. Jackson, *The Law of Cadavers* (New York, 1950).

Hermann Schütze, *Friedhofs und Bestattungsrecht* (Koln: C. Heymann, 1958).

E. S. Watkins, *The Law of Burials and Burial Grounds* (Bristol, England, 1948).

Afternote

I am happy to acknowledge my indebtedness to Professor Sigmund Diamond of Columbia University for aid in erecting the framework of this essay. We shared together the background of the Research Center in Entrepreneurial History at Harvard in the 1948–58 period, and, when I turned to an effort at broadening the earlier field of business history, Professor Diamond suggested the possibility of utilizing the anthropological formulation for a group of ideas that then lacked cohesion in my own mind.

Arthur H. Cole is Professor of Business Economics at Harvard University and former Director of its Research Center in Entrepreneurial History. [This article appeared in Vol. XIV, No. 4 (Winter, 1962).]